SQUATTERS IN THE CAPITALIST CITY

To date, there has been no comprehensive analysis of the disperse research on the squatters' movement in Europe. In *Squatters in the Capitalist City*, Miguel A. Martínez López presents a critical review of the current research on squatting and of the historical development of the movements in European cities according to their major social, political and spatial dimensions.

Comparing cities, contexts, and the achievements of the squatters' movements, this book presents the view that squatting is not simply a set of isolated, illegal and marginal practices, but is a long-lasting urban and transnational movement with significant and broad implications. While intersecting with different housing struggles, squatters face various aspects of urban politics and enhance the content of the movements claiming for a 'right to the city'. *Squatters in the Capitalist City* seeks to understand both the socio-spatial and political conditions favourable to the emergence and development of squatting, and the nature of the interactions between squatters, authorities and property owners by discussing the trajectory, features and limitations of squatting as a potential radicalisation of urban democracy.

Miguel A. Martínez is Professor of Sociology at the IBF (Institute for Housing and Urban Research), Uppsala University, Sweden. He was previously affiliated with the City University of Hong Kong and the Complutense University of Madrid. Since 2009 he has been a member of the activist-research network SqEK (Squatting Everywhere Kollective). He has conducted different studies about urban sociology, social movements, and participatory-activist methodologies. Most of his publications are available at www.miguelangelmartinez.net.

Housing and Society Series
Edited by Ray Forrest, School for Policy Studies, University of Bristol

This series aims to situate housing within its wider social, political and economic context at both national and international level. In doing so it will draw on the full range of social science disciplines and on mainstream debate on the nature of contemporary social change. The books are intended to appeal to an international academic audience as well as to practitioners and policymakers—to be theoretically informed and policy relevant.

Squatters in the Capitalist City
Miguel A. Martínez

The Tenants' Movement
Quintin Bradley

Social Housing, Disadvantage, and Neighbourhood Liveability
Edited by Michelle Norris

Young People and Housing
Edited by Ray Forrest and Ngai-Ming Yip

Beyond Home Ownership
Edited by Richard Ronald and Marja Elsinga

Housing Disadvantaged People?
Jane Ball

Women and Housing
Edited by Patricia Kennett and Chan Kam Wah

Affluence, Mobility and Second Home Ownership
Chris Paris

Housing, Markets and Policy
Peter Malpass and Rob Rowlands

SQUATTERS IN THE CAPITALIST CITY

Housing, Justice, and Urban Politics

Miguel A. Martínez

NEW YORK AND LONDON

First published 2020
by Routledge
52 Vanderbilt Avenue, New York, NY 10017

and by Routledge
2 Park Square, Milton Park, Abingdon, Oxon, OX14 4RN

Routledge is an imprint of the Taylor & Francis Group, an informa business

© 2020 Taylor & Francis

The right of Miguel A. Martínez to be identified as author of this work has been asserted by him in accordance with sections 77 and 78 of the Copyright, Designs and Patents Act 1988.

All rights reserved. No part of this book may be reprinted or reproduced or utilised in any form or by any electronic, mechanical, or other means, now known or hereafter invented, including photocopying and recording, or in any information storage or retrieval system, without permission in writing from the publishers.

Trademark notice: Product or corporate names may be trademarks or registered trademarks, and are used only for identification and explanation without intent to infringe.

Library of Congress Cataloging-in-Publication Data
Names: Martínez, Miguel A., author.
Title: Squatters in the capitalist city : housing, justice, and urban politics / Miguel A. Martínez.
Description: New York : Routledge, 2020. |
Series: Housing and society series | Includes bibliographical references and index. | Description based on print version record and CIP data provided by publisher; resource not viewed.
Identifiers: LCCN 2019018423 (print) | LCCN 2019018778 (ebook) | ISBN 9781315719023 (ebook) | ISBN 9781138856943
(hardback : alk. paper) | ISBN 9781138856950 (pbk. : alk. paper) | ISBN 9781315719023 (ebk)
Subjects: LCSH: Squatter settlements--Political aspects--Europe. | Housing--Political aspects--Europe. | Squatters--Political activity--Europe.
Classification: LCC HD7287.96.E85 (ebook) | LCC HD7287.96.E85 M37 2020 (print) | DDC 307.3/36--dc23
LC record available at https://lccn.loc.gov/2019018423

ISBN: 978-1-138-85694-3 (hbk)
ISBN: 978-1-138-85695-0 (pbk)
ISBN: 978-1-315-71902-3 (ebk)

Typeset in Bembo
by Swales & Willis, Exeter, Devon, UK

 Printed in the United Kingdom by Henry Ling Limited

CONTENTS

List of Tables	*viii*
List of Figures	*ix*
List of Images	*x*
Abbreviations	*xii*
Acknowledgments	*xiii*

Introduction   **1**
Squatting and Urban Justice 4
Contents and Arguments 10

1   Squatting as an Urban Movement   **13**
Structural Constraints and Social Conflict 13
Critical Social Science 16
Capitalism, Democracy, and Urban Movements 20
    Practices, Movements, and Scales 22
    Socio-Spatialities and Socio-Temporalities 25
Back to the Grassroots 29
    Movement Effects Contextualised 32
    The Contentious Social Production of Space 37
Squatters' Movements 42
Squatting and the Right to the City 48
    The Right to Squat the City 48
    Legacies of Fruitful Associations 51

vi Contents

Squatting Rights in Contention with the Existing Capitalist
City 53
Social Justice in European Urban Politics 55
References 56

2 Autonomy from Capitalism   **63**
Converging Radicalisms 64
From the Factory to Metropolitan Struggles 67
Mobilisation and Liberation of Everyday Life 72
Diffused Autonomy and Interdependence 78
Collective Self-Determination of the Oppressed 83
Squatting and the Radical Left in Berlin 87
References 93

3 Socio-Spatial Structures   **97**
Housing Shortages and Vacancy Rates 100
Urban Renewal 106
    Are Squatters the Storm Troopers of Gentrification? 109
Legislation and Law Enforcement 113
Activist Networks 118
Social Recognition 122
Amsterdam: The Lost Paradise of Squatting? 124
References 134

4 Types of Squatting   **139**
Squatted Houses and Social Centres 141
Motivations and Outcomes 148
Overlaps and Splits 152
Interactions between Squatters and Migrants 160
    Beyond Deprivation 163
    Autonomous Agency: When Migrants Squat 166
    Squatters, Migrants, and the Global Justice Movement 168
    Migrants' Empowerment through the 15M Movement 171
    Interactions and Contexts 173
Squatting in Paris: Internal Divisions and Local Regulation 177
References 185

5 Anomalous Institutions   **190**
The Movements' Structural Dilemmas 191
Strategic Negotiations 194
    High-Level Negotiations 194
    Transactional Negotiations 196

Contents **vii**

Survival Negotiations 197
Forced Negotiations 198
To Be or Not to Be Legalised 200
Institutionalisation 204
Type I Institutionalisation: Integration of the Movement into State Institutions 205
Type II Institutionalisation: New Institutions Promoted by Social Movements 209
Type III Institutionalisation: Creation of Anomalous Institutions 213
Legalisation of Squats in Madrid 218
Fully Legalised Squats 220
Failed Attempts at Legalisation 222
The Rejection of Legalisation 224
Analytical Remarks 226
References 230

6 Criminalisation and Counter-Hegemony   **234**
The Performative Powers of 'Spectacular Narrations' 234
Are Squatters All the Same? 237
Soft Gentrifiers 242
Are There Good and Bad Squatters? 246
Internal Cleavages 251
Discursive Struggles and Counter-Hegemonic Discourse 254
Reversive Responses 256
Subversive Alternatives 258
The Criminalisation of Squatting Invigorates Class Domination 262
References 266

Methodological Note   **271**

Index   *275*

TABLES

1.1	Urban movements according to a political economy approach	36
3.1	Socio-spatial structures of opportunities and constraints for urban squatting	124
4.1	Dimensions of squatting configurations	142
4.2	Seven types of squatting	152
4.3	Likelihood of coexistence between squats for housing and social centres	155
4.4	Types of squats according to a political economy approach	158
4.5	Four modes of interactions between migrants and non-migrant activists in the squatting of buildings in Madrid (1990s–2015)	174
5.1	Types of negotiations in which squatters may be involved	195
5.2	Types of institutionalisation processes	212

FIGURES

1.1	Structures and agency	15
1.2	Urban movements	41
4.1	Types of squatting	147
5.1	Institutionalisation processes in squatting movements	217
6.1	'Homogenisation' narratives that stigmatise squatters	246
6.2	'Polarisation' narratives that stigmatise squatters	252
6.3	Counter-hegemonic narratives that legitimise squatting	255

IMAGES

0.1	Squat Casablanca, Madrid, 2010	2
0.2	Squat Joe Garage, Amsterdam, 2011	3
0.3	After-squat Casa Pumarejo, Seville, 2018	6
0.4	Squat Rozbrat, Poznan, 2014	7
0.5	Squat Palestra Popolare Polisportiva Etnea, Catania, 2018	9
1.1	After-squat Poortgebouw, Rotterdam, 2016	29
1.2	Squat Exsnia, Rome, 2014	42
1.3	Poster Occupy, London, 2016	47
1.4	Squat Forte Prenestino, Rome, 2014	53
2.1	Squat Metropoliz, Rome, 2014	66
2.2	Squat Metropoliz, Rome, 2014	71
2.3	Squat Rote Flora, Hamburg, 2014	77
2.4	Squat La Casika, Móstoles (Madrid), 2014	79
2.5	Squat Patio Maravillas, Madrid, 2014	82
2.6	After-squat Rote Insel, Berlin, 2011	87
2.7	After-squat Manti, Berlin, 2011	90
3.1	Floor painted in solidarity with squat Villa Amalias, Athens, 2013	100
3.2	Squat La Ingobernable, Madrid, 2018	105
3.3	Squat Teatro Coppola, Catania, 2018	108
3.4	Squat Odzysk, Poznan, 2014	113
3.5	Posters in Athens, 2013	118
3.6	White Book of squatting, Amsterdam, 2011	128
3.7	Squat Afrika, Amsterdam, 2007	132
4.1	Squat Colapesce, Catania, 2018	145
4.2	After-squat Hafenstrasse, Hamburg, 2014	151
4.3	Squat Metropoliz, Rome, 2014	155
4.4	Squat La Enredadera, Madrid, 2017	170
4.5	Squat Le Transfo, Paris, 2013	178

4.6	Squat Le Shakirail, Paris, 2013	181
4.7	Squat Jardin d'Alice, Paris, 2013	184
5.1	Evicted squat in Rotterdam, 2016	193
5.2	After-squat Cyklopen, Stockholm, 2015	204
5.3	Squat Patio Maravillas, Madrid, 2015	219
5.4	Squat Edifici 15-O, Barcelona, 2012	224
5.5	Squatting Handbook, Madrid, 2013	225
5.6	Squat Casablanca, Madrid, 2013	228
6.1	Squat La Porka, Barcelona, 2015	237
6.2	After-squat New Yorck in Bethanien, Berlin, 2011	243
6.3	Squat Scup, Rome, 2014	249
6.4	Squat Rozbrat, Poznan, 2014	258
6.5	Squat Barrilonia, Barcelona, 2012	261
6.6	Squat Mare Street, London, 2010	265

ABBREVIATIONS

15M	Spanish 15 of May (2011) social movement (also known as Indignados movement)
BR	Brigate Rosse (Red Brigades)
BVODH	Brigadas Vecinales de Observación de Derechos Humanos (Human Rights Watch Neigbourhood Brigades)
CIE	Centro de Internamiento de Extranjeros (Immigrants Detention Centre)
CSOA	Centro Social Okupado y Autogestionado (Squatted and Self-managed Social Centre)
DAL	Droit Au Logement (Right to Housing)
DIY	Do It Yourself
GJM	Global Justice Movement
IMF	International Monetary Fund
JN	Jeudi Noir
KSU	Kraakspreekuur (Squatting Advisory Office)
LGBTQI	Lesbian, Gay, Bisexual, Transexual, Queer, Intersexual
ODS	Oficina de Derechos Sociales (Office for Social Rights)
PAH	Plataforma de Afectados por las Hipotecas (Platform for People Affected by Mortgages)
RAF	Rote Armee Fraktion (Red Army Faction)
RAZ	Red de Apoyo Zapatista (Zapatist Support Network)
RES	*Semana de Lucha Social Rompamos el Silencio* (Break the Silence activists network)
SMI	Social Movement Infrastructure
SMO	Social Movement Organisation
SqEK	Squatting Europe/Everywhere Kollective
SSC	Squatted Social Centre

ACKNOWLEDGMENTS

Despite the hardships of writing individually, every research work is the result of many satisfactory collective efforts, insights, and cooperation. This book is no exception. However, I express my apologies for the impossibility of mentioning all the names of those who contributed in many ways. Pre-eminently, squatters, activists, and participants in the squatting milieus were the main inspiration for this research. Many of them instructed me, talked about their experiences and views, or showed me the squatted spaces. I truly appreciate their support as well as their struggle. A warm recognition also applies to all the SqEK (Squatting Everywhere Kollective) fellows who participated in our meetings over a decade—too many names, again, to single them out. These conferences made use of many resources from local squats, non-squatted social centres, after-squatted house projects, and universities. Once (in 2015) we also obtained a grant from the Antipode Foundation, which sponsored the expenses of many contributors. RC21 conferences and the seminars on the squatting history of Madrid (2008–2010) also gathered plenty of people who shared their knowledge, questions, and political will to challenge social injustice. In addition, I would like to remember all the scholars who sparked my intellectual curiosity since my undergrad years and especially those devoted to the study of squatting, social movements, and urban issues in general, such as Tomás R. Villasante, Ramón Adell, Christopher G. Pickvance, and Margit Mayer. Some of them are quoted in the book, but the references included here are only a limited selection among a larger number of academics who helped me forge a critical gaze in order to understand social phenomena.

The conclusion of this book has been possible due to the extraordinary positive working conditions and the great colleagues at the IBF (Institute for Housing and Urban Research), Uppsala University. In particular, I must highlight Dominika V. Polanska for all her outstanding support and intellectual collaboration even

xiv Acknowledgments

before I moved to Sweden when she introduced me to squatting activism in Central and Eastern Europe, and organised several inspiring conferences I luckily attended. Among the extraordinary researchers I have met in Sweden, Irene Molina, Catharina Thörn, Håkan Thörn, Don Mitchell, Carina Listerborn, and Kristina Boréus have been some of the most inspiring and cooperative scholars. Moreover, friends and devoted activists such as Julia Lledín and Fernando Arozarena, first, and a post-doctoral researcher, Evin Deniz, helped me to complete my fieldwork in Spain when I lived abroad.

During the final stage to produce this book (index, references, translations of notes from Spanish, selection of pictures, etc.), Alba Martínez Folgado, Luis Martínez Lorenzo, and Clarissa Cordeiro de Campos were vital aids too. Some conversations with Don Mitchell and his comments added to the final polishing of some parts of the manuscript. Not the least, my editors at Routledge became a kind source of patience and confidence in this project since the proposal was approved some years ago.

Previous versions of the present chapters or parts of them have been published in the following journals and books:

2013. The Squatters' Movement in Europe: A Durable Struggle for Social Autonomy in Urban Politics. *Antipode. A Radical Journal of Geography* 45(4): 866–887.

2014. How Do Squatters Deal with the State? Legalization and Anomalous Institutionalization in Madrid. *International Journal of Urban and Regional Research* 38(2): 646–674.

2014. Squatting for justice, bringing life to the city. *ROAR Magazine*.

2017. Squatters and Migrants in Madrid: Interactions, Contexts and Cycles. *Urban Studies* 54(11): 2472–2489.

2018. Urban emptiness, ghost owners and squatters' challenges to private property. In Hojer, Maja et al. (Eds) *Contested Property Claims. What Disagreement Tells Us About Ownership*. Abingdon: Routledge, 74–91.

2019. Good and bad squatters? Challenging hegemonic narratives and advancing anti-capitalist views of squatting in Western European cities. *Culture Unbound* 11(1): 165–189.

2019. The autonomy of struggles and the self-management of squats: Legacies of intertwined movements. *Interface: a journal for and about social movements* 11(1): 178–199.

2019. European squatters' movements and the right to the city. In Flesher, Cristina & Ramón Feenstra (Eds) *Routledge Handbook of Contemporary European Social Movements* (forthcoming).

I am grateful to the above-mentioned journals and book publishers for their permission to reproduce large parts of the articles, albeit they have been updated and refurbished when needed. Journal and book editors, and anonymous reviewers who commented on the original papers equally deserve attribution for contributing to the enhancement of my arguments. As a non-native English speaker, assistance with language issues has always been essential to improve my manuscripts. In this regard, different parts of the already published pieces enjoyed the qualified and generous revisions of Alan W. Moore, Lucy Finchett-Maddock, ETC Dee, Carlos Delclós, Linus Owens, and Brad McGregor.

Finally, funds from three research grants have facilitated the development of this work: the MOVOKEUR project from the Spanish National Plan of I+D+i (Ref. CSO2011-23079), the MOVOUTCOMES project from the Research Grant Council of Hong Kong (Ref. 11612016-CityU), and the Betiko Foundation with the sponsorship of Pedro Ibarra. Two former colleagues, Mario Domínguez (Complutense University of Madrid) and Bart Wissink (City University of Hong Kong) were extremely kind with their support to manage these research projects when I moved to a different university.

INTRODUCTION

In 1989 I entered a squat for the first time. I was an undergraduate university student by then, very curious and enthusiastic about sociology but also about leftist and libertarian politics. Minuesa, as the squat was named, intrigued me from the very beginning. It was located in the city centre of Madrid, next to the picturesque street market of the Rastro I used to visit frequently on Sundays. The squatted building comprised two different spaces: a social centre and residential apartments where squatters and former workers of the factory lived. While studying in the universities of Madrid and Santiago de Compostela, my political concerns led me to participate in free radio stations, the pacifist movement, workers' and consumers' cooperatives, and community organisations. However, my multiple visits to squats in many Spanish cities raised a long-lasting fascination with that movement. Throughout the years, I became a supporter and researcher of squatting. Due to my family circumstances, it was not until 2007 when I became more actively engaged in the inner life of the squatting milieu. I went back to live in Madrid and joined several squats for a period of six years.

In the squatted social centre Malaya, circa 2008, I proposed holding a regular seminar where the history of squatting in the metropolitan area of Madrid could be discussed. Other scholars and activists joined, and together we ran this seminar in four different squats over the next two years (see Image 0.1). We ended up writing a collective book using the edited transcripts of the meetings. The purpose was to reach a wider readership beyond the squatting scene, but the intense experiences we all went through in the 2011 uprisings, known as the 15M movement, overwhelmed that endeavour. New evictions and occupations also kept me busy. A devastating wave of foreclosures gave birth to a strong housing movement, and squatting was revived in many unexpected ways. Obviously, in a squat you do many more things than intellectual debates, ranging from cleaning bathrooms to construction works and organising parties. Weekly assemblies and abundant management

2 Introduction

IMAGE 0.1 Squat Casablanca, Madrid, 2010
Source: Author

issues concerning the building, its legal affairs, its inhabitants, and the many other participants demanded as much as teaching, researching, and dealing with administrative work at the university. Hence, after years of reading and reflecting on the fundamental traits of activist-research, my life as a 'squatter academic' was a natural challenge I fully enjoyed, and not without occasional contradictions.

By 2013, the economic crisis and other reasons made me migrate to a distant city, Hong Kong, so my experience as a regular insider ceased. Nonetheless, I kept studying, writing, and discussing squatting movements, especially in Europe, but I also increasingly became more interested in similar phenomena in Asia and Latin America. Against this backdrop I envisaged this book as an academic synthesis of my knowledge on squatting across European cities.

Previously, in 1998, I had published my first sociological study of this subject while writing my PhD dissertation on different forms of urban activism and citizen participation. An extended version of that paper, based on new empirical analysis, was released as a book in 2002. Publishing in Spanish and with an independent house was tougher than imagined. The topic was not that attractive for the mainstream debates related to urban studies and social movements. This and an ensuing edited book in 2004, also in the Spanish language, sold out and were very popular among activists, but hardly had repercussions in academia. Although I never stopped following my curiosity in the many aspects of urban life (housing, urban planning, public spaces, migration, and so on) as well as the development of progressive social movements all over the world, my interest in squatting became a permanent research programme almost without noticing. From my first research stay at the University of Kent (UK) in 1999, I started engaging with the international scholarship on this matter under the insightful guidance of Christopher G. Pickvance. Early on, I often discussed Manuel Castells' original contributions to the field of urban movements with my doctoral supervisor, Tomás R. Villasante, but it was still difficult to find many works following that thread of inquiry. In addition to the key studies produced by Margit Mayer and others (such as various activist-research works conducted in the UK and Italy), I was very much impressed by Hans Pruijt's publications in 2003 and 2004.

A few years later, in 2009, I invited Pruijt and others to an international encounter of scholars who had published or were particularly interested in squatting. That year we met first in Madrid and nine months later in Milan. In our second meeting, we named ourselves SqEK (*Squatting Europe Kollective*) and wrote collectively a thorough activist–research agenda. Since then, we have continued organising meetings, at least one every year, in different European cities and writing books and special issues for academic journals together (see Image 0.2). Many affiliates have

IMAGE 0.2 Squat Joe Garage, Amsterdam, 2011
Source: Author

4 Introduction

also published articles and finished their PhD dissertations, which we promptly share with each other. News, incidents, and calls for solidarity circulate in our email list. Quite impressively, SqEK is vibrant and productive. When we met in Prague in 2017, we decided to change the meaning of the acronym to *Squatting Everywhere Kollective* in order to get rid of the limited geographical reference with the numerous political connotations we preferred to avoid. This activist–research network is still lively ten years later.

For me, SqEK has been the cradle of much fruitful collaboration. It has kept me intellectually active and also challenged me politically while studying and promoting squatting. Furthermore, our SqEK meetings have allowed me to access abundant empirical information that would be impossible to reach alone. The present book is in full debt to all the insights that emerged among the SqEK members and the local activists who hosted us. In particular, one of the first goals and drivers of such a network was to elaborate a systematic comparison of squatting movements across Europe. I had begun my own explorations of the special features of squatting in other European countries before 2002 but always felt that more insiders' views and first-hand knowledge was necessary. Additionally, participants in SqEK had very different academic backgrounds ranging from history to anthropology, geography, sociology, political science, economy, criminology, architecture, and arts. This widened my perspective regarding meaningful comparisons of this, also, very diverse movement, with many transnational connections beyond the cities where it unfolded. In my view, comparisons such as these were not a mere academic requirement to engage with the international scholarship on squatting so as to frame my own investigations in Spain but became a substantial focus of interest themselves. Moreover, instead of taking for granted that there was a squatting movement in Europe with some internal differences, a comparative approach encouraged me to ask what are its distinctive features compared to other contemporary and past social movements, and how it was influenced by specific sociopolitical and urban contexts. Last but not least, I shared with many SqEK affiliates a political concern about the limitations and achievements of such a struggle. In sum, this book aims at responding to these questions.

Squatting and Urban Justice

As I conclude this book in 2018, we are witnessing the rise of conservative politics worldwide that are jeopardising human rights, democratic principles, and redistributive policies which were considered a foundation for the left (and also for many liberal right-wingers) hitherto. Four decades of neoliberalism have paved the way for this upsurge of far-right and authoritarian politics even at the heart of the wealthiest nations. If squatters' movements were able to thrive and resist throughout those difficult times, it seems that the challenge is even higher now. However, I am confident that understanding the squatters' historical trajectories,

Introduction **5**

diverse experiences, and contributions will shed light over important grassroots struggles for enhancing the prospects of progressive politics in a broad sense.

This book offers an analysis of the squatters' movements in various European countries and cities by combining my own fieldwork and all the significant evidence collected from others' research. It aims at disclosing similar patterns that transnationally connect these local struggles. It also pursues a clarification of its internal diversity, the limits of its radical politics, and the significant circumstances, processes, and features that defined it as an urban movement. It does not draw a black and white picture. Many squatters promoted collective direct action, self-management, and communitarian lifestyles that challenged capitalist urbanisation, housing speculation, and unsustainable and alienated lives. However, not all squatters articulated their views in the same manner. Nor they did react unanimously to housing needs and social aspirations for a meaningful urban life. Some squatting projects were short-lived whereas others lasted for decades. In some cities or metropolitan areas, squats were tightly intertwined with other social movements, but this was not always the case. In some contexts, repression, legalisation, or a variable combination of both ruled the development of squatting. These political interactions were the sources of internal strains and divides. In particular, by examining multiple cases across Europe, this book investigates how specific structures of opportunities and constraints shaped the squatters' interactions with their opponents, and what kind of sociopolitical consequences were engendered.

Although I discuss the diversity of squatters at length, I do not deal here with some types of squatting that have a reactionary character (far-right squats, traffickers of vacant apartments, drug gangs who occupy buildings, illegal land occupations by developers, etc.) because they do not contribute to form squatters' movements—or even attack them when they are seen as interfering in their business. Some practices of stealth squatting can be also outliers and alien to even the most decentralised squatting movements, but they tend to share similar motivations and contextual embeddedness in the face of the housing crisis. So-called slums, shanty towns, and self-built houses in the derelict land of the urban outskirts are not the focus of my research either. Their association with urban movements in Europe is not as prominent as in other countries, although, as it will be noted, this has recently changed since the policies dealing with migration and refugees have accentuated urban poverty, marginalisation, and homelessness.

My knowledge stems mainly from squats in European cities, so these will set the scope of my analysis. Although all forms of occupying empty spaces must be regarded as essential parts of the urban history, their challenges are somewhat different. Hence, I refer to squats only as occupations of empty buildings or flats without the owner's permission. For instance, to mention a common misunderstanding, if a residence is broken into when their owners or tenants go on vacation, this is not a squat, but a distinct offence—a violation of a private domicile. A durable vacancy or abandonment of a house, factory, school, etc. is a prerequisite to setting up a squat. Only then is it manifest that the holder of the legal title of the property does not need it in the short run. His or her underuse of the estate and the lack of maintenance may even ruin the building and cause damages to other residents. Therefore, while using it, squatters help to keep the property in a liveable state.

Another common misleading judgement is that all squatters contest the right to private property. This is true according to the ideology of many squatters, but it does not apply to all. Most squatters pursue an affordable house or space for organising social activities. The prospect of buying the property is usually far outside their economic capacity, but it is not absolutely undesirable for many squatters. Social housing owned by state agencies or subsidised private property is demanded by some squatters (see Image 0.3). Some self-managed social centres also end up buying the premises they occupy if the authorities offer them a convenient deal. More often, legalisation agreements set rental fees below

IMAGE 0.3 After-squat Casa Pumarejo, Seville, 2018
Source: Author

market prices and may occasionally include state benefits to repair the buildings and run the social activities.

Opposition to the principle of private property indicates, in general, a strong criticism of the consequences produced by the unequal distribution of private property. It is more a cry for social justice around housing than a specific defiance of all forms of homeownership. Furthermore, the squatters who criticise the regime of private property express their reluctance to buy or rent houses as a pivotal amendment to how the elites use the real-estate market and housing policies to discipline large populations. However, by definition squatters only target properties which are vacant. This vacancy results from management decisions taken by their owners. If these are efficient in keeping their assets active and used, squatters could still discuss their wealth and speculative practices, but would not be able to take over their properties. They could demand requisitions instead. The direct action of squatters does not address all private property (and empty state-owned properties as well) but only that which is temporarily vacant. In practice, squatters' movements challenge real-estate speculation as well as failed housing and urban policies rather than the exclusive property rights (see Image 0.4).

In other words, in this book I am interested in squatters' movements because they tackle the very core inequities of the housing market and its laissez-faire

IMAGE 0.4 Squat Rozbrat, Poznan, 2014
Source: Author

8 Introduction

governance by state authorities. Urban planners, city managers, and property investors are responsible for the increasing production of unaffordable places, but they do not operate isolated from each other; they jointly participate in broader political and economic processes. For example, global financial speculation is pressing most governments to deregulate and dismantle welfare services so more for-profit niches can open up. Commodification of housing is not only a side effect of economic growth but an indispensable companion in the commodification of the whole built environment. If squatters represent crucial urban activism, it is not only because they are appealing to homeless people and anarchists but because they stand up and fight back against the above processes, which also threaten current tenants and even vulnerable homeowners. Housing violence, harassment, forced displacement, rising rents, and foreclosures for those financially broke are increasingly more visible phenomena in most cities. It is not only the concern of squatters, albeit they were often at the forefront of the struggle. Despite the apparent gaps, the claims of squatters may eventually engage other social groups who experience injustice in the allocation of housing. As I will show in the following chapters, squatting seems like a practical and immediate alternative to capitalism in everyday life, although it is also a limited tool in order to change housing and urban policies at large.

Another driver of this research is the criminalisation of squatting in most European countries. This issue, in particular, needs an insightful historical and comparative approach given that unauthorised occupations were usually a matter of civil regulation before being subject to criminal punishment. There are different ways of implementing the laws against squatting and also various legal aspects to take into account for each country. Nonetheless, historical shifts in terms of its criminalisation indicate that the dominant political forces are setting the core values of a society in accordance with a neoliberal framework rooted in privatisation, unlimited economic growth, and profit-making. As a consequence, squats are more easily evicted and squatters suffer greater state repression. My stance here is that most squatters and squats enhance cities in many ways that are not usually recognised by politicians, judges, the mass media, urban developers, and the public at large. Furthermore, their opponents tend to base repressive measures on either weak or insufficient evidence, if not on a very narrow-minded view of city life.

The purpose of squatting may vary between housing provision and the performance of a broad range of cultural, economic, and political activities (see Image 0.5). Hence, there are many types of squatters and squats. Their needs and impacts can be, accordingly, very different. One of the primary errors, then, is to pack them all under the same social category. At the other extreme, a no less wrong procedure is to simplify that diversity by, in a manipulative manner, splitting squatters between 'good' and 'bad' ones. Leaving aside the lack of tolerance towards the many criticisms of the capitalist system that squatters have, the dismissive attitude facing 'bad squatters' lies in the assumption that most of the squatting projects engender typical problems—for instance, noise that disturbs some neighbours or the spoiling of properties, something that can happen everywhere and not necessarily due to the presence of squatters. Quite to the contrary, what I have observed more often is

IMAGE 0.5 Squat Palestra Popolare Polisportiva Etnea, Catania, 2018
Source: Author

a great effort to take care of the occupied places, to promote communal ways of living, and to share their ideas with the surrounding neighbourhoods.

Sometimes squats are only known due to the protests that their eviction, or threats of eviction, ignite. However, outsiders, including journalists who cover the most repressive and contentious incidents, are rarely aware of the continuous exhibitions, concerts, workshops, talks, and sociability fostered by the voluntary work of several generations of activists and thousands of visitors in many squatted social centres. Beyond the pervasive stereotypes of squatters as young radicals, squats are open places for many different people who want to practice sports, learn foreign languages, create art, launch co-operative enterprises, organise meetings, and engage in political campaigning. Notwithstanding, when migrants, homeless people, and poor youngsters squat just for living or to promote radical politics, their struggle to reach a secure tenancy is more frequently hindered by fierce attacks. The hot issue for the decision makers is why they prosecute those who find an affordable means to house themselves while there are abundant empty apartments and a scarcity of social housing. According to figures collated by *The Guardian*, 'more than 11 million homes lie empty across Europe—enough to house all of the continent's homeless twice over. … There are 4.1 million homeless across Europe, according to the European Union' (Rupert Neate, *Scandal of Europe's 11m empty houses*, 23 Feb. 2014). In cities such as Berlin, Amsterdam, London, and Rome it was sometimes feasible to negotiate and legalise many of the former squats. Although authorities tend to praise the artistic squats over others, they forget that low-paid

10 Introduction

and precarious artists need accessible places to live too. Self-help squatting in response to shortages of affordable housing is ignored at the same time that some *creative* squats are tolerated. Moreover, it is also misguided to think of squats as a simple temporary solution since in many cases, both legalised and fully squatted, may last for several decades.

Without obliterating their unintended effects and contradictions, in this book I identify some of the prominent traits most squatters' movements feature. First of all, squats are built by squatters, active citizens who devote a great part of their lives to providing autonomous and low-cost solutions to many of the city's flaws—such as housing shortages, expensive rental rates, bureaucratic machinery that discourages grassroots proposals, or the political corruption in the background of urban transformations. Second, squatters move but squats remain as a sort of 'anomalous institution', neither private nor state-owned, but belonging to the 'urban commons' of citizenship, like many other public facilities. Third, since most squats have a non-commercial character, this entails easy access to their activities, services, and venues for all who are excluded from mainstream circuits, which is a crucial contribution to social justice, equality, and local democracy. Fourth, the occupation of buildings is not an isolated practice but a collective intervention in the urban fabric that avoids further deterioration in decaying areas by recycling materials, greening brown fields and urban voids, and, not least, by building up social networks and street life, which are palpable social benefits, though they are not easy to measure with official statistics. Finally, there is a long tradition of legal regulations that granted rights to the inhabitants of abandoned properties after a certain number of years of occupation—the so-called 'adverse possession' or 'usucapio'—though the hegemony of neoliberalism has fostered the increasing criminalisation of squatting instead.

Contents and Arguments

The contents of the book are organised in six chapters. Except the most of Chapter 1, the rest is a selection and improvement of my previous writings.

Chapter 1 introduces my structural-systemic approach. As presented above, my aim is to provide accurate accounts of the squatters' movements by describing their diversity all over Europe, explaining the structural conditions that foster their existence, and assessing their sociopolitical outcomes. I justify, in this chapter, why the analysis of urban movements needs to bridge political economy and contentious politics insights. Therefore, I define urban movements according to the influential contexts of capitalism and democracy, and I distinguish movements from short-lived and non-coordinated activist practices. I also incorporate multiple spatialities and temporalities into the investigation of urban movements. The review of the academic literature facilitates the identification of the salient structural-systemic conditions of urban movements and their contentious social production of space. Hence, I apply these assumptions and conceptual

Introduction **11**

choices to explain the surge, development, and consequences of squatting as a key expression of urban movements.

Chapter 2 examines the role that the notion of 'autonomy' played in the urban politics of the squatters' movements across Europe. Recent approaches based on 'the right to the city' and 'urban commons' usually replace or enunciate the idea of autonomy with a slightly different terminology. My aim in this chapter is to grasp how specific social movements from the autonomist tradition provided an identity reference for many squatters' movements, albeit sometimes in vague terms. In particular, I suggest a focus on the collective, feminist, and anti-capitalist dimensions of autonomy, which are absent from many studies on squatting. The approach to the legacies of movements contributes to the understanding of not only identity formation and protest repertoires based on specific activist practices but also the magma of political networks in which squatters' movements were embedded. Brief historical accounts of Italy, Germany, and Spain illustrate this analysis, with a special emphasis on the contemporary developments of squatting in the City state of Berlin.

Chapter 3 investigates how squats emerge and develop. It argues that squatters' intentions and strategic actions are mediated and constrained by specific structural conditions or contexts. I designate them, in general, as 'socio-spatial structures of opportunities and constraints' although a socio-historical dimension is also implicit in this approach. These structures may be local in nature, but they are often shaped at national scales and follow international trends, somehow in parallel with the transnational networks of squatters. Activists interpret these structures, react to them, reveal them, and try to find cracks that allow their transgressive practice to prosper. Authorities and power-holders exert their influence over these structures to suppress, regulate, or prevent the extension of squatting. The chapter examines five main socio-spatial and historical conditions of possibility for the occurrence and development of squatting. In particular, I single out the specific urban political economy and activist networks, which are seldom introduced in the study of urban movements. The discussion on neoliberal urbanism, gentrification, and regulated squatting is illustrated by a specific analysis of the trajectory of the squatting movement in Amsterdam.

Chapter 4 discusses the significant types of squatting, squats, and squatters. Classifications are problematic if they do not account for all the nuances of every case, its urban-metropolitan context, and its change over time. This chapter critically reviews various attempts to categorise urban squats and suggests an alternative typology. I highlight the distinctions between squats for housing and squatted social centres, on the one hand, and tactical and strategic squatting, on the other, in order to clarify the political dimension of squatters' practices and movements. Following this, I move from a focus on squatters' differentiated motivations towards the most probable outcomes they produce. I also present a case study about the interactions between migrants and squatters in the City of Madrid in order to show how waves of protest and other contextual features are articulated in the types of squatted spaces effectively produced. The chapter

12 Introduction

concludes with an account of the splits among different kinds of squatters when it comes to dealing with the local authorities and urban policies of Paris.

Chapter 5 is focused on legalisation processes but approached from the broader standpoint of institutionalisation outcomes. Is the legalisation of squats a positive and desirable outcome? Is it likely or unlikely to occur? How can it be explained according to specific conflicts and contexts? In my responses to these questions, I first analyse the 'strategic negotiations' between squatters and their opponents in a way not attempted before by other scholars. Negotiations and policy measures for specific squats are crucial stages of the legalisation process. Next, I discuss to what extent legalisation is seen as a condition for a lengthy duration of a squat given the scarce opportunities to turn unauthorised occupations into legal forms of tenure. I distinguish three forms of broader 'institutionalisation' as the effects of legalisation and introduce the concept of 'anomalous institutions' as a way to understand squatters' resistance to state assimilation. Another in-depth case study from Madrid is included to adequately explain how the above processes unfold.

Chapter 6 addresses the following question: Why has the occupation of vacant properties without the owner's authorisation become increasingly criminalised in European countries? Although the criminalisation process varies across countries, I argue that there are common features that allow understanding these historical shifts over the last three decades. In this chapter I identify two rhetorical strategies used by mass media and political elites to spread stigmas about squatters. I also argue that there are symbolic contradictions within the dominant narratives which, in turn, are reframed by the squatters in order to wage discursive struggles about the legitimacy of squatting. The conflict between hegemonic and counter-hegemonic narratives further illuminates the structural considerations regarding the capitalist system and class struggles which are involved in the politics of squatting.

The squatters' struggles should not, and often are not, detached from other contemporary social movements. The most radical ones dismiss the reproduction of hierarchical and authoritarian modes of organisation and political action. In spite of their local battles, skirmishes, and defensive responses, squatters have pointed out remarkable cracks in the capitalist system of domination. The long-lasting duration of the squatters' movement also manifests underlying transnational patterns, networks, and linkages. A more detailed and comprehensive analysis follows next.

1

SQUATTING AS AN URBAN MOVEMENT

To what extent can squatting be studied as an urban movement? How do various theoretical insights from urban sociology and social movements intersect with each other? This chapter introduces the main concepts, assumptions, and theoretical approaches that help to investigate the squatters' movements in European cities. I suggest adopting a critical perspective in which class analysis and political economy take precedence; however, the incorporation of 'contentious politics' and other specific concerns related to the urban and housing questions are also crucial (Alford & Friedland 1985, Barker et al. 2013, Della Porta 2015, Goodwin & Jasper 2004, Judge et al. 1995, Pickvance 1995, Tilly & Tarrow 2007). This engages with a specific attempt at understanding how 'socio-spatial structural contexts' shape movements, how agencies and identities of movements unfold within those contexts, and which outcomes are actually produced (Martínez 2018a, 2018b, 2019). I also look at the 'effective radicalisation' of urban movements when facing the increasing commodification of housing, gentrification processes, and intersectional injustices (across class, gender, and ethnic lines) (Bhattacharya 2017, Lees et al. 2016, Madden & Marcuse 2016). In addition, the context of neoliberal urbanism over the last four decades (Mayer 2016, Rossi 2017) crucially shapes the uprisings of urban movements and their *right to the city* (Attoh 2011, Lopes de Souza 2010) coalitions with other social movements, especially at the peak of protest cycles.

Structural Constraints and Social Conflict

Social sciences are grounded on key, but often hidden, epistemological and theoretical distinctions. Galtung (1977: 65–68, 92–97), for example, echoed the conventional boundary between 'realists' and 'idealists'. The former would be 'seekers of invariances'; the latter could be seen as 'breakers of invariances'. As

14 Squatting as an Urban Movement

with many others later on, Galtung advocated for an integration of both camps: '[T]heories have to be *open-ended*, which means that they have to serve as a basis for understanding not only empirical, but also potential reality' (Galtung 1977: 70, italics added). Social scientists face other conventional dichotomies between positivism-empiricism and hermeneutics-relativism, on the one hand, and between agency and structure, on the other. Researchers who emphasise agency, for example, focus on the motivations of the individual, collective identities, and the micro scales of reality. When structure leads the analysis, researchers focus on processes of historical change, political and economic dimensions, and the macro scales of reality.

These splits have been also challenged by scholars who investigated social phenomena through 'theoretical experimentation' (Bourdieu et al. [1973] 1991: 94), generative and 'causal mechanisms' (Tilly 1998), and more generally through 'critical realism' (Bhaskar et al. 1998, Bhaskar & Callinicos 2003). For them and for me, society is not made of individuals, but of social relations and processes. Harvey's project to recreate historical-geographical materialism provides an additional inspiring view (Harvey 1996: Ch. 2–7). According to Harvey, one of the aims of a dialectical enquiry is to identify the 'moments' 'embedded within continuous flows which can produce radical transformations' (ibid.: 55). These 'moments' are not restricted to the material basis of social practices and relations but also include features from other 'fundamental moments of social life' (ibid.: 78) such as 'manifestations of power', 'institution building', 'language/discourse' and 'the imaginary' (values, beliefs, and desires). In particular, he incorporates the Enlightenment ideals of 'human emancipation' and 'self-realisation' into intertwined scientific and political purposes. According to the Marxist tradition, these ideals emphasise a collective dimension, a 'strict social and political control over market operations and, if possible, the radical transformation of power relationships in the realm of production as well as in the discursive and institutional spheres' (ibid.: 126). This approach thus calls for the interrogation of the domination of 'nature, the self, and others' (ibid.: 139) based on divides determined by class, gender identities, sexual preferences, ethnicity, religion, location, cultural lifestyles, physical abilities, social stigma, and age.

I translate the above insights into an epistemological framework based on nested, dependent, and non-deterministic hierarchies: '[E]ach lower order of complexity, being an open system, depends on (and is therefore constrained by) the orders above it (its environments) for the matter-energy and information required for its existence, survival, and eventual reproduction' (Wilden 1987: 73) (see Figure 1.1). Hence, on the one hand, structures constrain agency in a more powerful manner than agency is expressed within or against structures. On the other hand, structures enable action by distributing the resources and opportunities available to agents. Agents may, however, use them strategically in various ways while setting different goals and relying on specific ideas. Following the same logic of a 'dependent hierarchy', material structures (land and means of production, for example) are assumed to enjoy more ontological powers than

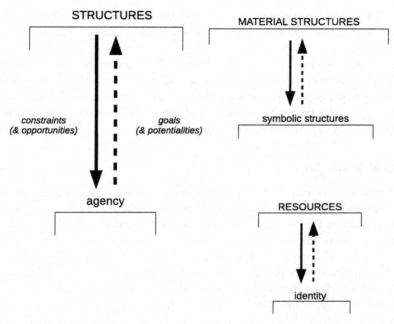

FIGURE 1.1 Structures and agency
Source: Author

symbolic structures (culture, in short). In parallel, social agents depend more on material resources than on symbolic representations (in other words, identity).

The non-deterministic nature of this approach suggests we must account for the constraints involved in the above hierarchical relationships (between structures and agency, the material and the symbolic, and resources and identity), but we must also examine how historical change of such structures occurs with the necessary participation of social agents' subjectivity and practices. Historical change may be incremental (usually in the long term) or discontinuous (often due to rapid moments of disruption in the short term). Hence, we need to identify first specific structures, agencies, and their dependent relationships; then, second, we must aim to explain their changing features over time. This implies an understanding of both vertical relations between the superior and inferior tiers of the hierarchies, and horizontal relations (not necessarily harmonious) among *equals* (elements within the same tier).

In Wilden's terms (1987: 77):

> For goalseeking, adaptive open systems—systems involving or simulating life or mind—constraints are the basis of complexity and the conditions of creativity. Only by using the constraints of the code of English can I write this sentence, for example. ... A constraint both limits and defines the ... relative

16 Squatting as an Urban Movement

freedom to use information to organize matter-energy or the relative freedom to use one kind or level of information to organize another kind or level.

At the risk of simplification, this abstract scheme could be well captured by Marx's celebrated statement: 'Human beings make their own history, but they do not make it just as they please; they do not make it under self-selected circumstances, but under circumstances existing already, given and transmitted from the past' (quoted by Cox & Nilsen 2014: vi).

Critical Social Science

At the theoretical level, I take sides with the broad legacy of 'critical sociology' that combines Marxian and Weberian inquiries on the major social and political forces shaped by the dominant economic mode of production and the configuration of the state (Alford & Friedland 1985). In my view, critical social sciences study, above all, power conflicts among social groups enjoying different structural conditions—vertically and horizontally situated. Instead of revealing the laws and individual values that underpin social cohesion, critical scholarship aims to reveal how every structural order is socially produced and the processes that trigger its historical change. Social structures, then, are made of contradictory and evolving social relations while also showing 'emergent' features in contrast with those shown by their constitutive elements (individuals and small groups). In the sociological tradition, this approach engages with concern about the 'problems of history, the problems of biography, and the problems of social structure in which biography and history intersect' (Wright Mills 1959: 224, Burawoy 2008). The social production of space is also, in my approach, an unavoidable dimension of historical processes.

In other words, critical social scientists should disclose what is hidden and dismissed (i.e. the contexts of structural domination and historical change) by the mainstream emphasis on order, integration, reproduction, stability, differences, individuals, subjectivity, choices, and identity (which mainly occupy the efforts of functionalism, interactionism, constructionism, pluralism, and rational choice approaches). Therefore,

> doing sociology in a critical way means looking beyond appearances, understanding root causes, and asking who benefits. ... The use of reason, science, and evidence to critically examine religious truth, established doctrine, and political authority ... [is also] devoted to a critical analysis of how social structures create relations of domination ... oppression, or exploitation.
>
> *(Buechler 2014: 12–14)*

In addition to debunking myths and beliefs that are taken for granted, I place power relations at the core of the analysis. The general notion of 'power to' (collective capacities to do, produce, create, think, speak out, cooperate, etc.) as a relational feature of agency within the constraints and opportunities of given structures, can be broken down into two subcategories: 'power over' and 'power against'. 'Power over' or 'domination' encompasses the capacities exerted by a specific social group (or an individual with the help of a social group) that result in the oppression of another group whose freedom and capacities are substantially restricted. 'Power against' or 'resistance' refers to the exercise of empowering capacities by the oppressed groups in order to oppose and overcome the domination they experience (Foucault 1975, Jessop 1982, Scott 2012). These concepts serve to frame the main vertical and horizontal relations involving class-economic, authority-political, gender-patriarchal, and ethnic-cultural dominations. Consequently, it is necessary to bridge Marxist and Weberian pursuits to explain the tensions between structures and agency, especially when there are collective demands of structural change at play.

The study of collective action and social movements meets this approach at its core when examining a basic triad:

1. how power relations are performed by both the dominant and the subaltern groups;
2. according to what specific structural constraints and opportunities those conflicts are expressed; and
3. what significant consequences in human history they produce.

Class struggles, contentious politics, and conflicts around hegemony (or 'cultural wars', 'symbolic violence', etc.) appear as the main areas of attention. As far as social scientists cannot claim to conduct research with an absolute value-free ethos, a critical stance implies a commitment to some of the aspirations of the subjugated groups without speaking on their behalf. As a consequence, scientific reports are not only about producing reliable knowledge but also about illuminating the potentialities of change opened and realised by the practices of resistance to domination. These potentialities and practices represent the central meaning of the goal-seeking, claim-making, and intersubjective framing activity that defines the collective identity of social movements. However, this bottom-up vertical relation is structurally constrained by the top-down historical rise of capitalism and nation states that crucially shape the demands and practices of social movements.

According to Alford and Friedland (1985), three levels of power can be distinguished:

1. 'Situational power' or 'power as influence'—when voters, interest groups, political parties, organisations, corporations, and labour unions compete for influence in government decisions.
2. 'Structural power' or 'power as domination'—when government agencies, technocrats, managers, and elites negotiate with each other in order to allocate resources and implement policies.

18 Squatting as an Urban Movement

3. 'Systemic power' or 'power as hegemony'—when societal forces, arrangements, and structures define the dominant social values, organisations, state institutions, and global development of capitalism towards crises.

These notions are aligned with three major theoretical perspectives:

1. Pluralist scholars give research priority to situational power, individuals, and small groups.
2. Managerial and elite theorists tend to emphasise structural power, large organisations, and state institutions (to avoid confusion, I would name it 'organisational power' instead).
3. Class-driven analysis privilege the observation of systemic power (I would name it 'structural-systemic power' or 'structural power' for short), global political economy, and the interests of labour and capital.

Following feminist and post-colonial critiques, the class perspective has increasingly incorporated gender-patriarchal and ethno-cultural sources of structural-systemic power (Bhattacharya 2017). As a consequence, the label of 'class' might simply be replaced by 'conflict', 'contentious', or 'critical' theory in order to account for all the differences, oppositions, and contradictions at play in the structural-systemic level of power relations.

Alford and Friedland suggest a 'synthetic analysis incorporating all three ... [and not] to collapse levels of analysis (and therefore levels of explanation) into each other' (1985: 8). This would entail a healthy eclecticism and simultaneous ambition to understand the whole, but it could also neglect two important aspects: (a) the 'critical' stance or political commitment of social scientists with the concerns of the oppressed groups to engender structural, systemic, and historical change; (b) the epistemological hierarchy of the macro dimensions of the social system, especially in terms of organising the state and reproducing the accumulation of capital that constrains (and enables) the operations at the inferior levels of society and power. Therefore, the class-critical approach offers a more consistent approach provided it includes my previous assumptions.

> The class perspective sees individuals, organizations, and society as being simultaneously held together and torn apart by societal contradictions. Capitalism, democracy, and the state are seen in terms of the dynamic relationships between capital accumulation and class struggle, creating the imperative to socialize the private and social costs of production. The multiple contradictions of this process lead to crises, which threaten the hegemony of class rule. ... Class power depends on the state, and the state is shaped by class power. ... The state is an agent or instrument of class rule ... [Some Marxists argue] for the systemic constraints on the capitalist state by the 'imperatives' or 'requirements' of capital accumulation. ...

> [Others stress] the active role of workers' resistance in shaping ruling-class strategies and the constant problems of maintaining workers' consent to becoming alienated objects in the production process.
>
> *(Alford & Friedland 1985: 285–287)*

In a capitalist society there are systemic-structural tendencies to commodify everything regardless of human needs, to replace public interest by class interests, and to polarise social structures between capital and labour—those who own the means of production and those who do not. Power is not an individual property but a social capacity that stems from structured and asymmetrical social relations. Therefore, the primary focus of a class-critical perspective is economic, political, and ideological class domination (Jessop 2012). Hence, democracy is usually considered 'a distorted and partial outcome of class struggle' (Alford & Friedland 1985: 281) and social movements, whilst the state is presumed to be class-biased, serving the interests of the dominant class.

However, there are also internal contradictions within the state because of the changing balance of forces, the different agencies and parties within the state, and its variable ideological hegemony over the whole society. According to Marx and Engels, "'the ruling ideas of any age are the ideas of the ruling class" ... [which relates] to the latter's control over the means of intellectual production' (Jessop 2012: 6). This led Gramsci and other Marxists to define the state as a combination of force and hegemony:

> Force involves the use of a coercive apparatus to bring the mass of the people into conformity and compliance with the requirements of a specific mode of production. In contrast, hegemony involves the successful mobilization and reproduction of the 'active consent' of dominated groups by the ruling class.
>
> *(Jessop 2012: 7)*

A remarkable implication is that 'power as hegemony' assembles and articulates (Alford & Friedland 1985: 288–332, Piven & Cloward 1979, 2005, Therborn 1980):

1. Economic exploitation.
2. Physical coercion by state agencies that exert the monopoly of violence (police and army).
3. Strategic actions by different social forces (typically, but not exclusively, by interacting with the state institutions) in order to consolidate or challenge dominant class interests (by 'rule-breaking' and building up 'counter-hegemony').
4. Strategic discourses to define reality, human needs, class interests, political alliances, laws, limits to capital accumulation, state autonomy, and state redistribution.

Agency is manifested within these systemic-structural powers, but it is neither insignificant nor passive in the pursuit of social change:

20 Squatting as an Urban Movement

> We need the concept of agency when we try to understand ... why [people] break the rules, defy the expectations of their community, and risk sometimes terrible penalties. ... Social structure itself encourages or inhibits self-consciousness and innovation, with consequences that can in turn lead to the power challenges that change structure, including both the rules governing social relations and the body of inherited meanings we call culture.
>
> *(Piven & Cloward 2005: 51)*

Capitalism, Democracy, and Urban Movements

Academic interest in urban movements still seems to occupy a subaltern position within the disciplines of urban studies and social movements. The most recent and comprehensive contributions (Andretta et al. 2015, Jacobsson 2015, Martí & Bonet 2008, Mayer & Boudreau 2012, Nicholls et al. 2013, Pickvance 1995, Pruijt 2007) express many unsolved tensions: the limits of liberal democracies and authoritarian regimes to cope with social movements at different spatial and political scales, the relations between the productive and reproductive realms when the urban and metropolitan spaces are shaped by social movements and governance dynamics, the problems of spatial fetishisation and location, the intersectional social composition of movements, the types of urban activism and outcomes in relation to the circulation of capital, etc. Squatting, in addition, is vaguely regarded as an urban movement by the literature, without a clear theoretical perspective. In order to clarify my critical and structural-systemic approach to urban movements in general, and to squatting, in particular, I will briefly elaborate on various fundamental aspects.

First of all, social movements are not necessarily progressive. Some can challenge domination while others can reproduce it. This suggests that social scientists must critically examine what activists say, what they do, and what consequences activism has. Social movements entail numerous contradictions rarely predicted by the enthusiasts who join the cause. Indeed, a true contentious approach looks not only at the conflicts between movements and their opponents but also at the internal conflicts within movements and within their opponents. There is always the risk of romanticising the movements we study, especially if we are deeply sympathetic to them or even a regular engaged researcher in their activities. At the same time, these movements' foes are seldom unified masters, oppressors, and objective systems. Contradictions within formal political regimes and within capitalism are not only opportunities to be seized for the movements to rise and prosper but also essential dynamics that can help explain their development and impacts.

Pickvance, for example, offered a restricted definition of urban movements by focusing on its specific organisations 'as mobilised groups, which make urban demands which challenge existing policies and practices, which make some use of non-institutionalised methods and which do not take the form of political parties' (Pickvance 1995: 198). This helps to distinguish movements from pressure groups 'although the degree of challenge is a continuum and the distinction ... is hard to make in certain cases' (Pickvance 1995: 198). Concerning their class composition, and despite the evidence of multi-class cases, Pickvance suggests a strong presence of the middle classes and highly educated activists among urban movements. When working-class participants are also involved, leadership tends to be taken by middle-class members (Pickvance 1995: 203).

Second, urban movements are a specific kind of social movements. For Tilly and Tarrow, for example, social movements are defined by durable practices of claim-making, including protest campaigns and other non-institutional performances (although institutional channels may be used too), and 'public displays of worthiness, unity, numbers and commitment by such means as wearing colors, marching in disciplined ranks, sporting badges that advertise the cause, displaying signs, chanting slogans, and picketing public buildings' (Tilly & Tarrow 2007: 8). Urban movements are concerned with urban matters related to the production, governance, and change of cities (and metropolitan areas). In doing so, urban activism unfolds within specific societal contexts and confronts some of their features. The grievances of activists originate in the articulation of specific political, economic, social, and cultural structures according to given spatial and historical conditions.

According to Pruijt (2007: 5115) 'urban movements are social movements through which citizens attempt to achieve some control over their urban environment. The urban environment comprises the built environment, the social fabric of the city, and the local political process'. In this definition contentious politics is implicit, but capitalism is not indicated as a necessary context in close interaction with movements. However, Pruijt divides citizens' concerns into three groups so that a political economy approach might be consistently elicited: (1) demands for collective consumption (what Castells also called urban trade unionism) such as housing shortages, rent increases, healthcare and education facilities, and basic supplies of water, sewage, and electricity, especially in shanty-towns; (2) contestation of urban planning due to insufficient or superficial participation, the effects of displacement, heritage conservation, environmental protection, etc.; and (3) 'specific urban issues' such as squatting, NIMBY (Not In My BackYard) protests, tax revolts, and anti-migrant local campaigns. As noted by Pruijt and others (Andretta et al. 2015, Cattaneo & Martínez 2014), the squatting of buildings may entail many purposes and motivations also related to collective consumption and urban planning issues which can intersect with the squatting of land (Aguilera & Smart 2017).

In my view, urban movements are also city makers—they contribute to the production of the city. They participate in conventional and unconventional politics by promoting certain services, land uses, and housing construction, or by opposing specific processes of urban development, renewal, and government. Contrary to the classic definition of cities as the simple combination of demographic density and social diversity, a critical socio-spatial perspective (Gottdiener 1994, Harvey 1996, Logan & Molotch 1987) conceives of them as the outcome

22 Squatting as an Urban Movement

of class, gender, and ethnic conflicts intertwined with forced residential moves; the work of builders, cleaners, retailers and many other inhabitants; and the specific interplays of economic, political, and cultural structures.

Urban struggles are expressions of those conflicts through the performance of various types of protest such as rent strikes, squatting, and alternative spatial plans (Pruijt 2007, Shephard & Smithsimon 2011: 38–44). They can also focus on the provision of decent and affordable housing; demands for schools; health services and green areas; the self-management of community gardens and counter-cultural social centres; the promotion of urban bicycling; and the improvement of conditions for the free expression of migrants, ethnic minorities, women, and LGBTIQ people in urban spaces. Opposition to urban neoliberalism in the form of privatisation, forced displacements, mega-events, corporate urban development, devastating tourism, and gentrification are ingrained in many contemporary urban conflicts. These examples indicate that there are, at least, four main domains of concern for urban movements (Martínez 2019, Pickvance 1995: 199): (1) the redistribution of wealth and urban commons; (2) the right to appropriate the city by the most vulnerable and excluded social groups; (3) the contestation of technocratic and limited participatory governance of cities; and (4) the self-management of spatial configurations and communities. These can be expressed with more progressive or regressive impacts, adding to the movements' internal contradictions.

Practices, Movements, and Scales

A third remark when it comes to demarcating the workings of urban activism refers to the distinction between practices and movements. Practices of protest and claim-making may hold political intentions and engender contention, but they can also be isolated, scattered, sporadic, and particularistic. Unless they are sustained over time, coordinated with each other, and challenging the powerholders (or whoever their opponents are), we cannot designate them as social movements. In addition, if activist practices do not tackle the power structures of the city, they can hardly escalate to the category of urban movements. For instance, every squatted place represents a protest practice, a form of activism, even if performed in a clandestine manner—as a 'hidden script' (Scott 1990). They can be indirectly associated or inspired by squatters' movements elsewhere but can hardly take part in them if they are not aggregated, regularly connected with each other, and also somehow coordinated in their actions when facing their opponents. Tilly also adds the engagement of 'third parties' such as 'other power holders, repressive forces, allies, competitors, and the citizenry as a whole' (Tilly 1999: 257). Since activists can be engaged in many different types of practices and movements can be also quite decentralised, without clear 'social movement organisations' taking the lead, it is a matter of interpretation to decide whether similarities and loose networks indicate the existence of a contentious social movement. This issue will be addressed many times in this book when dealing with the different manifestations of squatting, squats, and squatters.

Squatting as an Urban Movement **23**

In a similar vein, Andretta et al. interpret a risk 'that every urban mobilization or protest campaign could be considered as a social movement' (Andretta et al. 2015: 202). For them, the category of urban movements 'should be limited to conflict-oriented networks of informal relationships between individuals and groups/organizations, based on collective identities, shared beliefs, and solidarity, which mobilize around urban issues, through the frequent use of various forms of protest' (Andretta et al. 2015: 203). They also share the assumption that both socio-economic and political contexts create the conditions for urban mobilisations. In addition, 'going beyond institutionalized participatory processes and introducing some element of democratic innovation in processes of urban transformation can provide opportunities for urban movements' (Andretta et al. 2015: 204).

While introducing a collection of empirical works on urban movements in Central and Eastern Europe (CEE), Jacobsson (2015) heeds attention, above all, to the context of the 'liberalisation of housing and urban policy, often open fully to market forces ... [and] the complex nexus of state-society-market relations within post-socialism' (Jacobsson 2015: 2–3). The particular historical period under examination suggests a clear-cut contrast between the strong activity of NGOs sponsored by the USA and Western Europe during and immediately after the regime change, and the emerging urban activism 'domestically funded and grassroots-driven ... in response to local problems and needs, while often inspired ideationally by urban movements across the world' (Jacobsson 2015: 3). For decades, NGOs represented top-down and professionalised forms of activism and functioned towards the development of liberal democracies in CEE. Bottom-up urban movements explicitly declared a differentiated identity apart from NGOs, although occasionally they also evolved through processes of institutionalisation.

Jacobsson defines social movements as 'collective action efforts aimed at challenging the present state of affairs by people with common purposes and solidarity in sustained interaction with elites, authorities and/or opponents', and 'urban movements' next as a type of social movement 'concerned with shaping the life in the city' (Jacobsson 2015: 7). She explicitly adds Melucci's emphasis on the latent networks in everyday life (dispersed, informal, small-scale, and low-key activism) to the political economy and contentious politics approaches. Hence, she acknowledges types or degrees of urban activism and movements when mentioning the criteria of duration (short-lived vs long-lasting), institutions (non-institutional disruption vs institutional/moderate forms of protest), organisation (spontaneous vs formal organisation), origins (reactive vs proactive), and impacts (progressive vs conservative) in order to distinguish 'the rich variety of forms of urban protest' (Jacobsson 2015: 3).

Various case studies allow Jacobsson to identify three major contextual features especially significant in the explanation of urban movements in CEE: (1) a massive and accelerated form of privatisation of housing by means of property restitution to purported former owners before the state-socialist period; (2) a belated implementation of urban plans after a long phase of 'haphazard and chaotic urban development following a permissive laissez faire' (Jacobsson 2015: 11); (3) very unresponsive,

24 Squatting as an Urban Movement

repressive, and corrupt authorities as opponents of urban activists. On another note, urban restructuring, commodification, and gentrification are considered to unfold in a similar manner to the processes underwent by Western cities, although at a much faster rate of change.

Fourth, urban spaces are not just a mere local scale of politics or the location-scenario where movements develop their capacities. Above all, they are the result of social (as well as political, economic, and cultural) processes that make and reproduce a dominant mode of production and consumption (Harvey 1996, Ch. 9). Other state levels and even international or transnational flows of capital, goods, people, and information may be implicated in the movements' concerns and interactions (Hamel et al. 2000: 1–12, Mayer & Boudreau 2012: 284). In particular, debates about global cities (Sassen 2001) and the consequences of the economic globalisation in cities prompted many scholars to note that urban movements are attached to the local, but not exclusively. According to these authors, urban movements represent communities but also less clear entities such as the 'rights and privileges of legal and illegal immigrants' (Hamel et al. 2000: 3), all subject to global flows and disjunctives. Urban movements are expressions of systemic crises and contradictions in the globalised world, so they point to 'the flow of capital and its effects upon the communities in which people live their lives' (Hamel et al. 2000: 4).

Urban struggles in increasingly globalised cities are still concerned about deficiencies and the erosion of local welfare (collective consumption), but some conflicts are also about the living conditions in the city in terms of poverty, marginality, and precariousness that affect the domains of work, housing, and the racialisation of public spaces; for example, campaigns against racial-migrant police raids and solidarity with the homeless. Others engage activists in contesting the social costs associated with the competition between cities—gentrification, displacement, congestion, and pollution—in terms of mega-events, transfers of public assets and foreign capital subsidies, the outsourcing of services, etc. These struggles may or may not be articulated with those related to urban policies and governance, the renewal of urban areas, and site-based economic development programmes (Hamel et al. 2000: 8–12). Thus, some researchers insist on the 'global sense of place' by which 'locations are traversed by a wide range of power networks, with actors in different sites engaging with one another through multiple relations' (Nicholls et al. 2013: 11).

As a consequence, many scholars point to 'scale shifts' as key processes for understanding urban movements (Martin & Miller 2003: 148, Nicholls et al. 2013: 8–10, Tilly & Tarrow 2007: 95). In short, despite most activism being initiated at the local level, it can further shift to other places and upward levels if the diffusion of contention and the coordination of collective action are deemed to be more successful. However, excessive attention given to the strategic interactions between opponents may ignore both their different power conditions, the capitalist development of urbanisation (Mayer & Boudreau 2012: 279, Hetland & Goodwin 2013, Rossi 2017), and cyclical crises in the form of economic recession, regime change (Pickvance 1999), and so-called 'natural disasters'. Nicholls et al. (2013: 8–10) recall the focus on 'scale shift' when arguing that social movements 'often unfold at the intersection of a series of overlapping and hierarchical state spaces (municipality, regions, nation state, international agencies)' (Nicholls et al. 2013: 8). In spite of their prevalent geographical perspective, they put more emphasis on political and administrative scales of state institutions than to the social configuration of spatial scales such as neighbourhoods, city centres, urban peripheries, metropolitan areas, and urban regions. Interestingly, when authorities escalate resources, policies, and decision-making processes activists are forced to adopt 'multi-scalar strategies' (Nicholls et al. 2013: 9).

However, some researchers criticise the absence of 'urbanity' in Tilly and Tarrow's 'contentious politics' approach (Mayer & Boudreau 2012: 279). The so-called European or 'new social movements' perspectives had also ignored urban movements as such, despite being increasingly interested in cities as the loci where labour forces, in their changing composition, visibly manifest. It is within this context that Lefebvre's 'right to the city' became meaningful in order to account for the appropriation of urban spaces (streets, plazas, green areas, and, especially, the city centre) by those in need as well as those excluded, deprived, exploited, and alienated by the capitalist forces (Mayer & Boudreau 2012: 280). This entails a socio-spatial turn inviting research to focus on specific social groups (women, non-white and/or minority ethnic groups, migrants, the youth, the elderly, disabled people, homeless people, indigenous populations, diverse gender and sexual identities, street vendors, urban outcasts, etc.) and their spatial practices, needs, and demands (Marcuse 2012, Mitchell 2003, Wacquant 2007). Furthermore, the rise of 'global urbanity' due to neoliberal globalisation is engendering movements contesting and disrupting corporate urban development and socio-environmental injustice (Mayer & Boudreau 2012: 284). This suggests there is a transnational nature in many locally bound urban struggles. Notwithstanding, these authors provide a very ambiguous notion of 'urbanity' as 'a historically-situated and geographically unevenly distributed condition that affects the way we act politically' (Mayer & Boudreau 2012: 286–287).

Socio-Spatialities and Socio-Temporalities

A fifth aspect to reflect upon is to what extent urban movements are concerned with 'spatial claims' according to the social production of different spatialities and temporalities (McAdam & Swell 2001). A number of scholars made efforts to introduce a spatial perspective in the field of social movements research. Martin and Miller (2003), for example, engage with the contentious politics approach and emphasise their contextual and relational features in order to study 'how groups *shape, perceive* and *act upon* structurally based opportunities' (Martin & Miller 2003: 144, italics in original). For them, spatial variables do not simply add to the analysis of political conflict because society, history, and space

26 Squatting as an Urban Movement

altogether do structure and constitute every phenomenon. They borrow from Lefebvre his dialectical understanding of space as perceived, conceived, and lived:

> The potential for contention is often greatest where there are disjunctures among different types of space, e.g., when conceived spaces of order and equal opportunity are contradicted by material geographies of crumbling tenements, graffiti, pot-holed streets, dangerous parks, and resource-strapped schools.
>
> *(Martin & Miller 2003: 147)*

Accordingly, they distinguish between 'space' and 'place', the latter intended to be more specific, fixed, and situated: 'space is created through the flows, networks, and movements in the operation of capital, [whereas] place represents the interaction, interruption, or settling (however temporary) of flows in specific nodes' (Martin & Miller 2003: 147). Concrete locations, daily life experiences, and place-attachment may involve distinct spatial dimensions of political conflict. As for the notion of 'scale', they highlight the salience of 'jurisdictional hierarchies' as those represented by state institutions with different powers at various scales, but also the processes of 'scalar construction' and the 'underlying instability of scale' due to political action (Martin & Miller 2003: 148).

Nicholls et al. identify 'spatialities' other than scales such as territory, proximity, boundaries, networks, and mobility-flows. All these spatial features are meant to be 'relational' and 'play distinctive yet interlocking roles in the structures, strategies, dynamics and power of social movements ... Multiple spatialities intersect and shape social movements' (Nicholls et al. 2013: 2–3). The latter idea of place and space shaping politics, however, may lead to a spatial determinism that opposes the fundamental view of space as a product of social, political, economic, and cultural processes, as contended by political economy scholars (Harvey 1996). Spatial dimensions are as crucial as historical ones in the analysis of contentious politics, but social phenomena are ultimately caused by the influence of other social phenomena embedded in specific, significant, and connected contexts. Spatialities can result from those processes, participate in their constitution, or even intervene as mediators between them, but to claim their 'shaping role' or their capacity to 'empower activists' or 'ensnare them' (Nicholls et al. 2013: 6), for example, adheres to the assumption of space as an independent variable, which is at odds with the epistemology of both political economy and contentious politics. Miller alone (2013: 285–286) still echoes this mild spatial determinism but, more cautiously, defines the relational nature of space as 'the medium through which all social relations are made or broken' in accordance with its intermediating capacity. The Foucauldian notion of 'spatial technologies of power', as spatial practices (strategies and tactics) to mobilise and gain power (Miller 2013: 290), might serve that mediating purpose if discharged from the ultimate responsibility of shaping social relationships. Barricades, protest camps, and the occupation of vacant lots, for instance, are 'spatial infrastructures' of social movements (Feigenbaum et al. 2013) that mediate in their political contention with other actors.

According to Tilly (2000: 138),

> political actors can spell out their insistence by forming and/or referring to a spatial pattern, as when demonstrators march in well-disciplined blocks segregated by place of origin. They can also make claims with respect to spatial patterns and processes, as when rebels demand admission to a forbidden citadel.

This statement distinguishes the 'spatial dimensions' of social movements from their 'spatial claims'. Spatial dimensions or patterns may constrain social interactions 'including the interactions we call contentious politics' (Tilly 2000: 137). However, not all the spatial claims are the main ones in the political agenda of a social movement, which is exactly the opposite in urban movements—spatial claims, especially related to urban spaces, services, and governance, are usually the main content of their protest frame. Obviously, urban movements may also be understood by focusing on their various spatial dimensions, albeit these do not necessarily help define their urban character. Tilly also summarised the general relations between space and contentious politics in five propositions:

1. Time-distance costs and spatial configurations present opportunities and constraints to participants in public claim making.
2. Everyday spatial distributions, proximities, and routines of potential participants in contention affect the extent and character of their mobilisation.
3. Contentious politics intervene in the spatially organised jurisdictions of governments, and thereby incite governmental intervention.
4. Spatial configurations of routine political life shape non-routine contention.
5. Contention transforms the political significance of sites and spatial routines. (Tilly 2003: 221)

In the above propositions, spatialities both shape (#1, #2, and #4) and result (#3 and #5) from contention. In his 2003 shorter paper, Tilly focused on two main spatial dimensions (proximity and mobility) and conceived of them as 'spatial structures' able to facilitate or constrain contentious interactions. Their shaping or constraining power, however, must be considered, in my view, in association with other political opportunity structures such as the police control of certain urban areas according to 'comprehensive systems of governmental policing' (Tilly 2000: 143). Otherwise, an excessive emphasis on their independent nature might only lead to 'bare space'—the location and time-distance as proxies of non-spatial effects; 'phenomena that are spatially distributed but not intrinsically spatial, such as gender differences and class relations' (Tilly 2000: 152). Tilly also introduced the category of 'safe spaces'—those where activists can gather more easily away from police search and prosecution due to the

28 Squatting as an Urban Movement

shared meaning attributed to those urban areas by all the contending parties. Again, the prevailing social representation of 'safe spaces' stems from some physical traits (peripheral locations, hidden basements, etc.) associated with a certain legal status (privately owned land or clubs, for example) and political circumstances (tolerance of angry crowds next to symbolic monuments and privileges granted to protest in university campuses, for example).

> *Safe spaces* of one kind or another are a sine qua non of social movements. Oppositional movements need to control spaces in order to organize their activities and to recruit activists without being subject to crippling surveillance and repression by the state (or by landlords, employers, or other dominating groups or agencies).
>
> *(Sewell 2001: 69, italics in original)*

Finally, I assume that social movements in general, and urban movements in particular, are collective actions fundamental to understanding the limitations of liberal democracy as well as the contradictions of capitalism. Many people are ignored and marginalised from the decision-making processes within state institutions. Representative democracy cannot fully meet the needs, rights, and aspirations of the worst off, so unconventional mobilisation and contentious claim-making is often the last resort available for them. More privileged social groups can also be inclined to participate in social movements when institutional channels are closed off or due to opportunistic strategies. However, mainstream research on the political dimension of social movements tends to overlook how a capitalist organisation of the economy is not only deeply influencing society as a whole and the political system in particular, but also simultaneously spreading a devastating model of authoritarian rule, from the workplace to the stock markets. Furthermore, the increasing concentration of wealth fuelled by capitalism at a global scale destroys the possibilities of democracy, equality, and environmental sustainability.

Social movements are able to defy these trends and produce social change, but they are equally limited by the powerful forces that shape the contexts where activism is embedded. The analysis of workers' movements and class struggles is at the origin of social movement studies, but a biased emphasis on the novel emergence of some movements may ignore how class, exploitation, and productive processes are also directly or indirectly associated with their claims and social bases. Without the emancipatory current nurtured by many social movements, the degradation of democracy, with its internal flaws and authoritarian tendencies, will advance faster. Intimately related with the above are the ways in which liberal democracies, and many authoritarian regimes as well, legitimate and contribute to endless capital accumulation. When there is insufficient state regulation of the capitalist processes that undermine the pillars of democracy and social equality, social movements can either reinforce or replace the government in that endeavour.

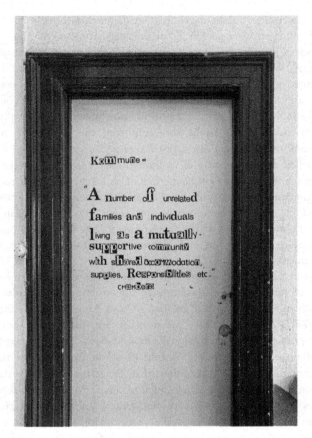

IMAGE 1.1 After-squat Poortgebouw, Rotterdam, 2016
Source: Author

Back to the Grassroots

My research about urban movements is in debt to the pioneering works of Castells and Villasante, especially their focus on the Spanish transitional period of the late 1970s, but also the further criticisms and analyses conducted by Harvey, Pickvance, Fainstein, Mayer, and other scholars in different countries of the Global North. Fortunately, the record of cases and approaches has been slowly expanded to the Global South in recent decades, which has also been an inspiration to my research. In particular, I was originally trained in the analysis of Latin American social movements and, more recently, have studied grassroots mobilisations in Asia as well, although I seldom deal with that literature here. In this section, I recall Castells' main insights and the theoretical discussions they provoked in order to frame my investigation of the European squatters' movements.

30 Squatting as an Urban Movement

I use the expression 'urban movement' in general, although I am aware that Castells and other scholars preferred 'urban social movement'. For Castells the additional 'social' meant the highest level of articulation and impact on the urban, cultural, and political spheres. He sometimes used 'urban movements' too as a category able to designate citizen actions with less leverage, weaker articulations, and low impacts. I designate the latter, simply, as activist practices—one-time, short-lived, low key, and poorly coordinated forms of protest. Pickvance (2003) noted that Castells also employed the notion of 'urban social movement' ambiguously in both a restrictive and a generic usage. Any action could be labelled as such in spite of its limited effects if the researcher considered the movement holds a higher *potential* effect. This leaves too much room for subjective interpretation and prevents an accurate assessment of the actual outcomes of movements. Instead, the term 'urban movement' (in a similar vein as we refer to the 'feminist movement' and the 'environmental movement') would not carry such a misleading connotation and, more importantly, obliges us to carefully evaluate its impacts.

In the first definition supplied by Castells, an 'urban social movement' consisted of 'a system of practices' able to 'transform the structure of the urban system or to substantially modify the power balance of class struggles and within the state' (Castells [1972] 1977: 312). These practices are articulated with social structures and specific political and organisational circumstances. The counterpart or main opponent of these practices is the 'system of urban planning and management' since it is from this instance where the urban fabric is shaped in order to reproduce the dominant conditions of production apart from the workplace. If the consequences of this contestation are not radical enough as to transform the whole 'urban system' and challenge the reproduction of capitalist relationships, instead of an urban movement there are only 'reformist/participative' collective actions (those just able to modify some elements of the urban system) or 'regulatory protests' that preserve the urban system. This approach, thus, excluded from the category of urban movements those which did not contest capitalism in the urban political arena—even more so if they did not establish alliances with leftist political parties and labour unions in order to stress the contradictions of capitalism (Castells [1972] 1977: 321–323). Therefore, most of the non-progressive urban claims, campaigns, and organisations would be considered limited forms of 'community participation', isolated protests, and easily manageable demands by the authorities. According to these categories, very few cases could strictly match the label of (a revolutionary) urban movement.

In spite of this limited definition, the structural analysis presented in *The Urban Question* entailed a valuable focus on: (1) the articulation of economic, political, social, and ideological dimensions in the analysis of the urban phenomena within the hegemony of capitalism, although the economic contradictions remain crucial; and (2) space as a dimension of class struggles when turned to the field of 'collective consumption'—the spatial means and public services necessary for the reproduction of the labour force (see a critical discussion in

Saunders 1983: 113–127). These tenets still ruled in Castells' next twist, *The City and the Grassroots* (1983), although not so overtly explicit. Urban movements occupied now the centre of attention. However, Castells did not consider them with the same revolutionary driver they had held before. Instead of being able to change the urban system and capitalist society, their main target was only the 'urban meaning'. This 'urban meaning' still refers to class and socio-economic struggles, but it incorporates a historical and cultural perspective that at times appears even more relevant than any other dimension:

> Cities are historical products, not only in their physical materiality but in their cultural meaning, in the role they play in the social organization. ... The conflict over the assignment of certain goals to certain spatial forms will be one of the fundamental mechanisms of domination and counter-domination in the social structure. ... The definition of the urban meaning is a social process, in its material sense. It is not a cultural category in the vulgar sense of culture as a set of ideas. It is cultural in the anthropological sense, that is, the expression of a social structure, including economic, religious, political, and technological operations.
>
> *(Castells 1983: 302)*

Urban movements aim to transform the hegemonic and institutionalised urban meaning which is shaped by the 'logic, interests, and values of the dominant class' (Castells 1983: 305), although grassroots mobilisations are not necessarily based on a particular social class. Furthermore, 'the autonomous role of the state, the gender relationships, the ethnic and national movements, and movements that define themselves as citizens, are among other alternative sources of urban social change' (Castells 1983: 291). By following closely the examination of the late-1970s Citizens' Movement in Madrid, he considered urban movements to be structured around three basic goals: (1) the city as a use value to satisfy collective needs (an incipient approach to the notion of the 'urban commons'); (2) the search for cultural identity and autonomous local cultures (a complementary view of Lefebvre's 'right to the city'); and (3) the decentralisation of government to local and differentiated neighbourhoods (oscillating between citizens' engagement in policies and communitarian forms of self-management) (Castells 1983: 319–320). Collective consumption, trade unionism, networks of collective identities-communities, and claims of political self-management must be articulated in order 'to accomplish a significant change in urban meaning' (Castells 1983: 323). Finally, urban movements should be 'organizationally and ideologically autonomous of any political party' but, nevertheless, keep themselves connected to them as well as to the media and the professionals—the so-called 'organisational operators' between movements and society (Castells 1983: 322). These mediations, in my view, should be supplemented with different degrees of engagement by other third parties (the police, by-standers, other social groups and organisations, etc.).

32 Squatting as an Urban Movement

Movement Effects Contextualised

This theoretical framework is of the utmost importance for the investigation of urban movements. Nevertheless, it has been critically reviewed in ways that also shed light over supplementary or alternative concepts. One set of critiques to Castells addressed early on the issue of movements' effects. Social change is not only due to movements' actions but also to the actions of state authorities and capitalists (Pickvance 1975: 32–34). The same may be applied to non-institutional means of action. Movements' mobilisations may be less successful in achieving their goals than institutional actions such as voting, petitions, and lobbying (Pickvance 1975: 37–39). Castells only conceived of 'urban social movements' as those able to combine the three main domains (urban, cultural, and political) in a high-level multi-dimensional impact on social change (Castells 1983: 373). Should they lack any of those dimensions, they still were classified as 'urban reform' (low-level multi-dimensional effect), 'urban utopia' (exclusive focus on urban-cultural change), 'urban corporatism' (exclusive focus on urban change), and 'shadow movements' (unable to produce any change). The more formalised the indicators to measure these effects, the more accurate the analysis would be.

However, it has been noted that Castells' formal theoretical models did not integrate well the indicators of the contexts in which every movement exists, such as 'the coexistence with a broader political movement, the presence or absence of political parties, and state structure and government policy' (Pickvance 1985: 35). The success or failure of urban movements, thus, hinges upon two different forces (agency and structure): (1) the movement's capacity to articulate multi-dimensional demands; and (2) the contextual conditions that favour or constrain the movement's capacity. Accordingly, Pickvance (1985: 40–44) highlights five key contextual features:

1. Rapid urbanisation associated with the material deprivation of housing, schools, water supplies, recreational facilities, etc.
2. State intervention of collective consumption that politicises formerly private issues or responds to movement demands with repression, the co-optation of movement leaders, or the funding of rival organisations.
3. The political context in terms of the existence of a protest wave of simultaneous movements, prevailing political ideologies and cultures, and the availability/openness of institutional channels to express demands.
4. A typically higher participation of the middle class in urban movements given their skills, social networks, affiliations, and values about the quality of life in cities. Working-class mobilisations about spatial claims may also imply alliances with middle-class groups.
5. General economic and social conditions due to the cyclical occurrence of crises and periods of relative affluence and growth.

Features 2 and 3, in turn, are tightly linked to the 'political process' theory in which the degree of cohesion among elites also plays a crucial role (Tarrow 1994). Regardless though of the number and type of relevant contexts we are able to identify, 'contextual features do not determine urban movement incidence or success but they supplement the analysis of mobilization, acting as conditions under which it is helped or hindered' (Pickvance 1986: 227). Hence, the success and failure of movements are crucial to illuminate their broad significance but are misleading when included in the definition of activist practices and social movements. Instead, it seems more sensible to assess movements' outcomes after a certain period of development according to the significant contexts at play (Pickvance 1995: 199).

Specific analyses of various urban movements in the US and Western Europe between the 1960s and early 1990s confirmed the validity of 'contingent factors' in the

> interaction between movements and context … [and] indicate how much a movement's strength and tactics depend on the socio-political framework in which it operates. Nevertheless, to the extent that movement activities shape this framework, the consciousness and tactics of participants have an independent role in affecting outcomes.
>
> *(Fainstein & Hirst 1995: 198)*

Castells' approach also emphasised the reproductive sides of capitalism in the urban sphere, the use value of urban goods and spaces, the connection of urban movements with class (until *The City and the Grassroots* when 'identity' became more central) and their tensions with other agents, such as political parties, in terms of autonomy, dependence, or convenient alliances. History and *transcultural* comparisons were warmly welcome to better furnish his approach. Although Castells was increasingly focusing on global phenomena and contexts, his conception of urban movements became more restricted as sources of 'defensive identities' (Castells 1997: 88, Marcuse 2002: 143) instead of turning to a more nuanced analysis of their interactions with local and global contexts. Conversely, the latter was attempted by various authors initially influenced by Castells' main views. For example, Fainstein and Hirst (1995) concluded their review of urban movements in Europe and the US since the 1960s by pointing to the following 'patterns of convergence':

> First [urban movements] are severely limited by their inability to sustain both mobilisation and programmatic gains without being routinized. … [Urban movements] have become absorbed into regular politics and the administration of state-funded programmes. Second, movements, typically characterized by a distrust of government, are frequently at odds with local authorities. While cooperation with the local state does tend towards co-optation, failure to do so undermines the ability of movements to harness

34 Squatting as an Urban Movement

the unique resources of the public sector. Third, 'collective consumption trade union' movements show a systematic inability to establish lasting coalitions with other groups. The relation of movements to political parties is consistently problematic. ... There is an overall trend towards middle-class movements in the West. The exception here are movements that are held together by ethnic or other identities, but such movements tend also to be circumscribed in their aims and restricted to narrow social groups.

(Fainstein & Hirst 1995: 196–197)

Also, while identifying the main shifts in the field of urban movements up to the mid-1990s, Mayer (1993: 149) stressed the 'specific West German (and later unified) political opportunity structure as well as in the context of a broader crisis and transformation of a mode of accumulation and regulation'. She also embraced a historical perspective and showed how strong 1970s urban movements, such as rent strikes, massive demonstrations against urban renewal, and squatting, were increasingly associated with other movements (such as the feminist and environmental ones) and that led to some electoral alliances. Later on, many community groups were incorporated in municipal programmes and moderated their demands. Instead of the inevitable pattern of institutionalisation, defeat and disappearance of most urban movements in Germany over those decades (1970s to 1990s), Mayer argued that they became more diverse, fragmented, sometimes even polarised, and occasionally able to mobilise supporters again. In the late 1990s and early 2000s, the anti-globalisation wave brought many urban movements into broader coalitions in order to oppose privatisation and the dismantling of the welfare state (Mayer 2006: 203). This brings about another omission in *The City and the Grassroots* that would challenge the general depiction of urban movements as progressive in the three areas of demands (collective consumption, cultural identity, and local power)—the rise of conservative and communitarian movements in many suburbs based on private consumption, exchange value, and exclusionary social identities (Miller 2006: 209).

Regarding the crucial waves of protest and other contexts of broader political mobilisation that create favourable conditions for the emergence of urban movements, Pickvance refers to

periods like the 1960s when protest was occurring over numerous issues [and] the likelihood that protest would emerge over one issue was much greater. This is because governments were believed to be likely to give in to demands, and because protests movements in one field created resources usable in others.

(Pickvance 1995: 204)

He also noted that many urban movements flourish in close relationship with political regime transitions. Movements may anticipate the collapse of authoritarian regimes and take the oppositional stance that forbidden political parties cannot.

Squatting as an Urban Movement **35**

Thus, urban movements may be tolerated because they 'are not explicitly political or anti-regime in aim' (Pickvance 1995: 206), which is, for example, the case of home-owners' associations and some environmental protests in China nowadays (Yip & Jiang 2011). Once political parties are formed, they incorporate many of the previously mobilised urban activists. This, in turn, undermines the activities of movements. Furthermore,

> Castells' research on the Madrid citizens' movement and on the Chilean squatters' movement showed that in each case the high level of success they achieved was due to their being part of a broader political movement. The concentration of social movements in Italy around 1970 is another illustration of the same phenomenon. In each case the process involved is an accumulation of political pressure in a situation of institutional weakness or loss of control capacity. The action of each movement is reinforced by the others, and increases the probability of concessions and reforms.
>
> *(Pickvance 1985: 41)*

The notion of 'collective consumption' as a central concern of urban movements was also challenged early by scholars such as Harvey (1973, 1982). Both Castells and Harvey approached the city by facing the same question (Merrifield 2014): How does the social production of urban space contribute to the reproduction of the capitalist system? While for Castells we should look at the conditions that permit the reproduction of the workforce, for Harvey we should worry about the conditions that grant the reproduction of capital accumulation. Obviously, both rejoinders might merge. What is important here is that the consequences for the analysis of urban politics differ. Collective consumption refers to the spatial conditions for the 'reproduction' of waged labour and, hence, the capitalist relations of production. State provision and management of collective consumption is thus the key driver of the social production of the urban space, whilst productive activities, spaces, and conflicts express the realm of labour exploitation and class struggles. As a consequence, urban movements primarily target the various domains of 'social reproduction' (from housing to urban planning and transport) (see an extended development of this theory with a feminist articulation in Bhattacharya 2017).

However, Harvey conceived of the city as a 'productive' force within capitalism. Cities are not only spatial conditions (locations) for capital accumulation, but a means to produce rents and profit in addition to exploiting labourers. Private property, real estate speculation, and financial investment in urban development constitute 'spatial fixes' in the 'secondary circuits' of capital (see a detailed examination in Jessop 2006). Therefore, urban movements would be defined by their association to opposing or favouring the circulation of capital through the built environment in order to deal with its crisis-ridden tendencies— by investing or/and disinvesting, building or/and destroying, appropriating or/and trading. Accordingly, urban movements would not necessarily be attached to the

36 Squatting as an Urban Movement

TABLE 1.1 Urban movements according to a political economy approach

Goals	Radical or moderate change of the capitalist economy and its functional system of urban planning and management Interruption of the circulation and valorisation of capital in urban space Promotion of use values vs exchange values Opposition to spatial financialisation, capitalist appropriation and accumulation by dispossession
Agency and structure	Articulation of economic, political, social, and ideological dimensions within the hegemony of capitalism
Space	A product of class struggles in the field of 'collective consumption' (the spatial means and public services necessary for the reproduction of the labour force) 'Urban meaning' incorporates class struggles into the cultural and historical configuration of urban spaces
Identity and social composition	Socio-economic class, gender, ethnicity, community residents, aspirations for self-management
Contexts shaping and interacting with protest	Protest waves, state structure, government's policies (redistributive vs neoliberal governance), urbanisation process (development, renewal, gentrification, housing, transport, environment), economic cycles of capitalism (growth/decline, globalisation), cultural trends (quality of urban life)
Life cycle	Institutionalisation, disappearance, co-optation, diversification, fragmentation, polarisation, re-activation

Source: Author

specific local places where they live and protest. Capital circulates throughout manifold spaces and scales despite its enormous accumulation in cityscapes.

The latter assertion entails a broader understanding of the relationship between movements, cities (both as the urban fabric and the local state), and capitalism beyond the local. That is to say, it calls for closer attention to the context of global flows of capital and the urban structures that they configure, occupy, and manipulate according to the capitalists' interests. As Merrifield contends, since the neoliberal turn initiated in the 1970s, even progressive municipal governments succumbed to state encroachment, divested from collective consumption budgets, privatised, and outsourced many of their services. In turn, they started subsidising capital in order to befriend spatially attached global investments landing in their cities. If 'extended reproduction of capital is achieved through financialisation and dispossession ... and reconfiguration of urban space ... on a planetary scale' (Merrifield 2014: 19), urban movements, then, have more targets in their agenda than merely the defence, if progressive, of local redistributive policies.

The Contentious Social Production of Space

By the mid-2000s, the study of urban movements was not as vibrant as before. Castells' legacies were widely ignored by those studying social movements. Many urban sociologists and geographers acknowledged his contributions but few continued by standing on his shoulders. Lefebvre's concepts (1968 [1996], 1991, 2016), on the contrary, were retrieved as more fashionable tools. Mayer's contention concerning the continuous fragmentation, institutionalisation, polarisation, and sometimes, in spite of the previous problems, the re-emergence of urban movements rightly questioned Castells' utopian assumption that 'they must have alternative visions resonating with radical leftist interests' (Mayer 2006: 204). Economic globalisation has transformed urban politics due to city-branding strategies, the construction of mega-projects, shrinking municipal budgets, the outsourcing of services, and competition for attracting capital investment. As Mayer indicates, this 'is the political and socio-spatial environment which has reconfigured the fault lines that furnish both opportunities and constraints for social movements' (Mayer 2006: 204).

The flaws in the comparative method attempted by Castells were also subject to criticism. He admitted that 'the intention was never comparative, but cross-cultural' (Castells 2006: 220). *The City and the Grassroots* was based on many case studies, but 'neither the same questions were asked nor the same mechanisms examined' (Miller 2006: 209). More particularly, Castells did not suggest any 'generative mechanism' or mutual constitution between agency and structures, society and space (Miller 2006: 209).

Castells' surprising turn to identity saw urban movements as agents who produce, make, shape, and transform the city but played down the structural-systemic powers of contexts: 'I decided to concentrate on agency and leave structure, and their interaction, for a later work ... Each context must be translated in the specificity of the language of social action taking place in the context' (Castells 2006: 220–221). However, he still acknowledged that movements' actions were constrained by specific contexts: '[W]here there is domination there is resistance to domination ... [and] resistance changes its forms with context and history' (Castells 2006: 221). For Castells, action and agency were at the core of social processes while the contextual forces only became seen as 'internalisations' or 'translations' of the outside. As an indirect response, Mayer asserts that

> if we combine analysis of their internal dynamics (their action repertoires, organisational structures, ideological frames, etc.) with that of their context (the structural contingencies, economic and political environments, relation to other movements and political parties) while paying attention to how contemporary conjuncture shapes our own research agenda and analytical models, we might move closer towards developing a persuasive theory of urban social movements.
>
> *(Mayer 2006: 205)*

38 Squatting as an Urban Movement

One of the books in Castells' trilogy *The Information Age* (Castells 1997) was devoted to social movements in which the urban ones mostly fell apart. Movements' agency became replaced by processes of identity creation. Class finally lost all importance in the understanding of movements. The material and spatial basis of movements was relegated too. As Marcuse critically pointed out, 'all identities are treated as reactions, and reactions against generalised processes. Enemies do not appear; processes operate without operators or subjects' (Marcuse 2002: 143). It is also striking that power was presented as diffused in global networks, less concentrated and dissociate from specific groups of people, the global capitalist class, or the political rulers. Marcuse also remarks that the abstract 'logic of space' 'becomes the cause, not the consequence of social change' (Marcuse 2002: 143), which contradicts Castells' prior emphasis on class relationships as triggers of differences in the use of space.

Going back to *The City and the Grassroots*, among the various urban movements under scrutiny, the Citizens' Movement in Madrid during the late 1970s was, without doubt, the case study that best represented powerful articulations of demands in terms of collective consumption, cultural-communitarian identity, and local empowerment-decentralisation. It was also the one that achieved the highest outcomes in changing urban life. However, there is at least one alternative interpretation of the same case (Villasante 1984, Villasante et al. 1989) that opens up quite valuable insights about the research on urban movements—and that has been ignored given its limited dissemination exclusively in the Spanish language. I summarise it in three bullet points:

1. The multi-class composition of the movement as a whole overshadowed the prevailing class composition of each of the main residents' organisations and the neighbourhoods in which they were rooted. Not only was class crucial to understanding material deprivations (instead of just a 'control variable' as it was used by Castells) but also, it was closely tied to the various kinds of movement organisations at play. Each performed different relationships with the residents and was organised according to different decision-making 'styles'. As a consequence, significant social diversity existed within the citizens' movement, but class divisions and organisational resources played more fundamental roles.
2. The observation of community bonds, mutual aid, and social networks in the everyday life brought about more specific identities of the social groups that took part in the mobilisations. The role of leaders, professionals, mediators, and the social base at large varied from neighbourhood to neighbourhood. So too did the composition of the social networks where local branches of trade unions, churches, sport associations, schools, retailers, etc. interacted with each other (Villasante 1984: 108–119). The coalitions and activist networks across districts were crucial drivers in explaining the process of mobilisation.
3. The historical roots of the movement date back not only to the rapid processes of migration and urbanisation in the late 1960s, and the squatted

settlements on the periphery of Madrid, but also to previous protest movements against the political regime—a dictatorship. Even some transnational protest waves influenced the ideological motivation of activists (Villasante 1984: 92–97). In addition, beyond the explicit material claims of the residents' organisations in terms of housing, transport, schools, and other public facilities, the citizens' movement participated in a broader political and counter-hegemonic movement trying to overthrow the ruling regime and to recreate the city bottom-up (Villasante 1984: 131–132).

Villasante's analysis connects with some Lefebvrian inspirations that Castells rejected in *The Urban Question*, although he became, in theory, more sympathetic to them in *The City and the Grassroots*; in particular, the attention paid to 'urban culture' as the social practices of everyday life, the changing appropriation of urban space, the claims raised by collective actors not necessarily unified by the same class ascription, and the need to address the main contradictions between urban struggles and the capitalist state (Gottdiener 1984). More systematic than Lefebvre, however, Villasante brought to the fore the specific socio-spatial and historical contexts where the internal dynamics of urban movements operate.

Unlike Castells, Harvey was not initially focused on the research of urban movements. This changed over the years, so he forged some analytical tools in accordance with his general theory, which was also partially influenced by the Lefebvrian notion of the social production of space (Harvey 2006). They are not as sophisticated as those of Castells, but they enhance the dimensions of the original and consequential contexts which frame movements' actions in a dialectical manner—from the 'personal is political' to the political economy of globalisation. I also find Harvey's interest in the social processes of mediation, negotiation, and *translation* (in short, the issues of hegemony and collective identity), which urban movements incur, coherent with my own scheme delineated in Figure 1.2. One of his most beloved notions is that of 'militant particularism'. His thesis holds that there are many particular grassroots struggles whose 'interests, objectives and organisational forms are fragmented, multiple and of varying intensity' (Harvey 2001: 190). The question would be to know: (1) their internal consistency, and (2) to what extent they are 'embedded in or metamorphosed into a broader politics' (ibid.). Whether progressive or reactionary on social, economic and environmental grounds, militant particularism entails community building, so Harvey suggests an understanding of 'the processes that produce, sustain and dissolve the contingent patterns of solidarity that lie at the basis of this "thing" we call "community"' (Harvey 2001: 192). Once we know how *particular* communities, urban struggles, and movements are produced, we should disclose how connected they are with more *universal* phenomena and structures such as the circulation of capital, environmental circumstances, class struggles, etc.

There is again a clear risk of interpreting the 'militant particularism' approach in light of the classical opposition between reform and revolution, and also according to Castells' low-level and high-level effects as integral parts of the

40 Squatting as an Urban Movement

definition of urban activism. However, I appreciate that Harvey's dialectical principles call attention to how urban movements may perform a mediator role themselves or may be implicated in negotiations with the key state institutions that mediate social relations in a capitalist society. 'What we identify are layers of mediating institutions, often organised into some rough hierarchy, operating as transmission centres through which social processes unevenly flow' (Harvey 2001: 196). And this leads to a more general theoretical warning that '[t]he context in which to understand local social movements is set by a fluid but highly complex interaction between processes and institutions operating at a variety of quite different spatial scales (such as national, regional, metropolitan and local)' (Harvey 2001: 196).

Table 1.1 and Figure 1.2 summarise Castells' contributions and the additional aspects raised by his critics. Two highlights of this approach are the distinction of movement outcomes and the contexts of opportunities and constraints. The latter are alternatively designated as 'socio-spatial structures', and I will dedicate a specific analysis to some of them in relation to the squatters' movements (see Chapter 3). The outputs produced by urban movements are closely related to the structural conditions in which they come into existence, but I here distinguish three main types: (1) the movement's self-reproduction over time; (2) the multidimensional impacts that movements can produce, either directly or indirectly, with higher or lesser degrees of intensity, and in more or less progressive directions (I add 'institutionalisation' to this category according to the discussion I present in Chapter 5); and (3) the major structural changes that, occasionally, some movements could bring about. Eventually, most outcomes are related to the same structural contexts that fostered the movement, albeit the three major types of outcomes demand a specific assessment.

The main rationale behind this graphic representation is that research on urban movements should focus not only, and not mainly, on their social components (social base, ideological motivations, resources, agency, identity, etc.) but also, and above all, on the contentious processes of strategic interactions between the main parties involved by taking into account the contexts that shape the movements and the impacts they, directly or indirectly, produce. Emphasis on a single aspect of these processes (movement, interactions, structures, or outcomes) will offer an unbalanced and biased knowledge. Notwithstanding the above statement, 'contentious interactions' occupy a central position in the chart. They represent social relations and practices in terms of power conflicts. This is the arena where activists meet their opponents, usually the powerholders, but sometimes other social groups in a horizontal position, and even subaltern social groups. Their interactions can take different strategic forms such as negotiations, reactions to each other and the contextual conditions, mediations and participation of third parties, brokerage, changing interpretations of the opportunities and constraints at play, decisions and non-decisions, etc. Castells' analyses were very limited in this respect, but scholarship in recent decades has delved significantly into these

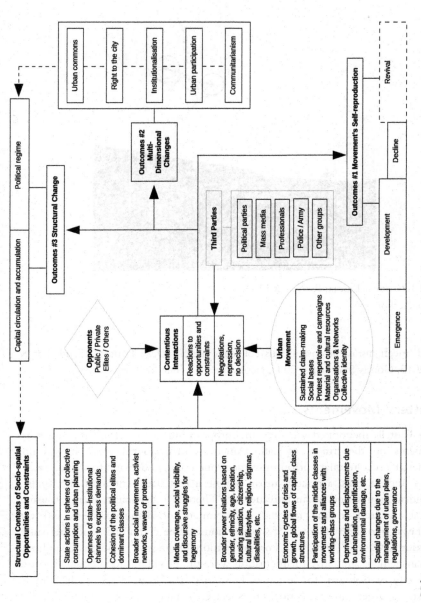

FIGURE 1.2 Urban movements

Source: Author

IMAGE 1.2 Squat Exsnia, Rome, 2014
Source: Author

central 'mechanisms' of contentious collective action (Della Porta 2015, Flesher & Cox 2013, Goodwin & Jasper 2004, Jacobsson 2015, Tilly & Tarrow 2007).

Squatters' Movements

When Castells mentioned squatting in European cities, apart from the squatters' settlements on the fringes of Latin American metropolitan areas, it was not considered a revolutionary urban movement but a limited demand for 'urban reservations' and, at most, a reactive urban protest against state centralism, the rigidity of political parties, and urban bureaucracy: 'There is a growing tendency towards political tribalism, calling for the abandonment of democratic life and the withdrawal into the wilderness of squatter houses, free communes, and alternative institutions' (Castells 1983: 317). For him, a more progressive paradigm for political self-management and citizen participation were the neighbourhood councils in the Italian city of Bologna, for instance. In spite of this limited approach, Castells suggested a larger and transnational perspective be taken into account:

> At the time the Italian movement was agonizing in the late 1970s, [and] the Spanish neighbourhood associations strengthened and had greater

Squatting as an Urban Movement **43**

impact. When, in 1980–81, the Citizen Movement in Madrid went through a devastating crisis, the squatter movements in Holland and Germany proposed many of the goals that had been forwarded by neighbourhood groups elsewhere.

(Castells 1983: 327)

In one of the early engagements with Castells' theories on urban movements, Lowe (1986: 138–151) dedicated some attention to examining the squatters' movement in the UK. By doing so, Lowe wanted to fill a gap in Castells' method: the understanding of how ideology operates in urban movements. In particular, Lowe noted that the squatting movement of the late 1960s and 1970s started criticising private property rights but 'rapidly became lost in a maze of negotiations and campaigns against [incompetent] local councils' (Lowe 1986: 142). Most squatters in privately owned properties did not focus on ideological concerns about private property either: '[P]eople squatted out of sheer necessity, having failed to obtain access to suitable or sufficiently cheap housing by other means' (Lowe 1986: 142). Of course, there was a third sector of squatters who rejected private property in accord with their anarchist ideology. However, Lowe explained the internal diversity of the movement according to very specific socio-spatial structures such as the management of vacancy by the local authorities and legalisation deals with some squatter organisations.

Despite the large numbers of squatters in Britain by the mid-1970s—around 50,000—the squatters' movement was relatively fragmented. Lowe identified another driver of the fragmentation beyond the squatters' ideology: the division between 'licensed' and 'non-licensed' squatters. Licensing implied that local councils made legal agreements with the squatters in council properties in order to grant them temporary accommodation.

The fact that most licensed squats were occupied by families was acceptable because it eased the waiting list of people for whom the housing authorities would otherwise probably have been responsible. Licensing is a classic example of the co-option of a critical social movement.

(Lowe 1986: 148)

By the mid-1970s there were around 3,000 squatters covered by licensing agreements in London. These concessions were possible after many criticisms to the ways in which local authorities managed their own vacant stock of housing. According to Lowe, vacancy in the public sector was due to complex allocation procedures, financial restrictions, lengthy management of renovation projects, and other bureaucratic bottlenecks (Lowe 1986: 145). Therefore, the image of the local authorities as providers of housing for need was eroded by these inefficiencies which, in turn, legitimised squatting of state-owned properties. 'Local authorities were more cautious in their use of private bailiffs. [In contrast,] illegal and clandestine evictions were more likely in private sector squats' (Lowe 1986: 146).

44 Squatting as an Urban Movement

Other early analyses of squatting as a social movement in the Netherlands and Italy took different approaches (see Image 1.1 and 1.2). The case of Amsterdam raised attention especially after the violent street confrontations and active resistance to evictions that took place around 1980. Draaisma and Hoogstraten (1983: 408–409) described the squatters' movement as a loose network of activist groups with a very diverse social composition: '[T]here is no organization, no committee, no chairman, there are no spokesmen ... there is no long-term strategy to solve the housing shortage'. They also characterised the movement as 'autonomous' and 'antiparliamentary' with a negative attitude to ally, negotiate, and compromise with the state authorities. This point, however, did not anticipate the deep institutionalisation effects that Dutch squatters experienced in the coming decades compared to other European countries. Consequently, squatters focused on direct action against real estate speculation. Their radical criticism of housing policies caused a breach in the coalitions they had forged with tenants' organisations. State repression also led the movement to barricade houses threatened with eviction and to increasingly resort to violent repertoires of protest that dwindled public support to their claims, according to Draaisma and Hoogstraten (1983: 412).

A more critical view of squatting in Amsterdam did not concern itself with the nature of the movement's activism (Priemus 1983). Instead, squatters were seen as either conservative or progressive. 'Bona fide squatters' behave as 'alternative urban managers' who allocate dwellers in the vacant apartments which, eventually, helps the local authorities to efficiently deal with the housing shortage.

> There are squatters who add living accommodation to the stock on behalf of priority home-seekers, and there are squatters who pinch allocation dwellings from under the noses of priority home-seekers. There are squatters with whom sympathetic local authorities can come to agreement in the struggle against speculators and squatters with whom no agreement can be reached.
>
> *(Priemus 1983: 424)*

Despite its shortcomings in terms of explaining squatters' mobilisations and protest repertoires, Priemus' approach indicated important aspects of the structural conditions and the legalisation outcomes that surround the interactions between squatters and their opponents.

Concerning Italy, Ruggiero (1992), for example, tried to merge 'new social movements' and 'resource mobilisation' standpoints. On the one hand, movements would pursue post-materialist values such as autonomy from bureaucratic rationalisation. On the other, organisations, leaders, and political alliances enabled movements to unfold. In order to search for common ground between both theories, Ruggiero pointed to the movements' networks and an increasing interest in their social institutionalisation, broadly speaking, without further elaboration on all the possible movements' outcomes. While focusing on the Italian occupied social centres emerging in the 1970s, he stressed their claims 'to abandon the [urban] periphery altogether and make their presence visible in the heart of the cities'

Squatting as an Urban Movement **45**

(Ruggiero 1992: 171) and to radicalise leftist politics: 'Straddling Situationism, Dadaism and libertarian Marxism, this movement came to regard the trade unions and traditional organizations of the left, which tried both to coopt and ostracise it, as the "new police"' (Ruggiero 1992: 171).

Treating squatted social centres in Italy as a social movement implied, for Ruggiero, the identification of the new forms of organisation and protest they invented (Ruggiero 1992: 181). In addition, he made two fundamental sociological observations. First, there were internal contradictions in the movement, such as the desire to 'stay together' or sociability 'cited by the [survey] respondents as the major motives for attending the *centri sociali*' (Ruggiero 1992: 179, italics in original) and the tendency to create 'closed enclaves' or ghettos that

> are far from hospitable. The reasons for this lack of hospitality, I believe, can be explained with the rejection by the *centri sociali* of any idea of activists recruitment. ... Also, the *centri sociali* refuse both to search for, and eventually represent, a majority.
>
> *(Ruggiero 1992: 181, italics in original)*

Second, he noticed the creation of new social and economic institutions fuelled by the alternative circuits of social centres. He designates them as 'pro-sumerist' lifestyles by combining both productive and reproductive-consumerist activities.

> There is thriving musical production in some *centri*, which are equipped with small recording studios and relevant accessories. ... This small-scale independent economy feeds a parallel market where other commodities and services are also available. Clothes, for example ... The term *pro-sumer* describes the figure of a producer-consumer located in an independent social niche where work serves the immediate needs of those inhabiting it. ... Finally, it includes voluntary work and co-operatives in all areas described as the *non-profit* sector.
>
> *(Ruggiero 1992: 176–177, italics in original)*

Squatting movements enjoyed marginal academic interest over the 1990s (among the exceptions: Corr 1999, Koopmans 1995, Mayer 1993). But a renewed strand of research since the 2000s manifested fruitful understandings in terms of the key dimensions that define urban movements according to what I have outlined in the previous sections (Martínez 2002, Mikkelsen & Karpantschof 2001, Mudu 2004, Owens 2009, Péchu 2006, Pruijt 2003, Uitermark 2004). As a novelty, recent accounts have focused on the relationships between squatters and broader autonomous and anti-capitalist mobilisations (Cattaneo & Martínez 2014, Steen et al. 2014, Vasudevan 2017), resistance strategies to the increasing criminalisation of squatting (Dadusc 2017, Finchett-Maddock 2016), and 'protest waves' and 'socio-spatial structures' (Martínez 2018a). I am not reviewing

46 Squatting as an Urban Movement

all these contributions here because I will engage in detail with some of the most relevant ones in the coming chapters. In particular, Pruijt's works over the years will deserve special attention since he made significant progress in terms of a structural-systemic approach—drawing upon political-economy and contentious politics—and the analysis of movements' outcomes. A comparative perspective across European cities and countries will also enhance our comprehension of the transnational character of this locally-rooted urban movement.

In sum, I agree with Mayer's (2013) appreciation of squatting first in terms of its singular features and, second, in terms of the urban and political contexts in which it unfolds. On the one hand, its configuration as an urban movement cannot be taken for granted unless some conditions are met:

> Squatting as a tactic can be used by individuals to improve their housing situation outside of any social movement, or it can be used, as a technique or action repertoire, by a variety of different social movements (including right-wing movements). ... [The progressive] squatting movement assertively operates in the open (rather than stealthily), engages in networking and coalition building with tenant organization and urban or environmental and/or other social justice movements; it makes explicit demands on the state, calling (most often) for affordable, decent housing and social centers, but also for (more or less) radical solutions to the underlying causes of the lack of adequate housing and social infrastructures. Crucially, it uses the occupied space not only for collective living arrangements, but also for collective self-organization and empowerment, in the case of the self-managed social centers for political and counter-cultural activities.
>
> *(Mayer 2013: 2)*

On the other hand, the neoliberalisation of capitalism has transformed many collective (both state-owned and commons-like) properties into exclusively private property by means of massive processes of 'accumulation by dispossession', privatisation, gentrification, and entrepreneurial forms of urban governance. The double-track processes of legalisation and repression of squatting are thus directly associated to various co-optation strategies of urban activists:

> Neoliberal urban policies thus on the one hand manage to hijack and incorporate alternative and subcultural activism including the creativity of squatters (who, in the process, may find it difficult to maintain their political autonomy), while on the other they entail intensifying repressive strategies, stricter laws, tougher policing, and hence more evictions and fiercer criminalization of squatting. Often local authorities implement both strategies simultaneously, which tends to sharpen the differences among and create collisions between cultural and political squatters.
>
> *(Mayer 2013: 5)*

Very often, squatters' movements have to face a dilemma between legitimising the neoliberal politics of authorities by signing agreements with them and opposing them so radically that state repression displaces squats from the visible city centres. Furthermore, the increasing financialisation of housing on an unknown world scale is revealing that squatting for social centres and squatting for housing are not so separate movements as have sometimes been considered. As a consequence, in the following chapters I will discuss more in-depth these constraining contexts over the squatting movements, their contentious interactions, and the main outputs of their development. Before doing so, in the following section of the present chapter I review another theoretical and political strand of the literature that has permeated contemporary debates about squatting movements in Europe—the right to the city approach.

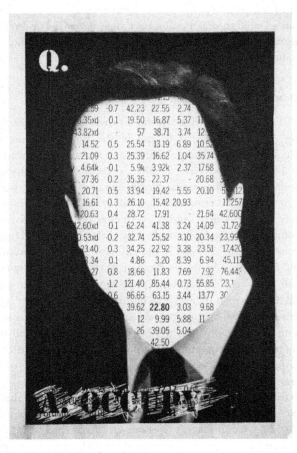

IMAGE 1.3   Poster Occupy, London, 2016
Source: Author

48 Squatting as an Urban Movement

Squatting and the Right to the City

The squatters' movement has evolved unevenly across European cities over the last four decades, although there have been recent attempts to understand their patterns and commonalities as well as their relations to other social movements. A very much discussed topic within these studies is the autonomous political identity of many of the squatters' movements, but less attention has been paid to frame their demands, practices, and achievements according to Lefebvre's notion of 'the right to the city'. In this section I argue that there are both strengths and weaknesses in that association. On the one hand, squatters' claims countered the exclusion of many social groups from the urban core and provided them with non-commercial and self-managed services, dwellings, social encounters, and opportunities for political mobilisation. This centrally engages with Lefebvre's main concerns on struggles to inhabit, appropriate, and recreate the city. However, the occupation of buildings was ignored in Lefebvre's agenda. Additionally, squatters have seldom adhered to urban coalitions united under the umbrella of the right to the city. Instead, most squatters aimed at challenging either the capitalist state broadly or specific speculative dynamics.

The Right to Squat the City

Henri Lefebvre's notion of the right to the city was formulated in the late 1960s when squatting movements started to rise in the European cities of Italy, the Netherlands, England, and Germany. There is a reciprocal resonance between both but only from a retrospective view. Lefebvre's ideas were highly speculative and fragmented, aiming at criticising capitalist cities and modern urban planning through Marxist concepts (use value versus exchange value, class struggles, historical materialism, etc.) while also proposing a normative theory for bringing forward an urban reform or revolution—a 'utopia controlled by dialectical reason' (Lefebvre 1968: 156). The normative side of the right to the city was defined by a number of tenets: (1) access for all (but, especially, the working-class) to a renewed city centre according to the social needs and use values; (2) appropriation of urban spaces in order to foster the full development of 'everyday life' and human creativity; (3) deep democratisation, citizen participation, empowerment of the excluded social groups, and self-management of the *urban* (both the built fabric or *habitat*, and the associated social activities to *inhabit* it); and (4) opposition to bureaucratic governance, alienated consumption, real estate speculation, commodification of all the components of cities, and socio-spatial segregation.

The right to the city was thus seen as an 'emerging' right along other more established liberal or 'civilised' ones such as the right to housing, health, education, etc. (Lefebvre 1968: 179). According to my observations and the literature about urban occupations, I argue that most squatting activists and autonomist movements all over Europe expressed similar concerns during the last four decades, despite often using a slightly different vocabulary. Without necessarily noticing it, squatters'

Squatting as an Urban Movement **49**

practices and discourses, limited in scope as they be, matched very well Lefebvre's plea for a post-capitalist city or 'urban society'. However, the identity of squatting movements in Europe has always been difficult to grasp and relate to a diverse range of experiences and organisations, so the label of the right to the city had few chances to articulate and unify the movement—even the earlier notion of 'autonomy' experienced similar troubles.

Urban studies scholars from English-speaking academia have revived attention to the right to the city since the 2000s, although there were occasional discussions in various contexts before. Mitchell (2003: 17–36), for example, put forward a compelling argument about the importance of public space in the realisation of the right to the city. Empirically, he identified homeless people and migrant workers as two of the most excluded social groups from the right to the city. Despite their exclusion, they strive for occupying public spaces and staying put. They protest in the streets, parks, and squares, but also in courts where they and their advocates contest the regulations that restrict their rights to assembly, to be represented, and to speak out. In doing so, those with no owned property show they are able to *produce* public space as a common good for all and, at the same time, to partially realise their right to the city according to Lefebvre's terms. Furthermore, the struggles of the dispossessed to appropriate some spots of the urban space reveal the violence of police forces—backed by state institutions and laws—and the interests of property owners.

Likewise, squatters expose the same primary contradiction 'in a world where some members of society are not covered by any property right and so must find a way to inhabit the city despite the exclusivity of property' (Mitchell 2003: 20). Children, women, prostitutes, street vendors, demonstrators, and other 'undesirable users' can also be subject to exclusions from specific public spaces and, as a consequence, deprived from their political empowerment and expression. According to Mitchell, the practice of appropriating public spaces and scaling up contention about policies, policing, and properties sheds light on the actual advancement or retreat of the right to the city.

Critical scholars also engaged in determining 'whose right is it about' and 'to what city'. Outstandingly, Marcuse (2012: 30–34) identified two crucial groups: the deprived and the discontented. The former refers to the 'most marginalized and the most underpaid and insecure members of the working class', with a special focus on

> those directly in want, directly oppressed, those for whom even the most immediate needs are not fulfilled: the homeless, the hungry, the imprisoned, the persecuted on gender, religious, racial grounds … those whose work injures their health, those whose income is below subsistence, those excluded from the benefits of urban life.
>
> *(Marcuse 2012: 32, 30)*

Squatters who demand decent and affordable housing provision definitely are key members of that group.

50 Squatting as an Urban Movement

Marcuse's discontented group comprises people from all social classes who are alienated, deprived from direct political participation, and also from a meaningful social life in order to express their creative potential. Students, cultural workers, and all sorts of counter-hegemonic dissidents represent this mixed group. Although this is a very loose category, it is applicable to the broad social composition of squatted social centres. Public squats congregate youth, left-libertarian activists, participants in various social movements, migrants, LGBTI-Q people, precarious workers, artists, and many others who have no say in urban planning and policies, who cannot afford commodified leisure, or who are simply displaced from quality urban facilities. Moreover, the city reclaimed is not just a physical space, but a whole urban society in the making. The aspiration to occupy the city centre also means the *centrality* of workers' power to determine production and enjoy its outcomes, including everything that urban life offers. Accordingly, squatters target specific built spaces, recreate community life within prior emptiness, and may desperately defend theses spaces as extremely valuable strongholds for enjoying true citizenship. However, it is social justice within a liveable city for which they eventually strive, above all. Direct democracy practices, anti-capitalist lifestyles, and feminist relationships, for instance, are some of the principal drivers of the prefigurative 'real utopias' that many squats promote in addition to meeting the housing and spatial needs of its participants.

The right to the city approach inspired some activist coalitions not only in Europe but also in North America and Latin America from the 2000s onwards. It became an explicit motto for broad campaigns in which squatting was only one of the branches, if included. This was the case, for example, of the Hamburg network who occupied Gängeviertel in 2009 (without using the term 'squat': Fraeser 2015). The area that hosted harbour workers in the past had been sold to Dutch investors (Hansevast) in line with other corporate buildings erected nearby. Activists created a cultural organisation, promoted public events, and ran art studios (Fraeser 2015). 'The tactics of emphasizing the architectural heritage and applying artistic playfulness to the process resulted in broad support from local elites and media' (Fraeser 2015: 174). This unexpected success—in a context where most squatting attempts are immediately suppressed—prompted local authorities to buy back the property and to legalise the occupation. The investor, indeed, had gone bankrupt during the global financial crisis (Birke 2016: 222). The Hamburg coalition Right to the City mobilised artists and precarious workers, but also leftist activists, urban gardeners, tenants, and even fractions of the middle classes (professionals, small retailers, civil servants, employees with secured jobs) because the effects of gentrification, privatisations, and peaking housing prices had disturbing economic, political, and spatial impacts on them as well. The coalition supported the protests against the eviction threat of the Rote Flora squatted social centre, the solidarity campaign with the Lampedusa refugees, the demolition of affordable housing, and the anti-austerity campaigns questioning the cuts in the local budget (Birke 2016: 219–228).

Other activist groups using the same slogan did not consider squatting a key issue in their political agenda. However, most right to the city coalitions shared a diverse social composition and focused their criticisms on neoliberal urban policies. As Mayer (2012: 68) pointed out: 'investments in glitzy new city centers, mega-projects for sports and entertainment, the commercialization of public space, and the concomitant intensification of surveillance and policing are all integral parts of the dominant pattern of corporate urban development'. In particular, Mayer argues that the cry for the right to the city has evolved since the 1970s according to political and economic contexts. Surprisingly, squatting in Europe as a protest repertoire can be found in all periods, despite its ups and downs (see, for a more detailed analysis: Martínez 2018c).

Legacies of Fruitful Associations

During the 'crisis of Fordism' (1970s) urban activists questioned the quality, efficiency, and service provision of, notwithstanding, generous welfare states. Squatters usually joined forces with various housing struggles and grassroots initiatives resisting urban renewal (recall, for example, the opposition to the 'upgrade' of the Nieuwmarkt area in Amsterdam: Uitermark 2012). New squatting waves also occurred when neoliberalism unfolded in the 1980s, although environmental issues, poverty, unemployment, and the revival of community life took the lead of the urban agenda. In this and the following decades, urban movements became more fragmented and some of their branches even turned to more cooperative relations with local governments, despite the cooptation and neutralisation of activism that these deals entailed. The global justice movement from the late 1990s and throughout the 2000s shifted priorities in a more interconnected European space for social movements, but squatters were still visible among these networks—for instance, in the alternative summits of the global powerholders, in Reclaim the Streets actions, and in anti-gentrification protests. The last offensive of hegemonic neoliberalism (2000s and 2010s) continued to shape opportunities for urban squatting given the rising rates of housing shortage, vacancy, indebtedness, commodified urban tourism, and the financialisation that guided urban development. Precarious jobs, workfare regimes, home insecurity, increasing socio-spatial polarisation, and the privatisation of urban amenities and basic services, such as health and education, motivated the revival of squatting movements for both housing and social centres—again, in coalition with other forms of urban activism (see Image 1.3).

The 2008 economic crisis represented a specific turning point for the upsurge of squatting in countries such as Spain, Italy, France, and Greece (Martínez & García 2018, SqEK 2018), which became even deeper with the increase of impoverished mortgaged families going through foreclosures, both working and middle classes facing rent increases without state regulation, and the violent border controls that endangered the lives of migrants and refugees moving into Europe (Mudu & Chattopadhyay 2017). The housing needs of all these social

52 Squatting as an Urban Movement

groups came to the frontstage of the European political agendas and, as a consequence, squatting was increasingly recognised as a *local* response to severe macro-structural turbulences.

As mentioned above, squatters in European cities, when visibly politicised, tend to emphasise the right to housing and other anti-systemic slogans in their banners, but the meanings and even the expression of the right to the city flood their discourses too, as many observers and activists have noted (Cattaneo & Martínez 2014). Grazioli and Caciagli (2018), for example, applied these notions to interpret two housing movements in Rome, Coordinamento Citadino di Lotta per la Casa and Blocchi Precari Metropolitani. They argue that the housing squats they studied do not merely satisfy housing needs but, more precisely, create conditions for

> the urban poor and dispossessed to keep living in the city, and thus to resist patterns of segregation and expulsion .... They re-appropriate the right to a central location that had been established as a prerogative of the well off and upper classes.
>
> *(Grazioli & Caciagli 2018: 9)*

However, the fact that precarious workers and undocumented migrants are the key social components of those movements suggests the need to consider more 'intersectional differences' (Grazioli & Caciagli 2018: 12) beyond the exclusive focus on the working class. Grazioli and Caciagli also remark the resemblance of Lefebvre's revolutionary call for the self-management and self-organisation of squats as 'urban commons' that challenge the prevailing *enclosures* of neoliberal urbanism—welfare cuts, privatisation of social housing, and for-profit urban management.

This move to the urban commons was initiated by prior anti-neoliberal campaigns around the mottos 'Cities for People, Not for Profit', 'Take Back the City', and 'The City is Not for Sale' in Italy, Spain, Germany, Austria, Ireland, and Switzerland. Evidence of this are the demonstrations promoted by squatted social centres such as La Ingobernable (and also non-squatted autonomous social centres such as EVA) in Madrid and various Spanish cities in May 2018 (La Ingobernable 2018). A similar initiative took place in Rome one year before, with several housing squats and social centres (Corto Circuito, Spartaco, Scup, and Lucha y Siesta) as members of the organising platform (DecideRoma 2017). The right to the city was also the driver of a critical architecture festival, BaBel2, that took place at Forte Prenestino in 2012 (BaBel2 2013). On the website of Forte Prenestino—occupied since 1986 and one of the eldest and largest squats in Rome—virtual visitors can still read the manifesto circulated by the Diritto alla Città network calling to oppose privatisations, evictions of squats, and urban financialisation (Forte Prenestino 2015, see Image 1.4). Another broad coalition of 18 groups named Take Back the City was recently formed in Dublin and occupied several buildings in 2018 in order to raise awareness about

IMAGE 1.4 Squat Forte Prenestino, Rome, 2014
Source: Author

homelessness and speculative vacancy. In their communiques to the media, activists rejected the label of 'squatters' and rather preferred designations such as 'concerned citizens' and 'political occupiers' (O'Keeffe 2018).

If we look at Eastern Europe, researchers have noted a parallel politicisation of squats such as Datscha in the city of Potsdam due to the housing struggles of 1993 and 1994, in a context where, in turn, more than sixty squats had mostly remained limited within a 'subcultural, self-sufficient alternative scene' (Holm & Kuhn 2017: 292–293). In Warsaw (Poland) squats such as Syrena and Przychodnia shared right to the city activism with tenants' associations formed in 2006–08 (Polanska & Piotrowski 2015: 286–290). This cooperation was especially fostered by the iconic figure of one of the founders of a tenants' organisation, Jolanta Brzeska, who was murdered due to her leading role in the movements of resistance to the reprivatisation of former 'communal housing' where they had been paying fixed and affordable rents until 1989.

Squatting Rights in Contention with the Existing Capitalist City

The normative nature of the right to the city approach has some benefits for conducting research on squatting movements. First of all, it provides key questions in order to interpret the political framing of squatters' claims and identity. Second, it suggests theoretical dimensions that further empirical analysis

54 Squatting as an Urban Movement

may test, elaborate, and expand. All the previous section has shown how fruitful these two paths are. However, I still see some problems too. In short, Lefebvrian speculations hardly indicate how to study actual activist practices, organisational resources and networks, strategic interactions, and broader relations with third parties and significant contexts.

On the one hand, the capitalist city is always designated by Lefebvre as the main ground to consider when envisioning future workers' forms of emancipation, but his emphasis on a 'right' to another city and *urban* society in the making blurs how neoliberal urbanism operates in relation to specific urban struggles, and vice versa, how grassroots movements respond to structural constraints. The loose definition of an abstract right could explain why the expression 'the right to the city' has been endorsed by very moderate political stances, international charters, and some legal statutes as a way to promote institutionally channelled citizen participation and a general access to the already existing capitalist city (Attoh 2011, Lopes de Souza 2010). This circumvents a careful examination of global capitalism currently manifested in the ways in which governments and financial institutions work in close collusion, with devastating consequences for many urban inhabitants.

For example, when European and IMF authorities pressed national governments to bail out banks subject to economic difficulties after 2008, whole housing and urban landscapes changed dramatically. Vacancy rates soared, unemployment led to mortgages arrears and foreclosures of primary homes, banks and social housing stocks were rapidly privatised, urban developments and renewal operations were accelerated to attract volatile and depredatory capital investments, and so on (Martínez & García 2018, Mayer 2016). Even more crucial for our purposes, impoverished and unemployed people did not enjoy the same benefits that states gave to the economic elites. On the contrary, many residents were evicted from their own homes, removed from the neighbourhoods to which they felt attached, or were forced to find affordable shelter in increasingly competitive and expensive housing markets. Housing exclusion and displacement to peripheral urban areas were the main consequences that urban struggles had to confront. Organisations such as the PAH in Spain framed these specific neoliberal policies as a massive scam and called for progressive social housing policies, emergency measures, and also squatting actions as self-help initiatives to remedy the most critical situations (Martínez 2018b).

On the other hand, Lefebvre ignored squatting struggles as drivers of possible urban revolutions despite surely being acquainted with occupations during the 1968 uprisings and also with housing movements in the after-war period, which, for example, achieved the legal concession of a 'winter truce' in France (i.e. the winter period during which squatters cannot be evicted). More specifically, most squatters are urban inhabitants who claim not only for the revolutionary right to the city according to Lefebvre, but for 'squatting rights' as well. For example, some explicitly question the right of private owners to keep their properties empty when housing exclusion is rampant and public resources limited. Furthermore, the most politicised squatters argue that local infrastructures and services are public expenses that ghost owners enjoy and dilapidate too when they keep their properties unused.

Squatting as an Urban Movement **55**

In addition, other squatters may urge authorities to be effective against all sorts of urban speculation. Otherwise, rent rises and inflation in housing prices will impact not only squatters-to-be but large swaths of the population as well. Even a liberal approach to squatting rights would agree that many human rights are usually violated when people are forcibly evicted from the place they live (domicile) (Fox et al. 2015). The increasing criminalisation of squatting thus indicates their capacity to reveal crucial mechanisms of social injustice in the capitalist city.

Squatting movements across Europe are more decentralised than, for example, tenants' and other non-governmental organisations devoted to housing issues (Cattaneo & Martínez 2014, Piazza & Genovese 2016, Polanska & Piotrowski 2015). Their anti-authoritarian views and a prevailing non-conventional repertoire of protest may, however, obscure their achievements in terms of the effective provision of housing and infrastructure for different social movements, refined methods of bottom-up and horizontal democracy, and legalisations. Take a look at, for instance, the work of specific activist collectives who advise how to squat and offer assistance, support, and militancy to those who initiate their squatting projects according to both the main traits of Lefebvre's right to the city and the daily anti-systemic struggles in which they are engaged (which excludes squatting as a business or for-profit activity, far-right racist and patriarchal squats, etc.): the Kraakspreekuur resources in The Netherlands (Pruijt 2013), the Advisory Service for Squatters in London (Finchett-Maddock 2016), the Oficina de Okupación (squatting office) and the Obra Social linked to the PAH in Spain (Martínez 2018b), and many others who promote squatting through textbooks, fanzines, art works, scholarship, and a myriad of affinity groups. They all have contributed to the steady persistence of squatting struggles over four decades, although variations in each context should not be overlooked.

In contrast to the utopian approach implicit in the right to the city, squatting represents concrete or immediatist responses to systemic oppressions. Concerns about the environmental, economic, and political implications of planetary urbanisation (Lefebvre's 'urban society') find a fertile ground of deliberation and criticism in most squatted social centres, but they do not usually appeal to housing activists in the same manner. This raises attention to the internal strains between different branches and expressions of squatting movements. Nevertheless, the material and spatial circumstances of living in extant cities, their uneven geographies and damaging social segregation, and the leverage of political power for the urban dispossessed centrally motivate most squatters. In conclusion, the right to the city paradigm does not suffice to capture the socio-spatial practices and structures of constraints (and opportunities) involved in struggles that claim for squatting rights while taking over strategic urban vacancy.

Social Justice in European Urban Politics

As argued above, the celebrated framework coined by Lefebvre as 'the right to the city' resonates with many of the squatters' discourses and politics, although

56 Squatting as an Urban Movement

there are only a few cases of explicit associations. Therefore, I contend that the right to the city approach illuminates the theoretical interpretation of squatting movements as far as: (1) these activists perform concrete appropriations of urban spaces; (2) squatted spaces are centrally located in relation to other urban facilities and social networks; and (3) beyond occupying empty properties for dwelling, squatters develop deep practices of self-management, self-help, direct democracy, the empowerment of the dispossessed and oppressed by capitalism, non-commercial services, social encounters, and infrastructures for political mobilisation. Furthermore, squatting struggles strive against the exclusion of various social groups not only from the existing city but also from the political right to participate in its transformation. However, the revolutionary impulse that animates many squatters and right to the city advocates needs to be tempered with the day-to-day struggles in which they are involved. In particular, squatters have shown to be excellent self-organised actors in monitoring urban vacancy and speculation, and to reveal processes of displacement, segregation, privatisation, and forced dispossession that have been increasingly boosted by neoliberal policies and the corporate powers of financialisation operating at both global and local scales. The right to housing and the right to a post-capitalist city are thus articulated in such a way that was hardly imagined by Lefebvre's insights.

Finally, Lefebvre did not sufficiently insist either in combining class analysis with other sources of oppression and social divides such as gender, ethnicity, citizenship status, and housing situation. Feminist and refugee squats must be highlighted here. On the one hand, this analysis also suggests that the study of legalisation, institutionalisation, and contentious interactions with authorities and owners will benefit from a deeper investigation of squatter rights and how they are articulated according to urban commons. This would entail more progress in the institutional arenas of legality and parliamentary politics that not many squatters would be eager to enter. On the other hand, the issue of urban centrality overwhelms the standard geographical location of squatting actions. It should include discussions about multiple centralities within metropolitan regions, and the kind of services and urban life that squatters wish to access and enable. In so doing, the analysis of alternative practices, campaigns, and policies that squatting movements promote would assess its outcomes in terms of housing needs, true participatory democracy, and measures to tame the markets, especially given the recent shifts to more exploitative economies based on urban tourism, luxury enclaves, persecution of undocumented migrants, and austerity policies. In this respect, squatting struggles are rarely alone but intertwined with other grassroots initiatives—and non-squatted social centres, in particular, too.

References

Aguilera, Thomas & Alan Smart (2017) Squatting, North, South and Turnabout: A Dialogue Comparing Illegal Housing. In Freia Anders & Alexander Sedlmaier (Eds)

Public Goods versus Economic Interests. Global Perspectives on the History of Squatting. Abingdon: Routledge, 29–55.

Alford, Robert R. & Roger Friedland (1985) *Powers of Theory. Capitalism, the State, and Democracy*. Cambridge: Cambridge University Press.

Andretta, Massimo, Gianni Piazza & Anna Subirats (2015) Urban Dynamics and Social Movements. In Donatella Della Porta & Mario Diani (Eds) *The Oxford Handbook of Social Movements*. Oxford: Oxford University Press, 200–218.

Attoh, Kafui (2011) What Kind of Right Is the Right to the City? *Progress in Human Geography* 35(5): 669–685.

BaBel2 (2013) Noi siamo la città. www.babelbabel.net/

Barker, Colin, Laurence Cox, John Krinsky & Alf Gunvald Nilsen (Eds) (2013) *Marxism and Social Movements*. Leiden: Brill.

Bhaskar, Roy, Margaret Archer, Andrew Collie & Tony Law (Eds) (1998) *Critical Realism. Essential Readings*. London: Routledge.

Bhaskar, Roy & Alex Callinicos (2003) Marxism and Critical Realism. *Journal of Critical Realism* 1(2): 89–114.

Bhattacharya, Tithi (Ed.) (2017) *Social Reproduction Theory. Remapping Class, Recentering Oppression*. London: Pluto Press.

Birke, Peter (2016) Right to the City—And Beyond: The Topographies of Urban Social Movements in Hamburg. In Margit Mayer, Catharina Thörn & Håkan Thörn (Eds) *Urban Uprisings. Challenging Neoliberal Urbanism in Europe*. New York: Palgrave Macmillan, 203–232.

Bourdieu, Pierre, Jean-Claude Chamboredon & Jean-Claude Passeron [1973] (1991) *The Craft of Sociology. Epistemological Preliminaries*. Berlin: de Gruyter.

Buechler, Steven M. (2014) *Critical Sociology*. New York: Routledge-Paradigm.

Burawoy, Michael (2008) Open Letter to C. Wright Mills. *Antipode* 40(3): 365–375.

Castells, Manuel [1972] (1977) *The Urban Question: A Marxist Approach*. Cambridge: The MIT Press.

Castells, Manuel (1983) *The City and the Grassroots. A Cross-Cultural Theory of Urban Social Movements*. Berkeley: University of California.

Castells, Manuel (1997) *The Power of Identity. The Information Age: Economy, Society and Culture Vol. II*. Oxford: Blackwell.

Castells, Manuel (2006) Changer la Ville: A Rejoinder. *International Journal of Urban and Regional Research* 30(1): 219–223.

Cattaneo, Claudio & Miguel Martínez (Eds) (2014) *The Squatters' Movement in Europe: Commons and Autonomy as Alternatives to Capitalism*. London: Pluto Press.

Corr, Anders (1999) *No Trespassing: Squatting, Rent Strikes and Land Struggles Worldwide*. Cambridge: South End Press.

Cox, Laurence & Alf Gunvald Nilsen (2014) *We Make Our Own History: Marxism and Social Movements in the Twilight of Neoliberalism*. London: Pluto Press.

Dadusc, Deanna (2017) *The Micropolitics of Criminalisation: Power, Resistance and the Amsterdam Squatting Movement*. Amsterdam: University of Kent [PhD Dissertation].

DecideRoma (2017) Appello Roma Non Si Vende. Att II. www.decideroma.com/romanonsivende-05-2017

Della Porta, Donatella (2015) *Social Movements in Times of Austerity: Bringing Capitalism Back into Protest Analysis*. Cambridge: Polity.

Draaisma, J. & P. van Hoogstraten (1983) The Squatter Movement in Amsterdam. *International Journal of Urban and Regional Research* 7: 406–416.

58 Squatting as an Urban Movement

Fainstein, Susan & Clifford Hirst (1995) Urban Social Movements. In David Judge, Gerry Stoker & Harold Wolman (Eds) *Theories of Urban Politics*. London: Sage, 181–204.

Feigenbaum, Anna, Fabian Frenzel & Patrick McCurdy (2013) *Protest Camps*. London: Zed.

Finchett-Maddock, Lucy (2016) *Protest, Property and the Commons. Performances of Law and Resistance*. Abingdon: Routledge.

Flesher, Cristina & Laurence Cox (2013) *Understanding European Movements. New Social Movements, Global Justice Struggles, Anti-Austerity Protest*. Oxon: Routledge.

Forte Prenestino (2015) Comunicato della rete per il diritto alla citta' verso la prossima assemblea. www.forteprenestino.net/mobilitazioni/diritto-alla-citta/836-diritto-alla-citta-verso-la-prossima-assemblea

Foucault, Michel (1975) [1995] *Discipline and Punish. The Birth of the Prison*. New York: Vintage.

Fox, Lorna, David O'Mahony & Robin Hickey (2015) Introduction: Criminalising Squatting. Setting an Agenda. In Lorna Fox O'Mahony, David O'Mahony & Robin Hickey (Eds) *Moral Rhetoric and the Criminalisation of Squatting. Vulnerable Demons?* Abingdon: Routledge, 3–10.

Fraeser, Nina (2015) Gängerviertel, Hamburg. In Alan Moore & Alan Smart (Eds) *Making Room. Cultural Production in Occupied Spaces*. Barcelona: Other Forms & Journal of Aesthetics and Protest, 172–177.

Galtung, Johan (1977) *Methodology and Ideology: Theory and Methods of Social Research, Vol. 1*. Atlantic Highlands: Humanities Press.

Goodwin, Jeff & James Jasper (Eds) (2004) *Rethinking Social Movements: People, Passions, and Power*. Lanham: Roman and Littlefield.

Gottdiener, Mark (1994) Debate on the Theory of Space: Toward an Urban Praxis. In Michael P. Smith (Ed.) *Cities in Transformation. Class, Capital and the State*. London: Sage, 199–218.

Grazioli, Margherita & Carlota Caciagli (2018) Resisting to the Neoliberal Urban Fabric: Housing Rights Movements and the Re-Appropriation of the 'Right to the City' in Rome, Italy. *Voluntas* https://doi.org/10.1007/s11266-018-9977-y.

Hamel, Pierre, Henry Lustiger-Thaler & Margit Mayer (2000) Introduction. Urban Social Movements—Local Thematics, Global Spaces. In Pierre Hamel, Henry Lustiger-Thaler & Margit Mayer (Eds) *Urban Movements in a Globalising World*. London: Routledge, 1–21.

Harvey, David (1973) *Social Justice and the City*. Athens: University of Georgia.

Harvey, David (1982) *The Limits of Capital*. Oxford: Blackwell.

Harvey, David (1996) *Justice, Nature & the Geography of Difference*. Cambridge: Blackwell.

Harvey, David (2001) *Spaces of Capital. Towards a Critical Geography*. New York: Routledge.

Harvey, David (2006) Space as a Keyword. In Noel Castree & Derek Gregory (Eds) *David Harvey. A Critical Reader*. Oxford: Blackwell, 270–293.

Hetland, Gabriel & Jeff Goodwin (2013) The Strange Disappearance of Capitalism from Social Movement Studies. In Colin Barker, Laurence Cox, John Krinsky & Alf Gunvald Nilsen (Eds) *Marxism and Social Movements*. Leiden: Brill, 83–102.

Holm, Andrej & Armin Kuhn (2017) Squatting and Gentrification in East Germany since 1989/90. In Freia Anders & Alexander Sedlmaier (Eds) *Public Goods versus Economic Interests. Global Perspectives on the History of Squatting*. New York: Routledge, 278–304.

Jacobsson, Kerstin (2015) Introduction: The Development of Urban Movements in Central and Eastern Europe. In Kerstin Jacobsson (Ed.) *Urban Grassroots Movements in Central and Eastern Europe*. Farnham: Ashgate 1' 1–32.

Jessop, Bob (1982) *The Capitalist State. Marxist Theories and Methods.* Oxford: Martin Robertson.

Jessop, Bob (2006) Spatial Fixes, Temporal Fixes and Spatio-Temporal Fixes. In Noel Castree & Derek Gregory (Eds) *David Harvey. A Critical Reader.* Oxford: Blackwell, 142–166.

Jessop, Bob (2012) Developments in Marxist Theory. In Edwin Amenta, Kate Nash & Alan Scott (Eds) *The Wiley-Blackwell Companion to Political Sociology.* Oxford: Blackwell, 3–14.

Judge, David, Gerry Stoker & Harold Wolman (Eds) (1995) *Theories of Urban Politics.* London: Sage.

Koopmans, Ruud (1995) *Democracy from Below. New Social Movements and the Political System in West Germany.* Boulder: Westview.

La Ingobernable (2018) Manifiesto #Madridnosevende / Nuestras ciudades #Nosevenden12m. https://ingobernable.net/2018/05/08/12m/

Lees, Loretta, Hyun Bang Shin & Ernesto López-Morales (2016) *Planetary Gentrification.* Cambridge: Polity.

Lefebvre, Henri (1968) [1996] *Writings on Cities.* Oxford: Blackwell.

Lefebvre, Henri (1991) *The Production of Space.* Cambridge, MA: Blackwell.

Lefebvre, Henri (2016) *Marxist Thought and the City.* Minneapolis: University of Minnesota Press.

Logan, John & Harvey L. Molotch (1987) *Urban Fortunes. The Political Economy of Place.* Berkeley: University of California.

Lopes de Souza, Marcelo (2010) Which Right to Which City? in Defence of Political-Strategic Clarity. *Interface* 2(1): 315–333.

Lowe, Stuart (1986) *Urban Social Movements. The City after Castells.* London: Macmillan.

Madden, David & Peter Marcuse (2016) *In Defense of Housing. The Politics of Crisis.* London: Verso.

Marcuse, Peter (2002) Depoliticizing Globalization: From Neo-Marxism to the Network Society of Manuel Castells. In John Eade & Christoper Merle (Eds) *Understanding the City. Contemporary and Future Perspectives.* Oxford: Blackwell, 130–158.

Marcuse, Peter (2012) Whose Rights(S) to What City? In Neil Brenner, Peter Marcuse & Margit Mayer (Eds) *Cities for People, Not for Profit. Critical Urban Theory and the Right to the City.* Abingdon: Routledge, 24–41.

Martí, Marc & Jordi Bonet (2008) Los movimientos urbanos: de la identidad a la glocalidad. *Scripta Nova* XII, 270 (121).

Martin, Deborah G. & Byron Miller (2003) Space and Contentious Politics. *Mobilization: An International Journal* 8(2): 143–156.

Martínez, Miguel A. (2002) *Okupaciones de Viviendas y Centros Sociales. Autogestión, Contracultura y Conflictos Urbanos.* Barcelona: Virus.

Martínez, Miguel A. (2018a) Introduction: The Politics of Squatting, Time Frames and Socio-Spatial Contexts. In Miguel A. Martínez (Ed.) *The Urban Politics of Squatters' Movements.* New York: Palgrave Macmillan, 1–21.

Martínez, Miguel A. (2018b) Socio-Spatial Structures and Protest Cycles of Squatted Social Centres in Madrid. In Miguel A. Martínez (Ed.) *The Urban Politics of Squatters' Movements.* New York: Palgrave Macmillan, 1–21.

Martínez, Miguel A. (Ed.) (2018c) *The Urban Politics of Squatters' Movements.* New York: Palgrave Macmillan.

Martínez, Miguel A. (2019) Framing Urban Movements, Contesting Global Capitalism and Liberal Democracy. In Ngai Ming Yip, Miguel A. Martínez & Xiaoyi Sun (Eds) *Contested Cities and Urban Activism.* Singapore: Palgrave Macmillan, 25–45.

60 Squatting as an Urban Movement

Martínez, Miguel A. & Angela García (2018) Converging Movements: Occupations of Squares and Buildings. In Benjamín Tejerina & Ignacia Perugorría (Eds) *Crisis and Mobilization in Contemporary Spain*. Abingdon: Routledge, 95–118.

Mayer, Margit (1993) The Career of Urban Social Movements in German Cities. In Robert Fisher & Joseph Kling (Eds) *Mobilizing the Community: Local Politics in a Global Era*. Newbury Park: Sage, 149–170.

Mayer, Margit (2006) Manuel Castells'. The City and the Grassroots. *International Journal of Urban and Regional Research* 30(1): 202–206.

Mayer, Margit (2012) The 'Right to the City' in Urban Social Movements. In Neil Brenner, Peter Marcuse & Margit Mayer (Eds) *Cities for People, Not for Profit. Critical Urban Theory and the Right to the City*. Abingdon: Routledge, 63–85.

Mayer, Margit. (2013) Preface. In SqEK (Ed.) *Squatting in Europe. Radical Spaces, Urban Struggles*. Vivenhoe: Minor Compositions, 1–9.

Mayer, Margit (2016) Neoliberal Urbanism and Uprisings across Europe. In Margit Mayer, Catharina Thörn & Håkan Thörn (Eds) *Urban Uprisings. Challenging Neoliberal Urbanism in Europe*. New York: Palgrave Macmillan, 57–92.

Mayer, Margit & Julie-Anne Boudreau (2012) Social Movements in Urban Politics: Trends in Research and Practice. In Peter John, Karen Mossberger & Susan E. Clarke (Eds) *The Oxford Handbook of Urban Politics*. London: Oxford University Press, 273–291.

McAdam, Dough & William H. Swell, Jr. (2001) It's about Time: Temporality in the Study of Social Movements and Revolutions. In Ronald R. Amizande et al. (Ed.) *Silence and Voice in the Study of Contentious Politics*. Cambridge: Cambridge University Press, 89–125.

Merrifield, Andy (2014) *The New Urban Question*. London: Pluto Press.

Mikkelsen, Flemming & Rene Karpantschof (2001) Youth as a Political Movement: Development of the Squatters' and Autonomous Movement in Copenhagen, 1981–95. *International Journal of Urban and Regional Research* 25(3): 609–628.

Miller, Byron (2006) Castells' the City and the Grassroots: 1983 and Today. *International Journal of Urban and Regional Research* 30(1): 207–211.

Miller, Byron (2013) Conclusion. Spatialities of Mobilization: Building and Breaking. In Walter Nicholls, Byron Miller & Justin Beaumont (Eds) *Spaces of Contention. Spatialities and Social Movements*. Farnham: Ashgate, 285–298.

Mitchell, Don (2003) *The Right to the City. Social Justice and the Fight for Public Space*. New York: The Guilford Press.

Mudu, Pierpaolo (2004) Resisting and Challenging Neoliberalism: The Development of Italian Social Centers. *Antipode* 36(5): 917–941.

Mudu, Pierpaolo & Sutapa Chattopadhyay (Eds) (2017) *Migration, Squatting and Radical Autonomy*. Abingdon: Routledge.

Nicholls, Walter, Byron Miller & Justin Beaumont (2013) Introduction: Conceptualizing the Spatialities of Social Movements. In Walter Nicholls, Byron Miller & Justin Beaumont (Eds) *Spaces of Contention. Spatialities and Social Movements*. Farnham: Ashgate, 1–23.

O'Keeffe, Alan (2018) 'We Have a Moral Responsibility to Invade' - inside the Take Back the City Movement. Independent. www.independent.ie/irish-news/we-have-a-moral-responsibility-to-invade-inside-the-take-back-the-city-movement-37320426.html

Owens, Linus (2009) *Cracking under Pressure. Narrating the Decline of the Amsterdam Squatters' Movement*. Amsterdam: Amsterdam University Press.

Péchu, Cécile (2006) *Droit Au Logement, genèse et sociologie d'une mobilisation*. Paris: Dalloz.

Piazza, Gianni & Valentina Genovese (2016) Between Political Opportunities and Strategic Dilemmas: The Choice of 'Double Track' by the Activists of an Occupied Social Centre in Italy. *Social Movement Studies* 15(3): 290–304.

Pickvance, Christopher G. (1975) On the Study of Urban Social Movements. *The Sociological Review* 23(1): 29–49.

Pickvance, Christopher G. (1985) The Rise and Fall of Urban Movements and the Role of Comparative Analysis. *Environment and Planning D: Society and Space* 3: 31–53.

Pickvance, Christopher G. (1986) Concepts, Contexts and Comparison in the Study of Urban Movements: A Reply to M. Castells. *Environment and Planning D: Society and Space* 4: 221–231.

Pickvance, Christopher G. (1995) Where Have Urban Movements Gone? In Costis Hadjimichalis & David Sadler (Eds) *Europe at the Margins: New Mosaics of Inequality*. London: Wiley & Sons, 197–217.

Pickvance, Christopher G. (1999) Democratisation and the Decline of Social Movements: The Effects of Regime Change on Collective Action in Eastern Europe. *Southern Europe and Latin America. Sociology* 33(2): 353–372.

Pickvance, Christopher G. (2003) From Urban Social Movements to Urban Movements: A Review and Introduction to A Symposium on Urban Movements. *International Journal of Urban and Regional Research* 27(1): 102–109.

Piven, Francis & Richard Cloward (1979) *Poor People's Movements. Why They Succeed, How They Fail*. New York: Random House.

Piven, Francis & Richard Cloward (2005) Rule Making, Rule Breaking, and Power. In Thomas Janoski, Robert Alford, Alexander M. Hicks & Mildred A. Schwartz (Eds) *The Handbook of Political Sociology. States, Civil Society, and Globalization*. New York: Cambridge University Press, 33–53.

Polanska, Dominika & Grzegorz Piotrowski (2015) The Transformative Power of Cooperation between Social Movements: Squatting and Tenants' Movements in Poland. *City* 19(2–3): 274–296.

Priemus, Hugo (1983) Squatters in Amsterdam: Urban Social Movement, Urban Managers or Something Else? *International Journal of Urban and Regional Research* 7: 417–427.

Pruijt, Hans (2003) Is the Institutionalization of Urban Movements Inevitable? A Comparison of the Opportunities for Sustained Squatting in New York and Amsterdam. *International Journal of Urban and Regional Research* 27(1): 133–157.

Pruijt, Hans (2007) Urban Movements. In George Ritzer (Ed.) *Blackwell Encyclopedia of Sociology*. Malden: Blackwell, 5115–5119.

Pruijt, Hans (2013) The Logic of Urban Squatting. *International Journal of Urban and Regional Research* 37(1): 19–45.

Rossi, Ugo (2017) *Cities in Global Capitalism*. Cambridge: Polity.

Ruggiero, Vicenzo (1992) New Social Movements and the 'Centri Sociali' in Milan. *The Sociological Review* 48(2): 167–185.

Sassen, Saskia (2001) *The Global City: New York, London, Tokyo*. Princeton: Princeton University Press.

Saunders, Peter (1983) *Urban Politics. A Sociological Interpretation*. London: Hutchinson & Co.

Scott, James C. (1990) *Domination and the Arts of Resistance: Hidden Transcripts*. New Haven: Yale University Press.

Scott, James C. (2012) Infrapolitics and Mobilizations: A Response by James C. Scott. *Revue française d'études américaines* 131(1): 112–117.

Sewell, William H. (2001) Space in Contentious Politics. In Ronald R. Amizande et al. (Ed.) *Silence and Voice in the Study of Contentious Politics*. Cambridge: Cambridge University Press, 51–88.

Shephard, Benjamin & Gregory Smithsimon (2011) *The Beach beneath the Streets. Contesting New York City's Public Spaces*. Albany: Excelsior-SUNY.

62 Squatting as an Urban Movement

SqEK (Squatting Everywhere Kollective) (Ed.) (2018) *Fighting for Spaces, Fighting for Our Lives: Squatting Movements Today*. Berlin: Assemblage.

Steen, Bart, Ask Katzeff & Leendert van Hoogenhuijze (2014) Introduction. Squatting and Autonomous Action in Europe, 1980–2012. In Bart Steen, Ask Katzeff & Leendert van Hoogenhuijze (Eds) *The City Is Ours: Squatting and Autonomous Movements in Europe from the 1970s to the Present*. Oakland: PM, 1–19.

Tarrow, Sidney (1994) *Power in Movement: Social Movements, Collective Action, and Politics*. Cambridge: Cambridge University Press.

Therborn, Göran (1980) *The Ideology of Power and the Power of Ideology*. London: Verso-NLB.

Tilly, Charles (1998) *Durable Inequality*. Berkeley: California University Press.

Tilly, Charles (1999) From Interactions to Outcomes in Social Movements. In Marco G. Giugni et al. (Ed.) *How Movements Matter*. Minneapolis: University of Minnesota Press, 253–270.

Tilly, Charles (2000) Spaces of Contention. *Mobilization: An International Journal* 5(2): 135–159.

Tilly, Charles (2003) Contention over Space and Place. *Mobilization: An International Journal* 8(2): 221–225.

Tilly, Charles & Sidney Tarrow (2007) *Contentious Politics*. New York: Oxford University Press.

Uitermark, Justus (2004) Framing Urban Injustices: The Case of the Amsterdam Squatter Movement. *Space and Polity* 8(2): 227–244.

Uitermark, Justus (2012) An Actually Existing Just City? the Fight for the Right to the City in Amsterdam. In Neil Brenner, Peter Marcuse & Margit Mayer (Eds) *Cities for People, Not for Profit. Critical Urban Theory and the Right to the City*. Abingdon: Routledge, 197–214.

Vasudevan, Alexander (2017) *The Autonomous City. A History of Urban Squatting*. London: Verso.

Villasante, Tomás R. (1984) *Comunidades locales. Análisis, movimientos sociales y alternativas*. Madrid: IEAL.

Villasante, Tomás R. et al. (1989) *Retrato de chabolista con piso. Análisis de redes sociales en la remodelación de barrios de Madrid*. Madrid: IVIMA-SGV-Alfoz. [http://oa.upm.es/14695/2/Retrato_de_chabolista_con_piso_2.pdf]

Wacquant, Loic (2007) *Urban Outcasts. A Comparative Sociology of Advanced Marginality*. Oxford: Polity.

Wilden, Anthony (1987) *The Rules are No Game. The Strategy of Communication*. London: Routledge.

Wright Mills, Charles (1959) *The Sociological Imagination*. London: Oxford.

Yip, Ngai-ming & Yihong Jiang (2011) Homeowners United: The Attempt to Create Lateral Networks of Homeowners' Associations in Urban China. *Journal of Contemporary China* 20(72): 735–750.

2

AUTONOMY FROM CAPITALISM

How do squatters' movements make a difference in urban politics? Their singularity in European cities has often been interpreted according to three major notions: 'autonomy', 'the right to the city', and 'urban commons'. However, few contributions have clarified the theoretical, historical, and political significance of these approaches (Cattaneo & Martínez 2014, Gil 2011, Katsiaficas 2006, Salamanca & Wilhelmi 2012, Van der Steen et al. 2014). In particular, autonomism has been identified as one of the main ideological sources of the recent global justice and anti-austerity movements (Flesher 2014) after being widely diffused among European squatters for more than four decades, though not often explicitly defined. In this chapter I examine the political background of autonomism as a distinct identity among radical movements in Europe, in general (Flesher & Cox 2013, Wennerhag et al. 2018) and the squatters, in particular. Instead of departing from the demarcation between autonomous and institutional left (Koopmans 1995, Pruijt & Roggeband 2014), I stress the social, feminist and anti-capitalist dimensions of autonomy that stem from the multiple and specific struggles in which squatters were involved over different historical periods (Cattaneo & Martínez 2014, Federici 2012, Van der Steen et al. 2014). These aspects have been overlooked or not sufficiently examined by the literature on squatting movements. By revisiting relevant events and discourses of the autonomist tradition linked to squatting in Italy, Germany, and Spain, its main traits and some contradictions are presented. Although political contexts indicate different emphases in each case, some common origins and transnational exchanges justify an underlying convergence and its legacies over time. I contend that autonomism is better understood by focusing on the social nature of the separate struggles by the oppressed in terms of self-management, collective reproduction, and political aggregation, rather than highlighting the individualistic view in which personal desires and

64 Autonomy from Capitalism

independence prevail. This interpretation also implies that autonomy for squatters consists of practices of collective micro-resistance to systemic forms of domination which politicise private spheres of everyday life instead of retreating to them.

Converging Radicalisms

Once squatters' movements become visible, articulated, durable, and challenging to the status quo there is an increasing elaboration of political discourse. This process is usually controversial, both internally and externally. Not all branches or factions of the movements agree with the major narratives about the nature of squatting. Some of these narratives in circulation are so intimately related to academic debates within the social sciences that the boundaries between both realms can also appear relatively blurred. This is the case with the notions of 'autonomy' and an 'autonomous movement' which have permeated many theoretical understandings of squatting over time, despite the indifference or disdain of some activists. In this chapter, I argue that autonomist approaches have widely circulated among squatters all over Europe and provided an often implicit or vague identity for most of them. However, what is the meaning of autonomy? By revisiting the accounts of autonomist and squatters' movements in Italy, Germany and Spain, I show the relevance of the social aspects of autonomy, which are sometimes obscured by more individualistic interpretations. In addition, I suggest that anti-capitalist stances, feminism, and solidarity with migrants have significantly contributed to the ideological meaning of autonomy, which has especially influenced the way squatters—especially its most politicised branches—manage their occupied spaces. This approach delineates the prevailing left-libertarian tenets as well as the squatting practices of houses and social centres, while helping to distinguish them from the occasional cases of far-right squats.

Italy and Germany are frequently considered the cradle of this trend (Geronimo 2012, Katsiaficas 2006), but autonomous movements emerged and unfolded in the metropolitan areas of many other countries all over Europe, including Denmark, Switzerland, the Netherlands, France, United Kingdom, Spain, Greece, the Czech Republic, and Poland, although the labels of 'anarchism' and 'radical left-libertarians' (Della Porta & Rucht 1995) attached to them have often blurred their characterisation (Flesher & Cox 2013, Van der Steen et al. 2014, Wennerhag et al. 2018). As I show below, autonomist politics emerged first from radical workers' struggles but squatters followed suit. During the 1960s and 1970s, squatting combined autonomist, countercultural, and feminist inputs, although the latter are not so frequently highlighted by the literature. The connection of struggles across urban territory and different social issues found fertile ground in the squatted social centres, usually in tight connection with housing campaigns and squatting actions too. Principles, memories, and examples from these autonomous experiences became adopted by the global justice movement around 2000 and, again, by the anti-austerity mobilisations a decade later (Flesher 2014), which indicates their long-lasting influence.

In my interpretation, the main misunderstanding about autonomism is the role played by 'individual autonomy' as a 'politics of the first person', a 'politics of desire' or the prevalence of individuals over organisations (Flesher 2007, Gil 2011, Katsiaficas 2006, Pruijt & Roggeband 2014). Although most authors mention this individualistic feature to distinguish autonomism from the more authoritarian, hierarchical, and bureaucratic organisations of the institutional left, I do not find this view very informative. Instead, as I shall argue, the expression 'social autonomy' seems to capture more accurately the central concerns of the collective practice of horizontal direct democracy and self-management fostered by autonomists. Even the feminist insights reveal that issues usually considered personal and private are politicised by making them socially visible and publicly debated. In addition, the radical independence of both the struggles and the oppressed groups is always voiced in a relational manner, not as individual independence: first, by identifying the social sources and dynamics of oppression; and second, and in a collective way, by empowering those who cooperate with each other in order to get rid of their perceived oppressions. More than a tension between the individual and the social dimensions present in all social phenomena, I contend that it is the specific emphasis given to the 'political method' of autonomism (self-organisation and self-management; autonomy from capitalism, patriarchy, and racism) and their 'immediatist' engagement in various contentious campaigns that makes it distinct compared to other political identities.

Although massive occupations of houses took place in some European countries in the aftermath of the Second World War, and many housing movements resorted to squatting as their main protest action (Aguilera 2018, Bailey 1973, Mudu 2014), squatters' movements developed their autonomist bases starting in the mid-1960s with the eruption of countercultural groups such as the Provos in the Netherlands:

> [A]n anarchic movement aiming at provoking the authorities and the norms of the Dutch society through performative direct action, and inspired by the situationists ... [who] started to squat empty houses ... [and] established *Koöperatief Woningburo de Kraker*, a place where homeless students could find support for occupying empty properties. Furthermore, the group also started the so-called 'White house plan' that aimed at locating empty buildings in the city and revealing the speculation of real estate owners.
>
> *(Dadusc 2017: 24)*

The Provos were mainly active between 1964 and 1967, but their subversive publications, political icons, and linkages between squatting and other social movements (feminism and urban cycling, for example) anticipated the youth revolts of 1968 (Smart 2014: 113).

The Provos shared countercultural inspiration with the Situationist International group (see, for example, Debord 1967, Knabb 1997, Sadler 1998), which was simultaneously active in France, Belgium, the United Kingdom, Italy, the Netherlands, Germany, Algeria, and the Nordic countries. Similar to other radical groups of the 1960s, the situationists sought an anti-capitalist revolution 'here and now', did not trust hierarchical organisations, and promoted workers' (and urban citizens') councils—the original meaning of 'soviets'—apart from political parties and labour unions. Their concerns about social domination through urban planning led them to support the occupation of universities, empty buildings, and public facilities, especially during the 1968 uprisings, although their most common practice consisted, mainly, of artistic performances (urban 'drifts', happenings, and communicative guerrilla).

In addition to situationism and the countercultural turn around the uprisings of 1968, feminism provided a framework to challenge 'everyday life' around social reproduction and housework beyond the housing question at large (provision,

IMAGE 2.1 Squat Metropoliz, Rome, 2014

Source: Author. Based on the artwork of LEROY S.P.Q.R'DAM, with permission

Autonomy from Capitalism **67**

access, affordability, policies, etc.). However, the self-management of social relations and spaces within squatted houses and social centres did not imply a fully liberated space from capitalism, patriarchy, and racism (Kadir 2016). Feminist groups and campaigns thus proved crucial in persuading autonomists and squatters of the need to incorporate their demands into radical politics. However, this was only possible through the autonomous organisation of women (and LGBTIQ people) themselves (Bhattacharya 2017, Federici 2012, Fraser 2008).

In the next sections, I review the main references in the literature that help to make my case. Only three countries are selected (two from Southern Europe and one from the North), but it suffices to disentangle the intertwined relations of autonomist struggles and the historical origins of the notion of autonomy. I recall this debate because I noticed its legacies in the squats I visited, read about, or joined as an activist during the past two decades all over Europe. However, the allusions to the autonomist notions and related events were seldom unequivocal.

From the Factory to Metropolitan Struggles

The influences of anarchism, heterodox (anti-state) Marxism, anti-institutionalism, and countercultural anti-authoritarian politics in the 'new social movements' and the 'new left' after-1968 were pervasive in squatting activism, although at different paces in each country (Van der Steen et al. 2014). These first trends of a vague autonomist movement had another precedent in the Italian Marxist-inspired *Operaismo* (workerism). This intellectual and political group had been sowing the seeds of autonomist politics since the early 1960s by focusing on the autonomy of workers' struggles from political parties and from labour unions. They also launched activist self-research (*coricerca*) with factory workers and favoured wildcat strikes, absenteeism, and sabotage on the assembly line (Balestrini & Moroni (1997) [2006], Katsiaficas 2006: 17–57). Leftist intellectuals and students engaged with class struggles in which the lowest tiers of the proletariat and the workers' viewpoint were expected to take the lead. A full opposition to salaried work and an invitation to take over the factories were a decisive inspiration for those who started occupying empty buildings and setting up squatted self-managed social centres (*Centri Sociali*) some years later, especially around the large mobilisation peaks of 1967–69 and 1976–77.

This move, as Geronimo recalls, had its roots in the defeat of many labour struggles, the transformation of the productive system, and the rise of the precarious class, which merged impoverished university graduates, casual workers, and unemployed people:

> The process of decentralization and automation led to a drastic reduction of jobs in the formal sector and to an enormous expansion of production in small factories and at home. Theorists like Negri described this development using the term 'fabbrica diffusa' ... *Operaists* ... shifted their focus

68 Autonomy from Capitalism

from the *operaio massa*, the 'worker of mass production' of the 1960s, to the *operaio sociale*, the 'worker of the social field'. This expanded the struggle to areas outside of the immediate workplace. It was a reaction not only to the decentralization of the production process but also to the women's and youth movements ... [Militants] looted supermarkets ... rode public transport for free, refused to pay for rock concerts and movie screenings ... [and some] used guns ... ravaged hotels, and hundreds of cars and buses [were] toppled and torched.

(Geronimo 2012: 42–45, italics in original)

Both Geronimo (2012) and Katsiaficas (2006: 65–66, 188) acknowledge that the Italian *Autonomia* was so influential in German extra-parliamentary politics that these activists changed their own name to the *Autonomen* by 1979–80. Danish political squatters did the same in the late-1980s, precisely when most political squats were evicted and anti-fascism, anti-racism, and anti-imperialism replaced the priority hitherto enjoyed by squatting (Karpantschof & Mikkelsen 2014: 188–193).

Workerism was the origin of autonomism, but the occupations of houses and social centres, along with tenants' struggles, were already in place and often supported by the Italian Communist Party (Mudu & Rossini 2018: 100). The turn to autonomism started with a wave of occupations around 1968, especially in large cities such as Milan. For example, located in Plaza Fontana, the very heart of the city, was the squatted Ex Hotel Commercio. Run by university students in alliance with many political groups and the local tenants' union, it was considered 'the largest urban commune ... in Europe' (Balestrini & Moroni (1997) [2006]: 276, Martin & Moroni 2007). Despite the call for the autonomy of the struggles, and as a reaction to harsh state repression and several fascist murders (Balestrini & Moroni (1997) [2006]: 363, 542), workerist activists set up multiple extra-parliamentary parties and organisations (Lotta Continua, Potere Operaio, Avanguardia Operaia, etc.) over the 1970s who joined anarchists, feminists, situationists, students, and housing activists in the squatted social centres of the following decades. These groups were short-lived, but their promotion of workers' autonomy has left a strong legacy among squatters, mainly since 1973:

Solidarity within proletarian communities has the power to organise the social conditions of exchange, production, and co-living, autonomous from the bourgeois legality; autonomous from the law of exchange, from the law of labour time, from the law of private property.... The proletarian sociality defines its own laws and practices in the territory that the bourgeoisie occupies by force.

(Balestrini & Moroni (1997) [2006]: 451)

As a consequence, beyond independence from electoral and institutional politics, autonomists fostered the autonomy of workers' power, knowledge, cooperation, needs, resistance, and struggles in order to take back the time, money, and spaces from the hands of the capitalist class. A diffuse political identity, multiple points of conflicts and insurrections, and decentralised actions aimed at mobilising large amounts of the proletariat were translated into the politicisation of new squatting waves from the mid-1980s onwards (Mudu & Rossini 2018: 101).

The Indiani Metropolitani and the Circoli del Proletariato Giovanile represented one of the countercultural echelons that connected autonomist politics and squatting. For example, a celebrated pamphlet of the latter from 1977 declared:

> We want it all! It's time to rebel! We throw parties because we want to have fun ... to affirm our right to life, to happiness, and to a new way of being together. We occupy buildings because we want to have meeting places to debate, to play music, and do theatre, to have a specific and alternative place for family life ... We hold assemblies about heroin because we want to find living alternatives, not death. And also, in order to expulse fascist and gangsters who attack us. We foster strikes because we want to work less and better, with the power of our hands ... This is our desire of communism, bread and roses.
>
> *(Balestrini & Moroni (1997) [2006]: 524)*

In addition to demands for affordable housing, the constraints experienced through conservative family traditions, a deep opposition to commodified and state-controlled leisure as well as the alienation engendered by salaried work motivated this mixture of autonomism and, often joyful and satiric, Situationism applied to urban squatting.

Internal ideological controversies among squatters adhered to different branches of autonomism, anarchism, and feminism were very frequent, but they also contributed to the creation of a vibrant political milieu in many cities (Mudu 2012: 416–418). In contrast to Anglo-Saxon countries, where anarchism and autonomism are almost synonyms, both branches had different historical trajectories and stances in Italy and Spain (Mudu 2012: 414–418). During the 1977 protest waves, for example, both shared an anti-authoritarian approach, but autonomists tended to lead and hegemonise the movement (Mudu 2009, Mudu 2012: 417). Nonetheless, in my interpretation, the collective self-management of squats, either for living or for socialisation, and in tight connection with the autonomy of the working-class and oppressed groups, represents the best theoretical and political coincidence among all the politicised squatters. This has hardly been noted in the literature on autonomous politics where squats are often seen as just another strand of activism (Wennerhag et al. 2018). Due to the decline of struggles at the workplace, the self-management of squats all over the metropolitan area took the lead, affecting different spheres of social life and helping to unite anarchists, punks, and autonomists in the second-generation social centres during the mid-1980s, as argued too by Mudu (2012: 420) and Piazza (2018: 503). In short, by considering all the above insights, a dominant

70 Autonomy from Capitalism

politics of what I designate 'social autonomy' increasingly found its own way, its own proponents, and its own practitioners in urban politics beyond the institutional labour unions and the parliamentary political parties of the left. Furthermore, this notion was also crucially nurtured by feminism.

Although less mentioned by the literature, during the 1960s and 1970s an innovative and challenging feminist movement emerged in tight connection with Italian autonomism. Active women in leftist politics called for their self-organisation without men in their groups, meetings, and protest actions. By doing so, they were able to politicise many issues conventionally considered personal and private, such as housework, sexuality, and violence against women. These topics were not yet at the centre of institutional feminism, which at the time was more focused on gender equality in terms of voting rights, access to education, and managerial positions.

> We learned to seek the protagonists of class struggle not only among the male industrial proletariat but, most importantly, among the enslaved, the colonized, the world of wageless workers marginalized by the annals of the communist tradition to whom we could now add the figure of the proletarian housewife, reconceptualised as the subject of the (re)production of the workforce.
>
> *(Federici 2012: 7)*

Autonomous feminists contributed to identifying housework as a pillar of the social-metropolitan factory. Instead of a consideration of domestic life as informal social relations or mere consumption, reproductive labour, even under a wageless condition, was seen as crucial for the continuation of capitalism. Adding to the state provision of welfare services (education, health, pensions, subsidies, etc.), feminists revealed that the production of meals, shopping, cleaning, having and raising children, taking care of the ill and the elderly, etc. was reproductive work, or 'housework', and it was an arena where women are oppressed, hidden, and dismissed by other male-driven struggles.

> The problem, then, becomes how to bring this struggle out of the kitchen and the bedroom and into the streets … Housework is already money for capital, capital has made and makes money out of our cooking, smiling, fucking.
>
> *(Federici 2012: 18–19)*

Campaigns such as Wages for Housework during the 1970s, demonstrations for the right to abortion and marches to 're-appropriate the night' (Balestrini & Moroni (1997) [2006]: 499) initiated a long-lasting wave of autonomous feminism that pervaded most squats as well as autonomist and anarchist groups. The frustrating experience of the sexual division of labour within radical organisations and the dominance of men when it comes to speaking out and writing, in addition to other forms of sexism in leftist politics, motivated the creation of only-women groups, campaigns, demonstrations, and squats (Balestrini & Moroni

(1997) [2006]: 491–494, 506, Martin & Moroni 2007: 162–163). Autonomy meant a separation from men that was conceived as a necessary step to demystify femininity, to make visible women's subjugation and resistance, and to further forge the unity of all the social categories of subordinated groups, including workers, but also gay people, prostitutes, ethnic minorities, migrants, etc. Autonomy also implied an exercise of women's power apart from state institutions, even from dominant discourses about women's rights:

> Overcoming our sense of powerlessness is indispensable for creative work … It is power—not power over others but against those who oppress us—that expands our consciousness … But feminism risks becoming an institution. There is hardly a politician who does not profess eternal devotion to women's rights, and wisely so, since what they have in mind is our 'right to work', for our cheap labor is a true cornucopia for the system.
> *(Federici 2012: 61)*

In order to appreciate the shifting contents of autonomy, it is also worth mentioning that Italian post-autonomist groups split during the 1990s into various factions (with anarchists also taking sides) mainly due to three contested issues that constrained the reach of self-management: the legalisation of squats, the participation of radical activists in electoral politics, and the introduction of waged employees in social centres. In particular, individual autonomy was a key basis

IMAGE 2.2 Squat Metropoliz, Rome, 2014
Source: Author

72 Autonomy from Capitalism

for many anarchists who, in turn, were less interested in the social dimension of class struggles. Individual leadership was criticised by all but was not a big issue for many post-autonomist groups represented by well-known spokespersons. The call to 'exit the ghetto' of the squats and reach out to a larger social sphere indicated a crucial concern for all kinds of radical activists—the size and scale of the 'social' feature of autonomous struggles. Therefore, the Italian radical-left scene was subject to 'both movements of convergence and divergence between post-autonomists and anarchists' (Mudu 2012: 421).

A landmark moment that signalled the main division between anarchist and post-autonomist squatters was the 2001 anti-G8 mobilisation in Genoa. Since then, their mutual interactions in practice have been scarce and limited to broader campaigns, such as the NO-TAV struggle against the high-speed train to connect Italy and France (Della Porta & Piazza 2008, Piazza 2011) and the referendum against the privatisation of water (Mudu 2012: 422). However, recent developments of squatted social centres and houses over the 2010s have kept reproducing the tenets of social autonomy while adding new meanings and tensions. For example, housing movements have included more subaltern groups such as poor migrants and homeless people in the squatting movement (Aureli & Mudu 2018, Feliciantonio 2017, Grazioli & Caciagli 2018; see also Images 2.1 and 2.2). The occupations of abandoned theatres and cinemas stirred larger political debates on the grassroots production of culture as a common good and the increasing precarious working conditions of the youth (Maddanu 2018, Piazza 2018, Valli 2015). Although these experiences remained attached to the legacies of autonomous self-organisation of oppressed groups and their active involvement in the self-management of squats, they were more prone to negotiating legal agreements with the authorities, and more experienced activists often led the initiatives.

Mobilisation and Liberation of Everyday Life

Even before being adopted as a political identity, autonomism in West Germany reshaped extra-parliamentary politics and urban struggles in a different manner compared to the 'new social movements' that had already emerged around 1968. For example, instead of focusing on self-management, Katsiaficas (2006: 3–6) recalled situationist and Lefebvrian concepts—alienation' and 'everyday life', above all—to define autonomy in that context:

> By 1980, a movement existed which was clearly more radical and bigger than that of the sixties. The new movement was more diverse and unpredictable, and less theoretical and organized than was the New Left. Despite their differences, they shared a number of characteristics; anti-authoritarianism; independence from existing political parties; decentralized organizational forms; emphasis on direct action; and combination of culture and politics as means for the creation of a new person and new

Autonomy from Capitalism **73**

forms for living through the transformation of everyday life ... More than anything else, the new radicals are distinguished from the New Left by their orientation to themselves—to a 'politics of the first person'—not to the proletariat or to the wretched of the earth ... In contrast to the centralized decisions and hierarchical authority structures of modern institutions, autonomous social movements involve people directly in decisions affecting their everyday lives. They seek to expand democracy and to help individuals break free of political structures and behavior patterns imposed from the outside. Rather than pursue careers and create patriarchal families, participants in autonomous movements live in groups to negate the isolation of individuals imposed by consumerism. They seek to decolonize everyday life.

Hence, Katsiaficas' interpretation of autonomist ideas in Germany highlights two aspects that might resemble individualistic views of autonomy: the 'politics of the first person' and the 'decolonisation of everyday life'. Within the autonomist scenes, individuals would feel free from party discipline, state control, capitalist-induced compulsive consumerism, and patriarchal domination. However, he also insists that German autonomist activists were well organised in small groups of militants and as a coherent movement. Furthermore, his definition also included 'self-managed consensus', 'open assemblies' without leaders, and 'spontaneous forms of militant resistance' to domination in all domains of life, society, and politics, which very much resembles the collectivist anarchism approach (Ward & Goodway 2014). Despite the frequent references to the 'politics of the first person', autonomy is defined as collective relationships, or 'social autonomy' on my terms, not as individual subjectivity:

> The Autonomen ... see their ideas as a revolutionary alternative to both authoritarian socialism (Soviet-style societies) and 'pseudodemocratic capitalism' ... They believe in diversity and continuing differentiation ... The Autonomen seek to change governments as well as everyday life, to overthrow capitalism and patriarchy.
>
> *(Katsiaficas 2006: 8)*

But what is 'everyday life'? And how can it be decolonised? According to Katsiaficas, everyday life is the sphere of civil society that is separate from state institutions. It is also a political sphere where direct democracy is possible in contrast to both the delegation of power to formal organisations and aspirations to conquer state power. Activism focused on everyday life tries to change the whole political and economic system through direct actions against established powers but, at the same time, against its manifestations in every domain of life (education, family life, friendship, dwelling, workplaces, and urban settings in general). Hence, Katsiaficas defines autonomism as an emergent social movement aiming to promote feminism, migrant rights, and worker cooperatives—for example, while suggesting that autonomy opposes universalising forms of oppression (Katsiaficas 2006: 14–16, 238). In

74 Autonomy from Capitalism

particular, what he designates as the 'colonisation of everyday life' refers to the rise of 'instrumental rationality' worldwide. This means that the forces of capital intend to commodify every aspect of our lives and needs (food, shelter, air, water, communication, mobility, affects, etc.) and make profit out of it. Individualisation, atomisation, privatisation, and alienation are the tools used by the capitalist *colonisers*. As a response 'collective autonomy' as it is represented in squats, appeals to the emancipatory will of youth, women, ethnic minorities, and precarious workers: 'communal living expands the potential for individual life choices and creates the possibility of new types of intimate relationships and new models of child rearing' (Katsiaficas 2006: 247).

Although there is no agreement about the meaning of autonomism, the 'theses' formulated by German activists in 1981 are eloquent:

> We fight for ourselves and others fight for themselves. However, connecting our struggles makes us all stronger. We do not engage in 'representative struggles'. Our activities are based on our affectedness, 'politics of the first person'. We do not fight for ideology, or for the proletariat, or for 'the people'. We fight for a self-determined life in all aspects of our existence, knowing that we can only be free if all are free. We do not engage in dialogue with those in power! We only formulate demands. Those in power can heed them or not ... We all embrace a 'vague anarchism' but we are not anarchists in a traditional sense. Some of us see communism/Marxism as an ideology of order and domination—and ideology that supports the state while we reject it. Others believe in an 'original' communist idea that has been distorted. All of us, however, have great problems with the term 'communism' due to the experiences with the K-groups, East Germany, etc.... We have no organization per se. Our forms of organization are all more or less spontaneous ... Short-term groups form to carry out an action or to attend protests. Long-term groups form to work on continuous projects.
>
> *(Geronimo 2012: 174)*

This political approach led to solid opposition to fascism, imperialism, and capitalism on the one hand, but also to the creation of lasting networks of self-managed houses, social centres, women's groups, and co-operative initiatives on the other. The influence of Italian autonomism was noted in some publications and debates of various political groups during the 1970s, which sometimes intersected with the squatting initiatives of the decade (Geronimo 2012: 48–57, 61–66).

However, more elaborate contents were explicitly added to the German version of autonomism in the early 1980s due to the resurgence of squatters' mobilisations (Geronimo 2012: 99–106). Originally, the remnants of 1968 anti-authoritarianism and the new peace, environmental, and feminist movements merged with multiple residents' protests (*Bürgerinitiativen*) all over the country and with countercultural situationist-inspired politics, such as the *Spontis*:

Autonomy from Capitalism 75

At the beginning of the 1970s, activists organized the first squats in Munich, Cologne, Hamburg, and Göttingen. In Frankfurt, squatters' struggles in the early 1970s were especially strong, and the city became the centre of the *Spontis* (spontaneists who engaged in direct actions and street fights without belonging to formal organizations) ... Like the Metropolitan Indians in Italy, *Spontis* loved to poke fun at their more serious 'comrades' and used irony rather than rationality to make their point. In 1978, *Spontis* in Münster helped elect a pig to a university office, and in Ulm, a dog was nominated to the Academic Senate ... [They organized] theaters of the absurd and other happenings.

(Katsiaficas 2006: 63, 65, italics in original)

In this milieu, according to Katsiaficas, 'the women's movement prefigured what would become the Autonomen. Feminists were the ones who made "autonomy" their central defining point' (Katsiaficas 2006: 67). They fought for the decriminalisation of abortion, equal pay for equal work, housing affordability, shelters for women subject to male violence and public subsidies for mothers, but, and no less importantly, they also focused on a radical change in the sphere of 'everyday life', demanding men (activists included) share domestic chores with women, creating self-help groups, launching campaigns to 'take back the night', and setting up feminist publications, centres, and residential spaces (squatted ones included) in which men were not allowed (Gaillard 2013). 'From the first big squatting wave in 1980/81, in which more than 200 houses in total were occupied, until 2013, around 20 houses in West Berlin and (united) Berlin have been squatted by female/lesbian/gay/queer/trans people' (azozomox 2014: 190). Their large mobilisations, direct actions, and even guerrilla groups added new meanings to what I term 'social autonomy' as women's power against male violence and complete independence from hierarchical structures and institutions (Katsiaficas 2006: 74–75). Although the motto 'the personal is political' might obscure this collective dimension, it was the politicisation of all hitherto considered private topics and 'everyday life', by questioning the social domination inside them and by making it visible, that justifies their autonomist insight.

Two other specific components of the German political context were the long-lasting peace and anti-nuclear movements, first, and the institutionalisation and co-optation of a substantial share of those activists by the Green Party, next. Members of those camps, as well as the Autonomen, were less involved with workers' struggles than their Italian counterparts due to the more generous welfare state and labour unions effective in obtaining concessions, which softened the precarious condition of many activists and attracted more middle classes to activism as well. However, squatting became a key icon for the autonomists, and, in neighbourhoods such as Kreuzberg in Berlin, poor Turkish immigrants, marginalised youth, punks, gays, and artists also became fully engaged in the movement.

76 Autonomy from Capitalism

> The squatters defied simple classifications: from rockers with working-class roots to feminists, recent immigrants from Turkey to the elderly, students to single mothers, and born-again Christians to ideological anarchists, they were more a motley collection than a self-defined collectivity of mainly students like the New Left was. As living behind barricades became a way of life for many squatters, the illegality of their everyday lives radicalized their attitude toward the state.
>
> *(Katsiaficas 2006: 91, 168–173)*

From the late 1970s to the early 1980s, squatters took over hundreds of houses (at least in the large cities), performed street fighting and demonstrations in which the black colour was dominant in both flags and dress codes, and created leaderless organisations, although they also had to face harsh police attacks, arrests and prosecution. This phase ended in partial legalisations that depoliticised part of the movement (Holm & Kuhn 2011) but still kept squatting as the primary identity sign for its remaining militant wing, especially where it was considered a victory against overwhelming repression, such as the Hafenstrasse squatted buildings in Hamburg in the late 1980s (Katsiaficas 2006: 91–96, 124–128, 178).

More generally, it is also worth recalling that another attempt to define autonomism in 1983 combined the general anti-capitalist stance (focused on exploitation and alienation) with concern about all forms of domination:

> Aspiring autonomy means first of all to struggle against political and moral alienation in life and work … It means to reclaim our lives …. This is expressed when houses are squatted to live in dignity and to avoid paying outrageous rent; it is expressed when workers stay at home because they no longer tolerate the control at the workplace; it is expressed when the unemployed loot supermarkets … and when they refuse to support the unions in their mere demand for jobs, which only means integration into a system of oppression and exploitation. Wherever people begin to sabotage the political, moral, and technical structures of domination, an important step toward a self-determined life has been made. Aspiring autonomy also means to engage in public debate with those who think differently and to make the ideas that motivate our life and our actions transparent.
>
> *(Geronimo 2012: 115)*

This author engages with the view of autonomy as collective self-determination. This implies the capacity of every social group to define the norms that will rule their own collective life. Most people are deprived from this right and basic source of power in both representative and authoritarian regimes, although to different extents. In so doing, autonomists need to deliberate in public, justify their stances, and reach consensus. This intense process of communication occurs prior to making decisions about the norms and actions to follow.

IMAGE 2.3 Squat Rote Flora, Hamburg, 2014
Source: Author

Eventually, autonomists had a contradictory relationship with the post-1968 alternative movement that became one of the moderate electoral bases for the Greens and for social democratic politics. Although food co-operatives, bars, bookstores, cultural events, self-managed clinics, playgrounds, etc. formed a convenient and ideologically sympathetic environment for autonomists, they usually criticised alternative infrastructures and enterprises because of their limited anti-capitalist impact (Geronimo 2012: 103–105). The contributions of autonomism to squatting were also accompanied with conflicts of violence among activists; sexism, homophobia, and transphobia (azozomox 2014); subtle forms of social control and uniformisation within the scene; extreme measures to prevent police infiltration; and even a nihilist rejection of intellectual analyses and affirmative political alternatives (Katsiaficas 2006: 177–180, Geronimo 2012: 174).

Squatting movements in Germany unfolded especially during the early 1980s and, after a combined policy of legalisation and repression of new squatting attempts, at the crossroads of its reunification with former East Germany, around 1990 (Holm & Kuhn 2011). As an illustration, between 1979 and 1984, there were 287 squatted houses and wagon places in West Berlin (azozomox & Kuhn 2018: 148). Another peak was reached between 1989 and 1991 when 214 buildings were squatted in Berlin, mostly in the former Eastern boroughs (azozomox & Kuhn 2018: 152). The issue of the squat legalisation was highly controversial and engendered splits among autonomists of the first period, but it became more widely accepted after the 1990s. In cities such as Hamburg, the language of social autonomy permeates both legalised initiatives (Hafenstrasse in the late 1980s and

78 Autonomy from Capitalism

Gängeviertel in the 2010s) and those partially tolerated (Rote Flora, see Image 2.3), but the strains with the authorities' attempts to institutionalise and co-opt autonomist activists keep going. On the one hand, the large numbers of legalised squats in those periods granted the Autonomen a long-lasting material infrastructure for continuing their political projects and struggles. On the other hand, although the German autonomists remained the main proponents and supporters of squatting actions, the more repressive contexts forced them to shift focus towards other campaigns, such as solidarity with migrants, anti-capitalist summits, environmental protests, tenants' rights, anti-fascism, and feminist claims at all the levels of politics.

Diffused Autonomy and Interdependence

Autonomism was well spread in other European countries such as Spain. The fascist dictatorship that lasted from 1936–9 to 1975 made a striking difference compared to other Western political regimes based on liberal democracy. Many workers' unions and strikes had to operate underground until the late 1970s when they unfolded massively in most industrial areas. Despite the hegemony of the Spanish Communist Party in many of these struggles, workers' autonomous organisations, and assemblies were quite significant in many sectors. Extra-parliamentary politics also consisted of manifold leftist organisations that often engaged with the demands of residents in urban neighbourhoods (Castells 1983). The practice of squatting buildings was not very frequent, but the revival of anarchism contributed to the establishment of Ateneos Libertarios, occupied social centres run by anarchist unions and various affinity groups, and countercultural social centres (inspired by the hippy and alternative movements around 1968) in the period known as 'transition to democracy' that lasted until the early 1980s (Martínez 2018a, Seminario 2014: 23–77).

During the first wave of political squatting in the mid-1980s, the autonomist identity was more imported from round-trip visits to Italy, Germany, and Holland than linked to their own legacy of autonomous factory struggles. Many squatters also preferred to associate their ideological roots with the core vigorous anarchist tradition from the decades before the dictatorship, which sometimes produced frictions with the 'vague anarchism' and heterodox-Marxism embraced by the autonomists. Some autonomists also felt akin to *workerist* and independentist armed groups (Estebaranz 2005), but the clandestine life, insurrectional militancy, and hierarchical organisations contradicted the experiences of most squatters. Moreover, the successful anti-militarist movement at that time (Martínez 2007: 380) achieved a high legitimation of non-violent direct action among most social movements, especially those who fully supported the anti-conscription campaign like most autonomists and squatters. In addition, nationalist-independentist militants and members of left-parties took part in some squats or initiated their own, especially in Catalonia, Galicia and the Basque Country.

IMAGE 2.4 Squat La Casika, Móstoles (Madrid), 2014
Source: Author

An autonomous branch of the feminist movement was also very active over the decades and was especially engaged in the squatters' movement, even founding their own social centres exclusively for women, such as Matxarda, La Karbonera, and Andretxe in the Basque Country (Padrones 2017: 227–235), Eskalera Karakola in Madrid (squatted in 1996), and La Morada-La Fresca in Barcelona (1997–8) (Gil 2011: 77–97). In a similar vein to what happened in Italy and Germany, there were endless debates between 'diffuse' and 'organised' forms of autonomy, especially among those who participated in the political scene around Lucha Autónoma in Madrid (Casanova 2002, Seminario 2014: 121–182). By 1987, the autonomists had presented a political agenda with an explicit social orientation in the squatted social centre Arregui y Aruej based on self-management, anti-authoritarianism, direct action, and anti-capitalism (Casanova 2002: 36–37). During the next decade and a half, squatted social centres and houses became a focal point of activity for all the autonomists, but there were many more squats in which 'autonomy' was no more than a package of multiple radical ideas in circulation. Anti-fascism as a political priority, for example, distinguished a certain number of squats from the rest (Seminario 2014: 130–131), which denotes the existence of significant social and political diversity in the squatters' movement. However, the regular practice of assemblies, direct democracy, self-organisation, and engagement with numerous social struggles around the squats disseminated a 'diffuse' politics of social autonomy among the most active and politicised squatters (Salamanca & Wilhelmi 2012).

80 Autonomy from Capitalism

An abundant publication of short pamphlets, fanzines (*Resiste, Sabotaje, El Acratador, Ekintza Zuzena, Etcétera, Contrapoder,* etc.) and some radical newspapers occasionally served to discuss theoretical and political aspects of autonomism. In Madrid, the squatted social centre Laboratorio (initiated in 1997) was one of the most prolific in recalling the post-workerist views and engaging with the Zapatista Uprising (1994 to date) and its anti-neoliberal discourse:

> This social centre is not the result of a determined identity, project, or organisation. ... It is the desire to bridge differences ... We aim to experiment with how to embed the squatted social centres in the metropolitan territory: struggles against real estate speculation against the deterioration of the urban peripheries, against the expulsion of residents in the city centre, against the militarisation of the land and CCTV surveillance, against total institutions, against the authoritarianism of urban planning, against new forms of fascism. ... This social centre is not only defined by struggles and confrontations; by needs of housing and liberated spaces; by mechanisms of protection and accumulation of forces and differences; by countercultural, neighbourhood-based and revolutionary politics. It is not just a means, but an end itself; the expression of a nomad community. ... Squatting is also to have fun ... to celebrate our here and now ... We aim to express the potential of an insubordinate life facing the void of capital, the creation of many [new] worlds, everyday practices of freedom ... forms of cooperation against hierarchy, control and separation.
>
> *(Casanova 2002: 162–163)*

As in Italy, precarious young workers and students were the most active social composition of the squatters' movement, although residents of all ages, migrants, artists, and activists from many other social movements were often attracted to participate in the squats. Therefore, anti-capitalism and concerns about labour conditions (precariousness) were crucial in their political approach to reclaim urban spaces and neighbourhoods.

In addition, the autonomist branch of Spanish feminism since the 1980s was intimately attached to squatting (see, for example, their publication *Mujeres Preokupando*), although not all the groups occupied spaces, and their political concerns were much broader (Gil 2011, Seminario 2014: 303–357). Interestingly, they nurtured autonomist urban politics by building upon insights from other international trends of radical feminism and by raising debates that were beyond the usual agenda of squatters. On the one hand, 'autonomy' for them meant independence from both institutional politics (parties, unions, and state agencies) and male domination in different spheres of life, including squats and autonomist organisations (Gil 2011: 57); on the other hand, 'autonomy' invited women to take matters into their own hands, to empower and liberate themselves by cooperating with each other and by establishing 'networks of counter-power' (Gil 2011: 46).

The legacy of the 1960s and 1970s in terms of the politicisation of private and personal matters (seclusion of family life, abortion, contraceptive methods, sexual freedom, domestic work, harassment and rape, etc.) paved the way for more ambitious concerns in the 1990s: rights for LGBTQI people; opposition to militarism; the precarious labour of women, especially those making a living through prostitution and domestic work; immigration; and even feminist porn. These topics hardly recalled the attention of the more institutionalised branches of feminism but, in turn, found a fertile ground of expression in the squatted social centres and, above all, in the feminist squats (Gil 2011: 46, 68–97, 295–298). Conversely, this development questioned sexism, LGBTQI-phobia, and racism within the squats and autonomist scenes. Furthermore, it revealed how neoliberal capitalism manipulates the notion of 'autonomy' in order to promote free individuals to consume, vote, and comply. This is manifest in the so-called 'crisis of care' for children, the elderly, the ill, the disabled, and its gendered and racialised dimensions. Self-determination and cooperation of the oppressed, thus, entail an essential 'interdependence' with one another and a systemic (anti-capitalist, anti-patriarchal, and anti-racist) search for alternatives to the crisis of care, which is on the shoulders of women, in order to halt the reproduction of capitalism:

> Capitalism ... has turned personal and collective autonomy upside down ...: atomised experiences, competition with each other, self-entrepreneurialism ... no future prospects ... vertiginous rhythms of survival and production ...fragile communities ... loneliness ... The ideal of independence ... [only applies to] personal and social situations in transit, casual ones, based on youth, health, strength, power, wealth, and without care for other people (their offspring, the elderly, the ill, etc.).
>
> *(Gil 2011: 305)*

Therefore, when individual autonomy is introduced in this approach, it is always defined together with issues of social interdependence and the constraints set in place by capitalist society.

Self-critical analyses within Spanish autonomist politics and squats are illuminating too; for example, the short-lived span of many organisations and squatting experiences, the superficial discussion of feminist concerns and the ineffective practices against sexism, the rejection of experts and professionals (except lawyers, to some extent) as well as accusations of vanguardism to the most devoted and politicised activists (Carretero 2012), to name just a few. When the autonomist experience cross-fertilised the global justice movement in the late 1990s and early 2000s (Martínez 2007), other shortcomings were brought forward: multi-militancy, irreconcilable tensions with the 'institutional left', scarcity of resources, a high diversity that resulted in the alter-globalisation movement's fragmentation, and a limited capacity for mass mobilisation (Flesher 2007). Nevertheless, autonomists contributed to this larger protest wave (and also to the 2011 upheavals [Flesher 2014]) with practical skills rooted in assembly-based organisations and with engagement in urban politics while bridging self-managed squatted buildings and more global issues:

> The autonomous actor actively attempts to negate the isolationism created by capitalist consumer society, through the nurturing of social relations that create community. ... Just as single total identities (e.g. worker) do not make sense from an autonomous perspective, neither do single issues ... The network form of organization and communication allows for the integration and interaction of multiple issues and identities, and for a connection between local, national and global levels of action.
> *(Flesher 2007: 340)*

IMAGE 2.5 Squat Patio Maravillas, Madrid, 2014
Source: Author

Although squatting was criminalised in 1995, the movement kept active in many cities over the following decades and even experienced a remarkable upsurge in the aftermath of the global financial crisis of 2008 (Martínez 2018a, see Image 2.4). Since the 2000s, an explicit autonomist identity has been reshaped by networks of squatted and non-squatted social centres, especially those more inclined to legalise their spaces and to interact more directly with some public policies and state institutions—despite all the difficulties they faced—such as the Casa Invisible shows in Málaga (Toret et al. 2008). A common theme of the so-called 'second-generation social centres', shared with many Italian post-autonomists, was their intention to get rid of stereotyped identities and to engage with broader publics—neighbourhoods, social and political organisations, migrants, precarious workers, and artists (see Image 2.5). However, a diffused notion of autonomy quite intertwined with anarchism and a strong anti-institutional standpoint has to date prevailed among the squatters of Madrid, Barcelona, Valencia, Seville, and Zaragoza, for instance. The main turning point was represented by the emergence of a housing movement led by a formal organisation, the PAH (Platform for People Affected by Mortgages), in 2009. This movement also occupied buildings but rarely developed social centres. Many of their activists had an autonomist background and still endorsed it, but they mainly claimed affordable housing, the increase of social housing and substantial changes in housing policies. As a consequence, a more institutional approach was combined with the social empowerment of those who became homeless due to the widespread financialisation of housing.

Collective Self-Determination of the Oppressed

The term 'autonomy' has been rightly criticised because it is charged with the burden of liberal and individualistic connotations, even when adopted by countercultural and anarchist trends (Bookchin 1998). As Flesher noted: 'Although the legitimate political actor is the autonomous individual, acting collectively, this does not translate into a rejection of collectives or affinity groups' (Flesher 2007: 340). She also argues that organisations are dispensable for autonomists because they only 'exist to serve the desires and goals of the individuals participating in them' (Flesher 2007: 339). Therefore, it is not uncommon to see individual self, subjectivity, autonomy and independence as the pivotal bases of the autonomist political identity. This is explicit in widely circulated texts such as the Temporary Autonomous Zone (Bey 1985: 114) and pamphlets engaging with individualistic anarchism and the 'radical criticism of any authority principle' (Mudu 2012: 414). Some post-workerist and feminist activist-scholars also attached the language of desire and subjectivation to autonomy (Berardi 2016, Gil 2011: 100), although they always interpreted them according to broader social conflicts of domination in late capitalism, not as an individualistic approach to autonomy. In particular, squatting movements following an autonomist orientation represented a practical way to refuse salaried labour and establish

84 Autonomy from Capitalism

free spaces for the emancipation of women and LGBTI-Q people. However, artistic squatters in France and Germany, for example (Aguilera 2018, Novy & Colomb 2013), have been frequently accused of adhering to the creative and individual view of autonomy rather than its more subversive, organised, prefigurative, and collective forms of class struggle and self-management. Squatted social centres such as Tacheles in Berlin and Gängeviertel in Hamburg, for instance, would exemplify individual self-interests in 'the seizing of cheap studio spaces' (Novy & Colomb 2013: 1828) and were instrumental to neoliberal city-branding policies aiming to attract well-educated but precarious creative classes. An additional feature that populates the distinctions between the autonomous and institutional left refers to decision-making processes. Autonomists oppose delegation and most prefer face-to-face assemblies and consensus over voting (Piazza 2013). This implies that specific individuals may veto collective decisions or force the collective into long discussions, postpone agreements, and even into stalemates and internal splits. Notwithstanding these risks, the relatively small-scale size and the decentralisation of autonomist networks posed no substantial threats to the persistence and predominance of consensual principles over time, although majoritarian voting has also been adopted by many squats.

In this chapter, I have argued that the meanings attached to autonomism by Italian, German, and Spanish squatters, in tight connection with the activists from intertwined movements, prompted me to prefer 'social autonomy' in order to capture their novel contribution to urban politics. This approach reminds of 'social anarchism' or 'libertarian communism' in its aspiration to set up 'communities of equals' (Bookchin 1998, Graeber 2004: 2, 65–66). Nonetheless, autonomists go beyond anarcho-syndicalism, the factory walls, the central role of the working-class, and the utopian models of a post-revolutionary future (Foucault 1982). Rather, they oppose all forms of domination spread throughout the metropolitan space by seeking cooperation with all oppressed social groups and by focusing pragmatically in the oppressions they all experience at present. Therefore, the emancipation is conceived as the political responsibility of the oppressed themselves. Instead of following vanguard leaders and external organisations, autonomists set direct democracy, assemblies, and horizontal cooperation at the top of their political agenda and practice. To fight the oppressors implies becoming separated from them and affirming the identity of the oppressed, temporarily, while the subordination and the resistance persist (Fraser 2008). Social autonomy thus indicates: (1) separation from the oppressors and the social relations where oppression occurs; (2) self-affirmation of the oppressed groups in direct social conflict with the oppressors; and (3) self-determination of the norms, decisions, and goals through the collective self-management of resources and spaces.

Their disbelief in future utopias and essentialist differences leads autonomists to attempt any possible revolution here and now. Thus, they aim to shape, in a prefigurative manner, spaces of equality, creativity, and resistance among those struggling together. As I argued above, the self-management and sociopolitical aggregation provided by squats (Martínez 2013, Piazza 2018) and other autonomous social centres (Hodkinson & Chatterton 2006) are the best materialisations of autonomist politics. Illegal and disruptive means of protest, when targeting empty buildings, supply affordable spaces to those who wish, in turn, to separate themselves from patriarchal domination and the capitalist dynamics of labour exploitation, mass consumption, and urban speculation. Squats also provide safe and self-organised spaces for immigrants and refugees (Colectivo Hinundzurük 2018, García & Jørgensen 2019, Refugee Accommodation 2018). Buildings are rehabilitated, resources are shared, domestic life is often articulated through collective decision-making, an ethics of do-it-yourself (DIY) and do-it-together (DIT) is put in practice, countercultural expressions and radical left ideas are promoted, and other movements' activists and campaigns are hosted (Cattaneo & Martínez 2014, McKay 1998, Notes From Nowhere 2003, Van der Steen et al. 2014). Everyday life as the sphere of social reproduction, consisting of welfare services as well as the collective self-management of the buildings and urban areas where they live, become a central concern for autonomism, squatting, and feminism:

> The rediscovery of reproductive work has made it possible to understand that capitalist production relies on the production of a particular type of worker—and therefore a particular type of family, sexuality, procreation—and thus to redefine the private sphere as a sphere of relations of production and a terrain of anticapitalist struggle.
>
> *(Federici 2012: 97)*

As a common thread shared by most autonomist and anarchist traditions, both state-driven socialism and capitalism (and, in its late stages, as global neoliberalism and financialisation as well) are confronted. Autonomism is nurtured by a strong anti-authoritarian concern that seeks the experience of freedom in all spheres of social life, for all, and as immediately as possible. This entails the need for the oppressed to exert their available power and to use their own capacities in order to be released from the chains of domination, which can be designated as an 'immediatist struggle':

> In such struggles people criticize instances of power which are the closest to them, those which exercise their action on individuals. They do not look for the 'chief enemy' but for the immediate enemy. Nor do they expect to find a solution to their problem at a future date (that is, liberations, revolutions, end of class struggle).
>
> *(Foucault 1982: 780)*

Not only are 'dictatorship of the proletariat' and one-party regimes resisted, but also all state institutions and formal organisations in liberal democracies that may reproduce social domination and inequality. Capitalism, patriarchy, racism,

86 Autonomy from Capitalism

fascism, and imperialism are thus seen as notoriously resilient in both authoritarian and pluralist regimes, which determines the multiple points of bottom-up resistance and the corresponding autonomous struggles. Squatted spaces are manifestations of this micro-politics (Dadusc 2017, Yates 2014) of the 'everyday life' (Katsiaficas 2006) in small living and self-managed communities, domestic and small-group relations, and horizontal affinity groups, while the squatters themselves also organise protest campaigns broadly and foster networks of solidarity with other autonomous and grassroots struggles worldwide (Mudu 2012).

My emphasis on the social features of autonomism also involves a long-lasting commitment to women's, LGBTI-Q, migrants' and ethnic minorities' struggles. The feminist call to politicise, disclose, question, and abolish oppression in every sphere of private life pervades the internal spaces of squats, which makes them more open and public but with a broader anti-systemic stance. Despite being subject to forced temporality and nomadism, squatters who take over abandoned buildings usually aim to stay as long as possible. The persistence of squatters' movements also indicates the existence of networks that make them more challenging to the status quo than isolated activism and insurrectional uprisings. The autonomist ethos, regardless of being expressed through vague and diffuse political identities, radiates from the specific urban spots of the squats to the neighbourhoods and other urban struggles intertwined with them, as far as coalitions are forged and are capable of articulating commonalities.

Nonetheless, autonomist projects are, more often than not, seriously constrained and menaced by the political and economic conditions that surround them. On the one hand, state repression and manoeuvres to institutionalise, integrate, and neutralise autonomous struggles severely reduce their radical reach and engender or accentuate splits among activists (Karpantschof & Mikkelsen 2014). Privatisation and outsourcing of collective consumption by the state also threaten how squatted social centres relate to social needs, public services, and the market (Membretti 2007, Moroni & Aaster 1996). Frequently, urban activists need to break apart from the isolated 'ghettoes' of many autonomist and countercultural scenes and connect with the society at large through institutional actors, professionals, and mass media (Castells 1983: 322), or use the resources of the 'institutional left' (Flesher 2007: 345). On the other hand, the concern for everyday life implies a continuous warning about the reproduction of social dominations inside autonomous movements. Sexism is the most prominent and overtly debated one but is far from unique. Tendencies towards dogmatism, retreating to individual and neoliberal forms of autonomy, *alternative* performances of vanguardism and hierarchy (Kadir 2016), exclusionary lifestyles and aesthetics (Flesher 2007: 350), exhaustion from long lasting conditions of illegality, an excessive and unwanted fragmentation of politicised groups, and endless dissatisfaction with the political achievements of the struggles due to their *limited* revolutionary capacity (Koopmans 1995) have been raised as the major internal troubles.

IMAGE 2.6 After-squat Rote Insel, Berlin, 2011
Source: Author

Squatting and the Radical Left in Berlin

In 2011 SqEK held its fourth meeting in Berlin. The city had been changing its appearance at a rapid pace since the fall of the Wall that had divided it from 1961 to 1989. In parallel, social movements of the radical left have also experienced significant shifts over the last few decades. In particular, squatting has become banned, and, in most attempts, squats have been quickly aborted in the first 24 hours of their existence since the early 1980s. However, it is still possible to feel the remnants of one of the most intense waves of squatting in Europe—around 1980, in the first instance, and a second during the 1989–90 process of reunifying the two Germanies (FRG and GDR). My interest in squatting here addresses the large and simultaneous activity of repression and negotiation that took place, unknown until that time in other European cities.

Carla MacDougall and Armin Kuhn were our guides through some of the historical landmarks of the Kreuzberg neighbourhood, which for the most part remained on the western side in the aftermath of the Second World War. Departing from Oranienplatz, they showed us abundant residential constructions

88 Autonomy from Capitalism

that were originally erected beside factories and storehouses, hosting modest German and Turkish immigrants, and which gathered a number of deficiencies in terms of living standards in the post-war years. Since the mid-1950s, the local authorities have prepared plans to renew the neighbourhood involving numerous demolitions of the whole district. However, step by step, the protests of the residents forced the urban planners to implement mechanisms of participatory planning and design. By the 1970s, urban redevelopment turned into a 'cautious renewal' approach that would not expel the working-class population and would bring back some industrial spaces and courtyards leading to the various small gardens and playgrounds that are visible nowadays. During this period of intense neighbourhood mobilisations, several committees were established such as the pioneer SO36, of which I saw abundant iconography and documents archived at the communal museum of Adelbergstrasse. Some even opted for the squatting of empty buildings as yet another means of intervening in the renewal process.

While telling us the historical memory of Kreuzberg, MacDougall and Kuhn estimated there were up to 160 squats in that period (late 1970s and early 1980s). Among them, around 120 gained a legal status later whereas the rest were evicted. At least in five cases, like those of Naunynstrasse and Mariannenstrasse (Schokoladenfabrik), the after-squats established feminist and LGTBIQ projects which are still in existence. Actually, despite the strength of the squatters' movement by then, the majority of the squatting collectives accepted legalisation deals both because the conservative government, in place as of May 1981, did not give them a single day of truce under illegality, and also because of the economic advantages that they were provided with. If the squatters negotiated an adequate contract concerning the property of the squatted building, the government of the city (with special status as a state or *Stadt*) could subsidise the renovation of the building if needed. Around 80% were non-refundable subsidies. The remaining 20% was covered by the work by the residents, often following some public programmes to support youth employment. In the end, the conditions of each contract were highly dependent on the type of owner (mostly, private owners), the physical condition of the building, and the organisational vigour of each squatting project. In the majority of cases, rental contracts for periods around 30 years were signed.

The problems, however, intensified when the contracts expired, and the landlords refused to extend them or alleged a breach of the terms. Police evictions of some after-squats (legalised squats or *hausprojekts*) have recently occurred again. This was the sad fate of Liebigstrasse 14, in the district of Friedrichshain, which closed its doors in February 2011 after an intense protest that resulted in a rally filled with damages, clashes, and detentions. In Berlin there are barely no new, visible squats taking place, although we were informed of some secret cases by their residents. In addition to the well-publicised eviction of Liebig 14, another remarkable case in recent years was the hausprojekt Yorckstrasse 59. Two private investors, whose pictures and residences became widely known from protest posters, acquired the property of the building and used legal tricks to force the eviction in 2005. Residents responded with the squatting of abandoned city-owned premises in the complex of buildings known as Bethanien, where a psychiatric hospital, a kindergarten, a dining room, and theatre rehearsal rooms were located. New Yorck was the name given to the new squatting project which, surprisingly, was not evicted the same day as the occupation. After two years of mobilisations, the district authorities feared an increase in the tension and waited five days. By then it was already too late because the police refused to enforce the eviction order as it did not comply with the established doctrine (the so-called Berlin Line). Several months later, the left-wing government of the district made a new attempt at eviction. It was also unsuccessful and, eventually, the local authorities ended up negotiating with the squatters. A legalisation contract was thus signed, and the squatters agreed to pay a monthly rental fee of 6,000 euros. New Yorck was divided into a hausprojekt with 30 rooms and a social centre with office and meeting spaces. Dwellers paid approximately 200 euros per bedroom which would amount to 5,000 euros. The remaining thousand was collected from the various political and social projects hosted in areas dedicated to the social centre.

The above could seem a high cost only if one ignored the stunning transformation that the city has experienced in the last decade and the growing inflation in both the rental and property markets. Spectacular architecture, gentrification processes, and an increasingly capitalist globalisation of the city have been promoted by most local authorities wishing to attract tourists, company headquarters, and capital investment. For that purpose, significant cultural and urban policies were developed consistently. On the opposite side, affordable social housing has increasingly been dismissed, despite the large public assets in this rubric. Just to mention one of the most notable transfers of goods, in 2004, 60,000 public houses were sold to the bank Goldman Sachs for a price per unit of around 6,100 euros. In 2009, the bank managed to sell 15,000 of those flats for around 50,000 euros each (Alas 2011). Kreuzberg and Friedrichshain are still the most popular and socially diverse areas of Berlin and is where the majority of the hausprojekts were located. However, in recent years their multicultural image and their animated urban life have invited wealthier residents, coffee-shops, alternative businesses, real-estate speculators, and more urban renewal projects.

S., one of the longest-residing dwellers of Rote Insel—the hausprojekt located on Mannsteinstrasse, in the district of Schoneberg, where we were accommodated (see Image 2.6)—lamented that in some cases the principle of 'living communally' had completely faded in most of the hausprojekts. The kitchens and the common rooms disappear, apartments are closed down with keys, and, on some occasions, the property of the housing is even bought individually, forgetting the relationships with the neighbours and previous activists. Rote Insel is one of the projects that has resisted that fate to a greater extent. In a long conversation with several of its members and while reviewing their memories through a photo album, we were able to reconstruct the dilemmas they had to face. Rote Insel was squatted in 1981 and, after numerous debates and internal divisions, they signed a tenancy contract with the district government in 1984. The rehabilitation works of the building, once almost in ruins, progressed very slowly and with many difficulties that almost nullified the state economic contribution. The renovation lasted for ten years and the first 25 inhabitants lived confined to a kitchen and in very few bedrooms. In 1997 they set up an association and signed a new contract for 20 more years which included a 'youth social centre' and several parking spots. M., K. and I.—some of the current residents with whom we talked—believe the renewal of this contract will be complicated once it expires. For the time being, they focus on solving their management conflicts in their bimonthly meetings.

The building has a grey and maroon façade, with a dividing wall painted in colourful graffiti and allusions to the collectives of the radical left. It has two independent entrance doors. There is a 'common kitchen' on each floor in addition to all the lock-less bedrooms. In one of the blocks there is a living room where meetings take place and visitors can temporarily sleep. Except for S. and her children, none of the original squatters remain living in the building. When asked about past conflicts, there is a unanimity in pointing out drug addictions as the main threat to collective living. When it came to heroin, expulsion by the collective was imminent. However, they declared that there are no written rules for cohabitation. Instead, they are only guided by two basic principles: the prohibition of violence among them and a collaboration in the common tasks. The frequent consumption of *drugs*, they argued, implies violent relationships

IMAGE 2.7 After-squat Manti, Berlin, 2011
Source: Author

within the community. Therefore, drug users are not allowed to stay. Cleaning toilets, stairs, and common areas is achieved without fixed shifts and relies instead on informal collective pressure.

Since October 2010 A., D., and S. have been provisionally hosted in the living room. They have come from Vitoria (Spain) to work in Berlin in jobs way below their academic qualifications, at least until they manage to be fluent in the German language. They are awaiting available bedrooms in Rote Insel. Together with Y., a Turkish archaeologist who escaped from mandatory military service in his country, and the Brazilian G., they are in charge of every Friday's 'solipizza' (solidarity pizza) in the social space (a sort of bar and dining room) of the building. The selling of home-made pizzas for two euros each and beers for one euro exemplifies one of the many gastronomic meetings (*voku* or popular kitchen) that are offered every day in the social spaces of a specific network of hausprojekts, announced punctually in the last page of the monthly bulletin *StressFaktor*. Last month they dedicated the money collected to solidarity with Liebig14. The voku is an essential part of Rote Insel's ability to foster political fundraising. Anyhow, the social space is managed without a specific legal license, so it is not fully open to the broader public and it is necessary to ring the bell to get in. The bicycle workshop is also not overtly advertised, although it is of utility for all the residents as well as their friends. This relative closeness is in contrast with the social centres of a few very well-known and socially busy hausprojekts such as the theatre and conference room, The Clash at the Mehringhof. In the old days, this was one of the main autonomist bastions. Another public project is the Schokoladenfabrik where there is a '*hamam*' (Turkish bath) only for women, and a coffee shop which in appearance is indistinguishable from that which are popping up in the area. For some activists, these projects of self-employment and co-ops, identity signs of the German 'alternative movement', can easily fall under the wave of depoliticisation, consumption, and gentrification.

At first sight it is not easy to discern a hausprojekt from any other building. Not even the presence of graffiti, eloquent sentences in the façades (see Image 2.7), or colourful murals are reliable indicators given that in some neighbourhoods these are very extended practices (the campaign RYC—Reclaim Your City, with its English spelling—for instance, was stencilled on many walls). Only the guidance of the people involved in the after-squats can help you to grasp their exact location and the subtle connections among them that still remain. The above-mentioned evictions or the threats of forthcoming evictions (such as that menacing the Kopi since 2006) have shown that they still enjoy wide support among the radical left of the city. M. adds that the other common ground among activists is the struggle against gentrification and the expulsion of working-class residents. But according to him the classical lines of division within the German leftist militants persist and cause great harm: the Israel–Palestine conflict, the resort to political violence, sexism, and anti-fascism. On another note, occasional overt or secret negotiations with political representatives are tactically

92 Autonomy from Capitalism

accepted by the majority of the radical groups despite being openly rejected overall, according to the opinion of the Rote Insel members we spoke to.

D., a member of the organisation-campaign Queerruption, highlighted the predominance of the anarchist-autonomist groups on the radical left in Berlin coexisting with some punk collectives, several extra-parliamentary communist organisations, anti-fascist, environmentalist, vegan, women's groups, artists as well as social enterprises (co-ops)—more or less, everything that shows up in the publication *StressFaktor* and which D. prefers to label only as the 'counter-cultural movement'. The May Day or alternative First of May celebration is still one of the pivotal expressions of some of the most militant factions of that movement in the streets, but the rest of the year it is not so common to observe an enduring convergence of all the branches comprising the radical left.

We were also invited to learn about the project Regenbogen Fabrik (Rainbow Factory) as another example of alternatives for a sustainable and self-managed social life, despite its relatively precarious legalisation. They never paid a single tenancy rent according to the deal they signed with the Senate of Berlin in 1984. Despite that refusal, they have recently obtained a subsidy of 100,000 euros from the same local authorities in order to fix the ceilings and renovate the theatre venue attracting a large audience from all over the city. A., one of the most veteran hosts, told us that the legalisation contract included the squatters' responsibility for the decontamination of the yard. A. explained that the pollution is now at a very low degree according to their regular checks. In fact, we held our collective talk there, where a playground centrally dominates the whole outdoor area. The day of the visit both the bike and the carpentry workshops were restricted exclusively for the use of women. Activists from Regenbogen Fabrik also run a coffee shop and a restaurant open to the general public with direct access from Lausitzerstrasse 22, beside the Spree Canal that goes through Kreuzberg. Among their different initiatives, they manage a 'hostel' with affordable prices (from 10 to 38 euros per night) in which, applying the principle of 'self-help', guests are expected to clean their own bedrooms.

The old factory premises and the block of 18 houses that belong to Regenbogen Fabrik were squatted in 1981 by some 50 people. The motivations of those youngsters were very diverse in their origins—from those who wanted to experiment with collective forms of cohabitation and sharing the maternity experience, to those who saw the occupation as a struggle against the local housing policies. They were the initiators of the Green Party in the city, who in turn supported them when they started gaining representative posts. This explains, partially, its anomalous survival. Activists had to reoccupy the space in 1991 when the property title shifted from private to public ownership. At present, they have a 30-year contract. They also collaborate with the municipal kindergarten and unemployment services, but the authorities, according to A., have not given up their intention to privatise the space devoted to social activities. The legal situation of the majority of the houses, however, seemed more consolidated and away from any realistic eviction threat, at least in the short-term.

In her review of almost three decades of activism in Berlin, S., from Rote Insel, stated that in the 1980s most activists had no-waged jobs, while nowadays almost everybody is employed with a salary and there is less time left for political activism. The German welfare state has substantially reduced the basic income and subsidies that it used to provide. For many, their unemployment periods in the past were dedicated to full-time unrest and to creating alternative ways of living. A. also stressed the same point and added that the official requirements for unemployed people are now greater and greater, such as the obligation to do internships, training courses, and to accept any offered job at the risk of losing all state support. Therefore, even some militants from the radical left, not so sympathetic to the Green Party, prefer to participate in alternative economic projects such as those run by Regenbogen Fabrik.

To conclude, Berlin is no longer the affordable city it used to be before its intense globalising urbanisation. The political infrastructure created by the squatters' movement first and the hausprojekts later kept providing hundreds of affordable housing facilities and common resources to a great part of the local leftist scene. Squatting in the past, and sometimes still attempted in the present, remains in the collective memory of today's activism. Although squatting seems to be less central to their political identity than before, it is still widely recognised as the original driver of alternative models of cohabitation and the critique of the capitalist city that is rapidly advancing.

References

Aguilera, Thomas (2018) The Squatting Movement(s) in Paris: Internal Divides and Conditions for Survival. In Miguel A. Martínez (Ed.) *The Urban Politics of Squatters' Movements*. New York: Palgrave Macmillan, 121–144.

Alas, Joel (2011) Gentrification: Stop blaming foreigners! *Exberliner*, 2 May. http://www.exberliner.com/features/gentrification%3A/

Aureli, Andrea & Pierpaolo Mudu (2018) Squatting: Reappropriating Democracy from the State. *Interface* 9(1): 497–521.

azozomox (2014) Squatting and Diversity: Gender and Patriarchy in Berlin, Madrid and Barcelona. In Claudio Cattaneo & Miguel Martínez (Eds) *The Squatters' Movement in Europe. Commons and Autonomy as Alternatives to Capitalism*. London: Pluto, 189–210.

azozomox & Armin Kuhn (2018) The Cycles of Squatting in Berlin (1969–2016). In Miguel A. Martínez (Ed.) *The Urban Politics of Squatters' Movements*. New York: Palgrave Macmillan, 145–164.

Bailey, Ron (1973) *The Squatters*. Harmondsworth: Penguin.

Balestrini, Nanni & Primo Moroni ((1997) [2006]) *La horda de oro (1968–1977). La gran ola revolucionaria y creativa, política y existencial*. Madrid: Traficantes de Sueños.

Berardi, Franco (Bifo) (2016) What Is the Meaning of Autonomy Today? Subjectivation, Social Composition, Refusal of Work. *Multitudes* www.multitudes.net/what-is-the-meaning-of-autonomy/

Bey, Hakim (1985) *The Temporary Autonomous Zone*. New York: Autonomedia.

Bhattacharya, Tithi (Ed.) (2017) *Social Reproduction Theory. Remapping Class, Recentering Oppression*. London: Pluto.

Bookchin, Murray (1998) *Social Anarchism or Lifestyle Anarchism: An Unbridgeable Chasm*. San Francisco: AK Press.

94 Autonomy from Capitalism

Carretero, José Luis (2012) La apuesta autónoma. In Francisco Salamanca & Gonzalo Wilhelmi (Eds) *Tomar y hacer en vez de pedir y esperar. Autonomía y movimientos sociales. Madrid 1985-2011.* Madrid: Solidaridad Obrera, 35–50.

Casanova, Gonzalo (2002) *Armarse sobre las ruinas. Historia del movimiento autónomo en Madrid (1995-1999).* Madrid: Potencial Hardcore.

Castells, Manuel (1983) *The City and the Grassroots. A Cross-Cultural Theory of Urban Social Movements.* Berkeley: University of California Press.

Cattaneo, Claudio & Miguel Martínez (Eds) (2014) *The Squatters' Movement in Europe: Commons and Autonomy as Alternatives to Capitalism.* London: Pluto.

Colectivo Hinundzurük (2018) You Can't Evict a Movement. From the Rise of the Refugee Movement in Germany to the Practice of Squatting. In SqEK (Ed.) *Fighting for Spaces, Fighting for Our Lives: Squatting Movements Today.* Münster: Assemblage, 16–37.

Dadusc, Deanna (2017) *The Micropolitics of Criminalisation: Power, Resistance and the Amsterdam Squatting Movement.* Amsterdam: University of Kent [PhD Dissertation].

Debord, Guy (1967) *The Society of the Spectacle.* New York: Zone Books.

Della Porta, Donatella & Gianni Piazza (2008) *Voices of the Valley. Voices of the Straits. How Protest Creates Communities.* New York: Berghahn.

Della Porta, Donatella & Dieter Rucht (1995) Left-Libertarian Movements in Context: A Comparison of Italy and West Germany 1965–1990. In J. Craig Jenkins & Bert Klandermans (Eds) *The Politics of Social Protest: Comparative Perspectives on States and Social Movements.* London: UCL Press, 229–273.

Estebaranz, Jtxo (2005) *Tropicales y Radicales. Experiencias alternativas y luchas autónomas en Euskal Herriak (1985–1990).* Bilbao: Likiniano Elkartea.

Federici, S. (2012) *Revolution at Point Zero. Housework, Reproduction, and Feminist Struggle.* Oakland: PM Press.

Feliciantonio, Cesare di (2017) Spaces of the Expelled as Spaces of the Urban Commons? Analysing the Re-Emergence of Squatting Initiatives in Rome. *International Journal of Urban and Regional Research* 41(5): 708–725.

Flesher, Cristina (2007) Autonomous Movements and the Institutional Left: Two Approaches in Tension in Madrid's Anti-Globalization Network. *South European Society & Politics* 12(3): 335–358.

Flesher, Cristina (2014) *Social Movements & Globalization. How Protests, Occupations & Uprisings are Changing the World.* New York: Palgrave Macmillan.

Flesher, Cristina & Laurence Cox (Eds) (2013) *Understanding European Movements. New Social Movements, Global Justice Struggles, Anti-Austerity Protest.* Abingdon: Routledge.

Foucault, Michel (1982) The Subject and Power. *Critical Inquiry* 8(4): 777–795.

Fraser, Nancy (2008) *Adding Insult to Injury.* London: Verso.

Gaillard, Edith (2013) *Habiter autrement: des squats féministes en France et en Allemagne. Une remise en question de l'ordre social.* PhD Dissertation. Tours: François Rabelais University.

García, Oscar & Martin B. Jørgensen (2019) Autonomous Solidarity: Hotel City Plaza. In Oscar García & Martin B. Jørgensen (Eds) *Solidarity and the 'Refugee Crisis' in Europe.* New York: Palgrave Macmillan, 49–72.

Geronimo (2012) *Fire and Flames. A History of the German Autonomist Movement.* Oakland: PM Press.

Gil, Silvia (2011) *Nuevos feminismos. Sentidos comunes en la dispersión.* Madrid: Traficantes de Sueños.

Graeber, David (2004) *Fragments of an Anarchist Anthropology.* Chicago: Prickly Paradigm.

Grazioli, Margherita & Carlotta Caciagli (2018) Resisting the Neoliberal Urban Fabric: Housing Rights Movements and the Re-Appropriation of the 'Right to the City' in Rome, Italy. *Voluntas* https://doi.org/10.1007/s11266-018-9977-y.

Hodkinson, Stuart & Paul Chatterton (2006) Autonomy in the City? Reflections on the Social Centres Movement in the UK. *City* 10: 305–315.

Holm, Andrej & Armin Kuhn (2011) Squatting and Urban Renewal: The Interaction of Squatter Movements and Strategies of Urban Restructuring in Berlin. *International Journal of Urban and Regional Research* 35(3): 644–658.

Kadir, Nazima (2016) *The Autonomous Life? Paradoxes and Authority in the Squatters Movement in Amsterdam.* Manchester: Manchester University Press.

Karpantschof, René & Flemming Mikkelsen. (2014) Youth, Space, and Autonomy in Copenhagen: The Squatters' and Autonomous Movement, 1963–2012. In Bart van der Steen, Ask Katzeef & Leendert van Hoogenhuijze (Eds) *The City Is Ours. Squatting and Autonomous Movements in Europe from the 1970s to the Present.* Oakland: PM Press, 179–205.

Katsiaficas, Georgy (2006) *The Subversion of Politics: European Autonomous Social Movements and the Decolonization of Everyday Life.* Oakland: AK Press.

Knabb, Ken (1997) *The Joy of Revolution.* www.bopsecrets.org/PS/index.htm

Koopmans, Ruud (1995) *Democracy from Below. New Social Movements and the Political System in West Germany.* Boulder: Westview.

Maddanu, Simone (2018) The Theater as a Common Good: Artists, Activists and *Artivists* on Stage. *Interface* 10(1–2): 70–91.

Martin, John N. & Primo Moroni (2007) *La luna sotto casa. Milano tra rivolta esistenziale e movimenti politici.* Milan: ShaKe.

Martínez, Miguel A. (2007) The Squatters' Movement: Urban Counterculture and Alter-Globalisation Dynamics. *South European Society and Politics* 12(3): 379–398.

Martínez, Miguel A. (2013) The Squatters' Movement in Europe: A Durable Struggle for Social Autonomy in Urban Politics. *Antipode* 45(4): 866–887.

Martínez, Miguel A. (2018a) Socio-Spatial Structures and Protest Cycles of Squatted Social Centres in Madrid. In Miguel A. Martínez (Ed.) *The Urban Politics of Squatters' Movements.* New York: Palgrave Macmillan, 25–49.

Martínez, Miguel A. (Ed.) (2018b) *The Urban Politics of Squatters' Movements.* New York: Palgrave Macmillan.

McKay, George (Ed.) (1998) *DiY Culture: Party and Protest in Nineties Britain.* London: Verso.

Membretti, Andrea (2007) Centro Sociale Loncavallo. Building Citizenship as an Innovative Service. *European Urban and Regional Studies* 14(3): 255–266.

Moroni, Primo & Consorzio Aaster (1996) *Centri Sociali: Geografie del desiderio. Dati, statistiche, progetti, mappe, divenire.* Milano: Shake.

Mudu, Pierpaolo (2009) Where Is Hardt and Negri's Multitude? Real Networks in Open Space. *ACME. An International E-Journal for Critical Geographies* 11(3): 211–244.

Mudu, Pierpaolo (2012) At the Intersection of Anarchists and Autonomists: Autogestioni and Centri Sociali. *ACME. An International E-Journal for Critical Geographies* 11(3): 413–438.

Mudu, Pierpaolo (2014) 'Ogni Sfratto Sarà Una Barricata': Squatting for Housing and Social Conflict in Rome. In Claudio Cattaneo & Miguel Martínez (Eds) *The Squatters' Movement in Europe: Commons and Autonomy as Alternatives to Capitalism.* London: Pluto, 136–163.

Mudu, Pierpaolo & Luisa Rossini (2018) Occupations of Housing and Social Centres in Rome: A Durable Resistance to Neoliberalism and Institutionalization. In Miguel Martínez (Ed.) *The Urban Politics of Squatters' Movements.* New York: Palgrave Macmillan, 99–120.

96 Autonomy from Capitalism

Notes From Nowhere (2003) *We are Everywhere: The Irresistible Rise of Global Anticapitalism.* London: Verso.

Novy, Johannes & Claire Colomb (2013) Struggling for the Right to the (Creative) City in Berlin and Hamburg: New Urban Social Movements, New 'Spaces of Hope'? *International Journal of Urban and Regional Research* 37(5): 1816–1838.

Padrones, Sheila (2017) *El movimiento de okupación como proceso emancipador. El caso de Donostialdea.* PhD Thesis. Elche: Universidad Miguel Hernández.

Piazza, Gianni (2011) 'Locally Unwanted Land Use' Movements: The Role of Left-Wing Parties and Groups in Trans-Territorial Conflicts in Italy. *Modern Italy* 16(3): 329–344.

Piazza, Gianni (2013) How Do Activists Make Decisions within Social Centres? In SqEK (Ed.) *Squatting in Europe. Radical Spaces, Urban Struggles.* Wivenhoe: Minor Compositions, 89–111.

Piazza, Gianni (2018) Squatting Social Centres in a SicilianCity: Liberated Spaces and Urban Protest Actors. *Antipode* 50(2): 498–522.

Pruijt, Hans & Conny Roggeband (2014) Autonomous and/or Institutionalized Social Movements? Conceptual Clarification and Illustrative Cases. *International Journal of Comparative Sociology* 55(2): 144–165.

Refugee Accommodation Space City Plaza (2018) Refugees' Struggles in Athens: Voices from City Plaza. In SqEK (Ed.) *Fighting for Spaces, Fighting for Our Lives: Squatting Movements Today.* Münster: Assemblage, 351–356.

Sadler, Simon (1998) *The Situationist City.* Cambridge: The MIT Press.

Salamanca, Francisco & Gonzalo Wilhelmi (Eds) (2012) *Tomar y hacer en vez de pedir y esperar. Autonomía y movimientos sociales. Madrid 1985–2011.* Madrid: Solidaridad Obrera.

Seminario (2014) *Okupa Madrid (1985–2011). Memoria, reflexión, debate y autogestión colectiva del conocimiento.* Madrid: Diagonal.

Smart, Alan. (2014) Provo. In Claudio Cattaneo & Miguel Martínez (Eds) *The Squatters' Movement in Europe: Commons and Autonomy as Alternatives to Capitalism.* London: Pluto, 113.

Toret, Javier et al. (Eds) (2008) *Autonomía y Metrópolis. Del movimiento okupa a los centros sociales de segunda generación.* Málaga: ULEX-Lainvisible.net-Diputación Provincial de Málaga.

Valli, Chiara (2015) When Cultural Workers Become an Urban Social Movement: Political Subjectification and Alternative Cultural Production in the Macao Movement, Milan. *Environment and Planning A* 47: 643–659.

Van der Steen, Bart, Ask Katzeef & Leendert Van Hoogenhuijze (Eds) (2014) *The City Is Ours. Squatting and Autonomous Movements in Europe from the 1970s to the Present.* Oakland: PM Press.

Ward, Colin & David Goodway (2014) *Talking Anarchy.* Oakland: PM Press.

Wennerhag, Magnus, Christian Fröhlich & Grzegorz Piotrowski (Eds) (2018) *Radical Left Movements in Europe.* Abingdon: Routledge.

Yates, Luke (2014) Rethinking Prefiguration: Alternatives, Micropolitics and Goals in Social Movements. *Social Movement Studies: Journal of Social, Cultural and Political Protest* 14(1): 1–21.

3

SOCIO-SPATIAL STRUCTURES

How do squats emerge and develop? What makes squatting possible? Large numbers of squatting practices over several decades and across various countries suggest that there is something beyond the will of squatters. Social movements, in my view, are better understood by accounting for the articulations between agency and structures. The intentions and strategic actions of squatters, in particular, are certainly mediated, constrained, and limited by specific structural conditions or contexts. I designate them, in general, as 'socio-spatial structures of opportunities and constraints', although a socio-historical dimension is also implicit in this approach. These structures may be local in nature, but they are often shaped at national scales and also following international trends, somehow in parallel to the transnational networks of squatters. Activists interpret these structures, react to them, reveal them, and try to find cracks that allow their transgressive practice to prosper. Authorities and powerholders exert their influence in these structures to suppress, regulate, or prevent the extension of squatting. In this chapter, I examine five main socio-spatial and historical conditions of possibility for the occurrence and development of squatting. In doing so, it is necessary to show how squatters' movements unfolded given these relevant contexts. In particular, I single out a specific urban political economy as well as activist networks, which are seldom introduced in the study of urban movements. This analysis contributes to an explanatory framework of squatting that also serves to investigate significant outcomes of squatting practices and movements.

Political experience, cultural differences, and material conditions of living enable squatters with various forms of resources and purposes to act within specific structural frameworks—socio-spatial and historical conditions of possibility. Squatting practices and movements can be explained by identifying each significant condition of possibility and their mutual interaction (see Image 3.1).

98 Socio-Spatial Structures

Sometimes severe housing shortages catalyse a wave of squatting. However, other contextual circumstances such as the existence of workers and tenants organisations with a certain background of past struggles and favourable policies may be necessary too.

Watson (2016), for example, provides a nuanced analysis of this context in the aftermath of the Second World War when at least 48,000 people took over empty premises all over the UK. Previous requisitions of property by the authorities to facilitate the production of weapons during the war period, the new comprehensive welfare policies launched by the Labour government afterwards, and the remarkable experience of rent strikes were crucial conditions for such a massive extension of squatting. Watson also emphasises the changing support to squatters given by the Communist Party. Leaders of another squatting movement in the UK, born in 1968, recognised the inspiration of the previous struggles despite the radically different context they faced (Bailey 1973: 21–24).

A similar increase of squatting actions in the post-war period took place in France:

> At the end of World War II, as the state engaged in a reconstruction plan to address a housing shortage, various associations demanded social housing policies, the requisition of vacant housing, and an end to evictions. Socialist-Catholic activists, inspired by London squatters (Colin 2005: 34, Péchu 2010: 49) resorted to squatting as civil disobedience. This movement, which was aligned with workers, against political parties, was mainly aimed at rehousing precarious families and homeless people. ... During this period [1945–1971], not all squats were repressed. In fact, some were supported by the state or even legalised (Colin 2005: 58).
>
> *(Aguilera 2018: 125)*

Sometimes the opportunities created by a regime change can be seized by activists. This is the case of East Berlin in 1989–90 (azozomox & Kuhn 2018, Grashoff 2017, Holm & Kuhn 2011, Sabaté 2012) and some Polish cities also after 1989 (Polanska & Piotrowski 2015, 2016).

In the case of East Berlin, starting in the 1960s, a 'cautious' and silent form of squatting (or 'black dwelling') was not unheard of, enjoying some tolerance from the local bureaucrats. By 1979, authorities listed 1,200 occupied apartments, and the numbers kept growing (azozomox & Kuhn 2018: 151). Economic difficulties in rehabilitating old buildings, a large amount of vacancy (around 400,000 empty flats by 1990: Grashoff 2017: 2), frozen rents, a wide dissatisfaction with the state allocation of houses, and a shortage of affordable housing all contributed to accommodate the arrival of new squatters, mostly from the Western area. Between November 1989 and October 1990, 134 new squats took place in East Berlin (azozomox & Kuhn 2018: 152).

In both Germany and Poland, a key political and economic condition after the fall of the Berlin Wall was the restitution of many properties to their owners before 1945 (and even before 1933 in Germany). Re-privatisation claims by owners, their heirs, and especially by private companies who bought their rights resulted in 'rent increases, causing the old tenants to move out and subsequent gentrification' (Polanska & Piotrowski 2015: 281); where these litigations faced unclear property rights, squatters were able to remain longer.

The above examples also spark intriguing empirical questions: Why did similar squatting waves not occur in other countries after the war period? Why did squatting not expand in a similar fashion in Central and Eastern Europe after 1989–90? Moreover, why did multiple squatting practices over the decades not scale up to form a more consistent movement, as occurred in Sweden (Polanska 2017)? Or why is squatting still active in cities such as Vienna, which has enjoyed one of the highest rates of social and affordable housing in the world (Foltin 2014)? Although this puzzle is beyond the reach of this chapter, a short answer is that the same contextual features play differently across cities and countries. In addition, we should look at the interplay of various structural conditions simultaneously. Drawing upon previous studies on squatting (for example, Cattaneo & Martínez 2014, Holm & Kuhn 2011, Koopmans 1995, Martínez 2018b, Mayer 1993a, Pruijt 2003, Mudu 2004, Piazza 2018, Piazza & Genovese 2016, Polanska & Piotrowski 2015, Steen et al. 2014; etc.), five major contextual conditions have been directly associated with the emergence and rise of squatting:

- housing shortage, rising rents, and high rates of vacancy;
- urban renewal regimes;
- applicable legislation and law enforcement (repression, tolerance, regularisation);
- activist networks involving squatters and other social movements; and
- mass media coverage of squatting, public opinion about it, and its significance for political agendas.

More specific conditions, such as those introducing this section, are:

- housing markets, dynamics of real estate speculation (gentrification included), and protection of owners' interests;
- housing policies, social housing, rent controls, rehabilitation of old buildings, city branding;
- local and national background of authorities implementing requisitions, adverse possession, and engaging in negotiations with squatters (and the owners of occupied properties);
- historical events of crisis such as economic recessions, wars, regime change, and the social struggles around them; and
- social structures in terms of poverty, homeownership, migration, cultural lifestyles and consumption, reproduction of social classes and gender inequality, etc.

IMAGE 3.1 Floor painted in solidarity with squat Villa Amalias, Athens, 2013
Source: Author

In the following subsections I briefly recall the main evidence and interpretation for the five general socio-spatial structures of opportunities and constraints that explain the emergence and development of squatting.

Housing Shortages and Vacancy Rates

Above all, squatting consists of a set of collective actions aimed at the use empty or abandoned properties without the owners' consent for, mainly, housing purposes and/or for the promotion of social activities. The kind of owners, buildings, and the volume and duration of vacant properties vary. Squatters need a sufficient amount of buildings available to be occupied directly or after light works of rehabilitation. The higher the vacancy rate of houses and buildings, combined with acceptable conditions of damage, if any, the higher the likelihood that squatters take over. The cases of the UK, East Berlin, and Poland which open this chapter are good illustrations of this principle. Abundant vacant properties in Spanish cities such as Madrid were also tightly tied to the rise of squatters' movements (Martínez 2018a).

In the Netherlands, where squatting was practiced by large numbers of the youth, students, workers, artists, and homeless people many observers noted a correlation with both acute housing shortages and a lot of available empty properties (Dadusc 2017, Draaisma & van Hoogstraten 1983, Priemus 1983, 2015, Pruijt 2003).

Socio-Spatial Structures **101**

> The squatter movement grew steadily and is thought to have numbered around 20,000 people by 1980. ... Although the squatter movement in Amsterdam had internationalised, its numbers were shrinking: in the 1990s, there were reportedly around 4000 squatters, and by 2010, there were between 1500 and 2000 squatters in Amsterdam.
>
> *(Priemus 2015: 86–87)*

A partial explanation of this shift can be found in a relative improvement of the housing situation and a decrease of available empty buildings after the mid-1990s (Pruijt 2003: 153):

> [W]ith the urban renewal projects of the city centre complete, fewer buildings were being emptied. ... Owners developed new strategies to keep their houses in use, such as the *kraakwacht* (squat watch). Finally, the city was no longer experiencing a population exodus.
>
> *(Owens 2009: 226; italics in original)*

Squatters in the Netherlands took over not only empty apartments but also office spaces:

> We now move to the current phenomenon of increasing vacancy in office space in European urban areas and at the same time there is a huge shortage of affordable housing for young people. ... In 2013, more than 7 million square metres of office space (14.6% of all office space) in the Netherlands was unused. ... In the 1970s and 1980s, the aim of the squatter movement in Amsterdam and other Dutch cities was to reduce vacancy in social housing and business premises and to increase the availability of affordable housing. Nowadays, social housing estates are seldom vacant. Vacancy is concentrated more and more in urban offices.
>
> *(Priemus 2015: 89, 91)*

According to Buchholz (2016: 186), the vacancy rate in Amsterdam is 18%. Dutch authorities reacted both against squatters and urban vacancy. On the one hand, anti-squatting companies have been allowed to operate since 1980 (Buchholz 2016: 94, 188). On the other hand, the Squatting and Vacant Property Act (passed in October 2010) banned squatting and at the same time made local municipalities responsible for the management of vacancy.

> [The law] delegated the problem to local municipalities by encouraging them to constitute a vacancy register for an overview of the empty spaces in the city, and by giving fines to property owners who would leave their properties vacant. This aspect of the law was not well received by most municipalities. When the bill passed, vacancy was a major problem for most Dutch municipalities, and in particular for

102 Socio-Spatial Structures

> Amsterdam. Indeed, after the financial crises of 2008, there were a large number of vacant apartments and offices in Amsterdam, generally owned by housing associations and real estate investors, who could not afford renovations, or wait for the market value to increase before selling their properties.
>
> *(Dadusc 2017: 180)*

The economic crisis also prevented housing corporations such as De Key and Rochdale to complete their projects, resulting in higher numbers of empty blocks. These were thus intended to be sold as luxury apartments instead of social housing aiming for a quick cash in. 'In 2011, 4.2% of houses in the Netherlands were empty, according to the Centraal Bureau voor de Statistiek (CBS), namely around 300,000.' (Dadusc 2017: 180)

In addition, Priemus (2015: 91) argues that fines up to €7,500 for real estate owners 'who fail to register vacant properties with the council … is hardly a deterrent in real-estate circles. A much higher fine has to be introduced'. Since these anti-vacancy measures seem to have been ineffective, the same applies to the legislation that makes squatting a criminal offence. However, the active work of owners to protect their vacant properties by resorting to 'anti-squatting' firms has had a much deeper impact on the development of squatting in the Netherlands (and, partially, in the UK, Germany, Belgium, Ireland, and France—where Camelot, one of the largest firms in private security, operates—but rarely in other European countries yet).

> In place of an active vacancy policy, most municipalities, including Amsterdam let the vacancy problem to be managed by so called anti-squatting (*anti-kraak*) companies. Anti-squat-companies are private companies for temporary real-estate management, namely security companies that provide 'property guardianship', and secure the house on behalf of the owner. This practice implies that real estate owners engage private companies for placing 'live-in security guards' in vacant properties, with the aim of preventing squatters from moving in. Although the property owners have to pay for this service, the fee is generally cheaper than the fines they would receive for leaving the property vacant. Anti-squatters, or property guardians, are explicitly hired as security guards, but the practice is promoted as a form of temporary housing.
>
> *(Dadusc 2017: 184; italics in original)*

Anti-squatters pay to access an affordable dwelling but, in practice, they pay in order to work as security guards. They are not entitled to any salary and they do not have regular tenancy rights either.

> [They] are expected to pay water-gas-electricity bills and so called 'administration fees, at up to 300 €/month. Moreover, they have to make sure that the property is well maintained and the anti-squatting company

regularly checks them. The anti-squatting contracts often prohibit the user from receiving guests and to go on vacation or to leave the house for longer than three days. ... Both the owner and employees of the anti-squatting company can enter the property at any time, without previous notice, and fine the anti-squatters if they are not complying with the conditions of the contract. Anti-squatters are [notified] only two weeks in advance before they have to leave the property.

(Dadusc 2017: 184–185)

According to the estimates, nowadays anti-squatters 'far outnumber the squatters at any time in their history' (Priemus 2015: 89). Buchholz (2016: 94, 192) identified 70 anti-squat agencies in the Netherlands who officially managed around 50,000 anti-squatters ('live-in guardians'), although the real figure would amount up to 100,000—he estimates 40,000 Dutch squatters in the 1980s. Even 'housing associations' usually buy the services of anti-squat companies. This tendency also represents an increase in housing and job precariousness, simultaneously. Instead of enjoying tenants' rights, domestic privacy, and housing standards, anti-squatters work as property guardians as a way to satisfy their residential needs because of the shortage of unaffordable dwellings in convenient urban locations. As Buchholz (2016: 121–123) investigated, 'newcomers', 'outsiders', and 'starters' in the housing market (and the social housing sector) are the most likely social groups to be accommodated as anti-squatters—and in other low-budget options. The average live-in guardian in one of the anti-squat companies (Zwerfkei) is 27 years old. Therefore, anti-squatting, as with any other means of protecting unused private properties, replaces squatting when it comes to dealing with urban vacancy as a low-cost solution.

Squatters tend to do serious research on the specific legal and economic situation of each, apparently in disuse, building. Frequently, neighbours are the best source of information. Squatters and other activists were always prone to detect, publicise, and question urban emptiness, which has been lately facilitated with geo-coded maps and online platforms (Arnold 2015). Higher proportions of vacancy occur due to several dynamics: economic crisis and slumping construction, reduction in rental housing stock, privatisation of formerly public houses, increasing levels of private ownership of housing, changes in the use of specific buildings, a decline in industrial activities, urban renewal processes, etc. Accordingly, the opportunities for squatters seeking a place depend upon these macro dynamics to provide a quantity of effective spaces ready to be squatted.

Fortunately for squatters, capitalist urban speculation is based, among other things, on a convenient stock of empty buildings which allows owners to delay works or sales for a certain period of time, while negotiating a better price. The ideal speculator wants his or her ownership to be renewed, sold, or rented at the highest price and at the earliest moment, but they can wait a certain period of time if there is an expected—relatively high—profit to be gained. Only if there was a total occupation of the built environment in a given moment,

104 Socio-Spatial Structures

without any loss or waste of owned space, would squatting be impossible. That perfect balance is far from being achieved by the free flow of market forces, so different rates of vacancy (around 5%) are accepted by mainstream scholars and market operators to facilitate transactions, and there is abundant legislation that backs this conventional market arrangement. Furthermore, low rates of vacancy are meant to increase rents and prices in the absence of sufficient social housing provision.

More specific economic and social conditions have been pointed out in order to understand vacancy:

> Economic reasons for not using vacant property are at least threefold. Firstly, the nominal book value contributes to the overall value of the company, so renting out at a lower rate reduces the book value of the entire company, which again affects credits by banks etc. Secondly, vacancy can be deducted (to a certain degree) from income tax by the landlord. Thirdly, interim or temporary uses pose administrative challenges to ensure safety regulations. This often costs time, energy, expertise and money to meet semi-permanent or permanent legal housing standards.
>
> *(Buchholz 2016: 184)*

According to Martínez & Cattaneo (2014: 32), we can distinguish three general cases of vacancy:

1. Empty properties subject to ongoing rehabilitation works, actively offered for sale or rent, due to prompt occupation, or with the owners seeking to change their land use. This 'active vacancy', notwithstanding the above plans, may keep the property vacant for long periods. Banks and financial firms tend to operate according to these principles, but their portfolio may be very large, and their priorities vary according to short-term and highly-speculative expectations, especially when authorities do not force them to implement the written 'active plans'.
2. Some buildings are completely abandoned, in serious need of rehabilitation or even in ruins, closed and kept off the market, and also unavailable as social housing if they belong to state authorities or public housing organisations. This form of 'neglected vacancy' usually lasts for very long periods of time. Owners do not have clear and explicit plans for the property. They may wait for legal changes in the planning regulation that can bring them future profits. Sometimes, abandonment is simply due to conflicts among various owners and managers.
3. A third category of vacancy relates to 'long run family projects'. Individuals from many different social class conditions may keep these properties empty in cases where there is no urgent need for their relatives or their own. Frequently, the owner purchased the house or building in order to transfer it to their offspring in the future, to use it after his or her own retirement, for temporary occupation during holidays, and also to keep it as an investment that

can compensate periods of unemployment, a small pension, and financial crises in general. These owners keep their properties off the market because they do not experience an urgent need to sell or get revenues from rental agreements.

The profitable management of vacancy is only one of the possible sources of urban speculation, but the most direct source that squatters can fight against. This does not imply that a simple increase in the stock of vacant buildings, as is the case in the so-called shrinking cities, will determine the emergence of a squatting movement. If the homeless population and organised activists are also diminishing, the likelihood of squatting will decrease. Moreover, the indispensable availability of empty properties to be occupied should be constructively intertwined with the lack of effective police repression and the previous political experience of potential squatters. For example, in Valencia (Spain) one old neighbourhood (Cabanyal), subject to a very contested renewal operation, had a lot of empty houses, but the wave of squatting in that area only started once the neighbours firmly opposed the city plans and, at the same time, the evictions of squatters were effective in other parts of the city, such as the now rehabilitated historical centre with less evident vacancy (Collado 2007, other examples from Spanish cities in Martínez 2004, 2018b, see Image 3.2).

IMAGE 3.2 Squat La Ingobernable, Madrid, 2018
Source: Author

106 Socio-Spatial Structures

Urban Renewal

The crucial condition of emptiness often depends upon the urban planning and restructuring processes of specific areas; the displacement of industrial factories, vacant schools or public facilities which have moved to a different location, and residential units subject to new regulations all often occur when a whole area has been designated for accomplishing new functions. Authorities, planners, and investors would argue that old-fashioned areas, poverty, crime, ruins, substandard housing, and pollution demand a transformation of public space and, simultaneously, of the residential buildings and existing population therein. New roads or mega projects (like museums, stadiums, waterfronts, commercial malls, etc.) may also account for the elite-driven vacancy of a large number of dwellings in a particular urban area (Fainstein 1994). The slower the rhythm of these reconfigurations, the higher the opportunities for squatting and campaigning against the plans (Martínez 2004). Old owners and tenants appear as the natural allies of squatters opposing the authoritarian (or the restricted participatory) manner of these urban interventions.

Many of the experiences of squatting in late-1970s Milan (Martin & Moroni 2007: 178) and Berlin (Holm & Kuhn 2011, Mayer 1993a, 1993b) took place in working-class and industrial areas where different political groups besides the squatters (tenants, foreign workers, countercultural artists, environmentalists, autonomist and libertarian organisations, etc.) confronted the official urban plans. Old schools that did not suit the new regulations in Spain in the early 1990s were one of the favourite and more feasible targets of squatters in Madrid during that period (Martínez 2018b). In former industrial areas like Bilbao, before and after 'the Guggenheim effect', many factories and residential buildings around them were widely squatted beginning in the mid-1980s. One famous case was the social centre and houses of Kukutza, an abandoned industrial building located in the popular neighbourhood of Rekalde (Bilbao) and evicted in 2011 after 13 years of squatting while enjoying great social support (Egia & Kukutza Gaztetxeko Kideak 2011).

This background indicates that squatters' movements behave as 'early risers' in the struggles against gentrification (Lees et al. 2016). A quick look at the experiences of squatting in Germany may illustrate this point. On the one hand, this activism in the 1970s and 1980s in Berlin was known as a 'rehab squatting movement':

> When a powerful youth and alternative movement emerged and coalesced with local community groups, squatting became a form of self-help in which the squatters not only occupied vacant buildings, but also attempted to restore the properties into liveable condition after years of physical deterioration. ... During the movement's peak, about 160 buildings were 'rehab-squatted' in West Berlin, involving directly about 5,000 people.
>
> *(Mayer 1993b: 212–213)*

The self-organised rehabilitation of derelict buildings in areas subject to demolition and renewal has been a common achievement of squatters all over Europe. They did not invest large sums of money in these works, but they were not for free either. These actions implied criticism of the urban policies concerning goals, stages, citizens' engagement, and intended benefits of the renewal operations.

It is this collective opposition to the urban restructuring of certain areas of the city, frequently in alliance with other residents less politicised and radicalised than the squatters, which was heavily repressed by the authorities—rather than the unauthorised occupation itself. As an unexpected outcome of these struggles, a 'self-help rehabilitation programme' was institutionalised by the Berlin Senate in 1982 (Mayer 1993b: 213); a few legalised squats even enjoyed financial support from the programme (Holm & Kuhn 2011: 649). A more predictable and successful result of the alliances between squatters and residents aiming at achieving 'cautious urban renewal' was the replacement of 'the violent character, bureaucratic paternalism and inscrutability of these [renewal] plans with careful, step-by-step processes that were easier to comprehend and more socially adjusted, yet this would not come into effect for several years' (Holm & Kuhn 2011: 649).

Another lesson to learn from the above experiences is that the buildings with the least damage and, thus, no need for deep repairs, will presumably last longer. They tend to be located in consolidated areas of the city without facing major changes. Conversely, if abandoned buildings are in very dangerous and ruined conditions, as is frequently the case in old, either post-industrial or working-class quarters of the city, authorities may speed up the eviction process (Pruijt 2003: 147). This also explains why some developers and real-estate speculators prefer to demolish or set their own vacant properties on fire while still in good shape: they fear that squatters can take over, fix them, and strive to remain. Very often, these acts of purposeful demolition and destruction are liable, which is well known by the perpetrators.

Holm and Kuhn convincingly show the relationship between squatting and urban renewal. In particular, they distinguish three stages for the City of Berlin. Between 1963 and 1981, a bureaucratic, managerial, and authoritarian approach to urban redevelopment planted the seeds of discontent and unrest among residents who were joined by squatters. In the early 1980s, squatters contributed to the modification of the renewal schemes with their criticisms of the demolition approach and the lack of citizens' say. This period is interpreted as an 'experimental laboratory in which new instruments of urban renewal were trialled' (Holm & Kuhn 2011: 653). The legalisation of some squats and their institutional integration in the 'cautious renewal' plans as stakeholders also implied the end of any 'lawless space'.

Since then, the repression of squatting has been implemented faster and with almost no mercy. The third post-Fordist period mainly refers to East Berlin in the 1990s. The privatisation and restitution policy led to individual negotiations between owners, tenants' committees, and authorities. Town planning as usual,

108 Socio-Spatial Structures

instead of specific renewal plans, was meant to facilitate the renovation of around 180,000 apartments by resorting to the owners' financial resources. This time, squatters were more marginalised from the process and also from other urban protests in the following years, at least until the struggles brought about in the 2000s.

> Unlike the West Berlin squatter movement in the early 1980s, squatters in East Berlin did not play a central role in implementing a new redevelopment regime. Squatted houses were, in fact, an alien element in the new regime of urban renewal. As in West Berlin, the regulatory strategy the city's government was pursuing gave squatters huge scope for structurally renovating their houses. In East Berlin the authorities for the most part had recourse to solutions already tried out in the West. The routine unwinding of self-help programmes and collective tenancy contracts had absolutely no innovatory potential for implementing the new redevelopment model in East Berlin, focused as it was on individual negotiation and private investments. These programmes, on the contrary, brought about only cautious renewal of small niches. The special role of squatted houses not only created discord between East and West, but also explained the squatters' far-reaching avoidance of district conflicts. Their special status made cooperation with tenants and district initiatives difficult.
>
> *(Holm & Kuhn 2011: 654)*

IMAGE 3.3 Squat Teatro Coppola, Catania, 2018
Source: Author

According to azozomox and Kuhn (2018: 155), around 70% of the squats in Berlin were located in inner-city districts (Mitte, Schöeberg, Kreuzberg, Friedrichshain, and Prenzlauer Berg) where the problems of decay, neglected maintenance of buildings, extensive vacancy, and temporary tenancy contracts prevailed. The large concentration of speculative vacancy, grassroots mobilisations against the housing shortage, and a cluster of thousands of activists moving into the affordable decaying blocks and factory buildings of these areas were identified as the structural conditions that explained the eruption of squatting in the 1980–88 period (azozomox & Kuhn 2018: 156). However, the marginalisation that squatters experienced in the wave of occupations in the Eastern part of Berlin during the early 1990s could not change the rapid process of private investment, redevelopment, and gentrification that occurred in former squatting areas such as Friedrichshain-Kreuzberg (azozomox & Kuhn 2018: 158).

Are Squatters the Storm Troopers of Gentrification?

A systematic analysis of four cities in East Germany (Dresden, Leipzig, Potsdam, and East Berlin) since 1989 concluded that squatting and gentrification were not causally associated (Holm & Kuhn 2017: 282, 296). One key argument is the low proportion of squats (between 0.5 and 5%) within the overall housing stock of the areas under examination. In all cases, silent squatting was a practice initiated in the 1980s and more public squatters came about in the reunification year of the two German states (1989–90). After the restitution-privatisation policy, old buildings of the inner cities were rehabilitated and the areas were successfully upgraded, which entailed high rises in prices and rents. Squats overlapped with these processes but they had little to do with them; most of them were legalised early on and new attempts at squatting were swiftly evicted.

To illustrate this analysis, take the example of the Prenzlauer Berg neighbourhood in East Berlin, one of the most quickly gentrified areas. There, legalised squats did not even contribute to boosting the local cultural image as an attractive artistic and socially diverse hub, as happened in other districts such as Kreuzberg. According to the researchers, squats from Prenzlauer Berg remained largely isolated from their surroundings and even from other urban struggles (Holm & Kuhn 2017: 285–288). In most cases, squatters criticised and opposed official rehabilitation plans and the subsequent gentrification, but they often cooperated with local governments in order to preserve their squats after being legalised. Indeed, the long-term lease agreements obtained by the squatters, secured affordable rents below the average local level, which played against the gentrification trends. For example, 'in five former squats, purchased by the non-commercial co-operative Mietshäuser Syndikat (tenement syndicate), current rents are only 40 to 60% of average local rent expectations for a new tenancy' (Holm & Kuhn 2017: 292).

The debate about squatting and gentrification was also addressed early by Pruijt (2003). In the two cases Pruijt examined (Amsterdam and the Lower East Side of New York), he concedes that squatters were pioneer residents in areas

110 Socio-Spatial Structures

that were gentrified later on. They were pioneers by making visible their claims to housing and the neighbourhoods themselves in local media, but not because they participated in the redevelopment of the areas nor in upgrading their economic character. The squatters' milieus certainly added subcultural and countercultural activities such as art exhibitions and studios in rundown buildings, underground concerts and dance clubs, graffiti on the walls, community gardens, bicycle workshops, and the like. Some of these symbolic images were framed by private developers in such a manner that they could appeal to the middle and upper classes to move in. Squatters are not powerful enough to promote gentrification, but they can contribute, even unintendedly, to it. As he quotes them: 'I have some contradictions, I see that my person, my culture, my lifestyle facilitates gentrification. It's like I'm a tool of the system. I don't know what to do' (Pruijt 2003: 148).

However, Pruijt offers compelling arguments that mitigate the supposed gentrification effect. First, 'if squatters did in any way stimulate gentrification, this was contrary to their intentions. Both in New York City and in Amsterdam, squatters often sided with original inhabitants against developers of expensive apartments' (Pruijt 2003: 148–149). These alliances and practices of contestation are omitted by developers. Anti-gentrification campaigns were even pioneering in various German cities during the 1980s and 1990s (Mayer 1993b). In some cases (especially in London: Dee 2013), squatters also occupied luxury mansions in already upper-class areas, which creates more distress than benefits for their wealthy neighbours. When squatters are aware of the operations run by developers to gentrify the area they occupy, they avoid cooperation and start confrontation.

If a clothing brand uses images of demonstrations and revolutions in their commercial advertisements, we cannot conclude that activists held any purpose of fostering the revenues of companies selling jeans and sneakers. Likewise, squatters' performances and outlooks may be manipulated and portrayed in a biased and beneficial way for real-estate speculators. 'Many squatters are rich in cultural and social capital, although not in economic capital. However, squatting is not gentrification for the simple reason that it does not create luxury housing for the affluent' (Pruijt 2003: 148). In addition, none of the four cases examined by Holm and Kuhn allows the verification that squats contributed with 'symbolic effects' to gentrification (Holm & Kuhn 2017: 294). A contrary appreciation was made by Uitermark (2004), who explicitly identified 'artistic squatters' as the main resource for governmental cultural policies in Amsterdam in order to boost neoliberal agendas (interurban competition to attract foreign investments and pursue economic growth), although he did not refer to gentrification in particular but to the breeding places policy which was launched in 1999 and facilitated the legalisation of some squatted social centres. Pruijt (2004a: 704) replied that artistic squats 'are still low revenue-generating functions on expensive land, i.e. potential focal points for future conflicts'.

Second, squatters may also be associated with poverty, homelessness, noise, drugs, protests, riots, and other 'deviant' attributes that do not easily fit middle- and upper-class tastes. Property developers are only interested in this stigmatisation once they fuel the gentrification process in order to keep attracting well-off buyers. In this second stage of gentrification, both developers and authorities prefer to get rid of the squatters or, if it is not possible to do so in a peaceful manner, to tame and limit their presence by funding their art initiatives or by legalising the existing squats while exerting heavy repression of any new squatting attempts — the so-called Berlin Line. As Pruijt notes, 'putting policemen on nearly every corner of Lower East Side was a more likely stimulant of gentrification' (Pruijt 2003: 148).

Another effective way of pushing gentrification is the suppression of empty properties available for squatting by inciting their development and occupation with affluent individuals, households, or firms. This is evident in the Bospolder area of Rotterdam where around 500 squats that had taken place in the 1980s almost entirely vanished alongside the process of state-led gentrification (Dee 2018: 200–203). By 2000, the local government of Rotterdam, led by social democrats, decided not to build more social housing (Uitermark & Duyvendak 2008: 1495).

Third, a reverse argument can be made. Instead of promoting gentrification, squatters can stand as resources against it. Drawing upon Neil Smith, Pruijt argues that 'squatting is one of the factors that slowed [down] and partially stopped gentrification on the Lower East Side' (Pruijt 2003: 149). Squatters' resistance to gentrification does not seem to be very effective in most places, at least not without broader coalitions of urban activism. But their presence beside other low-income residents, their struggles to uncover abusive landlords and developers, and the implementation of policy measures such as rent control and social housing provision can alter or slow gentrification down. A successful example of these struggles was the early opposition of squatters and other residents to the restructuring plans of the Nieuwmarkt area in Amsterdam which, over the decades, also ended up as a gentrified area (Pruijt 2004b, Uitermark 2012).

Similar observations were made about the City of Madrid:

> The criminalisation of squatting helped to secure private properties, usually after a court trial, in a context of urban expansion and intense globalisation of capital. However, the already-consolidated networks of activists and the previous experiences of squatting provided a more variegated ground for social and political backlash. Most political squats continued within the city centre (57%), particularly the areas with higher rates of migrant residents and where the gentrification progress was slower (Lavapiés and Tetuán) compared to the neighbouring ones (Huertas-Cortes, Palacio and Malasaña-Universidad) where gentrification was faster.
>
> *(Martínez 2018a: 37–38)*

Despite the active contribution of squatters to halt the economic upgrade of these areas and the displacement of the worst-off population, gentrification,

112 Socio-Spatial Structures

helped by concomitant processes of urban tourism and the global financialisation of housing, also occurred. The former strongholds of squatters in the city centre were consequently displaced too.

This has also been reported in the case of Stockholm, but less rapidly achieved in the City of Hamburg, for example, due to the resistance showed by various urban movements (Franzén 2005). The case of the Haga district in Gothenburg has also been scrutinised in light of gentrification processes (Thörn 2012). Thörn argues that local activists engaged in the physical preservation of the area from demolition and renewal succeeded in shifting the prevailing stigma of it as a 'slum' to a more charismatic, attractive, and hip area— a 'nice old-working class neighbourhood'. Two different generations of activists, squatters included, influenced the successful preservation of the area according to the original struggle. At the same time, they also criticised the social displacement produced by the new conservationist but also city-branding policies for the neighbourhood, the rising prices of apartments, and the increasing attraction of wealthy newcomers. 'As the rents rose, the groups inhabiting the district in the 1970s almost completely disappeared ... One witness stated that "the operation succeeded but the patient died"' (Thörn 2012: 161). Thörn thus concludes that local activists and squatters inadvertently contributed to the gentrification of the area by destigmatising its identity, which was, in turn, used by authorities and private developers to boost reinvestment processes. The final breaths of resistance were not capable to halt the rising gentrification. He also mentions the shortcomings of the movement's agency, caused by weak activist alliances and a very loose assemblage of countercultural groups unable to alter the gentrification process once fuelled by the urban elites.

Nonetheless, Holm and Kuhn suggest an alternative conclusion, partially in line with Pruijt's (2003) quote above:

> The squats did not disrupt the realisation of real estate interests; however, they provided a sheltered segment of affordable housing provision in gentrification areas. ... In comparison to fixed-term funding initiatives and rent caps in the context of rehabilitation, self-help programmes prove to be the most sustainable and effective tool in the politics of housing over the last twenty years.
>
> *(Holm & Kuhn 2017: 295)*

According to them, squatters were skilful in their negotiations with authorities to secure some proportion of affordable housing with different tenure options in gentrifying urban areas. In most cases, the authorities purchased the buildings, if not their own property, and transferred them directly to the squatters. Conversely, confrontations with private owners and developers were exceptional. These outcomes, anyhow, relate more to the legalisation of squats than to the phenomenon of squatting overall.

IMAGE 3.4 Squat Odzysk, Poznan, 2014
Source: Author

Legislation and Law Enforcement

Concerning the legal issues, we can distinguish now three options: strong criminal persecution, light criminal persecution, and specific legal arrangements that permit squatting temporarily or permanently. When the first option applies, and authorities work hard to implement that legislation, squatting becomes too difficult, marginal, and infrequent, although not absolutely impossible. Denmark, Germany, and Sweden, for example, are the national contexts where this policy rules. However, it is important to note that the squatted community of Christiania in Copenhagen survived for almost five decades in a difficult environment where most squatting experiences were repressed without concessions (Mikkelsen & Karpantschof 2001, Thörn et al. 2011). Eventually, the legal and political pressure forced Christiania squatters to purchase the land and houses they had occupied (or even newly built):

114 Socio-Spatial Structures

> *Freetown Christiania*, the largest inner city squat in northern Europe, is inhabited by approximately 800 people and situated on 34 hectares, along Copenhagen's protected, medieval ramparts. It remains the only autonomous freetown created and retained in the center of any European capital city (Thörn et al. 2011: 68). Here, military barracks have been transformed into homes, music venues, cafés, workshops, kindergartens, a communal bathhouse, post office and a number of collectively owned businesses.
>
> *(Steiger 2018: 169; italics in original)*

Even when Christiania was granted a 'social experiment' status in 1973 by the social democratic government, the community was subject to many police assaults over the years, especially targeting the trade of hashish. By 2004, the freetown was no longer protected under the status of social experiment:

> [They were forced to] purchase the land for a total of 76 million Danish kroner with a loan secured by the Danish government. This loan was partly financed by the sale of a public Christiania stock, further embedding the collective ownership of the land. Despite its tumultuous history, Christiania has remained an enclave for alternative culture and self-organized, communitarian living, as well as a desired tourist attraction, while continuing to receive popular support from the Danish cultural and academic community.
>
> *(Steiger 2018: 169)*

Legalisation of some squats and the quick repression of new attempts at squatting, if publicised, epitomise the context of Copenhagen—Christiania represents a long-lasting exception. Likewise, in Germany the squatters' movement gained great strength during its first phases, and it was able to preserve part of its radical identity and self-managed practices after waves of either hard repression or comprehensive negotiation and legalisation took place (in the early 1980s in general as well as in the early 1990s in Berlin, for example) (Holm & Kuhn 2011). Legalisation did not always mean complete safety for all the former squatters, but even under a heavy-handed policy dealing with squatting, there was room for some new initiatives to resist or even obtain legal agreements.

> Properties also changed hands many times. Some bought a house for 300,000 euros in East Berlin and later sold it for 1.3 million euros when Berlin was becoming the new hip trending place to be for tourists and investors. This affected, for example, the legalised squat Brunnenstraße 183; their lease agreement expired after 16 years and they were evicted in 2009. Our records reveal at least five such cases of legalised and then evicted squats. ... Since 1992 squatting seemed impracticable. Most squats did not last long, so they could not develop any significant infrastructure for the movement, and they do not even remain for long in

Socio-Spatial Structures **115**

the collective memory. Despite these repressive conditions—including the sanction of fines, although very few criminal convictions—squatting has been ongoing.

(azozomox & Kuhn 2018: 161)

These researchers mention the case of *New Yorck im Bethanien* on Mariannenplatz 2A, which was squatted in 2005 and, against the odds, managed to gain a lease contract soon after. Another recent case is

the 'grannies' of Stille Straße 10 in Berlin Pankow—a group of pensioners, seniors (300 retirees altogether) aged 67–96—[who] squatted their seniors' centre in 2012. After more than 111 days of squatting, several demonstrations and widespread support, they signed a long-term option for a contract.

(azozomox & Kuhn 2018: 161)

A different legal context applies in Spain and France where a 'lighter' criminal prosecution of squatting occurred. Usually, French authorities urge negotiations immediately after every squatting action occurs, but there are special conditions, such as the 'winter truce' and the signature of tenancy contracts that can make squatting viable.

A number of important laws favouring the right to housing have been adopted in France in the last three decades. A respite from expulsions during winter (15 November to 1 March), grace periods, financial support, social accompaniment and re-housing of tenants in case of expulsion (1998 law against eviction) are some significant measures characterizing these evolutions. ... Yet, it is remarkable that all these measures contain restrictive clauses concerning squatters. If they confer rights on holders of lease agreements, it is left to judges to decide when the occupants have 'actually' occupied the space. Evidently, the legislator concerned with respecting private property did not wish to grant the occupant 'without right or title' the same security as a tenant. ... Even before an eviction procedure came to my notice, a significant part of the squats were subject to expulsion by the police. ... Finally the decision of expulsion does not imply that it is always effective, the prefect must order of the police force to carry out the eviction, which is not always the case.

(Bouillon 2013: 231–232)

Legalisation of some artistic and residential squats under different formulas in Paris, for example, have occurred in parallel to the eviction of many other artistic, residential, and militant squats over the decades (Aguilera 2018: 128–132). Legal and political battles were thus waged in many cases that in practice prevented the absolute protection of the constitutionally granted right to private property and, therefore, opened up multiple opportunities for the practice of squatting.

116 Socio-Spatial Structures

One of the key legal issues regarding squatting in Spain is the ability of the judge to clearly identify who has effectively squatted and who has the will to remain in order to obtain the possession of the squatted building (Baucells 1999, Seminario 2015: 185–187). Thus, even when evictions increased after 1995 (when the criminal law was passed on), few people were in the end sentenced to jail. The criminalisation of squatting facilitated faster eviction processes, but did not prevent it from occurring, sometimes even in higher numbers than before (Martínez 2018b). Squatted social centres were more subject to eviction because they publicised their occupation. However, these squatters were also more prone to being acquitted in court due to the collective nature of the occupation. Squatting for housing purposes was more frequently clandestine and, thus, less easy to detect by both owners and public authorities. When residential squatters faced court trials, guilty verdicts with fines or even prison sentences were more likely to be given. If the attorneys, on behalf of the squatters, are successful, criminal offences can be turned into civil liabilities, so squatters avoid prison sentences and the juridical process will grant more rights to the squatters (Seminario 2015: 216). This entails, as a consequence, the longer duration of the squats. Furthermore, the legalisation of squatted social centres was rare, and only after 2011 did some buildings, publicly taken by housing organisations, gain particular lease agreements (Martínez 2018a).

Until recently, both the Netherlands and England/Wales enjoyed the most favourable legal conditions for squatting. However, new legislation was passed in 2010 and 2012, respectively, which made squatting a crime, and a more systematic repression followed suit (Dadusc & Dee 2015, Manjikian 2013). Nonetheless, it is worth recalling the legal arrangements that were applicable before the criminalisation of squatting, because they illustrate the effective reach of some squatters' rights at the time. In short, Dutch squatters enjoyed the heritage of thousands of squatted places, taken over in past decades when there was a greater tolerance. Squatting was legal in the case of liveable buildings left vacant for more than one year and, crucially, in case the owner had no ready-to -act plan for the building. Especially after a 1971 court ruling, housing needs and rights were considered superior to property rights given that owners did not use their property and had remained vacant for more than one year (Buchholz 2016: 97). This environment of 'pragmatic tolerance' led squatting cases to civil courts instead of criminal ones.

> In 1971 the Dutch Supreme Court decided that the 'house right', which protects homes from being entered against the will of the occupants, applies to squatters. From that moment, it became illegal for landlords to evict squatters and squatters were no longer considered illegal, provided that the building was neither in use nor being worked on. Often, squatters would invite the police into a newly squatted building to allow them to see the owner was not using it. … More than a decade later, legislation was passed that only protected those buildings that were registered in

a special file for vacant buildings. At the same time, local governments obtained the right to claim registered buildings as housing for those in need. This legislation was not effective, and in 1994 a change in the law made it illegal to squat a building that had been standing empty for less than one year.

(Pruijt 2003: 145)

After the criminalisation of squatting in 2010, new squats became more rapidly evicted by authorities. However, the legacy of the abundant experiences of squatting, the legalisation of many of them, and the existence of organised groups who still support and promote squatting (the *kraakspreekuur* organisations, for example, still active in many Dutch cities), challenged the legal shift.

Likewise, in British cities such as London, squatting was regularly encouraged by veteran organisations like the Advisory Service for Squatters (ASS), who published updated versions of the celebrated *Squatters Handbook* (www.squatter.org.uk/). At least since the 1977 Criminal Law Act, squatting in residential premises had been introduced as a crime in England and Wales. A further regulation in 1994 came into force once the massive movements of the 1940s and 1960–70s declined due to legalisations, concessions of tenancies in social housing, and improved management of empty property (Reeve 2015: 138). Squatting was still widely practised until the criminalisation passed in 2012 (section 144 of the Legal Aid, Sentencing and Punishment of Offenders Act) due to acute housing shortages, campaigns by organisations such as SQUASH (2011), and the loopholes in the existing legislation. According to the ASS (1996: 7):

> The 1994 Criminal Justice and Public Order Act created an offence of failing to leave premises within 24 hours of being served with an Interim Possession Order. Other Possession Orders carry no criminal sanctions. Apart from that, there is nothing criminal or illegal in squatting. Squatting is unlawful, not illegal. This means it is a civil dispute between two people. ... The police have nothing to do with civil disputes.

This meant that lawsuits in civil courts and evictions could occur at a slow pace, and confrontation with police was not necessarily required if no violence was used at the moment of trespassing. In the event of eviction, squatters could also appeal based on the same 1977 Act and ask for the right documents issued by the owners (ASS 1996: 11–13, 39). Furthermore, before the reform of the rights to 'adverse possession', by 2003, in some cases, after a continuous occupation of a property for more than twelve years, squatters could also halt evictions threats or even be entitled to the property (see the 13th edition of the *Squatters Handbook* for an update after 2003). Squatters' knowledge of these particular rights was beneficial to keeping the practice of squatting widespread. After 2012, the unauthorised occupation of commercial or industrial premises was not included

IMAGE 3.5 Posters in Athens, 2013
Source: Author

in the criminalisation of trespassing, which still allowed the continuity of public squatting (Finchett-Maddock 2015: 209–215).

Activist Networks

Squatting practices become stronger when they scale up to durable struggles and form coalitions with other social movements. This is not so obvious when it comes to housing movements in which squatting is only one of the various tools that activists use to claim affordable housing without necessarily questioning other

Socio-Spatial Structures **119**

aspects of the capitalist system. However, many experiences of squatted houses and, above all, of squatted social centres are eager to intertwine the defence of their occupations with the campaigns, actions, and goals of other social movements such as solidarity with migrants, precarious workers, prisoners, animal rights, hacktivism, queer and trans-feminism, urban biking, anti-fascism, artivism, urban ecology, etc. This was a common ingredient of radical left and countercultural movements (Koopmans 1995: 21, 32–35, Rucht 1990) in contrast to the single-issue orientation attributed to other new social movements, such as environmentalism, feminism, and pacifism (Offe 1985). Squatters not only offered spatial infrastructure for many other movements, but often shared their motivations. In return, these coalitions provided new recruits for squatting as well.

Examples of fruitful coalitions between squatters and tenants' organisations have been documented in Warsaw and Poznan (Poland) in recent years (Polanska & Piotrowski 2015, see Image 3.4) as well as in Amsterdam, when squatters joined the resistance to renewal plans in the mid-1960s (Pruijt 2004b). In the first case, their respective differences in terms of organisational models, social composition, and goals did not prevent their mutual cooperation, despite some frictions. The coalition is explained by the openness of the local authorities to more participatory governance schemes but also by the informal ties among acquaintances. Moreover, Polanska (2015) identified the squatters' brokerage role as mediators in talks between one of the three tenants' organisations and the local government. This is a surprising result given that formal organisations in most cities hold closer contacts with authorities than informal groups of squatters.

> Squatters have helped the tenants' organisations both when gathering material resources for publication of information, providing meeting premises or disseminating information [on] the Internet. ... An outstanding example of alliance formation between tenants' associations and squatters is the initiation of the Tenants' Round Table in 2012, where tenants and representatives of the city (City Council and City Hall) would meet regularly. ... Squatters are given credit for the success of opening up a dialogue with the city.
>
> *(Polanska 2015: 205–206)*

As for Amsterdam, the struggles to preserve the city centre from planned highways, subways, and offices, in addition to the demolition of residential blocks brought together neighbourhood action groups able to successfully break up the cohesion among the political elites in the town hall. Bottom-up alternative urban plans, mobilisations, and continuous negotiations with the local authorities achieved substantial changes in mainstream city planning (Pruijt 2004b).

Global justice concerns and the contestation of liberal democracies and capitalism were usually claimed by the most politicised squatters (Martínez 2007, Notes from Nowhere 2003). This implies a coexistence of local and global perspectives. Each squat has local, urban roots in a specific neighbourhood. Squatting is, thus,

120 Socio-Spatial Structures

an end itself once it is publicly and intentionally advertised, and also defended. Without losing this local ground, squatting is a means to foster other local protests, even some more generally related to class and global issues. Tactics and strategy, then, reinforce each other. However, among the internal diversity of squatters, some can emphasise squatting only as an ends, while others emphasise squatting solely as a means. The expansion of both squatted and non-squatted social centres all over Europe in the aftermath of the global justice movement increased that diversity (Hodkinson & Chatterton 2006, Martínez 2004, Membretti 2007, Mudu 2004, see Images 3.3 and 3.5).

Another effect of the revival of autonomist movements was that boundaries between occupied and non-occupied social centres became more blurred in cases where the latter shared a similar practice of self-management and even supported squatters in their surroundings. See, for example, the analysis conducted on the development of autonomous social centres in the UK:

> Precursors of social centres sprung up in the form of Squat Cafés like the Anarchist Teapot in Brighton (1996–1999), the OKasional Cafés in Manchester (1998–2003), and Eclectic City in Newcastle (2000–2002) offering cheap organic vegan food, DIY cultural events and a living example of anarchist politics. Some collectives also sought to establish more permanent self-organized spaces in their own communities such as the Kebele Kultural Project in Bristol, which began in 1995 when a small group of residential squatters gradually opened up a disused charity office to the working-class neighbourhood for benefit parties, donation-based vegan food and a range of facilities for activist groups. In 1998, the occupiers negotiated an affordable lease with the owners. By the late 1990s, the destructive effects of neo-liberal globalization and multinational corporate power saw the groups and networks behind a decade of 'party and protest' morph into the much wider global anti-capitalist movement that directly targeted the institutions of the global elite (the Group of 8, EU, World Trade Organization, International Monetary Fund and World Bank) while supporting myriad struggles worldwide.
>
> *(Hodkinson & Chatterton 2006: 306–307)*

Demonstrations and innovative forms of protest such as Reclaim the Streets and 'carnivals against capitalism' contributed to animating the expansion of social centres all over the UK. Many of them had a legal status from the beginning: London Action Resource Centre (LARC) opened in East London by 2002, the Sumac Centre was established in Nottingham in the same year, so too the Cowley Club in Brighton one year later.

These authors explained the upsurge of autonomous social centres in the UK as being due to the need for permanent places to hold meetings and make their campaigns visible. The context of sprawl in cities like London and the increased repression of squatting were effectively combined with the activists' needs.

Socio-Spatial Structures **121**

A great deal of their inspiration came from the lasting Italian experiences in the development of social centres as non-commercial places for politics, meetings, and entertainment (Hodkinson & Chatterton 2006: 310). Thus, a network of various types of social centres and movements was consolidated while, simultaneously, creating the conditions to facilitate the emergence of new activist networks. This synergy is well illustrated as follows:

> Almost every day, these buildings are in use, be it for meetings, workshops, film nights, solidarity benefits, pamphlet writing, banner making, reading groups, drumming practice and large-scale gatherings. Although the campaigns and groups making social centres their home differ from place to place, it is rare not to find anti-war, environmental, animal rights, independent media networks (like Indymedia), Palestine and Zapatista solidarity and anti-corporate activism at the heart of any space. A clear emerging focus for all social centres is solidarity with asylum and migrant struggles through the No Borders Network, which fights for freedom of movement and against detention, destitution and deportation.
>
> *(Hodkinson & Chatterton 2006: 310)*

Finchett-Maddock (2016: 53) distinguished 'community-driven' and 'event and political meeting places' among the social centres in the UK. She also observed a great variety of people attracted to them and a certain intention to radicalise them as exerted by those running the spaces. For example, British social centres were engaged in anti-gentrification campaigns, raised awareness on land rights worldwide, and served student protests against rising fees and privatisation of the university.

> Social centres attract a pastiche of folk, some unemployed, others married with families and full-time jobs, those who live in the centres, and those who visit … The impulse to accommodate for the surrounding social demographic is twinned with the desire to change, shape and influence the thoughts of those that attend the events and meetings of the centres: this is referred to as 'radicalisation'.
>
> *(Finchett-Maddock 2016: 53–56)*

Despite their popularity, social centres were usually short-lived. However, the exceptions made them emblematic and infrastructural hubs for many other social movements.

> The rampART social centre was established in May 2004 and evicted in October 2009, a squatted centre throughout this time. The fact that it was a squatted space and one that lasted for over five years is quite rare in the UK. Spaces normally last for a matter of months due to the transiency of the squatting scene, the political climate and the legal restrictions. It held a vast number of events and benefit nights, and linked to the organisation

122 Socio-Spatial Structures

> of the G20 protests in London in 2009 as a meeting place. ... During the student occupations of 2011, the social centre format became a strategic protest mechanism, notably with the occupation of University of London buildings to create the Bloomsbury Social Centre (2011).
>
> *(Finchett-Maddock 2016: 53–56)*

An ethnographic study about three social centres in Barcelona showed how participants were deeply concerned about both changing their own lives and the world out there. They performed this double-track activism or 'prefigurative politics' by taking alternative (or overlapping) routes: micropolitics, community-building, mutual learning, and coherence between values and actions (Yates 2014: 12).

> Localia was a squatted space, eight months old when fieldwork began, situated close to Barcelona's city centre. Workshops, events and discussions included Mexican dance, Argentine rock music and workshops on Zapatism, reflecting the large number of Latin American organisers and participants. Politically, Localia members planned and participated in campaigns and mobilisations including solidarity actions with Latin American movements, anti-racism and queer politics.... FUGA, another centrally located social centre but in a rented space that had no communal living experience adjoining, was composed of activists with considerable experience from alter-globalisation protests and migrant advocacy.... [They were united based on] clear political goals around precarious workers such as immigrant street-sellers.... Can Tintorer, the third case study investigated, was a squatted social centre, composed mainly of environmentalists and anarchists, on the edge of Barcelona. Although the group had been heavily involved in anti-roads and food-related protests in the early years of the project, they now did less direct campaigning as a centre. However, most individuals continued to be part of movements individually.
>
> *(Yates 2014: 6–10)*

In addition to the activities organised in and from the social centres for larger audiences, and in cooperation with other movements, they tried to forge activism in their everyday life and informal ties with fellows from the same alternative scene in this and other cities. This informal socialisation was especially robust during the valley periods between protest cycles. Therefore, Yates contended that affective bonds, cultural activities, and 'free spaces' prepared a latent ground of political opportunities for future mobilisations instead of just responding to ongoing particular structural conditions (Yates 2015: 239–240).

Social Recognition

Autonomous politics also implies an aspiration to full independence from commercial and state-controlled mass media. The most politicised squatters regularly

Socio-Spatial Structures **123**

contribute to alternative and independent media, especially online since the 2000s. However, press conferences, interviews, and cooperation with mainstream journalists may be frequent in some countries. This has to do with specific political contexts and traditions. Movements aiming to house the homeless, for example, try to exploit mass media exposure as much as possible in order to move from squatting to state-run social housing. When squatters' movements are weak in terms of their connections with the political elites (governments and parliamentary parties, above all), an alternative alliance with mass media may help communicating the legitimacy of their struggle.

Accordingly, regular and not too aggressive mass media coverage, even if it treats squatters with some unfair stereotypes (see Chapter 6 on stigma and criminalisation), may help legitimate the autonomy and purposes of this struggle in the eyes of a wide audience. When the mass media offer a window for news about squatting, their basic contribution is to spread some of the existing cases and examples of squatting. This evidence of squatting may appear surrounded by controversies and opinions contrary to the squatters, although the message 'squatting is possible (and, often, effective)' cannot be easily avoided. In the case of squatting-friendly journalists, short stories of squats and living experiences of squatters also allow the general public to understand their motivations. Given the unusual and variable treatment of squatting by the commercial mass media, squatters themselves tend to be actively engaged in the promotion of their own identity through independent media, graffiti, stencils, banners, face-to-face communication, documentaries, fanzines, and self-published books. While these communicative practices enhance the autonomy of squatters in their public recognition and legitimation, they at the same time put them in close contact with other social movements equally engaged with alternative means of communication.

Long-lasting squats, either houses or social centres, aim to display solid examples and graphic symbols of the movement's success, although abundant flows of communication among activists and with the rest of society (i.e. visibility and networking) equally enhance the squatters' social portrait. The *Witboek* (White Book) published by Dutch squatters before the ban on squatting in 2010 (see Image 3.6), and a publication made by a squatting advocacy group from UK facing a similar threat (SQUASH 2011), represent excellent responses to the strategic challenge of communicating the goal that nurtures the core of this movement.

Before enacting the criminalisation of squatting in residential properties, the UK government undertook a consultation process entitled 'Options for Dealing with Squatters', which came to an end on 5 October 2011. Squatters Action for Secure Homes (SQUASH) accused the government of 'ignoring the consultation … by rushing through anti-squatting laws only three weeks after the consultation had ended' (SQUASH 2011). In total, 90% of responses (2,126 out of 2,217) protested against the intended criminalisation of squatting. The government recognised 'that the statistical weight of responses was therefore against taking any action on squatting' but still supported that making squatting in residential buildings a criminal offence will 'end the misery of home-owners whose

124 Socio-Spatial Structures

TABLE 3.1 Socio-spatial structures of opportunities and constraints for urban squatting

General conditions of possibility	Specific conditions of possibility	Outcomes
Availability of vacant properties	Sufficient amount of vacancy, not too damaged, and not too actively protected by owners	Squatting decreases urban vacancy and its use for speculative purposes
Urban renewal	Restructuring at a slow pace, and alliance of squatters with residents subject to displacement	Squatters self-rehabilitate derelict buildings at low-cost and slow down gentrification
Legislation and law enforcement	Legal loopholes, some protection of squatters' rights, and limited repression	Squatters can win legal victories in court, postpone evictions, and achieve lease agreements
Activist networks	Infrastructural synergy with non-squatted social centres and other social movements, local and global claims	Squats contribute to non-single-issue movements and coalitions, alternative urban plans, and prefigurative politics
Social recognition	Alternative and independent media, fluent and positive coverage by mass media	Squatting can be legitimised, its public outlook can be enhanced, and its history known

Source: Author

properties have been preyed on by squatters'. This stance ignored the existing legislation (Section 7 of the Criminal Law Act 1977) to protect residents from having their principal home squatted, as 160 leading legal figures expressed in an article published in *The Guardian*. SQUASH spokesperson, Paul Reynolds, added:

> The government is ignoring the results of its own consultation which shows that the criminalisation of squatting in empty residential properties will do nothing to protect residents who are already protected by strong legislation. This amendment will criminalise the homeless in the middle of a housing crisis who use squatting as the last remaining option to keep a roof over their heads.
>
> *(SQUASH 2011)*

I develop this contextual condition more in another chapter of this book (Chapter 6). Table 3.1 summarises the main contents of the previous sections. The following fieldwork notes I took after one of my visits to Amsterdam also illustrate some of the arguments presented hitherto.

Amsterdam: The Lost Paradise of Squatting?

5 July 2011. At 6.20 in the morning police vans begin to appear in all the surrounding streets. They clear the traffic and go straight to the building. Most of

Socio-Spatial Structures **125**

the city still sleeps or is slowly getting up. All of a sudden, we hear screams and feel ruckus all around. There are musicians on the roof of the squat. At the street level, a theatre play shows up with five performers dressed up as brides. The first thing the police must face when trying to enter the building is a lot of foam and soap bubbles. No one stays inside the house, but the activists gather around and start throwing paint and also some stones and bottles towards the police officers. Although the latter have already conquered the building, the nearby protest is crowded and cries out loudly at them. Squatters try to pressure the police into retreat but the opposite occurs. In less than half an hour almost all the protesters are surrounded by police forces and vehicles. One of these vehicles is a large water tank that threatens to empty its fury against the crowd. Demonstrators begin to be individually arrested, including two who had chained themselves with cement. The whole group of activists—around 60 people—are forcibly pushed to the corner of Prinsengracht Street. Some do not stop playing music during the almost three hours that the police confinement lasts. I am witnessing the scene among another 100 people who stay a few meters away, clapping and shouting our support. There are also many curious bystanders who are observing the tense situation. It seems that the end of Schijnheilig, a squat and autonomous social centre located in an abandoned school at Passeerdersgracht 23 in the historical centre of Amsterdam, is inexorably near.

More and more police vans arrive. From one of them I notice a group of a dozen policemen and policewomen hop out dressed in casual clothes. They look very strong and young (their portraits were later published on https://www.indymedia.nl/nl/2011/07/77185.shtml). These undercover bailiffs start walking fast among the group of supporters where I am. By following the instructions of their team leader, who is wearing an earphone, they chase and grab several young people off the police cordon. Afterwards, they approach the group of sieged protestors, punch them violently, and arrest two more guys. A few minutes earlier, several activists had tied themselves up to the windscreen of a moving police van. A group of journalists are taking photographs and record everything. Next to me, I identify the squatters' lawyer and other activists filming the incident. In addition, an undercover policewoman is also video-recording everyone's faces in the area, without exception. After a while, the journalists are forced to leave and two buses, belonging to the same company that offers public transport service in the city, arrive. Three activists jumped into the canal waters in order to escape the suffocating kettle-tactic, but a police boat harasses them towards the canal wall and the incognito commando runs fast to arrest them. From time to time, we all sing chants and slogans.

The activists, in a last-ditch effort to delay the operation, have sat on the ground and entwine each other's arms. Hence, they can only be lifted one by one. As a backlash, police officers kick and beat them. Once detained, plastic handcuffs tight flanges are placed around their wrists. Additional martial joint locks are applied to most of the detainees. Police troops—helped by vans, boats, motorcycles, buses, and a helicopter—widely outnumber the demonstrators. Eventually they will clear the area with a balance of 143 arrests according to the

126 Socio-Spatial Structures

newspaper *Het Parool*, and one less social project in the city. Similar police operations to evict 20 more squats were planned for the same day. However, according to R., a member of the Schijnheilig collective, some squats had already been evicted in the days before. Nine more were closed down just hours after Schijnheilig. In most of the cases, as two Spanish squatters of Zeeburgerpad 13 told me, there were only barricades behind the doors and on the rooftops in order to delay police actions. Therefore, if lucky, the eviction of some squats placed at the end of the day's court order could be postponed one month more. The list of evictions was drawn up, ordered by the so-called triangle (the city mayor, the local police, and judicial courts). Active resistance to evictions is no longer the most frequent attitude in comparison to some notorious cases from the 1980s. One of the last groups that tried it, the social centre Afrika, whose eviction in 2007 I also attended (see Image 3.7), simply brought together, like now, an overwhelming number of police dedicated to evicting squatters more efficiently. The day after the eviction of Schijnheilig, one journalist from the Volkstraat transcribed a police conversation in which they congratulated themselves on their success while mentioning that they *only* had 165 squats more to evict in order to finish the job.

This is the third wave of orchestrated evictions in Amsterdam since the new legislation that considers squatting a criminal offence came into force in October 2010. Before the parliamentary bill passed, the social democratic mayor of Amsterdam (in coalition with the Greens) declared that he opposed the law and that he did not intend to implement it. However, the new mayor of the same party, Van der Laan, ruling the local government in coalition with the Liberals, was fully compliant. He contended that Amsterdam could not be a national exception and that it would fulfil the cleansing mission against all existing and future occupations. This policy has added to a certain decline in the city's squatting movement, once much stronger and socially legitimised. According to R.'s estimates, about ten houses were squatted every week in Amsterdam in the 1990s, while that figure drops to three per week in 2006, and no more than one per month today.

In any case, why do evictions not go faster? R. offers several explanations: (a) there is still wide social support for squatting (around 70% according to a recent survey published in *Het Parool*), understood as a practical way to meet the needs for housing and cultural spaces; (b) eviction arrangements are expensive for the public purse; and c) resistance to evictions not only increases public spending, but also provokes an image of turmoil and violence that authorities want to detach from the tourist brand of the city, traditionally associated with tolerance and social diversity. Given the above, one might ask why is there not more resistance from the squatters' side? In the case of Schijnheilig there was a clear contradiction between, on the one hand, a public that used the building regularly and massively—mainly students, young people, and middle-class artists according to our informant—and, on the other, those who revitalised and supported it with a radical political orientation—activists, probably with a similar social background. Almost none of the first stayed to sleep overnight and protest early on the morning of the eviction. Only the 'political squatters' and other activists backing them gathered that day. A slightly larger crowd (around 500 people) protested the eviction the previous Sunday in a demonstration that took place in the Dam (the main square of the city). The number of supporters is becoming increasingly slim. Another symptom of the decline in squatting activism is the number of 'squatting offices' (*kraakspreekuur*). There used to be 35 in 1982, whereas one can only look for assistance at three kraakspreekuurs nowadays. As a result, many occupations endure, but the movement is weak, fragmented, and less visible than ever.

Schijnheilig is very significant because its cultural activity had been highly praised across the city, even by a councillor of the local government, as he confessed to one of the activists who, in turn, sneered at him during the performances of that Saturday in July. The project had existed in five previous locations in other squatted buildings. The last occupation lasted a year and a half. It was a former school, abandoned for more than ten years. The state sold the building to a 'real-estate mafia' that, a few years later, sold it back to the state for two million euros more of profit. There was no short-term plan to rehabilitate or use the building (which was a requirement for evictions before the 2010 legislative change), but the occupation was quickly reported within days. Furthermore, the state agency managing the building had hired an *anti-kraak* (anti-squat) company to locate residents without rights as guards/tenants. They only managed to accommodate two people under these conditions, so the activists blocked the access to their residences, which had an independent entrance on the street, and squatted just the ground floor. The activists predicted that the day after the eviction more people would be located in the building with another anti-kraak contract. This case represents how not only private owners but also state authorities overtly speculate with their vacant properties through all the means possible.

If the massive squatting experienced in Amsterdam at its height was exceptional, then the phenomenon of anti-kraak companies has also been quite remarkable. As the name implies, these companies are hired by the owners of empty properties to protect them and dissuade squatters from entering. The system they have found is to *rent* them under special conditions—that is, at a price below the market average (from 50 to 200 euros per month) as long as the tenant gives up their legal rights as a regular dweller and agrees to an express relocation if requested upon short notice. Actually, more than a rental agreement, it is an undercover work contract as a private security guard. The notice period to leave the building is usually no more than two weeks when urgently asked. This introduces a feeling of uncertainty similar to that embodied by most squatters. Ironically, anti-squatters are accommodated in order to prevent the autonomous accommodation of squatters; precarious people are pushed against other precarious people. In addition to the loss of rights, no less serious is the individualised control or discipline that is applied to candidates who apply for an

IMAGE 3.6   White Book of squatting, Amsterdam, 2011
Source: Author

anti-kraak contract. The most appropriate appointees are those who have neither political sympathies nor an aesthetic outlook associated with radical political groups (dreadlocks, t-shirts with insurgent messages, etc.). Furthermore, anti-squatters are preferred if they live without any family relatives and pets. Foreigners not as aware of the applicable laws and poor students saliently fill the spots. In short, these companies implement a neoliberal disciplinary device that targets a precarious social sector with similar housing needs than that of most squatters. The state, as shown, has not only legalised these predatory companies but also buy their services.

In a talk delivered by Justus Uitermark around the time of the eviction, he pointed out that anti-kraak firms are also the perfect agents to develop urban renewal and gentrification projects. The great amount of public housing that Amsterdam has come to own and promote (around 85% until a few years ago) is being progressively dismantled due to its rapid privatisation. Fake cooperatives and housing corporations that manage public states with very low rents speed up their investments thanks to the expulsion and substitution of poor tenants. They offer scarce economic compensation (about 5,000 euros) and, with municipal complicity, a preferential position on waiting lists to obtain alternative public housing, supposedly new and of higher quality, but in another area of the city—almost always more peripheral. As many of these tenants refuse the offer, real-estate harassment then begins with threats, thugs, destruction of the building, and misleading information regarding their legal rights. Every time real-estate agents manage to empty an apartment, they place an anti-kraak*er* in it. Once the

Socio-Spatial Structures **129**

whole building has been emptied and the demolition or rehabilitation operation is ready, the anti-kraakers are called to leave immediately as stated in their *tenancy* contracts. Then, everything is prepared so that the new houses are sold at high prices and acquired by wealthier homeowners.

According to Nazima Kadir, another squatting activist and researcher who organised a mini-SqEK encounter to discuss squatting a few months before—a similar process like the one described above took place at Celebesstraat 33–36 (located in Amsterdam East, quite close to the city centre). With different tricks aiming to expel poor families and immigrants, the coveted blocks were almost fully vacated. However, several squatters entered some of them before the anti-kraak companies could place their own flexible *residents*. The squatters gave legal advice to the remaining tenants and went to trial in their support. Although better economic compensation was obtained for those who opted to move out, their displacement and the eviction of the squatted houses were in the end unavoidable. The gentrification of the street culminated in the sale of the renovated houses to the taste of higher social classes.

Let's return for a while to Schijnheilig. The night before the eviction I attended a large assembly sitting in the school auditorium with typical fixed benches. Images of the previous demonstration were projected as part of the program of activities held between 2 and 5 July to protest the waves of evictions. The assembly was in English because nobody objected given that many in the audience were not native Dutch speakers. The film also expressed the activists' demands in the English language, seeking to raise awareness among the foreign, transnational, and also tourist public that flood the city centre. A white board was put out in front of the projection screen, explaining all the plans for the long night ahead. At 3:30 a.m. desks would be moved onto the street and bolted to the road pavement. Around 6 o'clock, artistic performances would begin on the street. The doors of the building would be torn out in order to indicate the absence of a threshold between the public and the private. Obviously, it was also intended to ridicule the entrance of the police.

Several people asked if there would be enough coffee during the whole evening. A very important question, apparently. Technical advice was given regarding how the Dutch police ask for personal identification and the telephone number of the lawyer in case of arrest. Participants were asked not to take pictures of other people in the assembly or inside the building. However, we were also told that several professional journalists would cover the entire process from inside the building during the whole process of eviction. In fact, one of those journalists was eventually arrested because he decided not to show his credentials and thus be able to tell the entire story as a true insider. At the tables and in the corridors, you could still see some of the documents that were distributed in a bilingual edition including, above all, the legal aspects that resistance and detention entail. It was also said that the resistance would be 'nonviolent' although there were also 'other plans'. 'If you want to know more, ask in the ear of whoever you see around.' In the hallway of the main entrance, movies,

130 Socio-Spatial Structures

music, and books were openly asking for new readers, shelves, and houses. Among the printed material, I found the *Witboeke Kraken* (White Book of Squatting) that was published in 2010 during the campaign prior to the criminalisation of squatting. Despite being in Dutch, I felt it was another wonderful gift for my collection of activist publications. In an atmosphere without much effusiveness but neither with excessive sadness, the rooms and the magnificent courtyard were finally emptied. Black 'cargo' bikes, sound equipment, and other valuable resources were evacuated. All that remained were the illusions of continuing to squat elsewhere.

Once the eviction was finalised, 12 activists were accused of 'public violence', which, in case of being sentenced, can entail two and a half years of prison. The rest of the arrested activists were accused of 'disturbing the public order', which could result in a fine of several hundred euros. Among the latter group, 70 people were released after passing the minimum of six hours of detention once they were voluntarily identified. Some 50 more decided to take advantage of a peculiar Dutch regulation that guarantees the right to not be identified at one's own will. Therefore, they were indefinitely in prison until their personal identities were confirmed. Alternatively, an authority can decree their release or deportation in case of being considered illegal immigrants. This process can involve several weeks of imprisonment, even months, which is also seen as a form of public protest by many squatters. In any case, the significant point here is Schijnheilig squatters chose not to remain inside the building during the eviction. Had they done so, they would have been accused of 'squatting' and most likely sentenced to one year in prison. The criminalisation of squatting partially shaped the repertoire of the protest.

Until October 2010, there were very favourable legal conditions for those squatting vacant properties in the Netherlands. A strong protection of the right to housing predominated. Once inside a house, it was customary to inform the police that a 'residence' had been established, the space met basic residential standards, and nobody was living in the property beforehand. Afterwards, different legal processes might be initiated. These processes could lead to eviction, legalisation, or entrance to some limbo of uncertainty. Regardless of the outcome of each case, the squatters were not considered to be committing any crimes. Violent confrontations with the police were the only cause of arrest and conviction. Over the years, various governments have tried to forbid squatting but, according to Hans Pruijt, another SqEK member who guided us through old and new squats, it was never a priority on their political agendas; therefore, despite some parliamentary debates, there were hardly any noticeable changes. Some specific reforms produced a situation that lasted for many years—it was necessary to verify the vacancy of a property for more than a year, and at the same time the owner had to show that they had viable plans to build, rehabilitate, or occupy it. Anyway, the singularities of each legal process and of each protest campaign could substantially alter the fate of every occupation. So, even under the prior legal umbrella, it was not so easy to predict how long each initiative would last.

Socio-Spatial Structures **131**

R. explained that the 'political identity' of Schijnheilig resided on very few premises, similar to many other squatted social centres: (a) it promoted non-commercial activities; (b) it was accessible to everyone free of charge, although donations were welcome; (c) it was based on the voluntary and unpaid work of the activists; and (d) any group independent from state subsidies and private sponsorships was permitted to participate. By that definition, no traditional anarchist, communist, or leftist clichés could be found, albeit they all underlie those principles. However, any utopian project of society or of life in common was also left aside. Finally, the criticism of urban speculation was not at the top of their political discourse, so squatting only seemed a means to autonomously develop the housed projects.

It is not surprising, then, that the boundaries between legalised and non-legalised squats are blurred in Amsterdam. Until the last minute, local authorities offered an anti-kraak deal to the squatters in Schijnheilig. This was interpreted as an attempt to avoid protests and public criticism. At the same time, authorities would have gained legitimacy when urging activists to leave the building at a later time The core group of squatters, about 30 people, did not accept. It represented, after all, a legitimation of the anti-kraak business. However, as R. told me, if the agreement had established a legal cession for at least one or two years, the attitude of the activists was favourable to compromise. Appearances (i.e. resistance to eviction and full autonomy from state institutions) are strikingly different to what one concludes when observing things from inside (likely legalisation) and from a broader perspective (their criticisms of urban speculation and gentrification reached a large audience in practice).

One squat that did achieve legal status after negotiating with the municipal authorities is Overtoon 301, formerly known as Peper, which is located on one side of Vondelpark, another spot that has seen a large tourist influx in the city. Its agenda of events is very much devoted to independent arts such as dance, theatre, and music. Unexpectedly, the cultural, social, and political activities of other squatted social centres such as Joe's Garage or Blijvertje are also widely advertised among others on the motley bulletin board of the building entrance. In the bar and in the dining area you can also appreciate an old lantern with a red squat symbol and Peper inscription on its screens, as a relic of times gone by.

The building is located in the back of a courtyard behind other buildings which have a direct façade on Overtoon street. After years of squatting and negotiations with the city, they secured a rental agreement and, a bit later, a purchase-sale agreement through which they acquired the property. On the upper floors there are private studios for artists. They sometimes reside there without declaring it openly, as it would contradict some regulations. S., a member of the collective that manages the bar, told me that it would be unaffordable to pay all the official taxes for the activities they carry out if they strictly observed the applicable laws. In addition, they are very careful with the possible complaints of neighbours in case evening events produce some noise. When paying for the food, they ask for something 'between seven and ten

IMAGE 3.7 Squat Afrika, Amsterdam, 2007
Source: Author

euros' just to 'cover the expenses of the project'. Among the people gathered in the venue I could see, in my second visit some years later, that there are people from a wide range of ages between 18 and 65, approximately, as it happens in my squatted social centres. But judging from their outfits, I would say that their appearance fits that of university students and middle-class people, which is not the regular public in other Southern European cities, for example.

One last aspect that emerged from the interviews with R. and with the Spanish and Polish squatters of Zeeburgerpad, is the one related to the 'modus operandi' of the beginning of each new squat. The tacit agreement is that most squatting actions are prepared in advance with the support of a kraakspreekuur. In this way it is possible to access legal and technical advice in addition to crucial information about the property and its ownership. On the day of the occupation, around 50 people convened by the kraakspreekuur gather outside the building and give support especially when the police arrive. In practice, the kraakspreekuur get together the most 'political squatters'—activists who share their knowledge on squatting—and those with less or no activist background but in urgent need of housing. So-called 'political' and 'social' squatting are, thus, very arbitrary distinctions, or just a matter of degree and changing roles. In my interpretation, kraakspreekuurs represent the best organisational devices aiming to build a squatters' movement based on self-help and mutual aid among many different existing and potential squatters. The squatters at

Zeeburgerpad told me that the support of the kraakspreekuur was essential in dealing with the difficulties of the Dutch language they barely knew. What is more, it also helped them to take into account another political principle: to occupy only speculators and owners with several empty properties. This political orientation framed their exclusively residential squat. In this case, the occupation targeted the owner of several industrial buildings and warehouses near a canal whose land has been significantly revalued in recent years. Upgraded residential buildings are now punctuating the vicinity. Once the squat was evicted, on 5 July, the owner recovered his property and planned its demolition, making way for luxury homes—sadly, a very frequent story around squatting projects.

A very different case is that of the West Pole where R. resides as a squatter together with ten other people. It is an old school owned by the local government of a popular district in the west of the city, run by social democrats and the Greens. After years of abandonment and occasional use by drug addicts, its squatting was planned with the support of a kraakspreekuur. A day before the scheduled date, they found out that around six people had already occupied a part of the building. Nonetheless, they followed through with their plans and squatted another part of the building. As a consequence, both groups of squatters have a very conflictive relationship and are even forced to share the entrance door to the building. R. and other squatters refer to the other group as 'free riders' or *crusty* squatters that knew beforehand the intentions of his group. R. also describes their opponents as lazy people who spend the day drinking beer. On the other hand, R.'s group is identified as university students that lived a *normal* life and have *political* motivations. As a matter of fact, the second group frequently held talks with the district representatives. Hence, the local authorities decided not to sue the squatters and were even exploring the possibility of legalisation through a rental or purchase agreement. In contrast to Zeeburgerpad, there are no black flag nor squatting symbols on the façade of West Pole. As R. argued, their intention was to have a relationship with the rest of the neighbours unmediated by 'political stigmas'. However, he did not object to the display of such symbolic paraphernalia in the squatted social centre where he was also involved, Schijnheilig.

On Saturday 9 July, the documentary *Creativity and the Capitalist City* was screened in the after-squatted social centre Plantagedok, followed by a debate with the director, Tino Buchholz; a member of Schijnheilig; and Justus Uitermark. Most speakers pointed out that neoliberal politicians fill their discourses with trendy terms such as 'innovation' and 'the creative class' just to hide the processes of privatisation and gentrification that they promote simultaneously. When *arty* social centres such as Plantagedok or OT301 participate in those 'breeding policies' to achieve their legalisation, they first have to show their members' qualified 'curriculum vitae' and a track record of cultural activities. Afterwards, once the contracts are signed, they can go back to enjoying a considerable margin of freedom in order to keep their self-managed routines as long as they pay rents, taxes, insurance, and bills as agreed upon. And then there

134 Socio-Spatial Structures

are also 'political fees': Some cases of after-squats ended up highly dependent of state subsidies which undermined their political independence when it comes to public debates and, many suspected, also in the content of their public activities. With these models of co-optation, the world urban model of tolerance evolved into 'repressive tolerance'—without legalisation and compliance with neoliberal policies, squats are evicted and activists are charged with criminal offences. Drawing on the narrative of the documentary, the debate also revolved around the fading squatting movement. Coalitions with other social movements and concerns about the extraordinary development of the anti-kraak business were also considered of the utmost importance for the future of squatting.

When writing these notes (2011), the City of Amsterdam was experiencing a rising conservatism that endangered many of its past assets: plenty of affordable housing, buoyant social diversity, sustainable mobility, urban planning according to a reasonable human scale (enough built and social density without many high-rise towers, abundant public spaces, and large preservation of the old urban fabric), and participatory and redistributive policies. The squatters' movement emerged from all this magma in the decade of the 1960s. The economic growth of the 1990s altered many of those structural conditions, increasing the commercialisation of the city, intensifying mass tourism, releasing control over real-estate speculation, and increasing the economic, ethnic, and spatial forms of social segregation. These changes are coupled with more racism and xenophobia, rising electoral support for conservative political parties, and certain economic recession. Neoliberal policies were also embraced by social democratic governments, especially in relation to the management of land uses. As a matter of fact, some 150,000 inhabitants are registered as applicants for social housing with urgent need. In addition, some 450,000 people—approximately half of the dwellers of the urban core—are also registered on the waiting lists for social housing, which is seen as a ritualised practice with the purpose of improving housing conditions in terms of stability, size, location, etc. At the time of writing (2011), the average waiting period was around seven years, according to the manager of a housing organisation, Staddgenoot, located in Bos en Lommer, that we visited during the activities of the RC21 conference. In sum, the fiercer attacks to the squatting movement are framed and fuelled by those political and economic conditions. The one-time squatting paradise is disappearing at a rapid pace.

References

Aguilera, Thomas (2018) The Squatting Movement(S) in Paris: Internal Divides and Conditions for Survival. In Miguel A. Martínez (Ed.) *The Urban Politics of Squatters' Movements*. New York: Palgrave Macmillan, 121–144.

Arnold, Gregor (2015) Online-Offline Strategies of Urban Movements against Vacancies. The Crowdsourcing Platform Leerstandsmelder.De As a Collective and Critical Mapping Tool. *Observatorio (OBS★) Journal, Media City: Spectacular, Ordinary and Contested Spaces*: 145–176. [http://obs.obercom.pt/index.php/obs/article/view/888]

Socio-Spatial Structures **135**

ASS (Advisory Service for Squatters) (1996) *Squatters Handbook. 10th edition.* London: ASS.

azozomox & Armin Kuhn (2018) The Cycles of Squatting in Berlin (1969–2016). In Miguel A. Martínez (Ed.) *The Urban Politics of Squatters' Movements.* New York: Palgrave Macmillan, 145–164.

Bailey, Ron (1973) *The Squatters.* Harmondsworth: Penguin.

Baucells, J. (1999) L'ocupacio' d'immobles en el nou Codi Penal. In Assemblea d'Okupes de Terrassa (Ed.) *Okupacio', repressio' i moviments socials.* Barcelona: Kasa de la Muntanya-Diatriba, 63–74.

Bouillon, Florence (2013) What Is a "Good" Squatter? Categorization Processes of Squats by Government Officials in France. In SqEK (Squatting Europe Kollective) (Ed.) *Squatting in Europe. Radical Spaces, Urban Struggles.* Wivenhoe: Minor Compositions, 231–245.

Buchholz, Tino (2016) *Struggling for Recognition and Affordable Housing in Amsterdam and Hamburg. Resignation, Resistance, Relocation.* PhD Thesis. Groningen: University of Groningen.

Cattaneo, Claudio & Miguel Martínez (Eds) (2014) *The Squatters' Movement in Europe: Commons and Autonomy as Alternatives to Capitalism.* London: Pluto Press.

Colin, Baptiste (2005) *Les squatts parisiens depuis l'Après-Deuxième Guerre mondiale jusqu'en 1995.* Master's dissertation, Paris: Université Paris 7.

Collado, Francisco (2007) *Abriendo puertas. Okupaciones en Valencia 1988–2006.* Valencia: La Burbuja.

Dadusc, Deanna (2017) *The Micropolitics of Criminalisation: Power, Resistance and the Amsterdam Squatting Movement.* Amsterdam: University of Kent [PhD Dissertation].

Dadusc, Deanna & E.T.C. Dee (2015) The Criminalisation of Squatting: Discourses, Moral Panics and Resistances in the Netherlands and England and Wales. In Lorna Fox O'Mahony, David O'Mahony & Robin Hickey (Eds) *Moral Rhetoric and the Criminalisation of Squatting. Vulnerable Demons?* Abingdon: Routledge, 109–132.

Dee, E.T.C. (2013) Moving Towards Criminalisation and Then What? Examining Dominant Discourses on Squatting in England. In SqEK (Ed.) *Squatting in Europe. Radical Spaces, Urban Struggles.* Wivenhoe: Minor Compositions, 247–267.

Dee, E.T.C. (2018) The Political Squatters' Movement and Its Social Centres in the Gentrifying City of Rotterdam. In Miguel A. Martínez (Ed.) *The Urban Politics of Squatters' Movements.* New York: Palgrave Macmillan, 187–208.

Draaisma, J. & P. van Hoogstraten (1983) The Squatter Movement in Amsterdam. *International Journal of Urban and Regional Research* 7: 406–416.

Egia, Lutxo & Kukutza Gaztetxeko Kideak (Eds) (2011) *Kukutza Gaztetxea. Ellos por dinero, nosotras por placer.* Tafalla: Txalaparta.

Fainstein, Susan (1994) *The City Builders: Property, Politics, and Planning in London and New York.* Oxford: Blackwell.

Finchett-Maddock, Lucy (2015) The Changing Architectures of Adverse Possession and a Political Aesthetics of Squatting. In Lorna Fox O'Mahony, David O'Mahony & Robin Hickey (Eds) *Moral Rhetoric and the Criminalisation of Squatting. Vulnerable Demons?* Abingdon: Routledge, 204–223.

Finchett-Maddock, Lucy (2016) *Protest, Property and the Commons. Performances of Law and Resistance.* Abingdon: Routledge.

Foltin, Robert (2014) Squatting and Autonomous Action in Vienna. In Bart van der Steen, Ask Katzeff & Leendert van Hoogenhuijze (Eds) *The City Is Ours: Squatting and Autonomous Movements in Europe from the 1970s to the Present.* Oakland: PM, 255–277.

Franzén, Mats (2005) New Social Movements and Gentrification in Hamburg and Stockholm: A Comparative Study. *Journal of Housing and the Built Environment* 20(1): 51–77.

136 Socio-Spatial Structures

Grashoff, Udo (2017) Cautious Occupiers and Restrained Bureaucrats: Schwarzwohnen in the German Democratic Republic. Somewhat Different from Squatting. *Urban Studies*. DOI: 10.1177/0042098017734813.

Hodkinson, Stuart & Paul Chatterton (2006) Autonomy in the City? Reflections on the Social Centres Movement in the UK. *City* 10: 305–315.

Holm, Andrej & Armin Kuhn (2011) Squatting and Urban Renewal: The Interaction of Squatter Movements and Strategies of Urban Restructuring in Berlin. *International Journal of Urban and Regional Research* 35(3): 644–658.

Holm, Andrej & Armin Kuhn (2017) Squatting and Gentrification in East Germany since 1989/90. In Freia Anders & Alexander Sedlmaier (Eds) *Public Goods versus Economic Interests. Global Perspectives on the History of Squatting*. New York: Routledge, 278–304.

Koopmans, Ruud (1995) *Democracy from Below. New Social Movements and the Political System in West Germany*. Boulder: Westview.

Lees, Loretta, Hyun Bang Shin & Ernesto López-Morales (2016) *Planetary Gentrification*. Cambridge: Polity.

Manjikian, Mary (2013) *Securitization of Property. Squatting in Europe*. New York: Routledge.

Martin, John N. & Primo Moroni (2007) *La luna sotto casa. Milano tra rivolta esistenziale e movimenti politici*. Milan: ShaKe.

Martínez, Miguel A. (2004) Del Urbanismo a la autogestión: Una historia posible del movimiento de okupación en España. In Ramón Adell & Miguel Martínez López (Eds) *¿Dónde están las llaves? El movimiento okupa: Prácticas y contextos sociales*. Madrid: La Catarata, 61–88.

Martínez, Miguel A. (2007) The Squatters' Movement: Urban Counterculture and Alter-Globalisation Dynamics. *South European Society and Politics* 12(3): 379–398.

Martínez, Miguel A. (2018a) Socio-Spatial Structures and Protest Cycles of Squatted Social Centres in Madrid. In Miguel A. Martínez (Ed.) *The Urban Politics of Squatters' Movements*. New York: Palgrave Macmillan, 25–49.

Martínez, Miguel A. (Ed.) (2018b) *The Urban Politics of Squatters' Movements*. New York: Palgrave Macmillan.

Martínez, Miguel A. & Claudio Cattaneo (2014) Squatting as a Response to Social Needs, the Housing Question and the Crisis of Capitalism. In Claudio Cattaneo & Miguel Martínez (Eds) *The Squatters' Movement in Europe: Commons and Autonomy as Alternatives to Capitalism*. London: Pluto Press, 26–57.

Mayer, Margit (1993a) The *Career* of Urban Social Movements in German Cities. In Robert Fisher & Joseph Kling (Eds) *Mobilizing the Community: Local Politics in a Global Era*. Newbury Park: Sage, 149–170.

Mayer, Margit (1993b) The Role of Urban Social Movement Organisations in Innovative Urban Policies and Institutions. In Panagoitis Getimis & Grigoris Kafkalas (Eds) *Urban and Regional Development in the New Europe*. Athens: Topos, 209–226.

Membretti, A. (2007) Centro Sociale Loncavallo. Building Citizenship as an Innovative Service. *European Urban and Regional Studies* 14(3): 255–266.

Mikkelsen, Flemming & Rene Karpantschof (2001) Youth as a Political Movement: Development of the Squatters' and Autonomous Movement in Copenhagen, 1981–95. *International Journal of Urban and Regional Research* 25(3): 609–628.

Mudu, Pierpaolo (2004) Resisting and Challenging Neoliberalism: The Development of Italian Social Centers. *Antipode* 36(5): 917–941.

Notes From Nowhere (2003) *We are Everywhere: The Irresistible Rise of Global Anticapitalism*. London: Verso.

Offe, Claus (1985) New Social Movements: Challenging the Boundaries of Institutional Politics. *Social Research* 52(4): 817–868.

Owens, Linus (2009) *Cracking under Pressure. Narrating the Decline of the Amsterdam Squatters' Movement*. Amsterdam: Amsterdam University Press.

Péchu, Cécile (2010) *Les Squats*. Paris: Presses de Sciences Po.

Piazza, Gianni (2018) Squatting Social Centres in a Sicilian City: Liberated Spaces and Urban Protest Actors. *Antipode* 50(2): 498–522.

Piazza, Gianni & Valentina Genovese (2016) Between Political Opportunities and Strategic Dilemmas: The Choice of 'Double Track' by the Activists of an Occupied Social Centre in Italy. *Social Movement Studies* 15(3): 290–304.

Polanska, Dominika (2015) Alliance Building and Brokerage in Contentious Politics: The Case of the Polish Tenants' Movement. In Kerstin Jacobsson (Ed.) *Grassroots Movements in Central and Eastern Europe*. Farnham: Ashgate, 195–217.

Polanska, Dominika (2017) Reclaiming Inclusive Politics: Squatting in Sweden 1968–2016. *Trespass* 1: 36–72.

Polanska, Dominika & Grzegorz Piotrowski (2015) The Transformative Power of Cooperation between Social Movements: Squatting and Tenants' Movements in Poland. *City* 19(2–3): 274–296.

Polanska, Dominika & Grzegorz Piotrowski (2016) Poland: Local Differences and the Importance of Cohesion. *Baltic Worlds* IX(1–2): 46–56.

Priemus, Hugo (1983) Squatters in Amsterdam: Urban Social Movement, Urban Managers or Something Else? *International Journal of Urban and Regional Research* 7: 417–427.

Priemus, Hugo (2015) Squatters in the City: New Occupation of Vacant Offices. *International Journal of Housing Policy* 15(1): 84–92.

Pruijt, Hans (2003) Is the Institutionalization of Urban Movements Inevitable? A Comparison of the Opportunities for Sustained Squatting in New York and Amsterdam. *International Journal of Urban and Regional Research* 27(1): 133–157.

Pruijt, Hans (2004a) Squatters in the Creative City: Rejoinder to Justus Uitermark. *International Journal of Urban and Regional Research* 28(3): 699–705.

Pruijt, Hans (2004b) The Impact of Citizens' Protest on City Planning in Amsterdam. In Léon Deben, W. Salet & Maria Theresia Antoinette van Thoor (Eds) *Cultural Heritage and the Future of the Historic Inner City of Amsterdam*. Amsterdam: Aksant, 228–244.

Reeve, Kesia (2015) Criminalising the Poor. Squatting, Homelessness and Social Welfare. In Lorna Fox O'Mahony, David O'Mahony & Robin Hickey (Eds) *Moral Rhetoric and the Criminalisation of Squatting. Vulnerable Demons?* Abingdon: Routledge, 133–154.

Rucht, Dieter (1990) The Strategies and Action Repertoires of New Movements. In Russel J. Dalton & Manfred Kuechler (Eds) *Challenging the Political Order. New Social and Political Movements in Democracies*. Cambridge: Polity, 156–175.

Sabaté, Irene (2012) *Habitar tras el Muro. La cuestión de la vivienda en el este de Berlín*. Barcelona: Icaria.

Seminario (2015) *Okupa Madrid (1985–2011). Memoria, reflexión, debate y autogestión colectiva del conocimiento*. Madrid: Diagonal.

SQUASH (Squatters' Action for Secure Homes) (2011) *Criminalising the Vulnerable: Why We Can't Criminalise Our Way Out of a Housing Crisis—A Parliamentary Briefing*. [www.squashcampaign.org]

Steen, Bart, Ask Katzeff & Leendert van Hoogenhuijze (2014) Introduction. Squatting and Autonomous Action in Europe, 1980–2012. In Bart Steen, Ask Katzeff & L. Hoogenhuijze (Eds) *The City Is Ours: Squatting and Autonomous Movements in Europe from the 1970s to the Present*. Oakland: PM Press, 1–19.

138 Socio-Spatial Structures

Steiger, Tina (2018) Cycles of the Copenhagen Squatter Movement: From Slumstormer to BZ Brigades and the Autonomous Movement. In Miguel A. Martínez (Ed.) *The Urban Politics of Squatters' Movements*. New York: Palgrave Macmillan, 165–186.

Thörn, Håkan (2012) In between Social Engineering and Gentrification: Urban Restructuring, Social Movements, and the Place Politics of Open Space. *Journal of Urban Affairs* 34(2): 153–168.

Thörn, Håkan, Cathrin Washede & Tomas Nilson (Eds) (2011) *Space for Urban Alternatives? Christiania 1971–2011*. Vilnius: Gidlunds Förlag.

Uitermark, Justus (2004) The Co-Optation of Squatters in Amsterdam and the Emergence of A Movement Meritocracy: A Critical Reply to Pruijt. *International Journal of Urban and Regional Research* 28(3): 687–698.

Uitermark, Justus (2012) An Actually Existing Just City? The Fight for the Right to the City in Amsterdam. In Neil Brenner, Peter Marcuse & Margit Mayer (Eds) *Cities for People, Not for Profit. Critical Urban Theory and the Right to the City*. Abingdon: Routledge, 197–214.

Uitermark, Justus & Jan Willem Duyvendak (2008) Civilising the City: Populism and Revanchist Urbanism in Rotterdam. *Urban Studies* 45(7): 1485–1503.

Watson, Don (2016) *Squatting in Britain 1945–1955. Housing, Politics, and Direct Action*. London: Merlin.

Yates, Luke (2014) Rethinking Prefiguration: Alternatives, Micropolitics and Goals in Social Movements. *Social Movement Studies: Journal of Social, Cultural and Political Protest* 14(1): 1–21.

Yates, Luke (2015) Everyday Politics, Social Practices and Movement Networks: Daily Life in Barcelona's Social Centres. *The British Journal of Sociology* 66(2): 236–258.

4

TYPES OF SQUATTING

Which are the significant types of squatting? Squats are hardly dedicated to one single and exclusive activity. Squatters can sleep, work, study, meet their peers, raise children, rest, and even promote public events for outsiders in the buildings they occupy. Classifications of squats are problematic if they do not account for all the nuances of every case, its urban-metropolitan context, and its change over time. The names attached to the different types of squats and the political use that might be made of them entail practical consequences too—in the eventuality of a lawsuit, for example. This chapter critically examines attempts to categorise urban squats (especially Aguilera 2018, González et al. 2018, Martínez 2013, Polanska 2017, Pruijt 2013) and suggests new comprehensive classifications. Rather than merely focusing on the activities or functions accomplished by squats, my approach aims to relate the types of squatting to the most relevant socio-spatial and historical conditions of possibility examined in the previous chapter. Accordingly, I highlight the distinctions between squats for housing and squatted social centres, on the one hand, and tactical and strategic squatting, on the other, in order to clarify the political dimension of squatting practices and movements. Besides this, I move from a focus on the differentiated motivations of squatters towards the most probable outcomes they produce. The discussion of the literature also invites a focus on the overlaps and intersections between different forms of squatting. Splits among squatters when it comes to dealing with the local authorities and policies are also among the main distinctive features of squatting. Finally, I present a case study of the interactions between migrants and squatters in the City of Madrid in order to show how waves of protest and other contextual features are articulated with the types of squatted spaces effectively produced. A supplementary report from my fieldwork in Paris will also offer more nuanced accounts of various types of squatting.

140 Types of Squatting

Indeed, scholars and activists hold many different views on the classification of various types of squats, squatting practices, and squatters themselves. To some extent, these views identify another series of outcomes that add to those already presented in relation to the socio-spatial structures of opportunities and constraints. Squatters contend that most of these outcomes are beneficial to themselves, to other social groups, and, eventually, to the democratic quality of urban politics. My focus now is not on the assessment of all the possible outcomes of squatting, but only on those closely related to a meaningful typology of squatting practices and movements.

Squatting is sociologically seen as a special subcategory of informal housing, which is embedded, in turn, in a broader set consisting of 'informal strategies of survival' in the market (Ledeneva 2018). This particular nested position is challenged by the political dimension that the squatters' movement entails. Moreover, the realm of housing is not the only one where urban squatting makes specific impacts. Social centres, for example, unfold a variegated display of cultural, environmental, and social activities. Another criticism to that association targets the binary opposition and clear-cut distinction between 'informality' and 'formality' because it does not leave much room for understanding their interdependency, if it is the case.

For most scholars, the housing question is at the core of the development of squatting. This is not only a historical observation regarding the social practices that always occurred in anticipation of private property rights, but also according to the development of squatters' movements and practices worldwide. Research on slums and squatters' settlements on vacant land tends to be separated from research on urban squatting of empty buildings, although there are recent attempts to bridge both fields (Aguilera & Smart 2017, Davis 2007, Manjikian 2013, Vasudevan 2015). These theoretical proposals also explore the connections between squatting in the Global North and the Global South, and emphasise the heterogeneity of practices and contexts attached to them. For example, the legal recognition of many slums (or favelas, shanty-towns, informal settlements, etc.) in the South, their solid self-built structures erected and in place for many decades, and the property and market relations that follow suit indicate both connections and gaps with the usual forms of unauthorised squatting.

Since this book aims to illuminate how the squatting of buildings in European cities operates in relation to urban activism and movements, the global context of diverse squatting practices serves to frame them beyond the 'informality' approach. Social practices in relation to the vacancy of built stock and urban land, the social self-organisation of squatters and other related activists, and their interactions with specific urban political and economic contexts (at local, national, and even transnational scales), in my view, are the crucial dimensions that help classifying and advancing explanations of many forms of squatting, or, as Aguilera and Smart (2017) call them, 'the political economy of persistence and toleration' in both the Global North and the Global South. The methodical review of past contributions will reveal the state of the art and my proposed approach to this subject.

Squatted Houses and Social Centres

Pruijt's (2013) categories have become very well known and valuable for this purpose. He distinguished: (1) 'deprivation-based squatting'; (2) 'squatting as an alternative housing strategy'; (3) 'entrepreneurial squatting'; (4) 'conservational squatting'; and (5) 'political squatting'. Pruijt refers to this typology as a set of 'configurations', these being sort of ideal types: 'Combinations of features that are logically consistent and fit to the environment, and can therefore be expected to be efficient and effective' (Pruijt 2013: 21). Table 4.1 summarises the main contents of each configuration:

Pruijt argues that 'squatting projects' are the units of analysis so that various squatting projects can share the same building. In fact, all configurations may easily combine their main activities with housing (of activists and non-activists alike), although the residential feature is only salient and overtly presented to the public in (1) and (2) (see Table 4.1). Furthermore, I deem it necessary to highlight the distinction between tactical and strategic squatting when it comes to meeting housing needs. Tactical squatting implies a practical prevalence of other ends different from squatting, so this becomes a means to those ends. Strategic squatting designates a priority of squatting in practice as a political end, despite its coincidence with other goals, which makes squatting also a consistent means.

On the one hand, most housing movements resort to squatting in order to accommodate homeless people, migrants, and other deprived social groups. This is the case, for instance, of the Plataforma de Afectados por las Hipotecas or PAH (Platform for People Affected by Mortgages) in Spain, Droit Au Logement or DAL (Right to Housing) in France and the Movimenti Per Il Diritto All'Abitare (Movement for the Right to Housing) in Italy. They frame and practice squatting as one possible action repertoire among others, not the central one. Squatting is a means to grant and fulfil the right to housing for marginalised people. When immigrants and refugees are involved (as they are in squats in Greece, Italy, and France, for example) one major goal is to get full citizenship rights, so squatting is considered a temporary solution or a transitional step (see Image 4.3). Although it is not always the case, I agree with Pruijt that a crucial divide within this category encompasses activists who do not experience the same housing needs as those who end up living in the occupied buildings, which frequently leads to an internal hierarchy. When tactical squatting unintendedly lasts for long periods of time, many participants can reframe it as strategic and turn to endorse it as their main social and political concern. Furthermore, tactical squatting for dwelling purposes, either integrated in movement organisations or independent from them, is the most likely form of squatting to be practised in a stealth manner.

On the other hand, squatters who autonomously satisfy their own housing needs, without being as deprived as the aforementioned social groups, also tend

TABLE 4.1 Dimensions of squatting configurations

	(1) Deprivation-based squatting	(2) Squatting as an alternative housing strategy	(3) Entrepreneurial squatting	(4) Conservational squatting	(5) Political squatting
Activists' goals	Providing housing for needy people	Creating housing for themselves	Setting up an establishment (social centre)	Preserving a cityscape or landscape	Building up a counter-power to the state
Demands	Modest; temporary housing or alternative accommodation; (better) place on waiting list	To be left alone	To be left alone	Reversal of planning	Confrontation is the essence, demands are at most supplementary
Framing	Clear message: insensitive bureaucrats ignore needs of homeless people	Focus on action, framing not very important	Valuable role of the squat in the community	Against technocratic planning and environmental destruction	Depicting social democrats (or institutional left) as traitors
Cultural and political embedding	Sometimes a tenuous link with radical politics	Embedded in counterculture; ties with other movements	Embedded in counterculture; ties with other movements	Embedded in counterculture; ties with other movements	Links with Marxist or anarchist organisations
Class	Working-class squatters supported by middle-class activists	Middle class (but not exclusively)	Middle class (but not exclusively)	Middle class (but not exclusively)	Middle class (but not exclusively)
Organisation	Top-down, division between activists and beneficiaries	Horizontal	Mixed	Mixed	Top-down
Type of buildings	Regular low-income housing stock left empty	Buildings that are either too bad or too good to be rented out as low-income housing	Non-housing spaces, mainly	Buildings emptied because of a planned change in land use	Few restrictions

Source: Author based on Pruijt (2013: 23) Note: I have added a few details or shortened the descriptions to clarify the meaning. I have also reorganised the dimensions (goals, demands, framing, and cultural and political embedding are first because of their significant contiguity), and suppressed the rows dedicated to 'specific problems' and 'outcomes'.

Types of Squatting **143**

to frame and publicise their action as a protest against housing shortage, speculation, and policies. However, they are more eager to set up horizontal organisations, alternative lifestyles, and participation in broader social movements. For them, squatting is both a means and an end. Other political ends may be claimed, but squatting is one of the most important ones, especially while they are fully involved in practising it. This makes squatting a strategic priority in their political agenda and practical dedication. It holds a prefigurative nature since squatting is simultaneously a means of protest and a key goal of their political activity. Therefore, every occupied building is a victory, a stronghold to defend, an example of efficient direct action in the eyes of the society at large, and an interference in the flows of capital and the state allocation of resources without public scrutiny. When squatted 'living communes' (not necessarily aspiring to follow the example of the 1960s and 1970s communes) last a long time and are mutually interconnected (as has been the case for the legalised 'house projects' in Berlin and Hamburg—see Image 4.2—the 'freetown' Christiania, and networks of squatted houses in the neighbourhoods of Lavapiés and Tetuán in Madrid for some decades), they are prone to organise community events and activities in their own buildings and the surrounding public spaces, in a similar vein as the squatted social centres do.

Even radical squatters do not expect to squat for the entirety of their lives; this is, in fact, very unlikely. For most people who squat for a living, squatting is a stage along the way to a permanent residence, regardless of its tenure. In sum, the more deprived they are in the housing market (or non-eligible for social housing), the more likely they are to consider squatting as a political tactic, tool, or means.

This analysis leads us to a sharper grouping:

1. Squatting for housing as the main purpose.

    1.1 Tactical squatting to meet the housing needs of the poor, deprived, and homeless people, as part of housing movements—as well as movements in solidarity with migrants and refugees. Sometimes it is kept invisible from the public eye. Sometimes, as autonomous self-help initiatives, it is practised without the support of established organisations.
    1.2 Strategic squatting to meet the housing needs of activists, in the form of autonomous self-help initiatives, as a protest practice focused on squatting—and also, usually, embedded in broader movements. Squatting for housing is considered an alternative urban politics.

2. Squatting where housing is not the main purpose but, mostly, the self-management of 'social centres'.

    2.1 Tactical squatting to preserve historic buildings, urban areas, public facilities, or natural landscapes from demolition and restructuring (not necessarily by promoting social centres, though).

144 Types of Squatting

> 2.2 Strategic squatting to promote political, cultural, social, and economic activities as a protest practice open to the public and focused on squatting and broader movements. These are usually the most visible forms of squatting.

A similar argument can be made about the other three types of squatting ('entrepreneurial', 'conservational', and 'political')—there are tactical and strategic differences to incorporate in the classification. First, it is not unusual that activists sleep overnight in the buildings they want to save from demolition, but also in 'entrepreneurial' social centres where they are actively engaged for many hours every day, not the least in all kinds of buildings serving as the headquarters of very specific political groups who would not allow anyone to forbid them to do so. I verified these dynamics in squats all over Europe, although on some occasions activists did so secretly because it was against their legal defence strategies (this occurred in most Spanish cities after 1995) or because it was banned in the legal agreements reached with the authorities in cases where the squat had become legalised (above all, in many artist squats in Amsterdam, Paris, and Copenhagen, for example). Thus, although the provision of dwelling is not the main purpose of these occupations, they often intersect with the practice of housing as an alternative housing strategy. Moreover, they lend support to all cases of squatting solely for housing, even if they do not enjoy the same reciprocal support back.

Second, the 'political squatting' configuration is the most controversial type in Pruijt's approach because in all tactical and strategic cases there are political stances at play, which Pruijt himself acknowledges too (Pruijt 2013: 36). According to my observations, the contents Pruijt attributes to 'political squatting' refer to exceptional cases in which some strongly politicised groups in the left-libertarian spectrum and established political parties used squatting in a tactical way exclusively in order to advance their political agendas. They preferred to stay apart from other forms of squatting, although they could join them as a means to recruit members and expand their views. In my view, in contrast with the cases he mentions in the Netherlands, German, and Italy, it is more frequent to find autonomists, anarchists, and highly politicised activists involved in all forms of squatting (especially in social centres), promoting their views from inside in a very open and mixed practice with other groups and participants, than being isolated as a 'hardcore partisan' group in specific squats (or as independent groups within larger squats). Pruijt mentions internal hierarchy, hidden agendas, active opposition to other leftist or mildly progressive organisations, sectarianism, and violent repertoires of actions attached to the most radical squatters. However, I do not consider these features intrinsic to the radical politics that squatters usually perform and adhere to. In practice, radical and more moderate positions often cohabit in the same squats or across the local squatting scene, and there are also many approaches to the meaning of radicalism within the squatting movements.

My observations in 2017–18 as well as talks with squatters in the Italian city of Catania, for example, illustrate this complexity. Militants of a political party, Potere al Popolo, occupied an old fish factory (Colapesce, see Image 4.1), which became a social centre closely in touch with the local population and offering a diverse range of public activities. Despite the massive and exclusive propaganda of the party, the squat had an open door policy similar to many other social centres, resulting in the most demanding political activity the activists had yet faced. Another group of hardcore politicised activists in the autonomist area occupied various spaces (Liotru, Palestra, and Studentato) where the walls showed posters related to multiple anti-capitalist, feminist, and solidarity struggles. They also managed these social centres with similar open door and diversity policies, and also cooperated with other squats (included some just for housing) where they organised music concerts, for example. Less radical views and politicisation were observed in two more arts-oriented social centres of the same city (Lupo and Teatro Coppola), but leftist and progressive claims were also part of their discourse, decisions, and practices in addition to self-managing the occupied spaces and promoting a wide range of social activities for publics of different ages, tastes, backgrounds, and political inclinations.

Third, I suggest the combination of 'entrepreneurial' and 'conservational' squatting into one single category of 'social centres' as a squatting movement, where housing is not the main issue at stake and different claims related to

IMAGE 4.1 Squat Colapesce, Catania, 2018
Source: Author

146 Types of Squatting

urban life take the lead. 'Conservational' squatting tends to focus more on specific buildings or cityscapes threatened with demolition, restructuring plans, and mega-projects. It could be long-lasting and be strongly based on the provision of housing for activists, but the justification of squatting is closely associated with the disputed urban fabric. It is therefore a case of tactical squatting dependent on the more strategic goal of conservationism. Conservational squatting is a political endeavour that needs to be open to the public, so it is prone to organising public activities and, when possible, social centres in the occupied buildings. Entrepreneurial squatting applies in a more comprehensive manner to all public activities and prefigurations beyond dwelling that are developed within non-residential squats but also, sometimes, in mainly residential squats. The less squatted social centres are attached to the conservation of particular buildings, the more they become strategic, persistent, networked with other activists and social movements, and open to visitors, participants, supporters, and outsiders in general.

In addition, it is remarkable that squatted social centres provide a public resource for meetings, information, leisure, expression, and sociability, which are essential both to getting in touch with kindred people and launching new squats. Beyond its value as a material infrastructure for activists, squatted social centres are the most visible examples of squatting (for public opinion, mass media, local authorities, and neighbours) and the most open to recruiting new activists and attracting participants, visitors, and sympathisers with lesser degrees of commitment. Some housing movements are also skilful in making residential squats socially visible, especially as a bargaining chip when it comes to gathering public support, positive recognition, and legitimation in dealing with eviction procedures or potential concessions from the authorities. Some of the buildings that work as social centres host many political discourses and events closely-related to other social movements (migrants' and precarious workers' rights, hacktivism, artivism, urban gardens and organic food, etc.). They also offer their facilities to different social and political organisations. Some others combine weaker political concerns with a stronger dedication to organising music concerts, workshops, art exhibitions, or cheap meals and drinks. Artists, militants, and several social groups mix together in most of the countercultural or entrepreneurial social centres, but they can also split off into more specialised venues. In the case of successful self-employment initiatives (for example, a brewery in an Amsterdam squat or a handmade craft jeweller in a Barcelona squat) they tend to move out of the squats and run their own businesses.

When residence and social centre coexist within the same building, a neat separation of both activities tends to be established, although the latter usually plays the most visible role in the symbolic legitimation and promotion of squatting as a radical tool for grassroots urban intervention. In Italy, Spain, and the UK many activists and scholars embraced the notion of a 'social centres movement' (Common Place 2008, Hodkinson & Chatterton 2006, Mudu 2004, Toret et al. 2008) including non-squatted self-managed social centres.

Certainly, some of the latter can be considered as part of larger autonomist and squatters' movements when both squatting and self-management are placed at the centre of their political priorities. This is the case of Patio Maravillas, a squatted social centre in four different locations of Madrid that was linked to both the autonomist network RES (Rompamos el Silencio), who occupied buildings for a few days every year, and more stable autonomous, non-squatted (Candela in Terrassa and Tabacalera in Madrid, for example), and (fully or partially) legalised squatted social centres (Seco and Eskalera Karakola in Madrid, Casa Invisible in Málaga).

Social centres often substitute for the lack of established organisations and city coordination of all kinds of squats. Social networks of activists arise from demonstrations and informal encounters, but social centres add a direct and tangible example of how things can be organised collectively and without paying rent should they manage to remain occupied. These valuable outcomes are more difficult to attain for buildings just dedicated to the residential function.

As Figure 4.1 suggests, there are many shared category possibilities between tactical and strategic squatting as well as between residential squatting and squatted social centres. Thörn, for example, interprets that Freetown Christiania, in Copenhagen, combined all five configurations proposed by Pruijt (Thörn 2012: 156). However, while attempting a comparison with an area of Gothenburg (the Haga neighbourhood), also hosting a creative counterculture of squatting and resistance to urban renewal between the 1970s and the 1990s, he suggests an additional configuration designated as

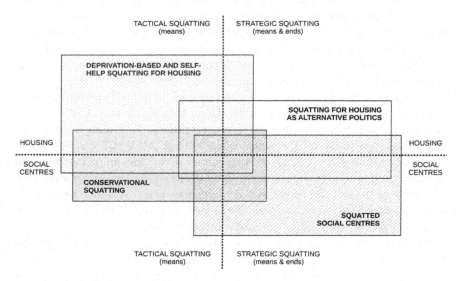

FIGURE 4.1 Types of squatting
Source: Author based on Pruijt (2013) and Martínez (2013)

148 Types of Squatting

the place politics of open space' which 'overlaps with Pruijt's second and third configurations ... The goal of place politics of open space is to combine autonomy and public-ness ... [It] involves the construction of a distinct place identity ... [and] a place-bound public sphere.

(Thörn 2012: 156–157)

This contribution calls attention to the role played by significant urban areas where squatters operate in a two-way direction: the materiality of the urban areas is appropriated by squatters and other activists who, in turn, influence the identity of the neighbourhood with their politics of housing and public activities. In the following sections, I develop more nuanced observations in order to understand the many overlaps and implications of Pruijt's categories.

Motivations and Outcomes

In historical research conducted on squatting experiences in Sweden between 1968 and 2016, it is contended that 'the goals of providing housing, creating free spaces, and preserving areas from clearance and demolition have been present in all periods' (Polanska 2017: 40). 'Free spaces' refer to what I designated as 'social centres' above, which is a label inspired by Italian autonomist politics mainly after the 1980s and is not necessarily shared by all squatters across Europe. Despite difficulties articulating squatting movements due to the repressive policies in this matter and the subsequent short-lived duration of the squats, Polanska accounts for the long-term continuity of this practice as related to its broader motivations such as the 'critique of national politics [welfare cuts] and environmental protection ... [and the] overtly political [and contentious] nature' (ibid.) of the squats. The three goals of housing, free spaces, and preservation were jointly claimed in the case of Gothenburg's Haga district from the late 1960s to the 1990s (Polanska 2017: 41, Thörn 2012), and a similar overlapping of goals was found in many other cases across Sweden.

In contrast to Pruijt, an important point about the Swedish case is Polanska's inclusion of 'demonstrative squatting' in the analysis. For Pruijt, only 'relatively long-term occupations ... intended to make relatively long-term use possible, though not necessarily by the same people' (Pruijt 2013: 22) are considered. However, as Polanska notes, an abundant number of early aborted occupations and the continuity of the whole set over a significant lifespan (various decades) contribute to shape a consistent field of contentious practices, a low-key form of urban activism. Therefore, it seems sensible to take the sustained duration of a set of practices with similar political motivations—and not just their isolated and limited existence—as a criterion to identify the contentious nature of this urban activism and movement in case it scales up to more consistent unity, worthiness, numbers, and commitment (Tilly & Tarrow 2007: 8).

Notwithstanding, Polanska includes in the same pool both 'squatting projects' intended to last and squatting practices as 'protest events' of disruption

Types of Squatting   **149**

performed by different social movements. In my view, the latter are too demonstrative and away from the former, so this combination disturbs the appreciation of existing squatters' movements. The boundary is more difficult to draw when it comes to conservational squatters, so often inclined to host resisting dwellers and mobilise communities around the defence of buildings threatened with demolition. Within the same category we could include the defence of specific buildings as providers of public services (hospitals, schools, sport facilities, etc.). But I would apply the boundary when, for example, students' movements occupy university premises to protest a specific policy without any relation to the claim of spaces, when workers occupy the factory floors or offices to demand a pay rise, or when activists occupy administrative buildings to protest against an economic, environmental, or transport policy. Although every form of tactical squatting could be seen as a weak relation to the occupied spaces because of their dependent role in the major goals, the extension of 'modular performances' (Tilly & Tarrow 2007: 12) across different forms of contentious politics does not suffice to identify a shared field of grievances and aspirations.

As a consequence, I suggest an alternative classification of squatting with a clear focus on the social problems and policy fields that motivate squatters to occupy buildings and remain in them. The duration of every squatting project is not questioned, but the goals should persist in time through many experiences that can also be tied together transnationally (Owens et al. 2013). I also assume that various goals can overlap in the same squatting project as non-single-issue concerns are very frequent in social centres and not unusual in-house projects.

1. Provision of housing. This includes tactical 'deprivation-based squatting' (either with non-squatter activists involved or without them, as in self-help experiences) and 'squatting as an alternative housing strategy'.
2. Resistance to home eviction and solidarity with people threatened with evictions. This occurs especially in areas affected by renewal projects and can lead to experiences of both tactical and strategic squatting for housing. It can also apply to people evicted from their own house anywhere in the city because they cannot pay off their mortgage to the bank or the tenancy rent to the landlord.
3. Conservation of specific threatened buildings and the areas where they are located, the social communities hosted by them, the public facilities they provide, or the surrounding natural landscapes, resources, and its collective use. In short, all these categories could form 'urban commons'. This tactical form of conservational squatting may also lead to the three previous forms of squatting for housing (resistance to eviction and provision of housing for marginalised and non-marginalised people) but also to the self-management of social centres.
4. Environmental benefits. This is a specific feature of conservational squatting based on the environmental value that the use of empty buildings imply in terms of avoiding new construction, pollution, and damage to nature.

150 Types of Squatting

Rehabilitation and reuse of buildings adds to associated practices of low-cost lifestyles, dumpster diving, sharing resources, and the use of renewable energy in the occupied buildings. It is closer to strategic squatting than the above forms of conservational squatting but may apply equally to housing squats and to squatted social centres.

5. Alternative cultural activities opened to other activists, local residents, and the city population at large. Most squatted social centres organise a diverse array of events, shows, exhibitions, concerts, performances, parties, film screenings, theatre plays, circuses, reading groups, artistic workshops, etc. apart from mainstream, commercial, and state-sponsored culture.

6. Political infrastructure for social aggregation and democratic empowerment. Social centres may also offer a meeting space for political groups—either exclusively the one who squats the building or many other affinity groups, organisations, and movements from the local, metropolitan or transnational arena. The convenient location of the squats and its use for free (or according to agreed exchanges or affordable fees) invigorates activist networks. Practices of direct democracy, horizontality, self-management, civil disobedience, negotiation skills, and legal knowledge add to the experimental and prefigurative politics that can ferment in squatted social centres.

7. Safe spaces for women, LGBTQI people, ethnic minorities, and immigrants-refugees to claim and practice their right to the city. Some squats, either for housing or functioning as social centres, are exclusively occupied and operated by one of these social groups, which adds empowerment to safety. Sometimes, their specific demands of emancipation permeate mixed squats or even become a central concern of their politics.

According to one publication put out by Barcelona squatters (VVAA 2004), squatted socials centres involve 'struggles against the destruction of neighbourhoods by speculators', 'workshops for collective learning without money', 'raising funds for the social centre and other projects', 'popular culture', 'non-commercial leisure', 'assemblies and meetings', 'networks of affects and solidarity', 'independent and horizontal media communication', and 'constructive resistance'. Squats are thus capable of providing meeting spaces for activists belonging to different social movements. This provision is often administered through collective principles of horizontal and direct democracy, self-management, non-bureaucratic regulation or state control (Piazza 2011), and free or cheap access to goods and services. Recycling, dumpster diving, and sharing resources show how to live at low cost and be environmentally friendly in urban settings. Moreover, social centres and squatters' organisations encourage people to experiment with alternative and communal modes of living which are outside the mainstream of culture, politics, economy, and social relationships. Squatting offers immediate results in the practice of direct action and social disobedience against the unjust distribution of wealth. Both by means of creative cultural expressions and through organised opposition around broadly censored

Types of Squatting   151

issues (police brutality, political corruption, the current situation in prisons, unfair global trade, etc.), squatted places may expand the political consciousness of their participants into the realm of dissidence and resistance; however, they may also instil a sense of temporality and uncertainty.

For the homeless, deprived, underprivileged, working class, unemployed, and dropouts of the institutional systems—education, asylums, juvenile homes, etc.—squatting forms a key survival tactic and, sometimes, scales up to a political strategy in terms of both awareness and practical priorities. Not only is affordable shelter conquered, but one can also be actively involved in the satisfaction of basic needs. This is usually achieved thanks to interaction with wealthier and more skilled individuals, resulting in an increase of social capital and mutual learning for all. Most of those engaged in squatting benefit from the empowerment, skills, opportunities, and self-confidence that these collective actions entail.

It has not been widely recognised that, in comparison to other forms of activism, squatting comprises almost the whole everyday life of those involved. Domestic tasks, gender relations, and the emotional dimensions of activism are regularly

IMAGE 4.2   After-squat Hafenstrasse, Hamburg, 2014
Source: Author

152 Types of Squatting

TABLE 4.2 Seven types of squatting

Outcomes and motivations	Types of squatting	Main activity		Political agenda	
		Housing	Social Centres	Tactical	Strategic
Provision of housing	Deprivation-based and self-help squatting for housing	***	*	***	*
	Squatting for housing as alternative politics	***	**	**	***
Resistance to home eviction	All forms of squatting for housing	***	*	*	***
Defence of urban commons	Conservational squatting	**	**	***	*
Environmental benefits	All forms of squatting	***	***	***	***
Alternative culture		*	***	**	***
Political infrastructure and empowerment	Squatted social centres	*	***	**	***
Right to the city	All forms of squatting focused on gender, ethnicity, and nationality	***	***	***	**

Source: Author

tackled, obliging squatters to transform their previous approaches to these questions. Among the skills squatters gain is the capability to deal with their own physical space in the context of the urban affairs of the local neighbourhood, the city, and the metropolitan area. Private life and communal living demands as much effort as public life and urban struggle, especially in relations with city councils, officials, politicians, judges, lawyers, private owners, companies, real-estate developers, journalists, researchers, and all kinds of neighbours, be they in favour of squatters, against them, or seemingly indifferent. As shown in Table 4.2, squatted social centres and houses can generate positive social impacts in different proportions and with different combinations, but they usually reinforce each other.

Overlaps and Splits

The importance of housing in all forms of squatting has been emphasised by alternative classifications. For example, González et al. (2018: 275–276), distinguish four categories:

1. *Abolitionism.* All forms of strategic squatting, including occupied houses and social centres, when the abolition of private property is a crucial goal that is advanced through squatting.

Types of Squatting **153**

2. *Communalism.* Squatting for housing, as alternative-countercultural politics and the most horizontal forms of organising deprivation-based and self-help initiatives share an interest in reviving communitarian ways of life in squats.
3. *Pragmatism.* It refers to all types of tactical squatting, especially those in the housing sphere where activists even demand legal and affordable means of housing provision.
4. *Unitarianism.* This represents the central area of intersection, and effective solidarity, between all the major types of squatting. Tactical and strategic squatting become united in a broad movement. Social centres integrate housing on the one hand, and residential squats launch many public activities on their premises on the other.

These four categories were applied to nine European cities along three different historical periods and urban-economic contexts. The three Spanish cities (Madrid, Barcelona, and Seville), for example, show a similar development from abolitionist and communalist types in all the periods to emerging cases of pragmatism since the mid-1990s (after the criminalisation of squatting) and an increasing, though partial, convergence with housing movements from 2011 to date (unitarianism).

> In the 1980s, the immediate urban and social environment of Spanish squatters drove them to focus first on youth unemployment and the rising social housing shortage in close parallel to the first wave of urban speculation. They also held distrust in institutional leftist political parties and unions. Flagship SSCs [Squatted Social Centres] such as *Minuesa* in Madrid or *Kasa de la Muntanya* in Barcelona exemplify this autonomous politics. In the 1990s, the squatters' movement grew in importance among the youth radical-left scene. The relationship between SSCs and housing was predominantly articulated via configurations (1) [abolitionist] and (2) [communalist] ... The development of the PAH from 2009, a housing organisation separated from the squatters' movement, made squatting a pragmatic tool (3) [pragmatism] as a response to the financial crisis and its massive foreclosures. Some branches of the autonomous squatters' movement and the 15M local assemblies established close ties with the PAH (4) [unitarianism] in most cities (in Seville, for example, where the housing movement was known as *Las Corralas*). In parallel, many cases of abolitionist (1) and countercultural (2) configurations are still ongoing, especially in Madrid and Barcelona.
>
> *(González et al. 2018: 277, italics in original)*

In the case of Copenhagen, there were only a few cases of pragmatism in the first (1963–79) and final (1994–2004) phases. This led to some agreements towards legalisation, but also to a strict repression of the most dominant forms of squatting—abolitionist and communalist—over the three periods.

154 Types of Squatting

In Copenhagen we can observe the shift from communalist (2) and pragmatic (3) configurations in the beginning of the squatting movement (those who cooperated with the municipality to develop student housing in derelict buildings) to the development of a strong autonomous movement in different phases (*Slumstormer Bevægelse, BZ* and *Autonomous*) as a case of abolitionist configuration (1) [abolitionism]. *Freetown Christiania* remained as a clear-cut and world-famous example of configuration (2) [communalism] since the 1970s. Radical activists were able to legalise and consolidate some landmark SSCs such as the *Folkets Hus* (squatted in 1971) and *Ungdomshuset* (since 1982). ... If we consider youth as a deprived social group in the housing market, a light form of configuration (3) [pragmatism] also unfolded during the 2000s when some squats for youth housing were legalised (*Alderstrøst, Ryesgade 58*, etc.). *BumZen* in Baldersgade was also legalised but maintains its autonomous character through association with youth housing institutions, so it is closer to configurations (1) [abolitionism] and (2) [communalism]. Some forms of secret squatting for housing were sometimes associated with the social centres of the 2010s, but there was no specific housing movement that resorted to squatting as a privileged tactic.

(González et al. 2018: 280, italics in original)

A similar scenario applies to Berlin (long-term persistence of abolitionism and communalism) with the main difference that the origins of the two strong waves of squatting (in the early 1980s and early 1990s) emerged from the breeding background of an original unitarian movement in the first period (1969–78) that paved the way for numerous pragmatic agreements between squatters and the authorities by the end of the main peaks of squatting in the city.

An important contribution of the above approach is the emphasis on the interactions and overlaps between squatting for housing and squatting for social centres. It also shows how a local squatters' movement can evolve from some particular combination to others. Finally, it indicates that even the most radical positions (squatting as a strategy to abolish private property) may coexist with pragmatic, tactical stances or even evolve to merge with them. This is why I have drawn dotted lines in the axes of Figure 4.1—tactical and strategic squatting are neither static nor mutually exclusive distinctions under certain local circumstances, depending on the strengths of the activists' networks, the institutional context, and the market forces. Table 4.3 aims to represent the most probable combinations in terms of degree of likelihood according to the evidence provided in Martínez (2018).

Aguilera provides a similar insight when it comes to classifying squats, squatters, and manifestations of squatting:

Ideal-types simplify and exaggerate the characteristics of each type. We never find perfect ideal-types in social reality. In practice, squatters from different groups combine different tactics. They can also change their

IMAGE 4.3 Squat Metropoliz, Rome, 2014
Source: Author

TABLE 4.3 Likelihood of coexistence between squats for housing and social centres

	Abolitionism	Communalism	Pragmatism	Unitarianism
Abolitionism	–	xxx	xx	xx
Communalism	xxx	–	xx	xx
Pragmatism	xx	xx	–	xxx
Unitarianism	xx	xx	xxx	–

Source: Author

> attitude depending on the context. Their positions and representations may evolve over time depending on previous positive and negative experiences. Finally, they can circulate across different types of squats.
>
> *(Aguilera 2018: 130)*

He uses three dimensions to differentiate squatting: resources (closely related to the social class of squatters and related activists), goals (in my terms, the political agenda according to tactical and strategic orientations), and attitudes towards policies. The historical and socio-spatial examination of squatting in Paris allows him to distinguish the following types:

156 Types of Squatting

1. Policy-oriented squatting. This category corresponds to the housing movements with a neat internal hierarchy between activists (wealthy in terms of economic, cultural, and political resources) and squatters (usually poor, deprived, and marginalised). Squatting is eminently a pragmatic tactic to achieve social housing, so the legalisation of the squats and relocations with affordable rents are their main claim. DAL and Jeudi Noir (JN) are the main representative organisations of this deprivation-based form of squatting. There is almost no extension here to develop public activities as is usual in social centres. When migrants, for example, are the main social group in these squats, their right to housing is supplemented with demands of the right to the city and to citizenship. Strong connections with mainstream mass media and political parties are common with these two organisations, which is a difference to similar groups in Italy and Spain, for example.

   > JN's activists are middle-class students (in architecture, urban planning, journalism, sociology), artists (musicians, writers, comedians) or precarious workers. The leaders of the collective are public officials or representative (City Council, Regional Assembly, European Parliament) and are usually members of political parties (mainly far-left wing or Green parties). Thus, they can use an impressive network of political actors and journalists who always come to support them when they open a squat.
   >
   > *(Aguilera 2018: 130)*

2. Survival squatting. Housing is the basic and unmet need for many marginalised people living under conditions of extreme precarity. Self-help initiatives for housing themselves drive the needy to resort to squatting. These squats are often short-lived and hidden. Sometimes they are also operated by organised traffickers who 'change the locks and sell illegitimate leases to families who sometimes ignore the trickery' (Aguilera 2018: 132). This parallels renting and subletting phenomena in slums: 'the poorest of the poor rent from the squatters' (Davis 2007: 43). In contrast to Aguilera, I interpret their practices more as means than ends because the squatters' main aspiration is to access a legal, affordable, and permanent house. They are pragmatic rather than abolitionist in regard to private property. If they live in communitarian squats, it is more out of necessity than by choice.

   > Without resources, their goal is mainly to find a roof for one or more nights within a larger trajectory of wandering between different solutions (street shelters, hotels, friends, tents provided by NGOs). They do not necessarily have an explicit anti-institutional attitude because they are quite disconnected from and abandoned by authorities and administrations.
   >
   > *(Aguilera 2018: 132)*

Types of Squatting **157**

3. Autonomous squatting. The radical politicisation of squatters may lead them to live apart (in squatted buildings as an alternative politics, communitarian lifestyles, and within countercultural networks) and to promote squatted social centres with an agenda of public activities not merely focused on arts and culture. The occupied buildings are considered as strongholds of their politics, so they usually take a strategic approach which, in this case, implies resistance and opposition to authorities more than cooperation and negotiations. Legalisation of these autonomous squats hardly goes far.

> If the autonomous squatting movement was very strong at the end of 1970s, it markedly declined due to the combined effects of repression and the rise of artists, who attracted more would-be squatters. The autonomous squatted social centres (SSCs) seldom occur in the centre of Paris. Nowadays they are all located outside Paris, in the eastern suburbs (Montreuil, Bagnolet, Fontenay-sous-Bois, Ivry). Their goal is to maintain a maximum distance from the state as well as from the institutional way of living in urban spaces. As a result, they are hostile to public authorities, considering them their major enemy.
>
> *(Aguilera 2018: 131)*

4. Substitution squatting. This category refers to squatted social centres (often with residential functions too) focused on arts and culture. Due to the shortage of affordable places for studios and exhibitions in the city centre, many artists occupy empty spaces. They 'substitute' the municipality in its duty to provide such cultural and community centres for the local residents. Whenever possible, most of these artists/squatters are willing to negotiate with the authorities with the aim of achieving legal agreements in order to remain in the building as long as possible. This implies, then, a strategic approach to squatting, although they are seldom connected to squatters' struggles and other social movements at large. Therefore, despite their strong attachment to the occupied building, their practices are also fully tactical in order to promote their professional careers. In Paris, this has occurred since the 1990s. For example, 59 Rivoli is a squat located in the core of the city centre, legalised after successful negotiations with the local government. However, the situation is less clear when squatted social centres enjoy local subsidies for some cultural events and artists find room for their own professional development but the squat is also highly politicised with many other public activities, and legalisation is not an urgent issue in their agenda (Rote Flora, in Hamburg, might serve as an illustration).

5. Recognition squatting. Aguilera applies this label to the squats where precarious and undocumented migrants obtain a temporary shelter but, above all, claim their regularisation as full citizens. This form of squatting is aligned with deprivation-based squatting for housing and can also entail the distinction between squatters and activists from a middle-class background (affiliated with non-governmental organisations [NGOs], trade

158 Types of Squatting

unions, and solidarity groups). It holds, then, a tactical character: The building is not their main priority, and squatting is not their main political struggle. Communal living and public activities around their main demands may lead them to open up social centres too. Some occupations of this kind may be performed, however, as an exclusive demonstrative protest, without much relation to the claim for shelter. In a similar fashion, although it is not mentioned by Aguilera, feminist squats operate under the same umbrella of recognition and the right to the city. Gender-oriented policies, services, and safe spaces are at the core of their agenda, so they often enter into negotiations with the authorities concerning these topics in addition to the legal status of the squat. In this case, it is more likely that these activists belong to the middle classes. Eskalera Karakola in Madrid illustrates this final category.

Interestingly, Aguilera's classification takes into account not only the squatters' attitudes to policies and authorities but also the reaction of the latter to squatters. This observation underlines the distinction between artistic and autonomous social centres, on the one hand, and between deprivation-based and self-help squats for housing, on the other. Otherwise, without incorporating this relational dimension, we would not identify crucial patterns within the main fields of squats for housing and squatted social centres. In the case of Paris, for example:

TABLE 4.4 Types of squats according to a political economy approach

	Resources and social class	*Political agenda*		*Attitudes towards policies*
		Tactical	*Strategic*	
Policy-oriented (Deprivation-based squatting for housing)	Activists: wealthy and middle-class Squatters: poor	Yes	No	Legalisation and provision of social housing
Survival (Self-help squatting for housing)	Squatters: poor	Yes	No	No interaction with policies/authorities
Autonomous (Alternative housing and social centres)	Activists/ Squatters: middle class	No	Yes	Radical opposition to negotiate and legalise
Substitution (Art squats/social centres)	Artists/ Squatters: middle class	Yes	Yes	Legalisation and provision of cultural-community centres
Recognition (Deprivation-based, alternative housing, and social centres)	Activist/ Squatters: poor and middle class	Yes	No	Demands of citizenship for immigrants and gender policies

Source: Author based on Aguilera (2018)

The officials from the housing and cultural departments who are in charge of squatting affairs clearly distinguish 'animators' (policy-oriented and substitution groups who create services) and 'troublemakers' (autonomous, survival and recognition squatters who criticise or ask for services). They tolerate and legalise the 'animators' who accept to negotiate, who are institution-friendly and officially organised through tangible structures like associations. They evict the 'troublemakers' who perpetuate a strong anti-institutional discourse and who self-organise in fluid and decentralised networks.

(Aguilera 2018: 137)

More fine-tuned internal differentiations have been attempted. Among the most politicised squats in Italy, for example, Mudu (2012) noted how internal leaderships, the type of public activities in which squatters were engaged, and the existence of waged labour within the squats added to the controversial issue of their relations with the authorities. As a consequence, post-autonomists groups (such as Disobbedienti) and anarchists grew significantly apart in their approaches to squatting.

The relationship between *Disobbedienti* and anarchists became increasingly distant over the 1990s ... with the latter accusing the former of spectacularism and leaderism ... Music is another medium through [which] fractures have arisen, with some Social Centers promoting and others rejecting hip-pop and ragamuffin groups over differing political and strategic considerations, especially in the content of the message and the relationship to the music industry ... In the anarchist Social Centers there is a preference for selling food and drinks at their cost, with no surcharge, and entry to concerts is free or covered by donation ... The dismantling of welfare states opened many opportunities for some Social Centers to cover social needs until then covered by state welfare, but this is viewed negatively by many anarchists because it undermines self-management by introducing self-exploitation. ... This contrasts with the view of the *Disobbedienti*, who have no compunction regarding having people working in Social Centers for a wage.

(Mudu 2012: 421–422, italics in original)

As Mudu observes in the above quotation, ideological differences are often accentuated by the context of economic and political conditions that force squatters to make decisions accordingly. The debates on waged labour and co-operative self-employment were especially urgent for many squatters when the rates of unemployment and precarious jobs rose, and public services became seriously eroded through privatisation and subcontracting by neoliberal policies. Housing unaffordability added to these economic crises, but this did not add significant cleavages among squatters since the use of squats

160 Types of Squatting

for residential purpose was a widely accepted resource, even in many social centres. The possible legalisation of squats and the issue of some squatters running for local elections (members of Leoncavallo in Milan and members of Disobeddienti in Rome and Venice, for example) fragmented movements that in some historical periods were more united.

In a similar vein, Piazza (2013: 91) went further and distinguished different branches of autonomism and networks across the country: '[T]he SCs' area is currently and continuously split into several groups and networks, very fluid and unstable' (Piazza 2013: 90). Dealing with negotiations and legalisations also became a heterogeneous reality even among members of the same network. Furthermore, Piazza examined different organisational structures and decision-making models in order to understand more subtle aspects of the diversity of squatted social centres.

Interactions between Squatters and Migrants

In this section I examine an alternative approach to the classification of squatting practices and movements by paying attention to a specific social group: immigrants and asylum seekers. My own research on the ways in which migrants participated in the squatting of abandoned buildings and interacted with other squatters in the City of Madrid led me to distinguish four major forms of interactions. I argue that deprivation-based squatting is not necessarily the prevailing type. Forms of 'empowerment' and 'engagement' were increasingly developed while 'autonomy' and 'solidarity' were continuously present. These variations occurred because of specific drivers within the cycles of movements' protests and contextual conditions which facilitated cooperation between squatters and migrants, although language barriers, discrimination in the housing market, and police harassment constrained them as well.

The so-called refugee crisis experienced in Europe since 2015 and the rise of far-right politics and anti-migrant movements since then has shaped the context for examining the involvement of migrants in squatting. However, there are significant precedents to take into account too. For example, from 2012 onwards, global mass media covered the occupations of a Berlin square and a nearby school by asylum seekers. While the protest camp in Oranienplatz hosted around 200 refugees and existed from October 2012 until April 2014, the renamed school was squatted.

> In December 2012, a group of refugees and activists occupied a school, which was vacant save for some offices on the ground floor, in Ohlauer Straße 12, Berlin, and named it Refugee Strike House. These refugees-squatters had been occupying the public square in Kreuzberg (Oranienplatz) since October 2012. One floor of the occupied school was converted into a woman-only refugee space called the International Women's Space.
>
> *(Colectivo Hinundzurück 2018: 19)*

Types of Squatting   161

The purpose of the occupation was [to get a shelter against] the very cold weather and we had families and sick people who needed to be in a warm place. So we organized the school as a place for sleeping, and everything concerning our political activities should take place at Oranienplatz ...

(Langa 2018: 8)

Both spaces served the same purpose: the defence of human rights for asylum seekers in terms of free movement, the right to work and education, access to emergency medical care, decent accommodation (instead of the isolated and inhumane conditions of the refugee camps), and opposition to deportations (see http://oplatz. net; azozomox 2014: 206). The remaining 40 squatters in the school announced in June 2014 that they would jump from the roof in the case of eviction.

Some 50 refugees on the roof and inside the building of the squatted Refugee Strike House (the former school Gerhardt-Hauptmann), resisted a siege and eviction attempt by police who had deployed daily some 500 officers for nine days. The situation finally ended with an agreement between the refugees and the district council of Kreuzberg-Friedrichshain.

(Colectivo Hinundzurück 2018: 19)

The heavy-handed siege by the police required roadblocks and a whole area to be cordoned off. Many local businesses and schools were forced to close. In parallel, solidarity activists camped near the police blockades and set up an information centre and a popular kitchen. In addition to debates and film screenings, they expressed their support for the refugees with many protest actions in various institutional settings—including those of the Green Party, which governed the district. Ironically, one Green Party politician, who had been a squatter for years, determined the eviction of the squatted school on the fifth day of the siege.

Hans Panhoff (The Greens), the councillor responsible for construction (who in 1980 himself had squatted a house in which he still lives in Cuvrystraße 25, Kreuzberg) signed the eviction order with the support of the Green mayor Monika Hermann, handing the matter to the police. ... In the meantime, the refugee squatters from the school were terrorized constantly by the police. From the surrounding roofs, the police, using flashlights, shined light all night and made noise in order to keep the occupants sleepless. They also insulted the refugees in a racist manner and sneered at them holding up handcuffs and bananas. All this time the press was still not allowed to enter the school, although the refugees demanded the press be let inside to give interviews.

(Colectivo Hinundzurück 2018: 24–25)

The final agreement granted squatters six-month residency permits, but the threat of deportation was still permanent for most of them. Afterwards, access to

162 Types of Squatting

the school was under the control of a private security firm; no visitors were allowed to enter. Other squatting and solidarity actions followed that year. However, Nazi and racist attacks proliferated as well. Buildings where the refugees lived in various German cities, for example, were set on fire. In January 2018, the remaining squatted floors of the school were evicted following the instructions of the local Green government.

Similar observations can be made about migrants and squatters in other European countries. Solidarity is the prevailing form of interaction—as has happened often in Amsterdam, for instance. In 2006, an office building located on a bridge over a highway on the periphery of Amsterdam was squatted by native activists (mostly Dutch-born people) and eventually handed over to the local Moroccan community, which had for years demanded a place to pray. Although the Kraakmoskee (squat-mosque) was evicted in 2010, 'squatting had provided them [migrants] with a place and with visibility. The Kraakmoskee project also gave the squatters the opportunity to step out of their own neighbourhoods and explore the outer ring area of the city' (Moore 2015: 206). As is well documented elsewhere, immigrants in the Netherlands may squat alone (Kadir 2014: 21, 32) or join squats where other natives live (Aoussar 2010).

The 'We Are Here' movement started occupying spaces in 2012 by first settling in the garden of a protestant church in Amsterdam. This was followed by the occupation of buildings such as empty offices, state-owned properties, and former churches, hospitals, and schools (Dadusc 2017: 276). Housing needs were usually met in simultaneity with socio-cultural and political activities such as debates, music events, educational projects, legal assistance, and medical aid.

> Living in squatted buildings has been used by undocumented migrants as a tool of protest and to gain visibility, but also to open collective spaces where it becomes possible to organize their struggles in a systematic manner.
>
> *(Dadusc 2017: 275)*

However, the narrative of social inclusion and diversity within the squatting scene has been overshadowed by the dominant stereotype of 'Dutch squatters—young, white, politically articulate, militant and skilled activists who heroically battle the police to defend their squats' (Kadir 2014: 22). Mass media, academic accounts, and the native squatters themselves tend to reproduce that myth and neglect the contributions of migrants to the production of urban space. In addition, a rising xenophobic discourse has been widespread over Dutch society as well as neighbouring countries in the last decades. This entails discrimination against foreigners, including those from Southern and Eastern European countries such as Spain and Poland, respectively, who are portrayed not only as abusers of the welfare state but also as those 'who exploit a Dutch protest tactic and who lack the political ideals of squatters "during the movement's height in the 1980s"' (Kadir 2016: 49).

Another example comes from Greece. Long lasting squats such as Villa Amalias (1989–2012), located in urban areas with large migrant populations, served to keep fascist attacks away (Souzas 2018: 238). The most significant case of a refugee squats after the 2015 'long summer of migration' was City Plaza, a seven-floor former hotel occupied in April 2016. Since then, more than 2,200 refugees from 13 countries have lived there, and about 350 were currently residing there in 2018 (Refugee 2018: 352). Compared to other government or NGO-run detention camps, squatters-migrants at City Plaza felt much more freedom, dignity, and mutual support. Activists from many parts of the world joined the squat in order to provide healthcare, education, and relocation services to the refugees.

> [It was] an example of self-organisation in the common struggles of refugees and locals and their daily life. We believe that it is through fighting together for practical demands in common struggles, rather than through general humanitarian declarations, that societal configurations and authoritarian and neoliberal policies can change, the far-right can be deterred, and a common front against racism and austerity can be constituted.
>
> *(Refugee 2018: 353)*

Many migrants face exclusion, socio-spatial segregation, marginalisation, detentions, attacks by racist and xenophobic groups, and murders. When they squat or become allied with left-libertarian squatters, migrants become 'agents of resistance and emancipation … [not] poor and helpless, victims of persecution and pogrom, always at the mercy of philanthropy and pity' (Makrygianni 2017: 250, 254). Other experiences of migrant squats in Athens were, for example, the former Court of Appeal, squatted in 2003 and housing around 500 people (mostly men) from 2006–9. This squat was labelled a 'hygienic bomb' by the state and the media due to the lack of water and electricity, which prompted their eviction with the help of the fascist political party Golden Dawn (Makrygianni 2017: 252). Another group of 400 highly mobile migrants dwelled in The Refugees (Ta Profigika) in 2015, although the complex of buildings was first occupied in 2003.

> For the last three years two assemblies have been running, one of the inhabitants and one of inhabitants and people in solidarity, while they have organized collective kitchens, a kindergarten and a barbershop. Some of the squatters also take part in [a] wider Athenian anti-fascist network. … [The] Prosfigika space keeps developing through its contradictions and antagonisms.
>
> *(Makrygianni 2017: 253)*

Beyond Deprivation

When migrant people squat, they tend to do it out of necessity. Their squats are considered more 'social' than 'political' (that is to say, in political terms, more reformist than radical) in a very quick and superficial approach.

164 Types of Squatting

This fits what has been designated as 'deprivation-based squatting', characterised by the following features:

> This configuration involves poor, working-class people who are suffering severe housing deprivation. ... It is tightly organised ... [There is] an organisational pattern that makes a clear distinction between activists and squatters. The activists open up buildings for the squatters and support them ... [It] is susceptible to co-optation, i.e. transformation into a form that is useful to state officials.
>
> *(Pruijt 2013: 22–24)*

Thus, deprivation-based squatting is more frequently an illegal means to enter into legal modes of accommodation (Aguilera 2013: 217) rather than a countercultural lifestyle or a key protest repertoire in a broader anti-capitalist movement. DAL in France as well as different groups in Italy represent perfectly this trend of helping the homeless, who are mostly migrants, by adopting a sharp organisational division of work and keeping a favourable attitude towards negotiation with the authorities for a formal housing solution (Aguilera 2013: 220–222, Mudu 2014: 147–156). In spite of this evidence, not much attention has been paid to other forms of involvement in squatting by migrants.

Before the recent publication of a collection of works on the relationship between squatting and migration (Mudu & Chattopadhyay 2017), the most ambitious attempt in this regard (Manjikian 2013) framed both groups as subjects to an increasing rhetoric of securitisation at the state level all over Europe. However, the 'politics of emergency and exceptionality' made up of higher legal and police pressures does not imply necessarily similar or joint reactions by migrants and squatters. As for the research made on the various forms of squatting (Cattaneo & Martínez 2014, Steen et al. 2014), it did not usually regard migrants as autonomous subjects that can resemble the radical politics and alternative cultures put forward by most squatters.

Although squatting for housing purposes is overwhelmingly portrayed as a non-political practice, I contend that many squatters and migrants are aware of their broader political and spatial role in challenging some taken-for-granted assumptions in capitalist societies. That is to say, the rigid or absolute right to private property and the arbitrariness of setting and managing the state boundaries are continuously questioned by both squatters and migrants. Moreover, the unequal distribution of property and the unequal access to national citizenship are in direct conflict with the right to decent and affordable housing, on the one hand, and the right to be granted a decent migrant or asylum status, on the other. Whenever this underlying conflict comes to the surface in public urban life, squatting and migration become key components of current politics. No matter how secretly the actions of squatting and migration are performed, their actors all participate in a situated political struggle about agenda, policies, representation, governance, etc. Whether to remain silent, hidden, clandestine, or the

Types of Squatting **165**

opposite corresponds either to tactical decisions or to their social involvement within explicitly political scenes. Just as a convention then, 'social' squatting labels the cases where political ideology is loose or not at the foreground because the urgent economic needs are emphasised above all, while 'political' squatting refers to the dense networks of activists where a political discourse contributes to their identity and cohesion. However, empirical nuances may portray a less neat distinction.

The practice of squatting helps to shape the city in a contentious manner by opening up anomalous (non-commercial and non-regulated) residential and coun-tercultural spaces. The participation of squatters and migrants in city life is usually performed through challenges to dominant inequalities. However, it would be mis-leading to equate their structural living conditions. In particular, many squatters and most of the migrants (especially the undocumented ones) have experienced similar situations of badly paid jobs (precariousness), social exclusion, police bru-tality, fascist attacks, spatial displacement, marginalisation, and stigmatisation, although not many squatters are so frequently harassed by the police because of their ethnic appearance or arrested because of the expiration of a residence permit. Native squatters, compared with most migrants, enjoy wider, safer, wealthier, and denser social networks made of friends, relatives, job acquaintances, political com-rades, etc. Furthermore, 'immigrants and people of colour have always been a minority portion of the squatter community' (azozomox 2014: 206).

Among migrants there are internal and striking differences too. Some may be rich or may hold passports from countries dominant worldwide so that the squatting scene is not an appealing one for them. Migrants who do not hold legal documents to stay in a particular country may face additional risks when they attend squats under the threat of eviction or police surveillance. Moreover, on some occasions, migrants approach squatting not only as a way to satisfy their need for housing and a social life, but also as a political tool to claim their citi-zenship rights, especially if they enjoy the support of political squatters and other native activists. This social context of overlapping and different living conditions constrains any given interaction between native squatters and migrants.

When the squatting scene is politicised and nurtured by leftist, autonomist, and anarchist perspectives, solidarity with those in need and oppressed, which includes many migrants, is a founding principle. From the 1960s onwards, the most outspoken political squatters in Europe had to face the historical circum-stances of the aftermath of the Second World War as well as the crisis of welfare policies in the following decades. This led, first of all, to defensive struggles against fascism in all its dimensions—not only neo-fascist groups and political parties but also their ideological roots. Anti-fascism, then, became one of the main pillars of identity for those squatters whose politics pointed beyond the walls of the occupied spaces. Accordingly, the opposition to racism and xeno-phobia was considered a logical consequence of that stance since fascist politics is based on ethnic supremacy, conservative nationalism, hate towards those seen as inferior (not only ethnic minorities and foreigners, but often homosexuals,

166 Types of Squatting

disabled and homeless people, punks and hippies, communists, and even women), and a pervasive violence. The threat of fascism and racism surrounding the squats provoked squatting activists to delegitimate these imaginaries and take defensive actions to halt their proponents. As an output of this attitude, rich anti-fascist and anti-racist iconography, information flows, and specific activities (workshops, sit-ins, border camps, etc.) have been produced by squatters and, sometimes, migrants involved in squats too (Moore & Smart 2015, Mudu & Chattopadhyay 2017). These affinities ease the practice of solidarity between native squatters and migrants but their interactions may also be subject to limitations, disruptions, and non-linear evolutions.

Autonomous Agency: When Migrants Squat

Squatting in Madrid began as a public action in the years of transition to liberal democracy, following Franco's death in 1975, although the first squat sounding similar to other autonomous spaces in Europe is dated to 1985. In 1992, there was a notorious incident which established the association between squatting (in abandoned buildings, not in slums) and migration. A black Dominican woman named Lucrecia Pérez was murdered while having dinner collectively in a squatted and almost ruined building—a former discotheque. She was 33 years old and had a daughter. She had neither residence nor work permits. Another Dominican man was shot in the same raid. According to the judicial sentence, the protagonists were four men, three minors, and one policeman aged 25. They were all known in Madrid for associating with fascist gangs and far-right football hooligans, and they also had a record of previous violent assaults. The court sentence stressed hate, xenophobia, and racism as motivations for the shootings (Calvo Buezas 1993). The building was located in an upper-class neighbourhood of the metropolitan area of Madrid (Aravaca). There was neither electricity nor water supplies in the occupied premises, which contributed an image of marginality and decay associated with squatted places. In 1993, as an attempt to question those stereotypes, a group of autonomist students occupied a building on the campus of the University Complutense of Madrid and named it 'Lucrecia Pérez' (Caravantes et al. 1995: 32).

International incoming flows of migration rose in Spain from the mid-1990s onwards at higher rates than ever before (Martín-Pérez & Moreno-Fuentes 2012). At its peak in 2005, undocumented and non-authorised migrants amounted to 1.2 million (Clandestino Project 2009), and at the end of 2010, the total number of foreign-born people settled in Spain had reached 6.7 million. In relative terms, the number of foreigners in Spain shifted from less than 2% of the population in the 1990s to 12% at the end of the 2000s. Notwithstanding this, in some neighbourhoods (such as those in the city centre of Madrid, where squatting was very popular) the concentration of migrants meant rates above 20–27% in the Centro district and 22% in Tetuán, for example, in 2011 (Schmidt 2012: 2). In 2011, the four main countries of origin for immigrants in Spain were Morocco, Romania, Ecuador, and Colombia.

Types of Squatting   **167**

The above indicates a regular increase of migrants in Spanish cities until the late 2000s—when the global financial crisis interrupted the flow of incoming migrants. Thus, it could be expected that migrants participated in squats at a similar rate. Given the absence of accurate calculations, I estimate that the presence of migrants in political squats slightly augmented over the years, although their percentage was in general lower than the local average. For example, according to my regular observations of political squats in Madrid since 2007, migrants rarely represented more than approximately 10% of the members or visitors. In the 1980s and early 1990s there were even fewer migrants attending squatted social centres. Moreover, not all the foreign nationalities were equally represented. Latin American immigrants were the first to arrive in Spain and faced an easier adaptation process given their mastery of the Spanish language. However, the racist or xenophobic attitudes of many homeowners determined their exclusion from the rental market once their Latin American accent was noticed. On the other hand, the interest in the revolutions and political struggles of Latin America meant that many squats organised events and invited people from that region. Therefore, Latin American migrants were the first to be seen in political squats. In any case, when migrants squatted buildings on their own, autonomously, they tended to do it away from the political squatting scene, as the Dominicans did in Aravaca, for example. This pattern is also evident in other cases widely covered by the mass media.

Outside of Madrid, for example, between 2002 and 2004, around a thousand people (most of them undocumented migrants from Africa and Eastern Europe) occupied the abandoned military barracks, known as Cuarteles de San Andreu, in a working-class neighbourhood of Barcelona. Their living conditions were very harsh: without water, electricity, toilets, and waste management. After the police evicted the occupiers, around a hundred residents were rehoused by municipal agencies and the Red Cross. The occupation showed the autonomous initiative of homeless poor people to get shelter but they were not able to implement any collective self-organisation of the place. Different NGOs, local associations, neighbours, and political squatters from the area helped them occasionally and rallied to stop the clearance of the barracks (Blanchar 2004, Canal Solidario 2003).

In 2008, the Palacete Okupado in the working-class district of Carabanchel (Madrid) popped up in the local news. One day after it was reported, the police arrested 12 undocumented migrants out of the 20 who lived in the building, although there was no official eviction. Most of them came from Senegal and arrived in the Canary Islands on a fragile boat. After their detention in the squatted building, they were subject to a deportation order. The multi-storey house had been squatted for more than one and a half years. One of the squatters was a Spanish citizen who claimed to have signed a rental contract, which he found out later to be a scam. In contrast with the previous case, this household was collectively run and the neighbours got along well with the migrant squatters (Herráiz 2008). A formal association Coordinadora de Inmigrantes or COIN (Immigrants' Coordination) supported them with legal advice and opportunities for professional qualifications.

168 Types of Squatting

In another area called Majadahonda, an upper-class municipality in the metropolitan region of Madrid, a luxury development that did not meet planning regulations remained empty from 2000 onwards, although the ground floors were occasionally used by homeless people, drug addicts, and youngsters. Later on, an estimated hundred Latin American migrants grouped as families (and mainly coming from Ecuador, Bolivia, and Dominican Republic) occupied all the apartments of the building. The replacement of the previous transitory occupants granted the new ones some support by neighbours. The squat was mentioned in the news in 2010 and still remained occupied in 2014 thanks to the absence of any judicial lawsuit against the squatters (Medrano 2010, Rivera 2014). Journalists used the term '*okupas*' (squatters) to name these migrants, although no direct connection with political squatters was known. In addition, the prior media-created image of filth, scuffles, male dominance, lack of self-organisation, and rejection by the neighbours shifted to a more positive one in which diverse residents, grouped in families, and cohesively organised, enjoyed respect in their neighbourhood in spite of their anomalous form of housing tenure.

Squatters, Migrants, and the Global Justice Movement

Contacts between migrants and native political squatters increased in the 2000s. The latter approached the former by launching solidarity actions, fundraising, demonstrations, etc. The first landmark of this interaction was a campaign in 2001 when hundreds of undocumented migrants strived for their legal right to remain in Spain by resorting to lock-ins or self-confinement in different *encierros* (buildings) in 14 Spanish cities (Nodo50 2001). In the case of Barcelona, around 800 migrants (mainly of African, Asian, and East European nationality) occupied 48 churches. Although squatters were not the only activists who joined the campaign, the demonstrations and solidarity actions created a strong precedent for further cooperation. The campaign coincided with the demonstrations of the global justice movement against wars, neoliberal policies, and global capitalism, but also with a slight decline in the squatters' movement after the enforcement of the 1995 Penal Code in which squatting had become a crime. In Madrid, squatters from El Laboratorio 2 and from Seco were involved in one of the encierros, although the dominant role in the negotiations with the state authorities was played by labour unions and a formal non-governmental organisation (SOS Racismo).

This wave of solidarity and closer ties is illustrated by a case from September 2002. One building occupied by migrants in Madrid's Murcia Street was set on fire. Ten residents were evicted after the police arrived. Protesters who gathered in solidarity with the migrant squatters (COIN and political squatters from La Biblio and El Laboratorio 3) assumed the fire was intentionally caused by racist individuals. La Biblio was a long-lasting grassroots library project that operated in different squatted buildings where they also taught the Spanish language to migrants as a way 'to fight against the laws on migration and the social exclusion of migrants' (La Biblio 2002). After the frustrating experience of several evictions, the collective decided to rent a place in Lavapiés where they have continued with their usual activities to the present.

The alter-globalisation trend gave birth to the ODS (Office of Social Rights) in the mid-2000s (Arribas 2012, Toret et al. 2008). At least ten organisations became initial members of this network of activists in different Spanish cities and four of them were rooted in Madrid. The aims of the ODS went beyond solidarity with migrants because they had the intention of investigating, devising shared strategies, and acting on the circumstances of 'precarious living' in the productive, reproductive, social, and political spheres—all of them affecting both migrants and increasing portions of the native working- and middle-class population. This entailed alternatives to traditional and bureaucratic welfare policies based on assistance, subsidies, hierarchy of rights, and state discipline. In a similar vein, these activists opposed neoliberal policies because they drag individuals into a flexible and unsafe job market, manage state borders at the convenience of capitalist interests, and criminalise political dissent. ODS then called for the defence of social rights for all and the self-organisation of those disempowered through precarious living.

However, it has been admitted that their daily practice focused more on the concrete needs of migrants who approached their offices regarding legal documents that allow them to work and reside, the provision of attorneys and solicitors to deal with their arrest and threats of deportation, their economic subsistence based on the informal selling of goods on the streets, and their knowledge of the Spanish language (Arribas 2012, López et al. 2008). Some ODS groups were also criticised for reproducing, unintentionally or without sufficient resources to prevent it, a hierarchical and professional mode of assistance to migrants by white, European, middle-class, highly-educated activists. They would have also failed to engage all kinds of precarious natives and migrants because of their focus on the most urgent problems faced by some of the foreigners (Arribas 2012: 222–224).

One of the achievements of the ODS was to build bridges between the squatting scene and other autonomous but not necessarily squatted social centres where some ODS groups were located (La Piluka, Prosperidad, and Carabanchel, in Madrid). These ties challenged the dominant squatting identity where migration and precarity did not represent a central aspect of the political discourse of squatters. The ODS network called to 'exit the ghetto', they questioned the squatters' radical imagery of resistance without any compromise or negotiation with the local authorities, they named the purely theoretical antifascism and anti-racism as symbolic without a consistent practice, and challenged the acceptance of nomadism as a given fate. In Madrid, two of the squatted social centres where work with migrants was a key area of activism, Seco and Eskalera Karakola (in the latter case, as a feminist group they were engaged with migrant women earning their living as domestic workers and prostitutes: Precarias 2004), succeeded in their claims for legalisation. Therefore, migrants and their specific living conditions became more visible and well recognised among the squatting scene of Madrid, mainly due to the actions of the ODS. Two examples of this influence in the next generation of squats were the 'Bangla Thursdays' in Casablanca (where a group of Bangladesh migrants made a small income by preparing and selling dinner, in addition to showcasing films and music from their cultural background) and the multiple activities in La Enredadera de Tetuán such as hairdressing, 'Womens' Saturdays', Spanish language classes, computing workshops, the 'free shop', etc. in which Latin American and African migrants took part frequently (see Image 4.4).

In the declining years of the alter-globalisation cycle of struggles, the expressions of solidarity continued. For instance, political squatters launched the Mundialito Antirracista (Anti-racist Little World Cup) in 2006 and the Campaña contra el Racismo (Campaign Against Racism) in 2007. The former was a yearly event in which activists from all over the metropolitan region of Madrid shared a day of 'non-competitive sports competitions' (basketball, football, running, etc.). The Mundialito was organised by La Eskuela Taller (based in Alcorcón, a working-class municipality next to the City of Madrid). Their aim was to stop the growing racism around sports since they observed that fascist groups tried to book out public sport facilities in order to prevent migrants from using them. They also expressed their intention to unite 'natives and foreigners, anarchists, communists, autonomists, postmodernists and separatists' (Mundialito 2011). The Mundialito was celebrated for nine years in spite of the obstacles erected by the local authorities. In a similar vein, the Campaign Against Racism

IMAGE 4.4 Squat La Enredadera, Madrid, 2017
Source: Author

Types of Squatting **171**

gave priority to cultural activities and collective meals over more militant and overt political actions (Rivero 2007).

In this period, I also noted a more frequent presence of Latin American migrants engaged in political squats—not only in social centres but also, a few years later, in residential communes such as La Barraka or Cambalache. It is worth mentioning two examples of how this engagement occurred: (1) the tradition of international solidarity, which connected autonomist movements with, for instance, the Zapatista uprising was manifested in the organisation of groups such as the Red de Apoyo Zapatista de Madrid (RAZ), whose members usually lived in collective squats (La Juli) and participated in squatted social centres in order to raise funds and spread information about politics in Mexico (at Malaya, La Mácula, La Enredadera, etc.). At the same time, they served to incorporate migrants from Latin American into the autonomist life of Madrid. (2) Exceptionally, some Spanish squatters decided to marry undocumented migrants they knew well after years of mutual cooperation (within the ODS at the Patio Maravillas, for example) in order to halt the threats of deportation that the latter experienced.

In 2009, squatters and other activists formed the Brigadas Vecinales de Observación de Derechos Humanos or BVODH (Local Citizens Watching [Migrants'] Human Rights, similar to the US group Cop Watch) and made their public presentation in La Mácula. By wearing reflective vests and walking around in groups of more than ten, they surveyed, documented, and denounced the police as they implemented identity controls in the streets, at subway exits, the front door of associations, and in queues for administrative appointments. These controls mainly addressed poor, non-regular, and non-white foreigners. Although police inspections are considered illegal if uniquely based on ethnic criteria, the police raids were systematically orchestrated. In this new form of solidarity, activists collected data about the stop-controls, informed migrants about their rights and, if possible, prevented their arrest. In parallel to the claims made by other formal NGOs such as Amnesty International and SOS Racismo, the BVODH were able to gain media coverage of the police's violation of migrants' human rights. They also released three reports at one-year intervals with the results of their activity and analysis (BVODH 2014).

Migrants' Empowerment through the 15M Movement

After the huge mobilisation that took place on 15 May 2011 proved a turning point, the political context changed for both migrants and squatters. On the one hand, in 2012 the conservative central government excluded thousands of migrants (and also natives away from Spain for more than 90 days) from the free services of the public health system (this measure was partially reversed in 2018 by the social democratic government). This had a large impact on all the estimated half-million undocumented migrants at that time (BVODH 2014: 16) and provoked numerous actions of solidarity and civil disobedience (YoSí 2015).

172 Types of Squatting

On the other hand, since 2013, the Campaña Estatal para el Cierre de los CIEs (Campaign Demanding the Closure of the Detention Centres for Migrants) intensified the criticisms of abuses, deaths, privatisation, absence of public scrutiny, and the illegitimacy of the detention-and-deportation centres. Many organisations were involved in this long-lasting campaign. After 2011, however, the number of participant groups, demonstrations, individual case follow-ups, and investigative reports made and spread by different grass-roots collectives increased significantly. Squats in Madrid such as Patio Maravillas (and, in particular, the special committee of Ferrocarril Clandestino) actively took part in the campaign. Even the annual traditional New Year's Eve anarchist march to jail was replaced by a march to the CIE, located in the area of Aluche, and was supported by various political squats (La Gatonera 2013 and https://cerremosloscies.wordpress.com/).

A third key circumstance that occurred after 2011was the soaring number of both foreclosures of homes with owners unable to pay their mortgages and evictions of tenants unable to pay the rents, combined with the absence of any emergency solution provided by the disappearing public housing system. Migrants were among the ones most affected by those events because of their entry into the housing market at the peak of the speculative construction bubble. The protests organised by the PAH since 2009 were ongoing but, above all, they gained wider support and influence after May 2011. In Madrid, an association of migrants from Ecuador was the first to join the PAH. Members of neighbourhood associations as well as lawyers, economists, and psychologists also became regular participants in the PAH. With a similar methodology of civil disobedience at the time of the evictions and the will to negotiate feasible solutions in each case with the banks or local authorities, other 'housing groups' born out of the 15M popular assemblies extended this wave of protest. Some of these groups also joined the PAH and some of their members were former or present political squatters (in PAH-Centro, at least according to my observations and interviews).

In 2011, the PAH launched the campaign Obra Social, which consisted of the occupation of abandoned buildings, especially those owned by banks and real-estate developers. Instead of calling them 'squats' they preferred to use the adjectives 'recuperated' and 'liberated' to refer to the buildings. Therefore, they tried to get rid of the stereotypes associated with the squatting movement like the strong emphasis on a radical 'left-libertarian' political ideology and the manifold goals of the squatted social centres. The PAH occupations focused on the housing needs of evicted families, and at the same time they demanded 'affordable rents' from the owners of the buildings and 'emergency housing' alternatives from the state authorities. Pre-15M squatters also attended eviction resistance callouts and supported the new 'liberations' of buildings (Abellán 2015, De Andrés et al. 2015, Martínez & García 2018).

This political context became a tipping point that shook the whole squatting movement as we knew it. Negotiations and mass media coverage became more

Types of Squatting **173**

accepted by even the most militant activists. Squatting for housing became more visible, politicised, and collectively supported. Poor families with children, homeless people, and immigrants became more engaged in the organisation of protest actions and the self-management of occupied buildings. This empowered them to overcome their difficulties by resorting to squatting. The old imagery of squatting did not vanish at all (not even in some of the new occupations) and many old-school squats remained quite active. Most of them, however, supported this emergent housing movement and, above all, their squatting initiatives. In many of the occupations, branded as part of the Obra Social or taking a similar political perspective (Sebastián Elcano, La Cava Encendida, La Manuela, Las Leonas, Corrala La Charca, Calle Cadete 7, Calle Argente, Calle Callejo, La Dignidad de Móstoles, etc.), there were many Latin American migrants involved, although without any explicit distinction pointing to that identity (just as an indication, see the American accent of activists in the videos of the PAH Vallekas 2014, Cadete 7 2014). One of the squatted blocks (Sierra de Llerena, in the district of Vallecas), in which many of the residents are of African origin, remained out of the public eye for two years. Afterwards, they went public and associated themselves with the Obra Social of the PAH (Vargas 2014). This move was motivated by an eviction statement issued by the owners of the building.

The 15M movement also stimulated other forms of activism in the field of migration, and these were narrowly connected to the squatted social centres in use or promoted by the 15M popular assemblies in the different neighbourhoods. In particular, in Lavapiés, a 'group on migration' called Migrapiés was created early on. Their work focused on criticising police raids, the provision of legal assistance to migrants, and support for them when they needed to use the public health system. They also launched a co-operative for providing meals that operated in squatted social centres such as Casablanca and La Quimera before renting their own self-managed social centre (Mbolo Moy Dole) and extending their projects to organic agriculture, cleaning and moving services, painting, catering, and alternative tourism (Diso Press 2014). Migrants, mainly of African (sub-Saharan) origin, worked in an egalitarian and consensual manner with Spanish indigenous activists, and empowerment through mutual aid and support was the main approach instead of just providing help to low skilled and resourceless migrants (Méndez 2012).

Interactions and Contexts

The above analysis has revealed four specific configurations in the ways that squatters and migrants relate to each other (see Table 4.5):

1. *Autonomy*. When immigrants squat alone without the initial help of native political squatters, although some cooperation may occur later on.
2. *Solidarity*. Either migrants or political squatters launch protest campaigns, actions, or events in which the issues of migration, citizen rights, police

TABLE 4.5 Four modes of interactions between migrants and non-migrant activists in the squatting of buildings in Madrid (1990s–2015)

	Autonomy	Solidarity	Engagement	Empowerment
Nature of the interaction	Migrants squat alone without the initial help of native political squatters, although some cooperation may occur later on.	Either migrants or political squatters launch protest campaigns, actions, or events, and both groups cooperate with each other.	Migrants participate in the activities and the self-management of political squats, usually initiated and run by natives.	Political squatters help migrants to squat. They both may occasionally cohabit the occupied building.
Frequency within political cycles	Continuous but only noticeable from time to time because most cases remained stealth or with a low profile of visibility.	Continuous but dependent on the duration of cases. They can also work with other political mobilisations.	Increasingly occurred along with the rising numbers of migrants in Spain (since 2000s), but also due to the influence of ODS and the alter-global movement.	Mainly after the global financial crisis (2008) and the protests ignited by the 15M/Indignados movement (2011) and the struggle against foreclosures by the PAH.
Type of squat	Residential units or blocks, usually hidden—in reverse proportion to the number of dwellers.	Residential buildings overtly occupied and social centres open to the public.	Social centres although migrants tend to be specialised in some activities or spaces within them.	Residential units or blocks mostly, but their visibility depends on tactical decisions.
Political implications	Migrants learn how to provide housing by occupying empty properties as an alternative to the exclusion they face in the housing and job markets on top of the lack of social housing for them. Squatting actions contribute to opening up public deliberation on housing and migration policies.	Consistent practices with anti-fascist ideology. Migration, citizen rights, police controls, etc. are the main claims at play. Politicisation of both public (streets, social centres) and private (housing) spaces where migrants suffer discrimination.	Migrants learn from native activists how to manage squatted Social centres while political squatters learn from migrants about their concerns (in the global scale of capitalism) and how to promote them inside and outside the squats. More horizontal cooperation between them.	All forms of squatting enjoyed a higher social recognition and legitimation, despite remaining illegal. Migrants politically active and visible along with middle and working classes subject to foreclosures, precariousness, and impoverishment. Strong networks of mutual aid facilitate more frequent and better organised occupations by migrants.

Urban effects	Effective occupation of empty apartments and buildings in areas with high vacancy rates, real estate speculation, abandoned barracks, or failures in the completion of developments. Increased ethnic diversity in neighbourhoods.	Occupied residential buildings become symbols, communicative hubs, and meeting places for migrant struggles. Squatted social centres organise campaigns, talks, and fundraising on top of gathering local native residents, migrants, activists, and sympathisers from various metropolitan areas.	Migration issues and migrants themselves become active and usual participants in squatted social centres. Additionally, their local image as neighbours is enhanced with their political involvement in those social centres and other struggles in the same urban area.	Squatting becomes more popular and widely practiced all over the city. Visible squats as local landmarks to provide assistance to forthcoming squats and various housing alternatives. Squats as knots of a broader urban movements—less isolated than before. Less stigmatisation of households and individuals who squat—and higher pressure on municipal authorities to negotiate with squatters.
Limitations	Very limited cooperation between migrants and native activists. NGOs more involved in migrant actions than political squatters. Risks of isolation and marginalisation of migrants.	Squatting, housing vacancy and urban speculation policies, or urban speculation are not at the core of the interactions and struggles—migrants' problems take the lead. Tendency for hierarchical forms of organisation.	Owing to the harsher conditions of living as migrants, they may use squats in a more instrumental and personal manner to just get assistance. Language and cultural barriers hinder deep and reciprocal interactions.	Difficult cohabitation of different ethnic groups in the same houses and buildings. The housing question takes priority over the establishment of social centres.

Source: Author

176 Types of Squatting

controls, etc. are the main claims at play. Both groups cooperate with each other and the squatted spaces are used to develop these ties.

3. *Engagement.* Migrants participate in the activities and the self-management of political squats, usually initiated and run by natives, with different degrees of involvement and in different numbers in each case.

4. *Empowerment.* When political squatters help migrants to squat and they both may occasionally cohabit in the occupied building.

Obviously, these forms of interaction may overlap. The striking observation is that, beyond the expressions of ideological solidarity or the tendency towards hidden deprivation-based forms of squatting, different forms of interaction have prevailed in different historical periods. In particular, 'engagement' has increasingly occurred along with the rising numbers of migrants in Spain. Furthermore, the subordinated integration of large numbers of migrants has also boosted highly-segregated labour and housing markets. Against this backdrop, the influence of some initiatives, such as the ODS facilitated, the 'engagement' of migrants in squatting. The forms of 'empowerment' were more fully developed due to the rise of the 15M movement during the economic recession of the 2010s, which hit immigrants and many other precarious social groups especially hard. 'Autonomy' and 'solidarity' modes remained constant features, but their knowledge, public visibility, and political support grew up in parallel with the increased social recognition and legitimation of squatting, at least until the 15M movement experienced a notable decline around mid-2014.

An additional implication is that the political squatting networks remained relatively consistent with their left-libertarian discourse of solidarity in order to add the migrants' struggles into the range of their concerns. However, it is worth noting that the process of mutual cooperation was slow over the first decade and a half (1985–2000) and some structural limitations are still at play, such as the hierarchical relations that occur when migrants just ask for help from native political activists and no autonomous organisation emerges out of their interaction (a complaint which is usually expressed by PAH members as much as it was by ODS activists before). In addition, the language barriers that necessitate exhausting exercises of translation and tend to disengage migrants from struggles where natives are dominant (this is why, as an exception, Latin American immigrants are more prone to participate in squats), can occasionally damage the cooperation.

The various types of interactions between migrants and squatters and their change are due to some specific contextual circumstances—in particular, the rise of the global justice movement and the triggering experience of the ODS, on the one hand, and the 15M movement and the new housing mobilisation, which were born after the global financial crisis, on the other. The relevance of these social and political contexts is nuanced with some other political and economic dimensions. The rise of the Madrid metropolis as a global city during the late 1990s, the mobilisations called by the global justice movement, and the new waves of internationalism, such as Zapatismo in Mexico, gave birth to new modes of questioning the dominant border policies for people (while not for capital) and the devastation created in poor countries by capitalist modes of production, consumption, debt, exploitation of natural resources, etc. In addition, the restrictions set by the European governments in the last decades halted the requests of asylum seekers, reinforced the military control of borders, legalised detention camps where numerous illegal practices and human rights violations are reported, and implemented deportation flights of undocumented migrants. These policies have engendered more risky forms of migrant mobility and deadly tragedies over the last few decades. Paradoxically, they were combined with discourses of 'integration' and 'multiculturality' as well as privatisations and cuts in public services (Avila & Malo 2010), including those services that specifically address the migrant population.

Therefore, the incorporation of critical debates around these issues during the early 2000s in the political squatting scenes paved the way for more intense and practical forms of interaction with migrants. Accordingly, starting from an initially poor interaction and given the prevailing image of marginality over the autonomous migrants' squats, the political squatting scene in Madrid evolved into deeper concerns about migration issues, its involvement in migrants' struggles, and tighter cooperation in the practice of squatting. After the global financial crisis in 2008 and the 15M movement in 2011, the occupation of houses by migrants, political squatters, and other activists boosted and challenged the criminalisation processes which were generally applied to squatting. This, at least in Madrid and other Spanish cities, obtained more favourable media coverage and produced a shift in the tactics of negotiation. As a consequence, the politicisation of the blocks occupied for housing purposes resulted in increased engagement and empowerment of the migrants involved in squatting.

Squatting in Paris: Internal Divisions and Local Regulation

March 2013 was my second visit to Paris dedicated to understanding the squatters' movement in the city. Curiously, the term 'squat' is an Anglicism frequently used in France. Three years ago, together with Thomas Aguilera, I visited some buildings, although by that time I could not talk with many local activists. In 2013, Aguilera and other members of SqEK (Margot, Heidiman, and Jacqueline) organised a number of visits, thanks to which we held very enlightening debates and talks with some of the local squatters.

The legal context of squatting in France was described by several activists in the following way:

During the first 48 hours, a squatted building can immediately be evicted by the police as soon as they have knowledge of the fact—this occurs.

After that time, the squatters (having demonstrated that they have resided at least for two days by means of some type of supply bill or, even, some home delivery) must prove before the police (even calling them with that purpose) that the building meets the minimum conditions of dwelling (light, water, no threats of ruin, etc.).

From then on, it is the owners of the building who must proceed to denounce the squatters in judicial instances if they want to get possession of the building back.

During the winter months (that can be extended by government decree if the weather conditions of a particular year are particularly hard) no eviction is carried out. This is known as the 'winter truce'.

Once there is a court sentence, the police quickly evict the squatted buildings, although sometimes there is resistance or various circumstances that may delay the end of the occupation.

Therefore, occupying abandoned properties is not a criminal offence in France, but evictions follow very clear channels set for all actors. Due to this non-criminal consideration of squatting, the political, judicial, and police authorities adopt their decisions by trying to balance two fundamental rights of the republic's constitution: housing and private property. This opens a margin of discretion that allows the persistence of many squatting projects. On the one hand, during the 'winter truce' and in the absence of a property complaint (or by the time gained in judicial litigation against the complaints). On the other hand, due to the active intervention of some municipal authorities that use squatting as a way to develop their public policies and calm the revealed social conflicts. All of this can happen while there is no court sentence that requires the eviction of the squatted property.

How can municipal governments 'use' occupations? According to Aguilera, they can sign a *convention* (agreement) with the squatters, allowing them to use the property for a limited time (usually three years). In exchange, the squatters would have to pay a symbolic rent below market prices. It is like a form of

IMAGE 4.5 Squat Le Transfo, Paris, 2013
Source: Author

temporary legalisation and usually occurs at a very early stage, during the first days or weeks of the occupation. In the agreement, clauses are listed regarding the kind of activities the squatters will carry out in the space. Failure to comply with this may result in a unilateral termination of the agreement by the authorities, a file reported to the police or the court, and an eviction request. We refer here to state properties. Some privately owned properties can also be subject to the mediation of the municipal authorities if the signed agreement and rent are satisfactory to the owner; the municipal warrant and its control over the squatted space could be enough for an owner who did not have any plans for the building. The crucial aspect in these deals is that the agreed activities would increase the public services offered in the urban area where the squats are located. Thus, the 'project' presented by the squatters should be adjusted to the vision and to the cultural and social policies of the local authorities—or to offer innovative activities that are not in much contradiction with the official rules. According to Aguilera, around 85% of the occupations in Paris during 2010 would have adopted this sort of agreement with the town hall, all of which would have been entitled 'artistic'.

The second method of municipal intervention is to offer the squatters a *convention d'occupation en précaire* (precarious-use contract) of the property, also in exchange for cheaper rent than the market price. While regular agreements are preferably applied to occupations such as socio-cultural centres, the precarious contracts tend to be applied to occupations with residential purposes. The precarious contracts do not offer many guaranties of stability to squatters and depend principally on the plans of the property (public or private) with respect to the building (its sale, rehabilitation, demolition, etc.). In 2010 there were 18 precarious contracts throughout Paris.

Of course, it could also occur that there is no negotiation between squatters, owners, and authorities. In this case, the chances of survival for the occupation would be significantly reduced due to the legal conditions and the repression, which are rigorously applied. All this political and judicial activity means an underlying or implicit regulation that seldom appears clearly in the programme of political parties. One exception was the legalisation of 59 Rivoli (www.59rivoli.org), located at the heart of the commercial urban centre. The legalisation of this squat was included in the electoral promises of a social democratic candidate who won the municipal elections in 2001, being fulfilled later with a considerable economic investment in the renovation of the building. In general, regulation entails an inherent condition of 'temporality' for all the cases, even though many agreements can be renewed several times at three-year intervals.

The third feature of the regulation of squats is their integration in regular administrative procedures. Therefore, occupations are normalised and institutionalised, which increases the political and social tolerance towards them. This is the case for 'open call' agreements (*mise en projet*), when authorities establish a specific period in which to receive proposals of use for an empty property, or even a previously squatted one. In the former case, instead of punishing the squatters, they force them to

180 Types of Squatting

compete with other possible users. Moreover, in addition to keeping the property effectively in use, the policy stimulates the provision of relevant services to the neighbourhood and a low cost for the public purse.

Lastly, the doors are often closed to both mediation and regulation when it comes to the most undesirable squatters in the eyes of the authorities (poor, immigrants, drug addicts, and radical activists). In these cases, repression is practiced in a more relentless way. The distinction between 'good' and 'bad' squatters promoted by the authorities is neither strict nor clear. For example, Aguilera commented on a case in which a local politician requested one of the groups dedicated to housing homeless people and immigrants in an irregular situation (DAL and Jeudi Noir) to squat a specific property so, later, they could establish an agreement of temporary use.

The squats we visited in Paris were aligned according to these axes, sometimes overlapping positions and attitudes: (a) those negotiating a temporary legal status vs those who remained squatted without any agreement with the property or the state; (b) social composition of (probably lower) middle class vs members from socially excluded groups; c) preferably artistic activities vs a priority of radical political activities (left-libertarian); d) collective self-management vs exclusive management of a small group (association) or, even, an individual promoter. From the combination, in different degrees, of these factors and the networks that they constitute with each other, different families of squats in Paris are formed. Some examples will illustrate that configuration.

Two of the artistic squats located outside of the area where the majority of squatters are concentrated (north and north-east of the city) are Le Gare XP (Experimentale) [http://garexp.org/] in the south, and Jour et Nuit Culture [http://jouretnuitculture.blogspot.com.es/] in the south-west. The first is a group founded in 2004 that had occupied on five previous occasions. They split as a result of one of the evictions and are currently housed in their sixth building (Portes Ouvertes) through an 'occupation agreement'. The second was promoted by a Chilean migrant, Alejandro, after having collaborated for a season with another squat (Théâtre de Verre; www.theatredeverre.fr/) also led by another Latin American immigrant. In addition, Jour et Nuit Culture has a full name that aims to provide the squat with a positive image in a district with a conservative predominance and without any previous squat: Collectif Artistique Tranquille [Quiet Artistic Collective]. Since its opening, they have invited the neighbourhood to participate in the space. In this way, they earned the sympathy of the conservative government in the 15th arrondissement to such an extent that local authorities helped squatters face the complaint of the owner, an electricity company, in court. For two years, they had a 'precarious contract' and then they signed a more stable agreement with the local authorities for three years, paying a monthly rent of €3,000. Some 25 members, mostly artists, currently comprise the collective.

In the area of La Chapelle (north of Paris), there are several cases of squatting that bring together artists, such as the aforementioned Théâtre de Verre and, among the best known, the Jardin d'Alice (http://jardindalice.wordpress.com/, see Image 4.7) and Le Shakirail (http://shakirail.blogspot.com.es/, see Image 4.6), as well as architects, such as the Eco-Box community garden (www.urbantactics.org). Le Shakirail, in particular, consists of two buildings, (800 and 600 m², each) owned by the French railway company SNCF (a former training centre, union headquarters, and changing rooms), next to the railroads. They arrived at that place after two previous occupations and evictions. The place they were squatting in 2013 was occupied in 2011 and a few days later they signed a 'squatting contract' in exchange for an income of €1,200 per month, although they also pay civil liability insurance separately. About 14 artists live in the space.

The workshops, buildings, and garden that make up the Jardin d'Alice were evicted shortly after our visit because the city council decided to carry out a renovation of the area, including the construction of social housing. The artists-squatters accepted this ending with resignation and were looking for new empty spaces to move their activity. By that time, the same fate hovered over the Théâtre de Verre for the coming months. Curiously, none of these incidents implied a rupture in relations with the municipal authorities, who continued to sponsor many of their activities. In addition, many of these squats or squatted social centres (later legalised) maintain close mutual ties and a certain shared

IMAGE 4.6 Squat Le Shakirail, Paris, 2013
Source: Author

182 Types of Squatting

identity. They regularly work on the organization of the festival 'Intersquat' and in a network of the same name that serves as an information agenda for activities [www.paris.intersquat.org/].

All these groups of artists must establish legally registered associations before signing the agreements. They must also develop very detailed proposals of the cultural activities they will promote. Finally, any activity that displeases the authorities can lead to termination of the contract and the beginning of a judicial process that culminates in their eviction. Most of them assume that these are projects with an uncertain duration, especially after the expiry date of the deal. However, they also consider that these are very convenient agreements from an economic point of view, since they can access urban locations that otherwise would be very expensive to rent at market prices. Besides this, the exhibitions, parties, or plays that they offer to the public, at very affordable entrance fees, are developed as part of their own vocation, independent of enriching the official cultural agenda sponsored by the authorities. There is also an 'unwritten clause' that consists of the possibility that the artists reside in the same buildings where they have their workshops. The agreements do not usually refer to this use, but there are no complaints about it, and it is fully assumed by all parties that an artistic career is very precarious and that real-estate speculation in Paris makes access to decent housing very difficult. Therefore, in these squat-ted-and-legalised 'social centres' there are collective kitchens, hot water, showers, living rooms, etc. There is a very intense community life for several dozens of people who cross paths with the continuous and abundant visitors, as well as with those who attend the programmed activities.

The majority of squatters are concentrated in the north-west area of Paris. In particular, the districts of Belleville (mainly, the 19th and 20th arrondissements) and Ménilmontant stand out. Belleville has a long history as the site of revolu-tionary activism at different times since the nineteenth century as well as hosting numerous cases of autonomist and artistic squatting since the 1970s. It is also a traditional area of settlement for ethnic minorities and the immigrant popula-tion, with many social housing blocks stuffing the territory. It is in this area that we find more squats with a strong autonomous-anarchist orientation who reject negotiations with the authorities. In some cases, they did not even have the opportunity to initiate these relationships. They did not have any 'artistic pro-ject' to offer in return, nor a willingness to schedule activities that could be pre-sented with the municipal stamp. Many of them have mutual aid bonds and many informal relationships with each other.

In the neighbourhood next to Bagnolet, we visited Le Transfo [https://transfo.squat.net/, see Image 4.5]. The occupied premises consist of four huge buildings and the asphalted space between them. About 30 people reside in one of the buildings, while the others have many empty rooms and large spaces for all kinds of activities and workshops. They had been managing the space for a few months only. It was squatted in November 2012 and they had lost the trial that the property (the privatised electricity company EDF) filed against them. Therefore, as soon as the 'winter truce' ended, it would be evicted (it was finally evicted in 2014). Among its principles were the rejection of all negotiations with authorities and the gratuity of organised activities. Its priorities were, above all, solidarity with different current struggles and with other social movements. The groups using the space contributed financially to cover the common costs. In any case, nobody paid a set rent to live or use a workshop. They did not have much relations with the social organisations of the district except with one that opposes the gentrification of the neighbourhood and another one that helps irregular immigrants.

On the border between Belleville and Ménilmontant is La Miroiterie [www.guernicamag.com/daily/jacqueline-feldman-vive-la-miroiterie/]. It is an artistic squat that has been active since 1999. It was to be evicted in the coming weeks because the claim of the new owners finally prospered (it was effectively evicted and demolished in 2017). Previously, the property was divided and there was no agreement to denounce the squat, so there was no need for any accord to be reached in the form of legalisation via project or 'precarious occupation' contracts. Several people resided in the property throughout its 13 years history and some artistic workshops were also housed. Even so, the squat stood out as one of the most prolific places in terms of concert programming (in particular, punk, rap, and jazz).

Situated right on the street in front of La Miroiterie is the social centre Louise Michel (after the 1871 commune leader; www.louise-michel.org/), founded and financed by the anarchist Lucio Urtubia. He is known for having created counterfeit checks from several banks for years and distributed that money between various political groups. During our talk, Lucio made us understand that squatting is in a, somehow, different political and cultural circuit, so they did not have much mutual contact. Not far from there, we also discovered La Cantine des Pyrénées (www.rue89.com/2013/03/21/au-squat-cantine-des-pyrenees-menu-5-euros-et-police-au-dessert-240713), where you could eat at a very affordable price and attend French classes or film screenings. In this case, there was no contract or agreement that had legalised the squat. They told us that they had received visits from thugs sent by the owners, so they also feared an imminent eviction (it was eventually evicted in October 2013).

The last squat to which I will refer is located on Valenciennes Street, to the north of the city but more central, near the Gare du Nord train station [www.theatlanticcities.com/housing/2013/01/pariss-power-squatters/4480/]. This is one of the occupations carried out by the Jeudi Noir collective. They had the double goal of providing accommodation for people in need and to take part in broader housing policies. Therefore, it is not a social or cultural centre, although some artists collaborate with the collective. Jeudi Noir emerged among university students in 2006 and soon began to squat with the support of DAL. The organisation has resorted to this practice in order to house, above all, irregular immigrants since its foundation in 1991. Most of the squats have had an

184 Types of Squatting

ephemeral duration except one that lasted for a year. The most relevant aspect of the squats launched by Jeudi Noir and DAL is that they seek a large impact in the mass media. In addition, many of the members of both organisations are also militants of various political parties. They have built a strong relationship with many politicians and have contributed to a broad acceptance of squatting as a legitimate action in the claim for housing justice. In the case of Valenciennes, three buildings were squatted on 29 November 2012 and two social democratic ministers came to support the squatting before the media. However, it is private property and they expected a forthcoming eviction—all the inhabitants were later relocated by the authorities and social housing was built in the same location. About 60 people selected by DAL inhabited the building, including some 24 minors, although a dozen resident activists were sleeping in a separate building.

Judging from these observed cases, the 'squatting movement' in Paris is so internally fragmented that there is no single movement for many of its participants. The presentations and debates of SqEK helped some activists with different tendencies to get to know each other better, although deep incompatibilities emerged among them during the debates. The concept of 'social centre' from an occupation takes very different shapes in each of the trends. Having said that, it should be emphasised that in most of the cases, housing

IMAGE 4.7 Squat Jardin d'Alice, Paris, 2013
Source: Author

is combined with social, political, and cultural activities. Moreover, the 'winter truce' provides them with three to four months of relative calm in terms of evictions, although they narrated several cases of illegal evictions carried out during that period as well.

The strong pressure of the municipal government to normalise (integrate, regulate, and legalise) the squatters of a more artistic nature has generated a political culture of a certain tolerance towards squatting. In this way, squatting is understood as another means of protest that allows the forcing of authorities to grant rents at prices lower than the dominant ones. That is to say, for many artistic collectives, squatting is conceived as a negotiating and pressuring tool to access work, exhibition, and residential spaces that the municipality could sponsor. Something similar happens with the occupations of Jeudi Noir and DAL, who seek the rapid implementation of social housing policies to urgently house the most vulnerable groups. These forms of squatting avoid confrontation with the authorities. Moreover, they do not intend to maintain the squatting situation indefinitely. In fact, in this framework a general vision predominates of squatting as a way of using urban buildings and vacant sites assuming their fragile existence, a limited temporality not exceeding three years in the best case, when a relatively strong legal agreement has been reached. Finally, there is hardly any collective protest campaign and defence of squatting. However, the large libraries in some social centres; the critical orientation of many artists; and the common sensibility that sustains the legitimacy of squatting disused properties, with a long history already in the City of Paris and throughout the Île de France region, can be identified as the vectors of transversality that connect all this activist diversity.

References

Abellán, Jacobo (2015) Ciudad, crisis y desobediencia: Una aproximación a las luchas por la vivienda en Madrid. In Rodrigo Hidalgo & Michael Janoschka (Eds.) *La ciudad neoliberal. Gentrificación y exclusión en Santiago de Chile, Buenos Aires, Ciudad de México y Madrid.* Santiago de Chile: Pontificia Universidad Católica de Chile, 257–274.

Aguilera, Thomas (2013) Configurations of Squats in Paris and the Ile-de-France Region. In SqEK (Ed.) *Squatting in Europe: Radical Spaces, Urban Struggles.* Wivenhoe: Minor Compositions, 209–230.

Aguilera, Thomas (2018) The Squatting Movement(s) in Paris: Internal Divides and Conditions for Survival. In Miguel A. Martínez (Ed.) *The Urban Politics of Squatters' Movements.* New York: Palgrave Macmillan, 121–144.

Aguilera, Thomas & Alan Smart (2017) Squatting, North, South and Turnabout: A Dialogue Comparing Illegal Housing. In Freia Anders & Alexander Sedlmaier (Eds.) *Public Goods versus Economic Interests. Global Perspectives on the History of Squatting.* Abingdon: Routledge, 29–55.

Aoussar, A. (2010) Squatting, the Right of Living Together. [http://emajmagazine.com/2010/01/14/house-squatting-the-right-of-living-together/]

Arribas, A. (2012) Sobre la precariedad y sus fugas. La experiencia de las Oficinas de Derechos Sociales (ODSs). *Interface* 4(2): 197–229.

186 Types of Squatting

Avila, Débora & Marta Malo (2010) Manos invisibles. De la lógica neoliberal en lo social. *Trabajo Social Hoy* 59: 137–171.

azozomox (2014) Squatting and Diversity: Gender and Patriarchy in Berlin, Madrid and Barcelona. In Claudio Cattaneo & Miguel Martínez (Eds.) *The Squatters' Movement in Europe. Commons and Autonomy as Alternatives to Capitalism.* London: Pluto, 189–210.

Blanchar, C. (2004) Punto final a los cuarteles de Sant Andreu, refugio de los 'okupas'. [http://elpais.com/diario/2004/02/10/espana/1076367625_850215.html]

BVODH (2014) *Persecución y acoso policial. La persistencia de los controles de identidad por perfil étnico.* [http://brigadasveci-nales.org/wp-content/uploads/2015/05/Tercer-informe-BVODH.pdf]

Cadete 7 (2014) CADETEvsSAREB. [www.youtube.com/watch?v=8I- VEbZEAvhk]

Calvo Buezas, Tomás (1993) *El crimen racista de Aravaca.* Madrid: Popular.

Canal Solidario (2003) Concentración en solidaridad con los inmigrantes, hoy jueves 7 de Agosto en la plaza Sant Jaume de Barcelona. [www.rebelion.org/hemeroteca/spain/030807barna.htm]

Caravantes, C. et al. (1995) *La okupación como analizador.* Madrid: Peligrosidad Social. [https://distribuidorapeligrosidadsocial. files.wordpress.com/2011/11/la-okupacic3b3n-como-analizador.pdf]

Cattaneo, Claudio & Miguel Martínez (Eds.) (2014) *The Squatters' Movement in Europe: Commons and Autonomy as Alternatives to Capitalism.* London: Pluto Press.

Clandestino Project (2009) Project Results. [http://clandestino.eliamep.gr/project- results/]

Colectivo Hinundzurück (2018) You Can't Evict a Movement—from the Rise of the Refugee Movement in Germany to the Practice of Squatting. In Squatting Everywhere Kollective—SqEK (Ed.) *Fighting for Spaces, Fighting for Our Lives: Squatting Movements Today.* Berlin: Assemblage, 16–37.

Common Place (2008) *What's This Place? Stories from Radical Social Centres in the UK and Ireland.* Leeds: University of Leeds. [www.socialcentrestories.org.uk]

Dadusc, Deanna (2017) Squatting and the Undocumented Migrants' Struggle in the Netherlands. In Pierpaolo Mudu & Sutapa Chattopadhyay (Eds.) *Migration, Squatting and Radical Autonomy.* Abingdon: Routledge, 275–284.

Davis, Mike (2007) *Planet of Slums.* London: Verso.

De Andrés, E.A., M.J.Z. Campos & P. Zapata (2015) Stop the Evictions! the Diffusion of Net-Worked Social Movements and the Emergence of a Hybrid Space: The Case of the Spanish Mortgage Victims Group. *Habitat International* 46: 252–259.

Diso Press (2014) Migrantes de Lavapiés crean la cooperativa Mbolo Moy Dole como solución de autoempleo. [www.diagonalperiodico.net/movimientos/23845-migrantes-lavapies-crean-la-cooperativa-mbolo-moy- dole-como-solucion-autoempleo]

González, Robert, Ibán Díaz-Parra & Miguel A. Martínez (2018) Squatted Social Centres and the Housing Question. In Miguel A. Martínez (Ed.) *The Urban Politics of Squatters' Movements.* New York: Palgrave Macmillan, 271–288.

Herráiz, P. (2008) Inmigrantes y 'okupas'. Y del palacete a la comisaría. [www.elmundo.es/elmundo/2008/03/13/madrid/1205398170.html]

Hodkinson, Stuart & Paul Chatterton (2006) Autonomy in the City? Reflections on the Social Centres Movement in the UK. *City* 10: 305–315.

Kadir, Nazima (2014) Myth and reality in the Amsterdam squatters' movement, 1975–2012. In Bart Steen, Ask Katzeff & Leendert van Hoogenhuijze (Eds.) *The City Is Ours: Squatting and Autonomous Movements in Europe from the 1970s to the Present.* Oakland, CA: PM Press, 21–61.

La Biblio (2002) ¿Se acerca el día del juicio final? La Biblio amenazada de desalojo. [www. sindominio.net/labiblio/web1/doc/juicio_final.htm]

La Gatonera (2013) 30/12 Concentración en frente del C.I.E. de Aluche. [https://csolagato nera.wordpress.com/2013/12/27/3012-concentracion-en-frente-del-c-i-e-de-aluche-2/]

Langa, Napuli Paul (2018) Voices of Resistance: About the Refugee Movement in Kreuzberg, Berlin. In Squatting Everywhere Kollective—SqEK (Ed.) *Fighting for Spaces, Fighting for Our Lives: Squatting Movements Today*. Berlin: Assemblage, 4–15.

Ledeneva, Alena (Ed.) (2018) *The Global Encyclopaedia of Informality. Understanding Social and Cultural Complexity. Vol. 1 And 2*. London: UCL.

López, S., X. Marínez & J. Toret (2008) Oficinas de Derechos Sociales: Experiences of Political Enunciation and Organisation in Times of Precarity. *European Institute for Progressive Cultural Policies*. [http://eipcp-net/transversal/0508/lopezetal/en]

Makrygianni, Vasiliki (2017) Migrant Squatters in the Greek Territory. Practices of Resistance and the Production of the Athenian Urban Space. In Pierpaolo Mudu & Sutapa Chattopadhyay (Eds.) *Migration, Squatting and Radical Autonomy*. Abingdon: Routledge, 248–256.

Manjikian, Mary (2013) *Securitization of Property. Squatting in Europe*. New York: Routledge.

Martínez, Miguel & Angela García (2018) Converging Movements: Occupations of Squares and Buildings. In Benjamín Tejerina & Ignacia Perugorría (Eds.) *Crisis and Mobilization in Contemporary Spain*. Abingdon: Routledge, 95–118.

Martínez, Miguel A. (2013) The Squatters' Movement in Europe: A Durable Struggle for Social Autonomy in Urban Politics. *Antipode* 45(4): 866–887.

Martínez, Miguel A. (Ed.) (2018) *The Urban Politics of Squatters' Movements*. New York: Palgrave Macmillan.

Martín-Pérez, Alberto & Francisco Javier Moreno-Fuentes (2012) Migration and Citizenship Law in Spain: Path-Dependency and Policy Change in a Recent Country of Immigration. *International Migration Review* 46(3): 625–655.

Medrano, C. (2010) 'Okupas' de lujo en una ciudad rica. [www.elmundo.es/elmundo/2010/02/22/madrid/1266828519.html]

Méndez, J. (2012) Solidaridad y ayuda mutua. El grupo de Migración y convivencia de la Asamblea Popular de Lavapiés. *Teknocultura* 9(2): 267–286.

Moore, Alan (2015) *Occupation Culture. Art & Squatting in the City from Below*. Wivenhoe: Minor Compositions.

Moore, Alan & Alan Smart (Eds.) (2015) *Making Room. Cultural Production in Occupied Spaces*. Barcelona: Other Forms & Journal of Aesthetics and Protest.

Mudu, Pierpaolo (2004) Resisting and Challenging Neoliberalism: The Development of Italian Social Centers. *Antipode* 36(5): 917–941.

Mudu, Pierpaolo (2012) At the Intersection of Anarchists and Autonomists: Autogestioni and Centri Sociali. *ACME. An International E-Journal for Critical Geographies* 11(3): 413–438.

Mudu, Pierpaolo (2014) 'Ogni Sfratto Sarà Una Barricata': Squatting for Housing and Social Conflict in Rome. In Claudio Cattaneo & Miguel A. Martínez (Eds.) *The Squatters' Movement in Europe: Commons and Autonomy as Alternatives to Capitalism*. London: Pluto, 136–163.

Mudu, Pierpaolo & Sutapa Chattopadhyay (Eds.) (2017) *Migration, Squatting and Radical Autonomy*. Abingdon: Routledge.

Mundialito Antirracista de Alcorcón (2011) Comunicado. [http://mundialitoantirracista. blogspot.com.es/comunicado.html]

188 Types of Squatting

Nodo50 (2001) Encierros y movilizaciones contra la Ley de extranjería en el 2001. [www.nodo50.org/derechosparatodos/Encierros.htm]

Owens, Linus, Ask Katzeff, Elisabeth Lorenzi & Baptiste Colin (2013) At Home in the Movement: Constructing an Oppositional Identity through Activist Travel across European Squats. In Cristina Flesher & Laurence Cox (Eds.) *Understanding European Movements. New Social Movements, Global Justice Struggles, Anti-Austerity Protest.* Abingdon: Routledge, 172–186.

PAH Vallecas (2014) Obra Social PAH. [www.youtube.com/watch?v=ffnoqJCNHvU]

Piazza, Gianni (2011) Which Models of Democracy? Internal and External Decision-Making Processes of Italian Social Centres in a Comparative Study. *Center of Studies on Politics and Society—WP Series* 1(1): 3–54.

Piazza, Gianni (2013) How Do Activists Make Decisions within Social Centres? In SqEK (Ed.) *Squatting in Europe. Radical Spaces, Urban Struggles.* Wivenhoe: Minor Compositions, 89–111.

Polanska, Dominika (2017) Reclaiming Inclusive Politics: Squatting in Sweden 1968–2016. *Trespass* 1: 36–72.

Precarias a la Deriva (2004) *A la deriva por los circuitos de la precariedad femenina.* Madrid: Traficantes de Sueños.

Pruijt, Hans (2004). The Impact of Citizens' Protest on City Planning in Amsterdam. In L. Deben, W. Salet & M. van Thoor (Eds.) *Cultural Heritage and the Future of the Historic Inner City of Amsterdam,* Amsterdam: Aksant, 228–244.

Pruijt, Hans (2013) The Logic of Urban Squatting. *International Journal of Urban and Regional Research* 37(1): 19–45.

Refugee Accommodation Space City Plaza (2018) Refugees' Struggles in Athens: Voices from City Plaza. In Squatting Everywhere Kollective—SqEK (Ed.) *Fighting for Spaces, Fighting for Our Lives: Squatting Movements Today.* Berlin: Assemblage, 351–356.

Rivera, P. (2014) Los 'okupas' de Majadahonda sufren cortes en el suministro de luz. [www.noticiasdemajadahonda.es/201003311921/los-okupas-de-majadahonda- sufren-cortes-en-el-suministro-de-luz]

Rivero, Jacobo (2007) Una campaña para combatir el racismo. [www.diagonal- periodico.net/movimientos/campana-para-combatir-racismo.html]

Schmidt, H (2012) *Lavapiés. Fenómeno migratorio y claves de la convivencia.* Madrid: EPIC- CAM.

Souzas, Nick (2018) Squatting in Greece: An Open Case with Closed Doors. In Squatting Everywhere Kollective - SqEK (Ed.) *Fighting for Spaces, Fighting for Our Lives: Squatting Movements Today.* Berlin: Assemblage, 231–240.

Steen, Bart, Ask Katzeff & Leendert van Hoogenhuijze (2014) Introduction. Squatting and Autonomous Action in Europe, 1980–2012. In Bart Steen, Ask Katzeff & Leendert Hoogenhuijze (Eds.) *The City Is Ours: Squatting and Autonomous Movements in Europe from the 1970s to the Present.* Oakland: PM, 1–19.

Thörn, Håkan ((2012) In between Social Engineering and Gentrification: Urban Restructuring, Social Movements, and the Place Politics of Open Space. *Journal of Urban Affairs* 34(2): 153–168.

Tilly, Charles & Sidney Tarrow (2007) *Contentious Politics.* New York: Oxford University Press.

Toret, Javier, Nicolás Sguiglia, Santiago Fernández, P. Lama & M. Lama (Eds.) (2008) *Autonomía y metrópolis. Del movimiento okupa a los centros sociales de segunda generación.* Málaga: ULEX-Diputación Provincial de Málaga.

Vargas, J. (2014) La PAH pide un alquiler social para los tres bloques ocupados en Vallecas. [www.publico.es/actuali- dad/pah-pide-alquiler-social-tres.html]

Vasudevan, Alexander (2015) The Makeshift City: Towards a Global Geography of Squatting. *Progress in Human Geography* 39(3): 338–359.

VVAA (2004) *Centres Socials Okupats. Una Historia de Resistencies, Vides I Lluides.* Barcelona: independent edition.

YoSí Sanidad Universal (2015) Desmontando mentiras. [http://yosisanidaduniversal.net/mentiras.php]

5

ANOMALOUS INSTITUTIONS

Is the legalisation of squats a positive and desirable outcome? Is it likely or unlikely to occur? How can it be explained according to specific conflicts and contexts? Some squatting experiences are able to last for many years, even decades. Others are active for shorter periods, especially given the political and juridical pressures that force their swift eviction. Legalisation is usually seen as a necessary condition for a lengthy duration of such experiences. However, sometimes there are not many opportunities to turn unauthorised occupations into legal forms of tenure. Many squatters, especially those aiming for affordable state-subsidised housing, use occupations as a tactical move to press authorities in that direction. Negotiations and policy solutions for specific individuals are crucial stages of the process. On the other hand, there are squatters who express no intention to compromise. Their strategic protest goes far beyond the legalisation of squats, and they even confront those squatters who negotiate with the authorities. The radical gesture of squatting, they claim, is at stake. Instead of legalisation, I would use the term 'institutionalisation' in order to investigate a number of squatters' claims—the right to be relocated in affordable dwellings and buildings, the state's requisition of the occupied building and further transfer to the squatters, 'adverse possession' in the rare cases where there is still such a regulation in force, and so on. Therefore, I elucidate the legalisation of squats as a specific outcome of a larger process where previous negotiations and subsequent integration in mainstream institutions are also crucial components. The concept of 'anomalous institutions' is introduced as a way to understand squatter resistance to state assimilation despite the occurrence of some forms of legalisation.

In this chapter, I examine the controversial issue of institutionalisation among squatters, focusing on cases of legalised squats in European cities. I argue that 'anomalous institutionalisation' occurs once self-managed squats, whether legalised or not, become consolidated and socially accepted, despite

Anomalous Institutions **191**

its inherent challenge to prevailing capitalist relations. This can be considered a successful sociopolitical impact, but it is not always perceived as such by all squatters. Furthermore, it remains unclear whether the legalisation of squats may be considered straightforward instances of institutionalisation and state assimilation, which reduce the squatters' autonomy and radicalism, or whether these legalisations contribute to alternative forms of institutionalisation. My argument is that anomalous institutions grant substantial and relatively wide autonomy to activists, even after a process of legalisation. However, some of these processes may end up in forms of 'terminal institutionalisation', while autonomy can also be seriously constrained through the repression of existing squats. To clarify these nuances, I first examine the different types of negotiations between squatters, state authorities, and private owners. Second, I interpret the legalisation of squats by framing it as a social movement outcome. And third, I define 'institutionalisation' as a broader systemic consequence in which legalisation intervenes in various ways and other structural features contribute in explaining the resulting outputs. Different examples from my own fieldwork and from secondary literature will underpin this approach.

The Movements' Structural Dilemmas

According to Neidhart and Rucht's definition (1991: 450–451), a 'social movement' may be conceived

> as an organized and sustained effort of a collectivity of inter-related individuals, groups and organizations to promote or to resist social change with the use of public protest activities. ... People involved in social movements play very different roles ... core activists, participants, contributors and sympathizers ... Movements do not necessarily go through an inherent 'natural' life cycle to end up in the status of institutionalization, but rather follow an unsteady course.

Therefore, squatting becomes a movement when it is not an isolated action or an occasional tactic by other movements and organisations, but when 'squatting itself is a means and primary goal at the same time ... [and] is at the centre [of] a community of squatters who cooperate' (Pruijt 2003: 143). A collection of well-rooted tactical approaches, as with some housing movements, must be included in the definition as well. Squatters, as activists engaged in broader movements, produce numerous 'protest activities' mainly by using a 'non-institutionalised action repertoire' and the constitution of 'mobilised networks of networks' without formalised membership and decision-making (Neidhart & Rucht 1991: 452).

Legalisation and institutionalisation processes are possible outputs of the conflictual relations between squatters and their opponents. This follows Tarrow's definition of 'social movements' as 'sequences of contentious politics that are

192 Anomalous Institutions

based on underlying social networks and resonant collective action frames, and which develop the capacity to maintain sustained challenges against powerful opponents' (Tarrow 1994: 2). In the study of squatter movements, some scholars emphasise the strategic features of the interactions between the parties involved in the conflict, the instability of those relations and identities, and their particular evolution over time (Owens 2009: 31). In more concrete terms, Pruijt defines 'effective organised squatting' as 'a sustainable way to repair, heat and maintain buildings, and deal with owners, authorities and the community … contributing to the push for a lively, low-income people friendly city' (Pruijt 2003: 134).

Legalised squats are cut off from the stock of radical activists' material and symbolic assets. If a building or apartment is not squatted anymore, residents or users will stop using it as a political tool to oppose urban speculation—at least, in relation to that particular building. Dwellers in former squats are not squatters any more, although they can still help and support other squatters. Former squatters face different social problems in their daily lives compared to their previous living conditions. In addition, their political culture of radicalism; autonomy; and anti-systemic, anti-institutionalisation attitudes are easily replaced by more moderate, dependent, mainstream, and institutional arrangements. The intensity of contention decreases, although that can still be channelled within state institutions or remain latent until incidents and campaigns in the future are sparked anew. In addition, internal cleavages among squatters in favour or against legalisation could drive the movement to fade out.

The outcomes of social movements could be distinguished between (1) those that bear directly on a movement's claims and (2) those which 'are often indirect, unintended, and sometimes even in contradiction to their goals' (Giugni 1998: 386). Besides the political opportunity structures and the use of disruptive tactics mediating the interaction of movements and authorities, Giugni proposes to examine how impacts are also due to the way movements are organised and public opinion. Tilly (1999: 269) added another variable to assess movement outcomes: to what extent are the effects a result of a movement's actions, of others' actions and external events, or a combination of both. The effects can also bear on a movement's claims. Tilly advocated for a 'critical theory of causal processes', which is an ambitious goal given the many external conditions at play and the internal diversity of movements, albeit not an impossible task if the case study is well demarcated. As he remarked (Tilly 1999: 257), the minimum claim of a movement—and, therefore, the basic outcome to identify—is the toleration of the movement's existence by the power holders.

Squatters are very contentious actors because they persist in practices that challenge the prevailing regulation of private property. For them, occupations of buildings are not just an occasional disruptive tactic within broader social campaigns and mobilisations, but a regular political activity and a substantial component of their protest. In addition to being tolerated, squatters aim at keeping the occupied buildings in their own hands for as long as possible. The legalisation of a squat may be instrumental to that end, but what autonomous control of the building means may also change afterwards. More often than not, after a lease agreement is signed, former squatters start paying bills for supplies, home insurance, and tenancy rents. Therefore, legalisation processes are not necessarily equal to the squatters' claims but can have an effect of them once other external circumstances are met.

Early on, in a concise evaluation of the 1946 squatters campaign in the UK, Ward categorised the stages of 'popular direct action in housing in a non-revolutionary situation' as follows: (1) 'initiative' (first actions that spark the campaign); (2) 'consolidation' (sufficient growth of the movement is able to challenge property rights); (3) 'success', 'when the authorities have to concede to the movement what it has won'; and (4) 'official action', 'usually undertaken unwillingly to placate the popular demand, or to incorporate it in the status quo' (Ward 1973: 70–71). In his view, legalisations are 'official actions' that comes after the 'success' of the movement. The success of the movement occurs when its opponents (authorities and owners) accept their claims and start negotiations. Ward's subtle point may help to illuminate the controversies around a movement's success and other possible outcomes. However, we need to examine first the crucial social relations that either pre-empt or deviate from the legalisation process.

IMAGE 5.1　Evicted squat in Rotterdam, 2016
Source: Author

194 Anomalous Institutions

Strategic Negotiations

It is obvious that any legalisation process of a squat requires previous negotiations between the squatters and state officials, politicians, or the private owners of the building. However, it is more rarely noticed that squatters also negotiate with their opponents by pursuing goals other than legalisation. I conceive these negotiations as one type of 'strategic interactions' (Tilly 2007) and also as one of the multiple relations between dominant and oppressed social groups (Foucault 1982, Scott 2012). Negotiations are *productive* processes in the political arena, specific moments of contentious politics and social mechanisms binding actors and practices. Instead of approaching them as mere rational calculations, I examine negotiations according to incremental tensions between the parties involved. Instrumental goals, collective identities, and crucial contexts of policy, regulation, and economic condition, usually related to specific urban settings, are all combined during the interactions between activists and their opponents. Negotiations entail 'bargaining' processes 'in which two or more parties seek conflicting ends through the exchange of compensations' (Burstein et al. 1995: 279–281) but are not limited to them. Hidden agendas or basic defensive moves can define negotiations too. When performed outside state institutions (parliaments, government agencies, administrative procedures, etc.), but on a regular and usually informal basis, I argue that we should regard negotiations as a key mechanism of movement institutionalisation.

Negotiations between squatters and city officials are based on power relationships within particular contexts. In the case of Madrid, I observed squatters taking the initiative in the negotiations when trying to obtain legal status for squats. However, this proactive role was mediated by crucial conditions such as the mass media coverage of the squatters' pleas, the specific field of public policy involved (youth, education, culture, gender, etc.), and formal organisations supporting the squatter groups. No less important were the ideological cleavages and social networks existing within the local squatting movement. These had a strong influence on the course of the negotiations, and some internal splits, although not irreconcilable, occurred after legalisation. It is also significant that instead of squatted houses, only squatted social centres—and only a few of these—were legalised in Madrid before 2015. The political context that emerged in Spain after the 15M movement in 2011 and the ascendance of progressive governments in some major cities after 2015 facilitated the legalisation of many more squats, although internal divides in the movements largely remained.

I suggest classifying negotiations in regard to squatting according to the following four categories (see Table 5.1).

High-Level Negotiations

These are aimed at winning legal occupation of the building for squatters. Depending on who the owner is and which state agencies are concerned with the management of the building or area, negotiators may vary, although squatters demand

Anomalous Institutions **195**

TABLE 5.1 Types of negotiations in which squatters may be involved

Negotiations	Aims	Social actors	Outcomes
High-level	Legalisation of the squat Affordable rents	Private or public owners Local (or supra-local) state Mediators and facilitators	Legal security Spatio-temporal stability Socio-political recognition Access to state benefits Payment of rent, taxes, bills, etc.
Transactional	State subsidies and benefits Participation in urban plans	Local (or supra-local) state Mediators and facilitators (Independent planners, other formal organisations)	Socio-political recognition Access to state benefits Access to planning information
Survival	Avoid or postpone eviction Time to continue squatting	Private or public owners Judicial court Mediators and facilitators (Attorneys, municipal planners, mass media)	Defence of squatters' rights Public exposure of urban speculation Private deals for temporary use
Forced	Avoid or soften repression Protection of squatters	Judicial court Police Bullies hired by owners	Reduce personal damages and injuries Reduce penal punishment

Source: Author

meetings of higher-level (usually local) state representatives. In case of success, former squatters could remain for a short or long period of time (rarely indefinite) at the cost of paying rent, a mortgage, taxes, bills, and anything else stated in the lease agreement.

Aguilera (2010: 63–81) distinguished three types of high-level negotiations implemented in Paris: mediation, project, and temporary housing (*convention d'occupation précaire*). The empirical cases he describes display how tortuous the roads can be to achieve a legal, and not necessarily stable, status. These strategic negotiations take place as an informal or *ad-hoc* environment in urban politics. Squats, thus, are managed on a case-by-case basis, according to media resonance and specific political tools, taking for granted that authorities are willing (or forced by their opponents) to negotiate. Otherwise repression, in the form of sanctions and evictions, is always ready to be applied due to the strong prohibition of squatting.

In Prague, one of the first and more popular squatted social centres in the 1990s, Ladronka, 'managed to gain the municipality's permission to legally use its property' (Pixová & Novák 2016: 38). After the demise of the state-socialist regime, a new social fervour about private ownership encouraged squatters to focus on state-owned properties. The novelty of the squatting phenomenon for

196 Anomalous Institutions

the authorities made high-level negotiations for temporary uses easier. Mass media coverage was not especially stigmatising in that period, despite the notorious anarchist and countercultural orientation of many squats. Ladronka, in particular, was evicted seven years after its occupation in 1993, following 'the globalization protests against the IMF and the World Bank congress held in Prague in September 2000, which created a hitherto non-existent moral panic concerning anarchists among the public' (Pixová & Novák 2016: 38).

Another, more recent case from Prague was Klinika, occupied in 2014, re-occupied again after the first eviction, and followed by negotiations with the local and the central state authorities. Well-timed alliances with members of the Green Party facilitated the talks. Although the activists won a one-year, rent-free lease after the negotiations, the property was transferred between different public administrations later on (Pixová & Novák 2016: 43), shifting it to a new unauthorised status of occupation. Despite a failed eviction attempt in 2016 and being punished with a daily fine of 37 euros, in place since March of that year, the squatted social centre was still active as of 2018.

Squatters can also deal with the private property owners of occupied buildings in case there are chances of an agreement on tenancy contracts or of selling the building to the squatters. Many of these deals are secret in the first stages, although they necessarily become public once both parties have signed the paperwork. In the case of Od:zysk in the Polish city of Poznan, for instance, the occupied building was auctioned and sold to a private company. The new owner met the squatters and offered 30,000 euros in order to leave the building and move to a new location provided by the municipality (Polanska & Piotrowski 2016: 52).

Transactional Negotiations

These negotiations occur when squatters want to participate in public benefits, plans, or services. Frequently, this requires face-to-face encounters with authorities before proceeding with formal applications. Squatters, thus, attain both political recognition and basic resources, enabling them to persevere with their regular activities. Authorities can claim an inclusive attitude to all kinds of civic groups, squatters included, while simultaneously commanding home and squat evictions.

Holm and Kuhn (2011: 653), for example, noted how Berlin squatters participated in 'cautious urban renewal plans' in an alliance with groups of residents, the Alternative List-Green Party, as well as professional town planners and architects who 'agreed to reject the bureaucratic and authoritarian urban renewal of the past' Pruijt (2003: 135) also observed in Amsterdam that 'involvement in neighbourhood politics and planning allows squatters to find allies and show themselves as constructive citizens, which has a moderating effect on repression'. Few cases of this involvement of squatters in conventional forms of citizen participation can be found in Spain, although I observed in Barcelona how Can Masdeu squatters agreed to participate in the urban planning of Collserola Park, where the squat is located.

Anomalous Institutions **197**

Squatter engagement in participatory processes with local authorities can pave the way for future talks on legalisation. The same can be said about squatters who apply for funds to organise activities or repair the occupied buildings. Therefore, transactional negotiations can scale up to high-level negotiations if sufficient mutual trust has been created and other contextual circumstances contribute.

Survival Negotiations

There are defensive negotiations in which squatters engage mainly in order to prevent, or delay as much as possible, their forthcoming eviction. Hence, time is the most precious resource in play. By all legal means known, available, and ideologically acceptable to squatters they attend court cases and interact, at least, with judicial officials, owner attorneys, and lawyers who defend squatting. As many squatters argue, these lawsuits can result in a great deal of media attention on urban speculation and could provide social legitimacy to squatting by framing the injustice of the eviction.

Albeit not often extensively reported by media, or simply delayed until several years after the day of eviction, some famous lawsuits in Spain (Cine Princesa in Barcelona, Guindalera and Laboratorio 2 in Madrid, etc.) have proved to be excellent events for public debate of the squatters' movement (Asens 2004: 301, Cañedo 2006, Casanova 2002: 161, Martínez 2002: 155–177). Press releases and conferences as well as support from squatters' relatives, formal organisations, and public celebrities increased the media audience for these cases and the political value of this sort of judicial performance. In Madrid, the Laboratorio and Patio Maravillas, for instance, also accepted a visit and inspection by municipal architects in order to verify the structural conditions of the building. Thus, if the building was not officially declared to be in ruins, no one could claim a rapid eviction was necessary based on that aspect alone.

Survival negotiations also call on squatters to meet with private owners away from the courts; the latter can threaten squatters with legal action or illegal harassment. Property owners can also approach squatters to explain their future plans for the building in terms of renovation, selling, or use by relatives. A usual trade-off consists of offering some amount of money to the squatters so they silently leave the property. Another behind the scenes agreement is to concede to a temporary use, free of charge, until the economic or legal conditions of the building change. Most squatters prefer not to disclose these agreements to the whole movement in order to preserve its unity and radical identity. Almost never seen as concessions or successful achievements by other squatters, these compromises are instead often seen as a betrayal and selling-out because the deals do not challenge the speculative operations of the property owners. For the activists, these negotiations mainly pursue short-term goals such as postponing a probable eviction.

198 Anomalous Institutions

Forced Negotiations

Even more defensive negotiations with state factions happen when squatters feel forced to deal with the police. If squatters want to avoid detention, being beaten, and accusations of public disorder or resistance to authorities, sometimes speaking with police officers may help. As I have experienced directly in one of the squats (Malaya, Madrid, in 2008), in case of an immediate eviction, squatters can accept the convenience of establishing direct communication with police officers. These talks are carefully planned, aimed at reducing personal injuries and keeping their belongings safe during the eviction. I observed similar conversations in the first hours of a new squatting action (Cines Luna, Madrid, in 2009) as well as during the development of non-legalised demonstrations.

When police arrest squatters and file charges, forced negotiations directly lead to survival negotiations. An observation from Poland illustrates this point:

> Mostly, the detention of activists has resulted in court cases, and in the last 15 years all but one were won by the squatters, who not only have a sympathetic lawyer but have become more and more skilled in litigation and legal practice.
>
> *(Polanska & Piotrowski 2016: 54)*

It is worth noting that all types of negotiations involve the actors' will to interact. The 'forced' level is the most ambiguous one because it is mixed with the squatters' reactions to the threat of repression. However, this expected event can be planned in advance and negotiators can be appointed if the opportunity to talk appears. Often there is more time for planning and to decide whether to engage or not in other types of negotiations. However, some remarks about the structural conditions of those actors' will are necessary here.

Obviously, squatters wish to remain in the building they occupy. Thus, negotiations are a tool for fulfilling this desire, with some additional or alternative outcomes too. In lower-level negotiations—the defensive ones—only a few extra hours or months can be gained, but personal safety and protection from police brutality is the dearest value at stake. In the higher levels, an increasing political challenge to authorities may also steer the hidden agenda of the negotiations. In the case of successful legalisation, squatters can accept an alternative location in which to continue their activities.

Concerning squatting, I find the above classification more useful than others such as, for example, that proposed by Burstein et al. (1995). The purposes of each level of negotiation do not correspond exactly to their six types of 'policy responsiveness' as a way of measuring successful outcomes for the movement: 'access', 'agenda', 'policy', 'output', 'impact', and 'structural'. Apart from access to state institutions and agenda setting, most policy outcomes address legal and legislative dimensions, while in my classification, only high-level and some transactional negotiations share similar concerns. Yet most squatters follow the basic purpose of remaining radical

Anomalous Institutions 199

outsiders and anti-systemic while squatting, so scattered attempts to engage in negotiations within the institutional realm cannot be properly regarded as movement goals, except for some housing struggles. Disobedience to the socially unjust distribution of private property is still a good bargaining chip when it comes to bringing squatters to the negotiation table. Moreover, a radical approach to squatting among non-negotiators can ease the odd agreements reached by the negotiators. However, the most radical wing of the squatters prefer street riots, clashes with the police, illegal demonstrations, and a refusal of any mediating organisations in negotiations with 'the enemy'. A well-disseminated pamphlet, written by the anarchist Italian squats El Paso Occupato and Barocchio Occupato from Torino, has since 1994 summarised the major arguments against negotiations and legalisation:

> The social center [Leoncavallo] that chose the molotov to defend itself in 1989 now chooses to defend itself through negotiation with its evictors ... In essence, these social centers become aided and supplementary places for the reproduction of conformity and normalization through the administration of services that the state lacks for the increasing numbers of marginalized people in the big cities who might become a problem for the public order ... We will never seek dialogue with institutions (certainly not with parties either of the right or the left) except in the case of extreme necessity.
>
> *(El Paso 1995: 9–10, 14)*

In the Spanish context, when negotiations are aiming for the legalisation of a squat, the city council tends to be the main player or stakeholder, even when other state agencies or private companies own the disputed building. When it comes time to negotiate, local authorities will argue city policies, metropolitan and master plans, urban growth, the rule of law, and so on. Squatters may be presented as respected and responsible civil society actors endowed with their right to submit proposals and demands. Therefore, it is tempting to interpret negotiations from pluralist and institutionalist (or 'managerial') perspectives. For example, Burstein et al. (1995: 279–281) argue that 'outsider groups' like squatters may increase their 'bargaining resources' by means of protest and the activation of 'third parties'. Castells (1983: 322) verified the mediation of 'organisational operators' between urban movements, society, and the political system. In particular, he pointed to the mass media, professionals, and political parties as facilitators. Negotiations may also be regarded as a structural feature of liberal democracy, 'an institutional method for selecting leaders' (Alford & Friedland 1985: 250–253) and for conflict regulation, according to the 'managerial perspective' (Pickvance 1984: 46).

However, a 'class perspective' (Alford & Friedland 1985: 345–353) seems more appropriate to investigate these processes. First, real-estate developers are never very far away from the negotiations. They lobby local authorities and influence various policies even if they do not own a specific occupied

200 Anomalous Institutions

building. Second, squatters question housing, cultural, and welfare policies. The autonomy and self-management of squatters imply responses and also alternatives to the locally managed 'collective consumption' (Castells 1983: 319–320). Third, people who squat are not, in principle, wealthy enough to buy or rent a place. Moreover, even when some squatters are wealthy or belong to the middle or upper classes, they join a general claim for free access to abandoned properties and a better social distribution of spatial resources for all. That is to say, there is an immediate demand to accommodate themselves in the loopholes of capitalist urban speculation in parallel with a broader contestation of the capitalist system. Fourth, when squatters directly interact with property owners, it is not just a specific estate which is subject to negotiation, but class relations, capital accumulation, and land rents. If these negotiations are not overtly exposed, the potential to question that broader capitalist background is undermined too.

As a consequence, negotiations are specific stages in which to represent the squatters' challenges to the local authorities and the urban capitalist dynamics. Due to the overall effects of neoliberal policies, negotiations between civic organisations and the local government may simply diminish political contention by shifting movement organisations 'from direct action to service delivery' (Fainstein & Hirst 1995: 186; also Mayer 2006, 2016) unless negotiations are regarded as concessions following mobilisation and confrontation (Fainstein & Fainstein 1993: 65).

To Be or Not to Be Legalised

In theory, legalisation falls under the domain of policy outcomes (Bosi et al. 2016, Burstein et al. 1995). According to this perspective, social movements are usually more influential at the lowest levels of policymaking, such as 'agenda setting' (Bosi et al. 2016: 11), but they are seldom capable of 'changing laws and policies' in accordance with their demands, and even less effective when it comes to the 'implementation' of intended reforms. Legalisations of squats certainly go beyond gaining social recognition and raising the issue of squatting in the political agenda, but they are usually performed as an ad-hoc policy instrument, not necessarily based on a substantial legal change. Local authorities do lack many legislative powers that could decriminalise squatting and regulate occupations with evident social benefits. These powers lie more frequently in the hands of state authorities, including parliaments and central governments, despite the urban and metropolitan scale where the squatting and housing movements unfold. These institutional contradictions are a source of opportunity for both squatters willing to achieve legalisations and policymakers with a favourable attitude towards the legalisation of squats as a means to placate conflicts around squatting.

As other institutionalist approaches point out, policy outcomes can be achieved through 'incremental' or 'sequential' stages, and at 'rapid' or 'slow' paces (Bosi et al. 2016: 17). Some social movements interfere in the political party system by nurturing new organisations, mobilising voters, and engaging in specific alliances with parliamentary representatives. The movements themselves, after regular and trustworthy interactions with political elites, can become 'institutionalised'. This is to say, movement organisations that become more formalised and hierarchically structured, depend more on state and private funding, cooperate more with authorities in deliberative forums and planning processes, and even become outsourced service providers. This leaves room to ask how the particular legalisation of one or several squats in an urban region implies broader processes of institutionalisation, where a movement's success can quickly turn into demobilisation and a decline in protest, without removing the structural roots of the conflict.

A key contribution here is Pruijt's argument that 'effective organised squatting' tends to resist 'terminal institutionalisation' unless state repression, cooptation and, sometimes, legalisation, fatally undermine its legitimacy, support, and duration. By 'terminal institutionalisation' he refers basically to the shift 'in the repertoire of action [when] convention replaces disruption' (Pruijt 2003: 136). According to Pruijt, 'squatters themselves are drawn towards legalization because squatting is not only a political activity but an economic activity as well' (ibid.: 135), which steers most squatters towards some sort of 'flexible institutionalisation'—that is, where 'conventional tactics complement disruptive ones' (ibid.: 136) after negotiations with state officials or representatives.

Pruijt's argument may be summarised as follows: Squatting is characterised by the predominance of disruptive tactics so the legalisation of squats is a conventional tactic that alters the balance. If radicalism is still guiding most squatters' lives after a legalisation process, 'flexible institutionalisation' occurs. If legalisation is able to tame, weaken, and split the movement, or make it disappear and force its transformation into formal organisations and political parties, then 'terminal institutionalisation' occurs. Therefore, the process of legalisation is a crucial mechanism in either development, but not a determining one. It does not necessarily prevent squatters from remaining radical, nor lead them primarily into the institutional arena.

Legalisation of a given occupied building is a battle won against the urban speculation in which that building was involved and the social exclusion experienced by the squatters. As Pruijt observes, it is a very convenient outcome for many squatters, especially for those with a pragmatic and short-term attitude. The question is to what extent former squatters remain as part of squatting and housing movements once they enjoy safer living conditions. They can still break the rules, but seldom in relation to their own building. Authorities may also aspire to contain the whole movement by giving away some concessions in the form of legalised squats, but their general goal may fail when movements are large and their structural grievances not fully redressed.

In my view, Pruijt's analysis might be improved with an additional remark. Flexible institutionalisation follows legalisations when movement strength, self-management of former squats, and the predominance of radical repertoires of

202 Anomalous Institutions

action keep going, but also when most of the squatters are not co-opted as a result, so that neither they nor their activities become widely integrated into state institutions, state policies, and capitalist firms. Co-optation, in particular, is one of the usually unintended outcomes that emerges within legalisation and institutionalisation processes: 'A salient example of co-optation can be found in the history of squatting in the UK. There, some squatters' organizations were transformed into management offices that rented out short-life public-sector accommodation' (Pruijt 2003: 136) As a consequence, we should distinguish the institutionalisation effects concerning particular legalised squats from those concerning the movements to which they belong. In other words, the legalisation of squats may lead to terminal institutionalisation if former squatters are torn apart, split, fragmented, and detached from the local initiatives of radical politics, with the output being a weaker squatting or housing movement. However, after being legalised, squats can still enjoy a high degree of self-management and autonomy from formal organisations, the state, and the capitalists, and thus keep contributing to radical movements and even supporting new squats.

In short, I see the co-optation of activists as a usually unintended outcome of the movement's actions that follows legalisation and pre-empts institutionalisation. In combination with shifts in movement repertoires, unity, and autonomy, co-optation leads to either terminal or flexible forms of institutionalisation once squats are legalised. Contrary to Pruijt, I do not conceive of co-optation at the same level as institutionalisation or as a 'second integrative mechanism' (Pruijt 2003: 136). According to my arguments above, institutionalisation designates a broader set of outcomes, and co-optation operates as a mechanism that may lead to the systemic integration of activists depending on its scope and the mentioned synergistic effects.

In his seminal analysis, Pruijt also advanced the thesis of 'functional splits' between moderate (or more institutionally oriented) and radical (or anti-institutionally oriented) branches of the same movement: 'Institutionalization does not have to be associated with a movement's decline.

> A movement may only be partly integrated, while a radical wing continues to produce disruption. The integrated moderates can then reap the concessions made in response to the disruption wrought by the radicals.
> *(Pruijt 2003: 135–136)*

Therefore, movement splits are driven by concessions to the moderates in the form of legalisation. Due to that policy, radicals become isolated, repressed, and, eventually, fade. The movement as a whole loses leverage. In other words, the success of the 'institutional' wing runs parallel to the failure of the 'autonomous' one. If the intention to suppress the radicals was actually driving the authorities' concessions to the moderates, then we could interpret legalisations as a success for the whole movement, although the yielded benefits only go for the more institutionally oriented activists.

Aguilera (2018: 130–140) applies the same rationale to the analysis of Paris squatters. In that context, the autonomous and anti-institutional factions of the squatters' movements were a minority, with no interest in legalisations. However, their confrontation with the authorities made them a likely target of repression while enhancing the outlook of squatters seeking legalisations—housing activists and artists, mainly. The threat of radicalisation, Aguilera claims, facilitates the achievement of concessions from the authorities. In the case of the housing movement, the co-opted members are not the squatters but other professional activists and members of political parties, in addition to some formal organisations that support squatters.

> Autonomous squatters in Paris serve as watch-dogs against the full co-optation of the squatting movement. They regularly reactivate a critical point of view against legalisation and prevent consensus on the issue. Moreover, they work as a movable cursor that pushes the claims of the whole movement farther and farther. They periodically demonstrate to moderate squatters that more action is possible and more claims can be made to public authorities. ... Finally, autonomous squatters are a threat that disorients Paris officials, who prefer negotiating with substitution and policy-oriented squatters [than] facing the prospect of autonomous squats ...
>
> *(Aguilera 2018: 139)*

Artists use the legalised squats either as platforms to replace the local government in the provision of cultural services or as cheap studios to produce works destined for the market. Arguably, co-optation alone cannot explain the terminal or flexible institutionalisation effects for the social groups enjoying legal status or for the squatters' movement as a whole.

Aguilera also shows that the policy-oriented squatters' groups historically appeared before the autonomous squatters. The tolerance towards the former was followed by increasing repression of the latter. New housing policies in the 1990s and new cultural policies in the 2000s opened up the access of moderate squatters to state institutions, so legalisations became a more probable outcome. According to him, the 'functional split' works two-ways:

> If autonomous squatters had been acting alone, the end of the movement might have been precipitated in the late 1980s when they were strongly repressed. The emergence of pro-negotiation squatters seems to have contributed to the moderation of the repression of the movement as a whole. Indeed, substitution squatters have shown that squatting is a legitimate mode of action when it is used to identify and animate vacant spaces ... This institutionalisation contributes to stigmatising autonomous and survival squatters. But at the same time, it contributes to de-stigmatising squatting as a political practice.
>
> *(Aguilera 2018: 139–140)*

IMAGE 5.2 After-squat Cyklopen, Stockholm, 2015
Source: Author

It is finally worth noting that repression of squatting is always possible and actually probable no matter the stages of toleration, negotiation, legalisation, and institutionalisation taking place. When authorities apply a 'selective neglect' approach (Rossini, azozomox & Debelle 2018: 249), squatting is ignored, relegated to a minor political issue, or silently tolerated. Repression then occurs behind the scenes, far from the public eye. When squatters gain the recognition of local citizens, media coverage, and access to negotiate with state officials and representatives, authorities apply 'containment strategies' (Rossini, azozomox & Debelle 2018: 249). Legalisations are more likely to be granted, but repression also continues to target those who are, intentionally or against their will, excluded from that policy. Furthermore, evictions of previously legalised squats are not rare given the temporality of the agreements and the stringent regulations that the former squatters must observe, in addition to new speculative attacks by market forces.

Institutionalisation

In this section I distinguish three general forms of institutionalisation and discuss how squatting movements are involved in them. This analysis supplements the distinction between 'terminal' and 'flexible' institutionalisation.

Type I Institutionalisation: Integration of the Movement into State Institutions

The integration of a movement into state institutions ends up in both the total disappearance of the movement and the regular adoption of institutional means by its former members. In the case of squatting this implies, for example, the utilisation of buildings only within legal regulations (private property, renting, temporary permission, etc.), the changing of squatter groups into political parties, and the preference of activists to participate in formal and bureaucratic planning procedures. Former radical activists who claim that they defend from inside state institutions the same ideas that they defended before as part of an autonomous movement, tend to underestimate the constraints imposed upon them by both the institution and the ruling groups within it. Assimilation to the dominant patterns within the state, then, would be pervasive.

This kind of institutionalisation has been theorised as a highly probable stage in the evolution of movements in order to overcome their main disadvantages, such as instability, informal organisations and decision-making, lack of resources, exclusion from state institutions, repression, waning influence, and diminishing mobilisation capacity (Offe 1990, Piven & Cloward 1979, Tarrow 1994). Turning to bureaucratic and conventional politics would stem from either strategic choices of the movement's organisation or the macrodynamics of state democratisation involving movements (Pickvance 1999). This integration can also be considered as temporary, tactical, and fragile. Thus, insiders are able to spread their movements' goals inside the institutions; however, this window may be narrower at a later stage, so, albeit unusually, activists may go back to the streets again (Touraine 1978: 87–89, 131–132).

The squatters' movements in Germany and Denmark are good examples of those that have been almost eliminated due to a combined policy of repression and legalisation. During the first wave of occupations in Berlin (1968–78), most squats were willing to negotiate legal agreements, and these were implemented on a case-by-case basis given the limited numbers of squatted spaces—around 14 (Rossini, azozomox & Debelle 2018: 251). A much stronger extension of squatting took place between 1979 and 1983, with a total number of 287 squats. More than half of them were evicted and the rest were legalised. The legalisations in the 1980s started when the movement lost the political initiative and suffered harsh persecution, so that it 'established the division of the movement, making it easier to criminalize the autonomist *non-negotiators*' (Holm & Kuhn 2011: 649). The dominant policy of 'integrating and repressing' caused the internal divide of a notwithstanding previously united movement:

> As early as March 1980 a 'squatters' council' had been set up. In the first phase, it refused any negotiations with authorities, demanding the release of all arrested activists, the end of criminalisation of squatting, and the

206 Anomalous Institutions

> resolution of conflicts over all the squatted houses. But movement cohesion did not last very long. Evictions and demolitions repeatedly destroyed the results of the squatters' self-help works, so that more and more squatters began looking towards establishing some kind of mediating agent to represent their interests to the local state.
>
> *(Rossini, azozomox & Debelle 2018: 251)*

While most squatting groups accepted long-term legal leaseholds and participated in public self-rehabilitation programmes, the dissenting minority was rapidly evicted (Koopmans 1995: 170–179, Mayer 1993). Throughout these periods, at least 40 collectives purchased their formerly squatted buildings (Rossini, azozomox & Debelle 2018: 265).

Similar 'terminal' defeats were experienced in the second wave of squatting in the early 1990s. Another 'Berlin squatting council' (B-Rat) was formed, this time with a shared approach to negotiating and finding legal solutions for all the squats. However, state authorities applied the same formula of combined repression and legalisation. 'After the violent eviction of 12 squats in Mainzerstraße in November 1990 provoked a fierce three-day resistance by the squatters, most squats were gradually legalised in separate negotiations with the city-districts' (Rossini, azozomox & Debelle 2018: 252). Furthermore, the property regime of each building created different arrangements and, in turn, more divisions among squatters (Holm & Kuhn 2011: 652). Squatting is still supported by many of the former squatters, and occasional squatting actions are also openly promoted from time to time, but the squatters' movements of past decades have disappeared as a particular branch within the autonomist movement as a whole.

Mainstream institutionalisation also succeeded in Copenhagen. Christiania was, for several decades since its occupation in 1971, an exceptional case of sustained squatting that survived under pressure but ended in a legal defeat. In 1973 Christiania was granted the status of a 'social experiment' as a 'freetown' by the central government. This status was lost in 1978 when a high court ruled the clearance of the area—which, however, was not enforced. After a new parliamentary concession in 1989, Christiania enjoyed certain legal protections that also prohibited new constructions by the squatters. A later lawsuit between 2008 and 2011 resulted in a decision by the Danish Supreme Court against the squatters. As a consequence, Christianites became 'private owners'. In order to implement the verdict, buildings and land were transferred to a foundation whose board comprised both Christiania representatives and state appointees. The foundation, thus, became the full property owner of Christiania, especially after another legislative decision in 2013. Despite their long-lasting opposition to private property, the inhabitants of Christiania succumbed to market forces: '[R]esidents do not own the houses, but they pay rent to the Foundation who owns and governs the buildings' (Rannila & Repo 2018: 3002). After such a long process, most parties assumed that the legalisation process implied the full normalisation of Christiania and respect for the state building and planning regulations. Agreements between squatters and the state included the removal of houses built in conservational areas for cultural or environmental reasons. Five houses were effectively demolished and rebuilt in permitted locations. 15 houses more are expected to be removed by 2042 (Rannila & Repo 2018: 3003).

Once legalisation was imposed by the state authorities, internal splits among squatters occurred. On the one hand, residents were divided between those dwelling in 'legal' buildings and those houses considered illegal because they were self-built or located in areas of 'historical value'. On the other hand, the new property regime opened up two ways of enforcing private ownership: make a deal directly with the state or buy it from the foundation via approval of the Christiania assembly. Given the extremely low prices of the buildings compared to other close-by central areas of Copenhagen, a few of the so-called 'privatists' took the initiative to buy their houses directly from the state. This decision made them subject to harassment from other Christianites still more attached to the consensus decision-making process and direct democracy that defined the community hitherto:

> [I]solation, demonization, vandalism, throwing bombs, smashing windows, painting doors, painting the houses with graffiti, and booing out from meetings.... [t]hese acts are punitive in a sense that they confined the privatists to their homes and prevented them from taking part in the community as usual.
>
> *(Rannila & Repo 2018: 3006)*

This internal conflict expressed a late attempt by the majority of Christiania to preserve their prior anti-private property or 'commons' approach, even once the legal conditions had changed. In addition, the community still managed to select new residents according to family and friendship bonds with the members.

In the City of Copenhagen as a whole, the repression of squats and immediate evictions had become the general pattern well before Christiania was forced to accept privatisation. Local authorities had allowed and even subsidised a few legal social centres for radical and autonomist activists to meet. By 1990, after the first two waves of squatting, the harsh repression had culminated in the end of the squatters' movement. Nonetheless, some buildings were legalised and continue as partially self-managed spaces to the present day (Folkets Hus, for example—squatted in 1971). In other cases, such as the well-known Ungdomshuset (the Youth House), located at Jagtvej 69, the legal cession of the building was achieved after street battles with the police in 1982. The eviction, years later in 2007, sparked new riots, clashes, and large demonstrations that, again, resulted in a legal agreement with the authorities to set up a new self-managed Youth House in a less central area of the city (Steiger 2018: 177). Although the legalisation did not alter the autonomy of the activists who used the building,

208 Anomalous Institutions

their eviction reflected not only the repressive side of the Danish state against any form of squatting, beginning in the late 1980s, but also the tight nexus between repression and legalisation. Therefore, the terminal institutionalisation of the squatters' movement in Copenhagen implied more evictions than legalisations, and the latter were granted after a bargaining process, highly contentious negotiations, and confrontations between activists and state authorities.

As seen, legalisation is the main avenue that leads to state integration, but not the only one. In Italy, for example, at least three squatters obtained seats as city councillors during the 2000s (two in Rome: Rossini, azozomox & Debelle 2018: 258), and a political party was even born in a very well-known squatted social centre (Leoncavallo, in Milan) that had been attempting to become legal for more than three decades (Membretti 2007). Former squatters also became city councillors in Madrid after 2015, which facilitated the legalisation of some squats (Salamandra, EVA) and the tolerance of others (La Ingobernable) but did not integrate most of them. However, even when former squatters became political representatives and promoted the decriminalisation of squatting, their legislative efforts clashed with a jungle of mainstream forces. This quote from an analysis of squatting in Rome illustrates my point:

> The only way to institutionalize them is by means of the 1998 regional law on *autorecupero del patrimonio immobiliare* (self-managed real estate renewal, Regional Law No. 36/1998). The law recognizes housing occupations as an alternative way to address the housing emergency issue through self-renewal of mostly public property, as fostered by the housing movements. Just a year prior, in 1997, Nunzio D'Erme, one of the leaders of the housing movements, had been elected municipal councilman. He thereby inaugurated the movements' entry into local institutions to promote the movements' demands. Yet in the 17 years since its approval, the law has been applied in a very limited number of cases (11).
>
> *(Mudu & Rossini 2018: 113)*

While participation in formal party competition is never a requirement, the creation of formal organisations or private companies by the squatters is always an official request in case they want to achieve legal status for the buildings they occupy. In addition to being legalised, some 'artist squats' in Amsterdam (for example, Overtoom 301, Plantagedok, and Vrankrijk) and Paris (59 Rivoli, for instance) were expected to produce a regular programme of cultural events in order to contribute to the marketisation, touristification, and attraction of global capital to the city (Aguilera 2018: 128, Owens 2009: 228). Finally, we should recall that even wide-reaching policies addressing the legalisation of squats, as with the late 1970s 'licensed squatters' in the UK (Lowe 1986: 143), did not prevent a new squatters' movement from thriving in the same context.

Type II Institutionalisation: New Institutions Promoted by Social Movements

Apart from integration into already existing state institutions, structures, and regular dynamics, social movements can promote emerging institutions. When recognised by the dominant social groups, the state powers, and the society at large, new institutions become consolidated. Recognition means here an increasing social acceptance and legitimation, and often a demand for legal regulation. Movements that become active creators of new institutions are those able to transform issues once marginal into mainstream politics and culture. Feminist, LGBTIQ, civil rights, and pacifist movements were extremely efficient in doing this in many countries over the twentieth century, despite the waves of conservative backlash against them. Very often, the movements' mobilisation and spread helped to produce new legal rights, anti-discrimination policies, and a lot of media coverage and public deliberation on those topics (Eder 2003, Goodwin & Jasper 2009). The institutionalisation of strikes, collective bargaining, minimum wage, and paid holidays is an undisputed consequence of the workers' movement. This type of institutionalisation covers different impacts that the movement may obtain before, or instead of, achieving integration into state institutions, if any — for example, the opportunity to testify in congressional hearings, the inclusion of issues in the political agenda, desired changes in policymaking and legislation, etc. (Burstein et al. 1995). Another example is the participatory budget and the World Social Forum, which was born in Brazil as a result of the endeavours of various social movements and which obtained wide social backing and political acceptance all over the world (Santos 2003).

The will of activists to prevent repression and achieve respect, especially by means of new legal rights, policies, and state agencies is also behind the creation of new institutions, although that is not the key driver. Integration in already existing state institutions (type I institutionalisation) does not leave much margin for innovations brought about by newcomers. Conversely, activists who reject this type of full integration ask for new spaces within state institutions (type II institutionalisation), with their own political views and agenda. For type I, a harsh repression against the movement and the movement's reaction to it lead to a high degree of state integration. In type II, legalisation and acceptance within the state apparatuses are not aimed for at any cost. For the promoters of new institutions, their social legitimacy is of the utmost importance. Even if repression is not as fierce, activists will keep advancing their claims for new and distinct institutions through more or less contentious repertoires of protest.

Above all, squatting has the advantage of keeping open a continuous social debate about the housing question, the legitimacy of property rights, and the right to the city for the most vulnerable tracts of the population (Hojer et al. 2018). In the Netherlands and England–Wales, where it was for a long time considered non-criminal behaviour, squatting became a broadly legitimate and frequent practice. In particular, slightly more than half (53%) of the Dutch Parliament in 2009

210 Anomalous Institutions

voted in favour of criminalising squatting, while almost half (46%) voted against it. The same year, a survey was conducted among the Dutch population in which only 36.8% agreed with the statement that '[s]quatting an empty building should always be forbidden', compared to 42.5% who disagreed (Pruijt 2013). Despite the durable social legitimation of squatting over various decades, the full enforcement of its criminalisation, after 2012 in England and Wales and 2010 in the Netherlands, undermined its spread and popular support (see Image 5.1).

Social legitimation depends on public opinion but also on the frequency of practices. Sometimes both aspects may be in contradiction: 'In 1979, there were estimated to be 50,000 squatters throughout the UK, with the majority (30,000) living in London' (Finchett-Maddock 2016: 60). In 2011, the British government estimated the number of squatters in the UK at 20,000. In parallel, an opinion poll concluded that 81% of the population declared that the squatting laws should be changed to make it a criminal offence [http://yougov.co.uk/news/2011/11/11/criminalise-squatting/]. Squatting, then, did not reach mainstream status, but it was a subcultural resource widely used for decades by thousands of people. The regular editions of the *Squatters Handbook*, released by the London-based Advisory Service for Squatters over the decades (it 'has sold in excess of 150,000 copies since 1976': www.squatter.org.uk/about-ass/), testify to the activists' attempts to achieve the institutionalisation of squatting via the defence of squatting rights.

Legitimacy is closely related to tolerance. The Dutch model of regulating squatting before its criminalisation was similar to the tolerance applied towards issues such as drugs, prostitution, and immigration. Squatting was seen as 'the latest of the country's liberal institutions' (Manjikian 2013: 159). According to Dadusc, this regulated tolerance also implied a depoliticisation of the squatting struggles, a specific form of social control by codifying them still as deviational as well as a 'productive mode of power', providing a 'useful informal *service* from the perspective of local governments' (Dadusc 2017: 38–40). However, the tolerant Dutch approach drastically changed in the 2000s. Housing was intensively privatised, urban regeneration programmes expanded, and 'zero tolerance' policies against all kinds of minor offences were implemented. 'Policing ethnic minorities and the youth became a priority' (Dadusc 2017: 42), migrants and asylum seekers were stigmatised, and nuisances such as noisy music produced by the squats became outlawed. This political twist affected squatting as well after decades of soft-institutionalisation, so its criminalisation by the end of the 2000s was not a surprise.

We can also look at more exceptional and short-term episodes. For example, after the 2008 economic recession, squatting for housing in Spain was more practiced and enjoyed greater support than ever before. This was due to general criticism towards both the banks, which were bailed out by the government, and the wave of home evictions that followed suit (Martínez 2018). However, squatting in a country with an extremely high rate of homeownership was always a controversial protest practice and even its increasing legitimation during the worst times of the crisis did not last long. Once the new flows of real estate speculation through international investment funds infiltrated the Spanish urban economy again from 2014 onwards, property owners, landlords, the mass media, and political parties recovered their common front against squatting.

A different conclusion arises from the peak mobilisations of the 1970s in Italy. By then, the simultaneous occupations of factories and universities resulted in synergetic effects that favoured the consolidation of squatted (and non-squatted) social centres in most cities over the coming decades, regardless of their illegal status (Mudu 2004). Attempts to legalise squatted social centres in Rome according to a specific city regulation (Delibera 26/1995) was applied in eight cases. These enjoyed recognition of their singular role as self-managed spaces and a certain stability for a decade, but many had also received eviction notices by 2014. 'These evictions are being justified officially by the need to abide by national and local budgetary frameworks, linked to "stability pacts" that push the municipality into repossessing public property and monetizing them' (Mudu & Rossini 2018: 113).

A late development of the social centres movement came, for example, around 2011 when the campaigns for 'common goods' were embraced by a new wave of squats in abandoned theatres and cinemas all over Italy (Teatro Valle Occupato and Cinema Palazzo in Rome, Teatro Coppola in Catania, Macao in Milan, Teatro Marinoni in Venice, Asilo della Creativita in Naples, Teatro Garibaldi in Palermo, etc.) (Quarta & Ferrando 2015, Valli 2015).

> The occupiers are capable of reaching beyond those who are directly involved in the act of disobedience and of bringing the space to the community and the community to the space. Not only [do] they avert the tragedy of the commons by collectively managing the resource but they also share the utilities produced with the rest of the community. Not only [is] Hardin proved wrong, but through broader legitimacy the occupation takes a fundamental step toward recognition.
>
> *(Quarta & Ferrando 2015: 17–18)*

Based on these claims to endow the *commons*, including occupations as mentioned above, with a new legal status, squatters engaged with other movements against the privatisation of water and other public assets. As a result, cities such as Bologna (2017) and Naples (2016) passed local legislation to recognise and allow some self-managed squats to operate as 'common goods'. In the case of Naples, seven buildings were explicitly protected according to 'a self-regulated system of access, programming of activities, and operation developed by its civic communities and its inspiring principles' (Delibera 446/2016). Some Spanish social centres followed the same rationale while striving for institutional recognition as urban commons (Casa Invisible in Málaga, EVA and Patio Maravillas in Madrid, Astra in Gernika, etc.).

212 Anomalous Institutions

TABLE 5.2 Types of institutionalisation processes

	Focus of contention	Political-economic conditions	Strategic interactions between opponents	Institutionalisation outcomes
Type I. Integration in state institutions	Legality	Compliance with the rule of law and the laws of capital	(1) Legalisation, co-optation, and concessions applied to most in the movement (2) High degree of repression applied to the whole movement and non-negotiators in particular (3) Only or mainly conventional repertoire of actions	Terminal End of the movement (but not of isolated protest practices) Potential decriminalisation of squatting
Type II. Promotion of new institutions	Legitimacy	Contribution to new legal rights, social acceptance, and subcultural markets	(1) Legalisation, co-optation, and concessions only applied to some parts of the movement (2) Variable degrees and forms of repression applied to different parts of the movement (3) Prevalence of unconventional means of action but in combination with conventional ones	Flexible Continuity of the movement (but in different forms than before being institutionalised) Potential tolerance of squatting
Type III. Creation of anomalous institutions	Autonomy	Persistence of countercultural forms of opposition to mainstream politics and economy		

Source: Author

In general, squatting movements find numerous obstacles to making squatting a new social institution or even to spread its practice widely enough as to be a modular protest action for other social movements. The cases above indicate a spectrum of degrees and contexts in which this can happen. Even after being broadly accepted, the image of squatting in the mass media may remain a very negative and stigmatised one. In order to fight its image of marginality, a squatting movement sometimes appeals to society with nicely designed books and well-argued documents displaying the most positive sides of squatting (Egia & Kukutza 2011, Kraken Nederland 2009, SQUASH 2011). In the Netherlands,

Italy, Spain, and Germany, many social centres, whether still squatted or squatted only in the past, are extremely well known as venues for music concerts and cultural events, sometimes with a massive attendance. Squats, then, have contributed to institutionalising subcultural circuits and music scenes often as a well-established alternative.

Type III Institutionalisation: Creation of Anomalous Institutions

A third distinct category of institutionalisation (see Table 5.2) refers to the process that gives birth to 'anomalous institutions'. When social movements remain on the margins of mainstream society and institutional politics, they can contribute to the creation of anomalous institutions in addition to their claim-making activity and protest mobilisation. The boundaries with legitimation and legalisation processes are blurred, but the key feature is that activists produce and defend these sustained forms of organisation, rules, social relations, and material bases without much interference from the state, the economic elites, or established social groups.

Countercultural opposition to dominant institutions and markets, prefigurative lifestyles and practices (Yates 2014), 'free spaces', and the 'institutionalisation of resistance' and a 'hidden law' (Finchett-Maddock 2016: 40) are alternative designations of the same concept. Instead of classic 'counterpowers' or 'workers' councils' aiming at a coordinated substitution of the state (Debord 1967: 38), anomalous institutions give priority to the autonomy and self-management of the spaces, resources, and internal regulations according to the participants and their different membership status (McKay 1998, Piazza 2013). This may lead, eventually, to a claim for legitimation and legalisation, but to build up autonomous spaces away from the dominant social relations is the main concern. Anomalous institutions also recall the 'hacking ethic' (the transgression of established rules and private property as a way to promote general intelligence) (Stallman 2002), the 'rhizome' (multiple and horizontal connections) (Deleuze & Guattari 2004), 'constituent powers' (Negri 1994), and the Zapatistas *caracoles* (self-managed communal councils) (Klein 2002: 217). As long as these sociopolitical experiments stem from contentious protests and activism are able to last and are broadly accepted by most of the participants (not only by movement activists), the processes leading to them can be identified as anomalous institutionalisation.

Rucht (1990: 224) argued that some contentious repertoires of action, like civil disobedience, can also achieve a (albeit marginal) socially institutionalised status once state repression seriously discourages violent expressions of dissent. Even some political opportunity structures (pre-election periods or state crises, for instance) and ritualised 'strategic interactions' between activists and authorities can constitute a sort of 'secondary institutional framework' shaping collective actions as 'relatively permanent features of a country's political landscape' (Goodwin & Jasper 2009: 313–314; also Piven & Cloward 1979: 14, 21–23, Tarrow 1994: 51, Tilly 1984: 47–50, 76–80). Like expatriates who can live for

214 Anomalous Institutions

a long time with subaltern and unclear rights, some countercultural expressions by movements persist in society, relatively hidden but also relatively expected, as part of a pluralist political landscape.

Anomalous institutions are also referred to as 'movement institutions' for being 'flexible, mobile, nomadic institutions … stable laboratories of encounters … neither private nor public [but] community-managed … offensive Social Centres, proliferating war machines' (Toret et al. 2008: 121–127, Universidad Nómada 2008). In the case of squatting, some information desks (take, for instance, the *kraakspreekuur* in Amsterdam or the well-established London based Advisory Service for Squatters), underground bars and 'popular kitchens', radical bookshops, independent publications, alternative think-tanks, non-legal co-operatives, self-managed festivals (such as the Intersquat events in Paris and Berlin), and non-squatted autonomous social centres (which were often squatted before and still support squatting too) constitute a 'social movement infrastructure' (SMI) (Kriesi 1996: 223, Owens 2009: 175, Uitermark 2004: 228, 242) that serves as a material basis for anomalous institutions—with a similar value to the informal social networks that nurture every social movement (Della Porta & Diani 2006: 172).

Squatters recuperate empty buildings and challenge housing shortages, unaffordability, and exclusion from city centres. In principle, their claims for spatial justice only entail protest practices and direct action. However, they also self-manage the occupied spaces, over time they resist in the squats, and they create alternatives to both social conventions and legal regulations. Hence, they also build their own institutions or 'commons' (Stavrides 2016) by resisting enclosures, market privatisation, and state facilities for capital accumulation. Since a sustained duration of the alternative experiences is a crucial dimension of anomalous institutionalisation, the legalisation of the squats may contribute to that end. The more squats continue to be self-managed after their legalisation, the more they adhere to the anomalous nature of institutionalisation. Whether legal or not, experiments in the self-management of collective resources remain relatively tolerated while confined to small groups of people. The anomalous side of institutionalisation (type III) risks being increasingly lost once the movement enters the cultural/subcultural mainstream (type II) or gains full access to existing state institutions (type I).

Pruijt's 'terminal institutionalisation' is a more probable outcome of state assimilation, but 'flexible institutionalisation' is likely to happen in the type II and III processes (see Table 5.2). Co-optation of some squatters (e.g. as elected politicians, public managers, business owners, and university professors) or of some squatting organisations (as housing associations who quit squatting after obtaining state subsidies, for instance) can result in any of the three types of institutionalisation. When co-optation, concessions, and legalisation are not generalised to the whole squatters' movement of a city or metropolitan area, then the movement is characterised by flexible institutionalisation. For Piven and Cloward (1979: 33), co-optation is, above all, an elite response intended to integrate and moderate the movement. I thus assume that co-optation is a serious threat to the whole movement, especially in a declining phase, unless, as I contend, it only affects a tiny and not very influential minority of the movement. Consequently, anomalous institutions are equally menaced by the surrounding environment of co-optation, regularisation, and integration into state institutions, especially in a capitalist context where precarious labour and commodification of every service, good, space, piece of information, and social relation is rampant. Reactions to these tensions can take the form of hybrid transitions between autonomous and institutional grounds, as was argued during the 2011 15M movement in Spain, with the key participation of squatters in broader anti-austerity mobilisations (Martínez 2016).

Drawing on Koopmans (1995) and Kriesi (1996), we can associate countercultural movements with processes of anomalous institutionalisation. Countercultural identities are seen in terms of being 'essentially negative, defined by opposition to something else, [seeking] conflictive interaction with political opponents, from whom they tend to get similar reactions that will reinforce the group's identity' (Koopmans 1995: 19). This means they are primarily anti-institutionalisation, resisting in practice types I (full integration in the state) and II (emerging institutions) of institutionalisation:

> [T]he goals pursued are so radical that changes in their direction are almost by definition insignificant. ... [and activists] tend to interpret concessions as an effort to appease the movement and to keep it from attaining its ultimate goal. Therefore, countercultural activists sometimes fight those who favour such *reformist* changes even harder than they do their *true* opponents.
>
> *(Koopmans 1995: 32)*

Accordingly, success for the most countercultural and anti-systemic squatters is not linked to institutionalisation but to mobilisation, participation, and reaction to decisions taken by elites. 'Even when countercultural movements employ legal action forms they are confronted with much higher levels of repression and receive much less facilitation from established actors than instrumental and subcultural movements, which are less threatening to the status quo' (Koopmans 1995: 21). Following Koopmans' classification, 'instrumental' identities and purposes would fit in type I institutionalisation (state assimilation), 'subcultural' ones would correspond to type II (new institutions), and 'countercultural'-oriented movements would fall into type III (anomalous institutions) or outside the picture. For Kriesi (1996: 222–231), the institutionalisation of countercultural social movement organizations (SMOs) occurs when these increasingly turn their activities to the preservation of their own existence, resources, and membership. In so doing, they are more prone to interact with the authorities and avoid the direct participation of the broader 'membership' (supporters, participants, and neighbouring communities). In legalisation processes, for example, squatters

216 Anomalous Institutions

would engage in lower degrees of mobilisation and confrontation. Furthermore, they would perform actions aiming to achieve higher social legitimation. If the legalisation of a particular squat is achieved, the main dilemma faced by the activists is how to keep radical politics and autonomy alive—the anomalous character of their project—even while complying with many more conditions in the rule of law and more domination of capital than before.

Figure 5.1 represents the main ideas of this chapter. On the one hand, institutionalisation processes are constrained by contexts of repression and the resistance of movements to it. Squatters' dilemmas regarding the possibilities of legalisation are not merely dependent on their more radical or moderate will, but, above all, on the intensity and nature of the repression they face. The favourable or negative attitudes of authorities and owners to negotiations with squatters also depend on how the strategic interactions between repressive and defensive actions evolve. Dilemmas are also structured according to the dominant urban policies and the capitalist interests behind them. These determine the specific conditions of the legalisation agreements with squatters if they are ever able to be signed—how short or long term will the temporary use of the premises be, how many costs will the squatters have to bear, whether they can remain in the same building or are obliged to be relocated somewhere else, how much interference the current planning regulations and local policies will exert on the autonomous life of the after-squat, and so on and so forth. On the other hand, even if radical movements do not regularly and largely resort to institutional means of protest, they are often engaged in institutional relations such as negotiations with state authorities, formal organisations, and private firms. Some negotiations are a straightforward means of achieving legal status for the squat or social housing, but there are other forms of negotiations that do not necessarily lead to that destination. Squatters, like many other radical activists, are always forced into low-key forms of negotiations just to continue their activities. Talks with the police, aid by attorneys in court, and informal deals with property owners is evidence of this basic relationship behind the most obvious forms of institutionalisation.

Furthermore, I argue that legalisation of a particular squat should be distinguished from the combined conditions that affect a whole squatters' movement when legalisations are feasible and effectively implemented. Concessions other than the legalisation itself and various forms of co-optation of activists (especially leaders or key members) and their organisations (particularly once they are formalised) may accelerate a movement's decomposition if generalised to most of its components. However, the decline of squatters' movements may also be due to other circumstances apart from legalisations, such as internal conflicts, a lack of resources, weak identities and organisations, the higher appeal of other social movements, and the shift in the contextual conditions of capital accumulation and its related policies. By the same token, I have stressed the capacity of movements to promote new state (or social, cultural, and economic) institutions (type II), as well as create 'anomalous institutions' (type III). Legalisations of squats are not an essential obstacle in fostering these forms of 'flexible institutionalisation' when most of the

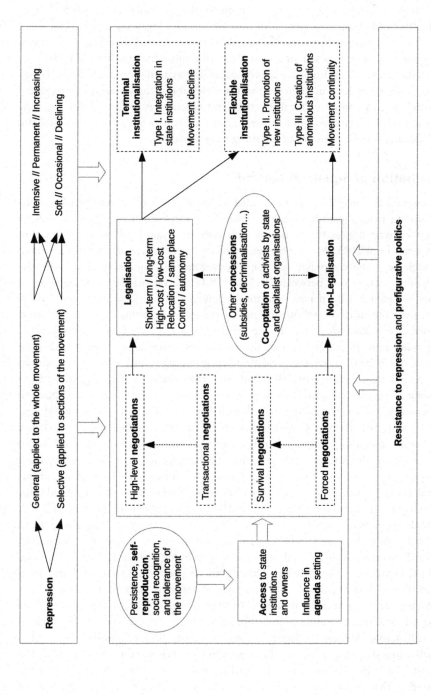

FIGURE 5.1 Institutionalisation processes in squatting movements

Source: Author

218 Anomalous Institutions

conditions causing the decline of the movement are not altogether met. What is even more striking about this interpretation, is the possibility for squatters to contribute to flexible forms of institutionalisation without legalising squats. The more they strive for squatters' rights, for respect towards diverse dwelling alternatives, and for the autonomy of self-managed squats, the more they push society, the political establishment, and market agents against the systemic contradictions. Long-term squats, their deep influence on social views about the housing question, the consolidation of countercultural practices and subcultural circuits, and their contribution to deliberations about urban injustice are strong forces that may facilitate the legitimacy and continuity of squatting over decades.

Legalisation of Squats in Madrid

Legalisations of squats have been unusual in Spain. They often were a taboo subject among many Spanish squatters—with the exception of those in the Basque Country—who opposed negotiations with authorities and legalisations of squats in most cities until 2011. More experiences of legalisation have occurred since then, although no consistent policy was implemented in the majority of cities, with the exception of Barcelona between 2015 and 2018. Nevertheless, the legalisation of squats in Spain has been rare. Squatting enjoyed a vague legal status until 1995. From then onwards, according to a new penal code, squatting became a criminal offence. Notwithstanding that, in the mid-1990s the wave of squatting was at its height and only at the end of that decade did the movement experience a slight decline. Since 2007, in cities like Madrid, squatting has spread again. The uprisings that started in the spring of 2011 with the 15M movement also gave birth to a strong resurgence of squatting all over the country along with a new housing movement more eager to achieve legal deals once they occupied empty buildings.

It was in the Basque Country where more cases of legalisation occurred due to its specific political situation and the conception of squatted social centres as 'youth houses' falling under the management of municipal youth policies. Yet there has been a recent case of a more genuine and ambitious 'social centre', Astra (located in Gernika), which was eventually legalised after several years of squatting, evictions, and hard negotiations beginning in 2005. In Málaga, another group of squatters and cultural activists negotiated from the start, in 2007, and reached an initial agreement with the local and regional governments, as well as a national museum, in order to legalise the occupied building, La Invisible. Despite those promising prospects, the local authorities did not concede and threatened eviction several times over the following years, especially in 2018. In Barcelona, there are notable cases of legalised community centres after their occupation in the late 1970s, such as the still active Ateneu 9 Barris. Another curious case of anomalous institutionalisation is Can Batlló, an old factory which was legally transferred to the activists by the conservative/nationalist local government in 2011, the same day that a large grassroots mobilisation announced the occupation of the property. The new progressive government, which included some former housing activists that had become city councillors in 2015, supported the legalisation of many squats if other plans for municipal facilities did not interfere. Nonetheless, not all the squatters were open to negotiations, especially if they were overtly exposed to the media, given the legacy of legalisation refusal by the most politicised squatters.

In the City of Madrid, there were only four cases of legalisation out of 155 publicly known squatted social centres from the late 1970s to 2015. Sometimes social centres also housed people. Exclusively residential squatted buildings or apartments are more difficult to count due to the fact that most remained secret. One of the legalised cases (La Prospe) was not exactly a squat, but more a sort of a free school for adults. One squatted social centre found in four locations (Patio Maravillas) made great efforts to be involved in high-level negotiations so as to obtain a state-owned building where a self-managed social centre could be developed, but it failed even when three of their members also ascended to the city council in 2015. The most salient case of a legal self-managed social centre, often referred to as a squat by the mass media, was never squatted, although some former squatters initiated and joined the project (Tabacalera). There were also some cases of informal agreements with private owners that allowed the squatters to remain without any fixed date, until the owner had plans for the building. The latter were seldom propagated among the local squatters' scene.

IMAGE 5.3 Squat Patio Maravillas, Madrid, 2015
Source: Author

220 Anomalous Institutions

Fully Legalised Squats

The case of La Prospe does not exactly belong in the squatting movement at first glance but became very close to it during its campaign against eviction. In 1977, this popular school for adults was one of a number of groups who squatted, as a social centre, a building owned by the official labour union (Falange) during the dictatorship. Once it had been evicted from the building in 1980, La Prospe alone moved into a property belonging to the Catholic Church, whose rent was paid by the, initially reluctant, municipality (Social Democrats) after a short period of squatting. In 1991 the rent contract expired, and the Church wanted the school out of the building. Activists then initiated a public campaign and a strong mobilisation to avoid eviction from that space, where they remained as squatters. After several years of losing all their cases in the courts, negotiations with the political parties and, in particular, with the conservatives, who were ruling both the local and the regional government, were fruitful. In 2001, the regional government gave them free permission to legally use a public-owned building in the same area (a former working-class neighbourhood in the north-east, now very close to the city centre) for a period of 50 years.

La Prospe was not seen by the authorities as a typical squatters' collective, but as an alternative school mainly for poor people, with a very long trajectory and international recognition, although closely linked to leftist and libertarian ideals. Since the Church's attempts at speculation had been revealed, La Prospe's activists both supported squatting in general and publicly expressed their will to squat again if negotiations failed. Although most of the squatters in Madrid did not want to legalise their social centres, there was warm support for La Prospe's high-level negotiations. La Prospe appeared as an example of well-conducted self-management and autonomous political commitment for all the progressive social movements of the city. After the legalisation they continued to practice the same autonomy with the same political connections (with autonomists and anarchists) and frequently offered their premises for events hosted by other radical organisations. Both before and after legalisation, La Prospe has continued to represent well a socially recognised anomalous institution within the city.

The second successful case of legalisation involved a group of feminist squatters, Eskalera Karakola, with previous experience in mixed-sex squats. In 1996 they occupied a very old building, almost in ruins, which was then used almost exclusively by women. The squat was located in the inner city, Lavapiés, which was subject to various renewal plans during the 1990s and 2000s, and it is experiencing a belated (compared to other central districts) gentrification that began in 2016. The private owner of the building reclaimed it in 2003, but activists had already begun a public campaign asking the city government (conservatives) to buy the building and transfer it for free to the squatters. The squatters lost a court case, but the campaign resonated widely in local media and also received international support. The city council did not buy the building but, in turn, by 2005, offered the use of two nearby public basements of social housing

Anomalous Institutions **221**

estates on the same street for very low rent. The former squatted building was finally demolished a few years later, and the vacant land waited for construction plans many years more.

It is significant in this case that squatting was never denied by these feminists (and post-feminists) as part of their political identity, but it never enjoyed the same level of importance as gender politics (involving related issues such as women's labour precarity, LGBTQI militancy, migrant house workers, prostitution, sexist violence, etc.) from a radical and autonomist perspective. Their independent feminist project was better accepted by the local authorities as a conventional civic claim than the multiple goals associated with other squatted social centres. In contrast to the previous case, the Eskalera Karakola's attempts to negotiate a legal solution caused controversies among the squatters' movement and did not receive unified support due to both the general taboo concerning the legalisation of squats and the different approaches towards gender issues. Notwithstanding this, the legalised women's social centre kept the same autonomy and self-management of the space as before. Most of these feminists also remained very much involved in other social movements.

The *Seco* social centre is another full legalisation of a squat. The squatted building was an old school subject to a renewal plan in a working-class area Puente de Vallecas not far from the city centre. The first squatters formed one of the groups of an extreme-leftist organisation (Lucha Autónoma) who participated in dozens of squatting actions during the 1980s and 1990s. The building was self-abandoned after a first period of squatting (1991–97), and the re-squatting (1998–2007) opened up a political orientation much more connected to the local residents and concerned about the current renewal plan, problems of social exclusion, citizen participation, and social housing. Therefore, these activists experienced a turn to more conventional urban issues beyond squatting. As a consequence, they joined the neighbourhood association, worked together with independent urban planners, and organised film festivals with the attendance of famous filmmakers supportive of the squatters' demands for relocation in a public building. After a very long campaign, combining disruptive and conventional means, in 2007 they were allowed to use a city-owned two-floor space with the obligation of paying normal rent that could be partially subsidised on a year-by-year basis.

Seco's activists did not conceal their long experience as squatters, but they consciously decided to separate from the predominant aesthetics, symbols, and political discourse of the squatters in Madrid. Instead, they adopted a more conventional image by linking themselves to the neighbourhood association and to the demands for citizen participation in the urban renewal process. Thus, they united their demand for a new location of the social centre with demands for the rehousing of poor and old residents. This legalisation process suffered the same harsh criticisms from many Madrid squatters as the process led by Eskalera Karakola. However, wide social solidarity and impressive media coverage gave them substantial support in conducting the difficult negotiations with the local

222 Anomalous Institutions

government (conservatives). The new legal social centre combined the traditional style of neighbourhood associations working hand in hand with traditional residents of different ages and the innovative contents of other squats, such as solidarity with migrants (even helping them to squat), hack-labs, free and copyleft culture, urban gardening, etc. However, further internal cleavages gave birth to the opening of other social centres in the same area aiming to develop more radical and anomalous projects.

Failed Attempts at Legalisation

Regarding failed attempts at legalisation in Madrid, most of the squatters tend to forget that the first local organisation of the squatting movement (Asamblea de Okupas) initiated a discussion with the social democratic mayor in 1987, asking for legally assigned self-managed spaces. This had no result and was not well known to later squatters, although the attempt was noticed in some fanzines and books. As a legacy of that squatter coordination, in the next decade the strongest organisation among squatters comprised libertarian and extreme-left groups (Lucha Autónoma). Squatting was one of the emblems of this organisation, but many other struggles were relevant too (precarious work, feminism, students' strikes, anti-fascism, anti-militarism, etc.). When this sort of social movement organisation was dealing with a strong internal crisis, the decision of the most popular and massive squat at the time (Laboratorio) to launch a negotiation process with the municipal authorities, together with the traditional neighbourhood associations, produced a huge controversy and a split the city's squatters into several factions. The social success of the Laboratorio, which had three different locations between 1997 and 2003, was mainly based on the massive attendance of people at its events. Most of these users did not care about the internal political issues of the social centre, such as the negotiation process with the city and the eviction threats. Apart from the large number of theoretical texts and debates that these squatters produced, and the support obtained from a new network of neighbourhood associations (Red Lavapiés), there were no high-level meetings with authorities.

It is evident that the squatters' will and initiative to conduct a process of legalisation are not enough. Neither are social legitimation and the help of formal organisations. The powerful cultural activities hosted by the Laboratorio changed the general image of squatting in the city and could have been used as a policy sector apart from political squatting, as education, neighbourhood participation, and women's issues were for the legalised squats. However, political campaigns like opposition to the Iraq War, which was strongly associated with this squat, and the refusal of the local government to recognise the project and legalise it were crucial to the feasibility of the negotiations. Apart from paving the way for the subsequent attempts at legalisation, in 2010 some of the participants of the Laboratorio reached an agreement with the Ministry of Culture to develop a similar experiment in anomalous institutionalisation inside a very big building, in the same urban area, and which had never been squatted before: Tabacalera. The new experimental but legal (without paying any rent and even enjoying some subsidies) self-managed social centre was promoted by some people who participated actively in the previous Laboratorios, but they were not the majority of the new collective. As a matter of fact, they declared that 'Tabacalera is not a squat. Our political struggle is not about urban speculation and there is no core group with a high degree of militant politicisation setting up the lines of the process'. To some extent, Tabacalera enjoyed the fruits of efforts made a decade before. Self-management and free culture were the main axes that defined this project, and usually the mass media identified it as a squat, regardless of its legal status from the beginning. Although the Tabacalera became a self-managed social centre standing relatively apart from the squatters' scene in Madrid, after May 2011 it was used frequently by many working groups that emerged out of the occupation at Puerta del Sol. Later on, internal conflicts and difficulties with the management of the building deteriorated the previous vibrancy.

In 2007, a new squatted social centre Patio Maravillas, located in an increasingly gentrified area of the city centre called Malasaña, opened its doors. From the initial meetings, a majority of the squatters expressed their aspiration to achieve legal status, thus provoking an early division within the group and the exit of dissidents. Attempts to negotiate were delayed and the first meetings with the municipality (conservatives) took place more than a year after the squatting action. After their eviction from the first location and the squatting of a new building, the same group tried several times to contact political representatives and continue the conversations, but the process was very slow; a few more meetings were held without reaching any specific agreement. A piece of vacant land that was offered by the municipality as a possible future location for a self-managed building in the neighbourhood was also squatted as a way of obtaining a guarantee for that uncertain promise. Some months later, along with several of the formal organisations (neighbourhood associations, NGOs, etc.) that supported the squatters' demands, the squatting of a city-owned building (almost in ruins and subject to obvious speculation) was also carried out, but the squatters were evicted some weeks later. Following the paths of the Laboratorio, the Patio Maravillas mobilised massive attendance to its activities, wide media coverage, and an innovative way of combining culture and politics, local networks, and broader movements.

Patio Maravillas always showed their intention to learn the lessons of previous legalisation cases and even got the support of state institutions such as the National Museum of Contemporary Art, following similar alliances previously established with La Invisible (in Málaga) and Tabacalera. Although independent arts and free culture were often the core of the favourable image of them presented by the mass media, and they were also incorporated into municipal planning documents (the Strategic Plan for the City Centre, for instance), they also showed a more mixed, ambiguous, and anomalous identity in combination with other militant activities such as solidarity with migrants, LGBTQI, hackactivism, neighbourhood festivals, and urban biking. In addition, the Patio's desire to

IMAGE 5.4 Squat Edifici 15-O, Barcelona, 2012
Source: Author

legalise their projects faced the opposition of other squatters who even once attacked the building with a small explosive device. The Patio activists always remained in close contact with other groups of squatters and alternative movements in Madrid, including the 15M, while trying to involve neighbourhood associations and wider formal organisations (leftist political parties, environmental groups, etc.) in the defence and utilisation of their squat. When three of their core members became city councillors in 2015, the local government evicted them from one location and, after some negotiations, argued that no available buildings in the disputed city centre could satisfy the squatters' demands. After other failed attempts at squatting, the group vanished, although some of their members have kept squatting in a more successful experience to date, *La Ingobernable,* also located in the highly gentrified city centre (Huertas).

The Rejection of Legalisation

Finally, as an example of the predominant attitude towards the rejection of legalisation among the squatters of Madrid, I present the case of a group of squatters who occupied seven buildings between 2006 and 2018: Escoba, Alarma, Malaya, Mácula, Casablanca, Raíces, and Quimera (I refer to them as Casablanca for short, since this was the best known, see Image 5.6). All of these squats were located in the city centre (Huertas, Lavapiés, and Arganzuela), which helped to attract activists and sympathisers from all over the metropolitan region. In these squats a more libertarian or anarchist trend to autonomism was dominant, which included the rejection of any kind of transactional and high-level negotiations. The novelty among other similar squats was that Casablanca combined strong support for squatting (for example, by hosting a squatting office which provided legal advice and published a how-to-squat book, see Image 5.5) with a respectful attitude towards pro-legalisation squatters. Although no more than ten activists from the original group were still involved in Casablanca and almost none in Quimera, the decisions and agreements reached over the years were still guiding everyday life and political principles. Like most of the Madrid squatters until May 2011, Casablanca's activists consciously dealt with current survival and forced negotiations, but firmly rejected any sort of transactional and high-level ones. Hence, squatting as a means and an end was quite important for them, politically speaking. The close connection between Casablanca and the many working groups and the local popular assembly that were born as part of the 15M movement increased the social legitimation of this squat, which lasted two and a half years.

IMAGE 5.5 Squatting Handbook, Madrid, 2013
Source: Author

226 Anomalous Institutions

The issue of legalisation was hidden and purposefully avoided in the political debates within Casablanca. It was a taken-for-granted issue. While squatting and social inclusiveness were explicitly pursued by Casablanca, the legalisation of the squat was considered a topic on which it would be extremely difficult to obtain a consensus among the most active members, so it was almost never mentioned in assemblies. One of the exceptions was a SqEK (Squatting Europe Kollective) conference I organised in February 2012 in which squatters from Berlin, Amsterdam, Paris, and Brighton presented their knowledge of legalisations in their respective cities. Strikingly, this event in Casablanca was full at that time—around 60 people attended, with a few regular members of the assembly.

Therefore, Casablanca represented the prevalent stance of the squatters: direct opposition to both the state and major urban speculators such as real estate companies and banks. Legal defence in court was considered the maximum degree of negotiation that should be maintained with the state. This did not prevent further cleavages between different political squats due either to their opinions about ongoing legalisation processes or to other conflicts (physical aggression, exclusive coordination, ideological views, etc.). This means that the rejection of legalisation was not a sufficiently key element to keep squatters united.

Analytical Remarks

The first observation is that the ownership of the building and the need to deal with the conservative party in the government were not relevant at all when squatters and state officials (from the city council, mainly) started to negotiate. All three cases of legalisation moved their project to a new location provided by the authorities, although the economic conditions varied very much between them. With similar strategies, previous (Laboratorio) and further (Patio) attempts at legalisation failed. The reason, according to the argument above, is that they were not able to neatly separate their strongest single-issue identity (creative, independent, and free culture, in these cases) from all the political dimensions tied up in their projects (squatting, the campaign against the war, the 15M anti-austerity and anti-corruption movement, etc.). An additional verification of this analysis is that the Tabacalera project was always defined as a basic cultural and artistic initiative with an additional emphasis on self-management, cost-free status, and sharing, instead of focusing on urban speculation or other social struggles. On the one hand, the Tabacalera experiment could prepare the terrain for coming cultural and touristic attractions in the area when the economic recession was over and once the central government, at that time in the hands of social democrats, could relaunch the project of a new museum in that location. On the other hand, the social democrats also wanted to open up a wedge in a very conservative political arena at that time (both the city and the regional governments were controlled by the conservatives).

There were no other major variables that could determine the success of the legalisation processes, such as the trajectory at the courts or the urban location.

Lawsuits were used as typical forms of legal self-defence and as a means to expand their claims, but they did not help to preserve the continuation of the project since Spanish criminal law always favours the owner in cases of squatting. The central location of all the cases also contributed to the mass media coverage, but it was not crucial in helping the attempts of Laboratorio and Patio. Furthermore, recent cases of legalisation (Montamarta) occurred in a peripheral neighbourhood (San Blas) and in a city-owned building. Again, the political context of previous experiences of legalisation, the support of formal resident organisations, and the shift in the squatters' attitudes after the 15M movement contributed to the successful legalisation of this squat, although it was again an exception among the more than 38 visible occupations that occurred in Madrid between 2011 and 2015.

All these well-known social centres described above, due to their very convenient and powerful city centre locations plus their unexpected permanence, were able to preserve a strong commitment to an autonomous and self-managed way of functioning and retain bonds with other radical movements, even after some of them became legalised. When legalisation was sought, alliances with formal organisations and increased involvement in the state bureaucracy were always necessary. Intense campaigns of solidarity and social mobilisation through the mass media were also very time-consuming. By contrast, the squats that were reluctant to legalise felt released from those kinds of work and constraints, thus concentrating on their regular countercultural affairs. In spite of those differences, however, I observed that all of them made instrumental decisions in order to obtain social legitimation in the eyes of a broader audience beyond the autonomous movements. Moreover, none of them jeopardised their countercultural strength, social diversity, and radical challenges to the dominant neoliberal order.

The fact that most squatters participated in 'survival' and 'forced' negotiations reveals the subtle forms of institutionalisation in which they are involved. This differs from the stigmatised image of squatters as living almost completely on the margins of society and the state, something that is reinforced by a parallel ideological self-identity displayed by some squatters. On the other hand, when some groups of squatters initiate 'high-level' negotiations with authorities in order to legalise the occupied buildings, this does not mean that the squatters want to be totally integrated into mainstream society and politics. Legalisation provides stability, a means to access new resources, and political recognition from the authorities. This entails a higher degree of institutionalisation and more and more intense relationships with politicians, state officials, and economic elites compared to squats that reject legalisation. However, 'transactional' and 'high-level' negotiations do not necessarily imply, as the evidence from Madrid shows at least, that squatters abandon the countercultural, experimental, autonomous, and self-managed styles of running social centres.

It is also worth noting that there is strong pressure on the squatters when their building is in ruins, subject to imminent demolition or intended speculation, so that negotiations must go fast and become more instrumental than ideological. In the absence of immediate threats, the squatters can delay their interactions with state authorities and owners, which makes the planning of negotiations in advance easier.

IMAGE 5.6 Squat Casablanca, Madrid, 2013
Source: Author

Apart from the case of La Prospe, most of the attempts to become legal involved many other actors as mediators and facilitators, such as members of formal organisations, professionals who contributed their technical skills to write official documents, and journalists who could produce positive narratives in the mass media. In addition, other squatters and activists from other social movements, even in the controversial context of Madrid, heeded calls to demonstrate and give support to the squats aiming at legalisation. Conversely, an excessive insistence on the legitimate critique of urban speculation and defence of the right to decent housing, or a refusal to form a legal association, to pay rent, or to move to alternative locations, tend to be seen as intransigence by city officials and local politicians. Thus, negotiations may be aborted if these radical discourses appear in the foreground of the negotiations.

With respect to the political context, successful cases of legalisation cannot be explained by the conservative political party in the city and regional governments of Madrid having any ideological affinity with the squatters. Not even parliamentary leftist parties could play a conclusive mediating role in support of these squatters. Instead, the stories of legalisation could be interpreted as the authorities' tactics of conflict regulation when facing strong networks and campaigns of civic actors. Before these particular campaigns, the authorities did not have any explicit plan either to fully integrate the squatting movement institutionally or to dissolve it, although they were aiming to repress it. Actually, pro-legalisation squatters brought about a more flexible and open opportunity structure as opposed to one that was otherwise rigid and closed in accordance with the elites' conservative and neoliberal policies. In particular, that was the case of Seco's activists when they proposed an alternative urban renewal plan based on principles of citizen participation, the right of the population to be rehoused in the same area, social housing for young people, and a new location for the squatted social centre. Facing this challenge and the social mobilisation behind it, the municipality was obliged to respond and to largely meet those claims.

Finally, my interpretation of the above cases and the flexible and anomalous forms of institutionalisation that framed them in general relies on another strand of analysis: the rising globalisation of the metropolitan area of Madrid. In particular, an unprecedented expansion of neoliberal urban growth unfolded during the decade between 1996 and 2006. Many public services and companies were privatised and the resulting corporations expanded their business overseas. Mega operations of urban redevelopment and huge inflows of foreign investment invigorated real-estate speculation all over the region, with a consequent rapid escalation in housing prices. In parallel, public housing supply diminished dramatically. International immigration provided cheap labour for the construction economy but also for many domestic services, adding to an increasingly precarious labour market also affecting the native female and youth workforce. Urban tourism and gentrification of the inner city increased the tensions in the current housing bubble and displaced the most vulnerable groups from the central areas.

Squatters were some of the few urban activists who engaged in a deep criticism of these trends. However, their occupations were also under pressure, so property owners and developers demanded faster evictions, especially in the most profitable parts of the metropolitan region. Capitalists also better protected their properties, renovating them more quickly, and harassing old tenants in order to force their departure, so the opportunities for squatting decreased (a similar situation with even more intense processes of speculation and expulsions took place again in Madrid between 2016 and 2018). Therefore, squatters engaged in legalisation processes pursued a survival strategy that could grant them a safe base to develop their local struggles with most of the issues related to the globalisation of the city and their lives. The central areas were the most contested battleground, which explains all the difficulties that activists experienced before achieving lease agreements. Furthermore, the entrepreneurial forms of governance fuelled by both the local conservative governments and the social democrats in the central state, left little room for bottom-up participation. Legalisations were thus unlikely and, when attempted by the squatters, clashed with the dominant trends to privatise and marketise the entire public sector, from housing to culture. The cases of full legalisation represented exceptional concessions to placate some noisy claims for the affordability of central spaces and radical social projects (Seco, Eskalera, Prospe, and Montamarta), with one special

230 Anomalous Institutions

case (Tabacalera) more explicitly aligned with the arts-based sector of urban growth and at 'low-cost' once the economic crisis drained the public purse as well.

References

Aguilera, Thomas (2010) *Gouverner l'illegal: les politiques urbaines face aux squats à Paris*. Mémoire de Recherche. Paris: Master Stratégies Territoriales et Urbaines, SciencePo.

Aguilera, Thomas (2018) The Squatting Movement(S) in Paris: Internal Divides and Conditions for Survival. In Miguel A. Martínez (Ed.) *The Urban Politics of Squatters' Movements*. New York: Palgrave Macmillan, 121–144.

Alford, Robert R. & Roger Friedland (1985) *Powers of Theory. Capitalism, the State, and Democracy*. Cambridge: Cambridge University Press.

Asens, Jaume (2004) La represión al movimiento de las okupaciones: del aparato policial a los mass media. In Ramón Adell & Miguel A. Martínez (Eds) *¿Dónde están las llaves? El Movimiento Okupa: Prácticas y Contextos Sociales*. Madrid: La Catarata, 293–337.

Bosi, Lorenzo et al. (Eds) (2016) *The Consequences of Social Movements*. Cambridge: Cambridge University Press.

Burstein, P., R. Eisenwohner & J. Hollander (1995) The Success of Political Movements: A Bargaining Perspective. In J.C. Jenkins & B. Klandermans (Eds) *The Politics of Social Protest. Comparative Perspectives on States and Social Movements*. London: UCL Press, 135–144.

Cañedo, M. (2006) *Lavapiés, Área De Rehabilitación Preferente. Políticas Culturales y Construcción yel Lugar*. PhD Dissertation. Madrid: Universidad Complutense de Madrid.

Casanova, Gonzalo (2002) *Armarse Sobre Las Ruinas. Historia del Movimiento Autónomo en Madrid (1995-1999)*. Madrid: Potencial Hardcore.

Castells, Manuel (1983) *The City and the Grassroots. A Cross-Cultural Theory of Urban Social Movements*. Berkeley: University of California.

Dadusc, Deanna (2017) *The Micropolitics of Criminalisation: Power, Resistance and the Amsterdam Squatting Movement*. Amsterdam: University of Kent [PhD Dissertation].

Debord, Guy (1967) *The Society of the Spectacle*. New York: Zone Books.

Deleuze, Gilles & Felix Guattari (2004) *A Thousand Plateaus*. London: Continuum.

Della Porta, Donatella & Mario Diani (2006) *Social Movements: An Introduction*. Oxford: Wiley-Blackwell.

Eder, Klaus (2003) Social Movements and Democratization. In Gerard Delanty & Engin F. Isin (Eds) *Handbook of Historical Sociology*. London: Sage, 276–286.

Egia, Lutxo & Kukutza Gaztetxeko kideak (Eds) (2011) *Kukutza Gaztetxea. Ellos por Dinero, Nosotras por Placer*. Tafalla: Txalaparta.

El Paso Occupato & Barocchio Occupto (1995) *Against the Legalization of Occupied Spaces*. [https://theanarchistlibrary.org/library/el-paso-occupato-barocchio-occupato-against-the-legalization-of-occupied-spaces.pdf]

Fainstein, Norman & Susan Fainstein (1993) Participation in New York and London: Community and Market under Capitalism. In R. Fisher & J. Kling (Eds) *Mobilizing the Community: Local Politics in the Era of the Global City*. Newbury Park, CA: Sage, 52–71.

Fainstein, Susan & Clifford Hirst (1995) Urban Social Movements. In David Judge, Gerry Stoker & Harold Wolman (Eds) *Theories of Urban Politics*. London: Sage, 181–204.

Finchett-Maddock, Lucy (2016) *Protest, Property and the Commons. Performances of Law and Resistance*. Abingdon: Routledge.

Foucault, Michel (1982) The Subject and Power. *Critical Inquiry* 8(4): 777–795.

Giugni, Marco (1998) Was It Worth the Effort? the Outcomes and Consequences of Social Movements. *Annual Review of Sociology* 24: 371–393.

Anomalous Institutions 231

Goodwin, Jeff & James Jasper (Eds) (2009) *The Social Movements Reader. Cases and Concepts.* Oxford: Wiley-Blackwell.

Hojer, Maja et al. (Eds) (2018) *Contested Property Claims. What Disagreement Tells Us About Ownership.* Abingdon: Routledge.

Holm, Andrej & Armin Kuhn (2011) Squatting and Urban Renewal: The Interaction of Squatter Movements and Strategies of Urban Restructuring in Berlin. *International Journal of Urban and Regional Research* 35(3): 644–658.

Klein, Naomi (2002) *Fences and Windows: Dispatches from the Front Lines of the Globalization Debate.* Toronto: Random House.

Koopmans, Ruud (1995) *Democracy from Below. New Social Movements and the Political System in West Germany.* Boulder: Westview Press.

Kraken Nederland (2009) *Witboek Kraken.* [www.witboekkraken.nl]

Kriesi, Hanspeter (1996) The Organizational Structure of the New Social Movements in a Political Context. In Dough McAdam, John D. McCarthy & Meyer Zald (Eds) *Comparative Perspectives on Social Movements: Political Opportunitiesm Mobilizing Structures, and Cultural Framings.* New York: Cambridge University Press, 152–184.

Lowe, Stuart (1986) *Urban Social Movements. The City after Castells.* London: Macmillan.

Manjikian, Mary (2013) *Securitization of Property. Squatting in Europe.* New York: Routledge.

Martínez, Miguel A. (2002) *Okupaciones de Viviendas y Centros Sociales. Autogestión, Contracultura y Conflictos Urbanos.* Barcelona: Virus.

Martínez, Miguel A. (2016) Between Autonomy and Hibridity: Urban Struggles within the 15M Movement in Spain. In Margit Mayer, Catharina Thörn & Håkan Thörn (Eds) *Urban Uprisings. Challenging Neoliberal Urbanism in Europe.* New York: Palgrave Macmillan, 253–281.

Martínez, Miguel A. (2018) Socio-Spatial Structures and Protest Cycles of Squatted Social Centres in Madrid. In Miguel A. Martínez (Ed.) *The Urban Politics of Squatters' Movements.* New York: Palgrave Macmillan, 1–21.

Mayer, Margit (1993) The Role of Urban Social Movement Organisations in Innovative Urban Policies and Institutions. In Panagoitis Getimis & Grigoris Kafkalas (Ed.) *Urban and Regional Development in the New Europe.* Athens: Topos, 209–226.

Mayer, Margit (2006) Manuel Castells'. *The City and the Grassroots. International Journal of Urban and Regional Research* 30(1): 202–206.

Mayer, Margit (2016) Neoliberal Urbanism and Uprisings across Europe. In Margit Mayer, Catharina Thörn & Håkan Thörn (Eds) *Urban Uprisings. Challenging Neoliberal Urbanism in Europe.* New York: Palgrave Macmillan, 57–92.

McKay, George (Ed.) (1998) *DiY Culture: Party and Protest in Nineties Britain.* London: Verso.

Membretti, A. (2007) Centro Sociale Loncavallo. Building Citizenship as an Innovative Service. *European Urban and Regional Studies* 14.3: 255–266.

Mudu, Pierpaolo (2004) Resisting and Challenging Neoliberalism: The Development of Italian Social Centers. *Antipode* 36(5): 917–941.

Mudu, Pierpaolo & Luisa Rossini (2018) Occupations of Housing and Social Centres in Rome: A Durable Resistance to Neoliberalism and Institutionalization. In Miguel Martínez (Ed.) *The Urban Politics of Squatters' Movements.* New York: Palgrave Macmillan, 99–120.

Negri, Antonio (1994) *El Poder Constituyente. Ensayo Sobre Las Alternativas De La Modernidad.* Madrid: Libertarias/Prodhufi.

Neidhart, Friedhelm & Dieter Rucht (1991) The Analysis of Social Movements: The State of the Art and Some Perspectives for Further Research. In Dieter Rucht (Ed.) *Research on Social Movements: The State of the Art in Western Europe and the USA.* Boulder, CO: Westview Press, 421–464.

232 Anomalous Institutions

Offe, Claus (1990) Reflections on the Institutional Self-Transformation of Movements Politics: A Tentative Stage Model. In Russel J. Dalton & Manfred Kuechler (Eds) *Challenging the Political Order. New Social and Political Movements in Democracies.* Cambridge: Polity, 232–250.

Owens, Linus (2009) *Cracking under Pressure. Narrating the Decline of the Amsterdam Squatters' Movement.* Amsterdam: Amsterdam University Press.

Piazza, Gianni (2013) How Do Activists Make Decisions within Social Centres? In SqEK (Ed.) *Squatting in Europe. Radical Spaces, Urban Struggles.* Wivenhoe: Minor Compositions, 89–111.

Pickvance, Christopher G. (1984) The Structuralist Critique in Urban Studies. In Michael P. Smith (Ed.) *Cities in Transformation. Class, Capital and the State.* London: Sage, 31–50.

Pickvance, Christopher G. (1999) Democratisation and the Decline of Social Movements: The Effects of Regime Change on Collective Action in Eastern Europe, Southern Europe and Latin America. *Sociology* 33(2): 353–372.

Piven, Francis & Richard Cloward (1979) *Poor People's Movements. Why They Succeed, How They Fail.* New York: Random House.

Pixová, Michaela & Arnost Novák (2016) Prague Post-1989: Boom, Decline and Renaissance. *Baltic Worlds* IX(1–2): 34–45.

Polanska, Dominika & Grzegorz Piotrowski (2016) Poland: Local Differences and the Importance of Cohesion. *Baltic Worlds* IX(1–2): 46–56.

Pruijt, H. (2013) Culture Wars, Revanchism, Moral Panics and the Creative City. A Reconstruction of A Decline of Tolerant Public Policy: The Case of Dutch Anti-Squatting Legislation. *Urban Studies* 50(6): 1114–1129.

Pruijt, Hans (2003) Is the Institutionalization of Urban Movements Inevitable? A Comparison of the Opportunities for Sustained Squatting in New York and Amsterdam. *International Journal of Urban and Regional Research* 27(1): 133–157.

Quarta, Alessandra & Tomaso Ferrando (2015) Italian Property Outlaws: From the Theory of the Commons to the *Praxis* of Occupation. *Global Jurist* 15(3): 261–290.

Rannila, Päivi & Virve Repo (2018) Property and Carceral Spaces in Christiania, Copenhagen. *Urban Studies* 55(13): 2996–3011.

Rossini, Luisa, azozomox & Galvão Debelle (2018) Keep Your Piece of Cake, We'll Squat the Bakery! Autonomy Meets Repression and Institutionalisation. In Miguel A. Martínez (Ed.) *The Urban Politics of Squatters' Movements.* New York: Palgrave Macmillan, 247–269.

Rucht, Dieter (1990) The Strategies and Action Repertoires of New Movements. In Russel J. Dalton & Manfred Kuechler (Eds) *Challenging the Political Order. New Social and Political Movements in Democracies.* Cambridge: Polity, 156–175.

Santos, Boaventura (Ed.) (2003) *Democratizar a Democracia. Os Caminhos da Democracia Participativa.* Porto: Afrontamento.

Scott, James C. (2012) Infrapolitics and Mobilizations: A Response by James C. Scott. *Revue Française D'études Américaines* 131(1): 112–117.

SQUASH (Squatters' Action for Secure Homes) (2011) *Criminalising the Vulnerable: Why We Can't Criminalise Our Way Out of a Housing Crisis—A Parliamentary Briefing.* [www.squashcampaign.org]

Stallman, R. (2002) *Software Libre Para Una Sociedad Libre.* Madrid: Traficantes de Sueños.

Stavrides, Stavros (2016). *Common Space: The City as Commons.* London: Zed.

Steiger, Tina (2018) Cycles of the Copenhagen Squatter Movement: From Slumstormer to BZ Brigades and the Autonomous Movement. In Miguel A. Martínez (Ed.) *The Urban Politics of Squatters' Movements.* New York: Palgrave Macmillan, 165–186.

Tarrow, Sidney (1994) *Power in Movement: Social Movements, Collective Action, and Politics.* Cambridge: Cambridge University Press.

Tilly, Charles (1984) *Big Structures, Large Processes, Huge Comparisons*. New York: Russel Sage Foundation.

Tilly, Charles (1999) From Interactions to Outcomes in Social Movements. In Marco G. Giugni et al. (Eds) *How Movements Matter*. Minneapolis: University of Minnesota Press, 253–270.

Tilly, Charles (2007) *Democracy*. New York: Cambridge University Press.

Toret, Javier, Nicolás Sguiglia, Santiago Fernández, P. Lama & M. Lama (Eds) (2008) *Autonomía y Metrópolis. Del Movimiento Okupa a los Centros Sociales de Segunda Generación*. Málaga: ULEX-Diputación Provincial de Málaga.

Touraine, Alain (1978) *The Voice and the Eye. An Analysis of Social Movements*. Cambridge: Cambridge University Press.

Uitermark, Justus (2004) Framing Urban Injustices: The Case of the Amsterdam Squatter Movement. *Space and Polity* 8(2): 227–244.

Universidad Nómada (2008) Mental Prototypes and Monster Institutions. Some Notes by Way of an Introduction. [http://eipcp.net/transversal/0508/universidadnomada/en]

Valli, Chiara (2015) When Cultural Workers Become an Urban Social Movement: Political Subjectification and Alternative Cultural Production in the Macao Movement, Milan. *Environment & Planning A* 47: 643–659.

Ward, Colin (1973) *Anarchy in Action*. London: Freedom Press.

Yates, Luke (2014) Rethinking Prefiguration: Alternatives, Micropolitics and Goals in Social Movements. *Social Movement Studies: Journal of Social, Cultural and Political Protest* 14(1): 1–21.

6

CRIMINALISATION AND COUNTER-HEGEMONY

Why has the occupation of vacant properties without the owner's authorisation become increasingly criminalised in European countries? Although the criminalisation process varies across countries, I argue that there are common features that allow understanding these historical shifts over the last three decades. In this chapter I examine first how media and political elites spread stigmas about squatters that prepared the ground for increasing legal prosecution of squatters. In particular, I identify a two-fold 'homogenisation' and 'polarisation' rhetoric as the main strands of hegemonic discourses that portray squatters with 'negative' traits. They lead to full or partial stigmatisation of squatters, on the one hand, and to mistaken stereotypes, on the other. The performative power of these discourses influence political and economic structures around urban vacancy so that squatting is rarely seen as a protest movement contesting them. In a following section I discuss how the symbolic contradictions within the dominant narratives are reframed by the squatters themselves in order to wage discursive struggles about the legitimation of squatting. The conflict between hegemonic and counter-hegemonic narratives further illuminates the structural considerations regarding the capitalist system and class struggles which are involved in most squatting actions.

The Performative Powers of 'Spectacular Narrations'

The term 'stigma' dates back to the Ancient Greece when it referred to visual signs which 'were cut or burnt into the body and advertised that the bearer was a slave, a criminal, or a traitor' (Goffman 1963: 1). Later on, it was generalised to encompass the identity attributes of specific social groups who in the extreme are seen as 'quite thoroughly bad, or dangerous, or weak ... sometimes it is also called a failing, a shortcoming, a handicap' (Goffman 1963: 3). The stigma accentuates undesirable or discredited attributes of the 'stereotype', or biased

Criminalisation and Counter-Hegemony **235**

social identity, held by the group members. Therefore, Goffman's sociological use of the term 'stigma' suggests negative connotations overall. Instead of taken for granted his interactionist and functionalist approach, I rather assume that stigmas, stereotypes, and social identities in general, are mainly, though not exclusively, the outcomes of dominant discourses. These discourses are produced according to the economic and symbolic means of production under the control of dominant social groups, elites and capitalists, which necessarily implies a certain articulation with class struggles (Harvey 1990, Jessop 1982, Therborn 1980). I will thus interpret stigmatisation processes of squatters according to the ideologies and hegemonic discourses that intervene in the reproduction of the capitalist city at large, and the neoliberal city specifically (Madden & Marcuse 2016, Mayer 2016, Rossi 2017). As a consequence, I argue that the dissemination of stigmas and stereotypes about squatters contributes significantly to their criminalisation, although other specific institutional dynamics (in national parliaments, for example) and economic interests (the anti-squatting and private security companies, among others) should be investigated as well. In addition, I understand the criminalisation process of squatting as a condition to reinvigorate the capitalist class domination in the urban sphere, which is hardly examined by previous scholarship.

The law changes in the Netherlands (2010) and England and Wales (2012) are the most recent landmarks in the criminalisation of squatting across European countries, so they instigated a significant amount of research (Dadusc 2017, Fox et al. 2015, Manjikian 2013, Pruijt 2013b). Hereafter I look at other European cases as well. Despite its prosecution, squatting continues to go on and has even proliferated in those territories more acutely hit by the global financial and refugee crises (Di Feliciantonio 2017, García-Lamarca 2016, Mudu & Chattopadhyay 2017). Beyond their illegal condition, many squats manage to last for years and decades while developing a rich variety of social milieus, activities and residential alternatives (Cattaneo & Martínez 2014, Martínez 2018c, Steen et al. 2014, Vasudevan 2017). This indicates the continuing existence of tensions and controversies about the nature and contributions of squatting, which are manifest in 'culture wars' (Pruijt 2013b) and discursive struggles (Bouillon 2013, Dee & Debelle 2015, Manjikian 2013).

According to many observers, mainstream mass media and politicians tend to portray squatters as 'folk devils' (Dee 2016), 'gangs of thugs, layabouts and revolutionary fanatics, parasites, invaders who steal people's homes' (Fox et al. 2015: 4). Breaking in and trespassing on private property is often clumsily equated with the occupation of empty premises. They all are quickly conflated into a representation of serious criminal offences before any research on the circumstances of an occupation or any legal verdict has been determined. These dominant narrations have the immediate consequence of criminalising squatters (Dadusc 2017). No distinctions between their income, residential and labour conditions are made—homeless people in need of shelter, those who cannot afford to buy or rent convenient venues for performing social activities, activists who squat as a means of protest

236 Criminalisation and Counter-Hegemony

against urban policies, etc. Rational discussions about the political, economic, social and urban contexts are usually neglected by media reports. Accordingly, capitalism, absolute property rights and real-estate speculation are naturally taken for granted, despite the multiple legal regulations at play. Home evictions and homelessness are seldom associated with the human rights violations involved in the eviction of occupied places.

In accordance with Debord's insights, the term 'spectacular narrations' may be used to designate the aforementioned set of assumptions. According to him, 'spectacles' first *separate* and alienate workers from the products of their work, workers from other workers (also as inhabitants of the same city), and subjects to a system of oppression from their potentialities to overcome it. Second, 'spectacles' are cultural weapons aiming to represent the world as a *unity* of interests, feelings, national identity and universal human values between the exploited and their exploiters, servants and masters, matter and culture, past and future.

> The unreal unity proclaimed by the spectacle masks the class division underlying the real unity of the capitalist mode of production. What obliges the producers to participate in the construction of the world is also what excludes them from it. ... While all the technical forces of capitalism contribute toward various forms of separation, urbanism provides the material foundation for those forces and prepares the ground for their deployment.
>
> *(Debord 1967: §72, §171)*

Mass consumption, political disenfranchisement and homeownership are some of the key areas that spectacular narrations bring together in order to foster an 'unreal unity' and to mystify the ongoing economic inequalities and spatial segregation which characterise capitalism and contemporary cities. When applied to squatting, it is worth questioning how the divisions among squatters and their supposed unity as a whole, in radical opposition to the rest of society, are disseminated. Furthermore, I wonder to what extent there are alternative narrations that manifest discursive struggles about the legitimation of squatting. Yet these questions have not been properly addressed by the literature on squatting. In particular, I have noticed a lack of distinction between 'homogenisation' and 'polarisation' narratives in the main works dealing with dominant discourses on squatting (Aguilera 2018, Bouillon 2013, Dee 2013, Dee & Debelle 2015, Fox et al. 2015, Manjikian 2013, Middleton 2015, Pruijt 2013b). While the split between 'good' and 'bad' squatters has been carefully disclosed, the accounts differ substantially. As a consequence, a more systematic categorisation of the cleavages among squatters imposed by the 'spectacular narrations' is needed. Moreover, the attempts to anchor counter-hegemonic responses and to legitimise squatting have not identified which dimensions are more oppositional to capitalism (Cattaneo & Martínez 2014, Hodkinson 2012, Madden & Marcuse 2016) and which ones do not imply such a radical view, although they may still help enhance the reputation of squatters.

IMAGE 6.1 Squat La Porka, Barcelona, 2015
Source: Author

While disclosing the ideological turn operated by spectacular narrations there is also the risk of representing a false homogeneity or solidarity among all kinds of squatters. This would prevent us from recognising their significant social diversity as practitioners and activists (azozomox 2014, Cattaneo & Martínez 2014, Martínez 2018c, Mudu & Chattopadhyay 2017). For instance, they can differ in terms of gender, race, age, cultural and economic capital, motivations, political affinities and alignments, organisational membership, etc. The variety of occupied properties also intersects with the squatters' social networks and communities. The land use of the urban area and the building, the time span of vacancy, whether the property is subject to heritage protection, the state of maintenance and age of the building, who the owners are and what they did with the building before its abandonment, etc. are not pointless features (Martínez 2018a). Therefore, squatters can share an opposition to private property as far as it entails unacceptable inequalities, but squatters can also occupy buildings under very much different circumstances, without invoking private property as a pillar of capitalism. The avoidance of the above variations by the literature on squatting requires clear identification of the radical (anti-capitalist) and moderate grounds that justify the occupations of vacant properties.

Are Squatters All the Same?

Borrowing from Debord (1967), the stigmatisation of squatters via hegemonic stereotypes may take two basic forms: (a) homogenisation ('all squatters are the same'); and (b) polarisation ('there are good and bad squatters'). Squatters themselves may equally adhere to these rhetoric strategies by filling them with own

238 Criminalisation and Counter-Hegemony

contents. They can also reverse them by: (a) revealing significant differences when its collective is seen as homogeneous; (b) underscoring the commonalities among all the squatters as subjects to market oppression and state marginalisation when they are distinguished as 'good and bad' squatters. Let's examine first how homogenisation operates.

Opposition to squatting may be backed for different reasons. For example, a rooted belief in the primacy of private property that allows almost absolute power to those granted ownership, regardless of the legal limitations applicable in each national jurisdiction (Fox et al. 2015). More often, it is due to urban elites' revanchism against poor people, migrants, racial minorities and young activists, all perceived as marginal, deviant and undesirable individuals whose mere existence in the city is not welcome (Pruijt 2013b). Smith illustrates this revanchism with declarations of New York's former mayor, Rudolf Giuliani: 'He identifies homeless people, panhandlers, prostitutes, curbside squeegee cleaners, squatters, graffiti artists, "reckless bicyclists", and unruly youth as the major enemies of public order, the culprits of urban decline generating widespread fear' (Smith 1999: 100).

Elite revanchism against those altering the status quo tends to occur in association with a 'moral panic' that frames squatters who actively resist their eviction as violent, unruly or even a sort of low-key terrorism. Pruijt recalls how a majority in the Dutch Parliament and Senate have always claimed a 'sense of urgency' to legislate against squatting since its first public manifestations in the mid-1960s. They only succeeded four decades later, after three incidents in 2007 and 2008 that triggered the moral panic:

> The police reported that squatters had left booby traps in barricade squats ... Prime Minister Balkenende expressed shock ... In 2008, the impression of a violent turn in the Amsterdam's squatters' movement was reinforced by a case in which the Amsterdam police reported having found various weapons during an eviction.
>
> *(Pruijt 2013b: 1121–1122)*

The Dutch anti-squatting law was passed in 2010 with a preface in which the association between squatters and violence justified the criminalisation. Dee (2016: 786–788) delved into the same three cases by citing the squatters' views. According to Dee's analysis, there was no compelling evidence for the accusations made by the police—i.e. no booby traps, no bombs and no guns. These counterarguments, however, were not reported by the mass media as much as the authorities' version. 'The panic was used for "agenda-setting" ... but it is important to note that it was based on completely fictitious grounds' (Dee 2016: 789). Interestingly, during the process of stigmatisation that resulted in the end of tolerance towards squatting, Dee interpreted the squatters framing as a 'symptom of the other' in a typical labelling process that assigns deviant properties to specific social groups 'as young, threatening, violent, disrespectful, foreign, different, and so on' (ibid.).

Squatters in the Netherlands enjoyed four decades of 'regulated tolerance' policies that shifted towards harsher repression in the 2000s. Tolerance does not mean an absolute protection of squatting, but its legal and political control within certain limits. Similar to Dutch policies related to drugs and prostitution, the regulation of squatting was left in a grey area between legality and illegality. Negotiations with squatters and ritual encounters with the police were the pattern (Dadusc 2017: 30–31). A partial criminalisation was already implemented in 1981 and 1993 by limiting squatting to properties vacant for more than six months, first, and more than a year, later (Manjikian 2013: 162). This indicates that 'culture wars' were at play all over the history of squatting, although intensified in the periods immediately before its criminalisation. For example, violent episodes of evictions and clashes between police and squatters had nurtured the media stigma of squatting since its inception as an urban movement and especially during the 1980s, at the movement's heydays: 'Whereas squatters, in private, were friendly, caring, and trusting individuals, the public squatter was tough, violent, and suspicious' (Owens 2009: 85). However, the context of regulated tolerance also matched 'the squatters' movement easily acquired sympathy by large parts of society, including politicians and the media' (Dadusc 2017: 26) during the economic recession of the 1970s and early 1980s. For example, in 1975, after a successful alliance between squatters and residents to prevent the demolition of affordable housing in the city centre (in the Nieuwmarkt area), a parliamentary bill to criminalise squatting in 1976 did not get endorsement by the Senate.

However, following the rise of neoliberal and 'zero tolerance' policies in the 1990s, homogenisation rhetoric depicting squatters as 'lazy', 'parasites' and 'foreigners who come to Amsterdam to have fun, use drugs, and live at the expenses of Dutch society and welfare' (Dadusc 2017: 1) culminated in the Black Book of squatting published by the liberal party VVD in 2008. Above all, squatting was framed as 'an immoral action against private property rights' (Dadusc 2017: 213). But this was also underpinned with ideological attacks launched from various flanks: squatters seize luxury apartments in the city centre that they do not deserve, they jump the queue for the allocation of social housing, and they are 'barbaric foreigners' that 'invade' the Netherlands, 'come here for mayhem' and threaten the Dutch democratic model based on 'consensus decision-making and social compromise' (Dadusc & Dee 2015: 118). In the Explanatory Memorandum dated on the same year, politicians from the VVD and two other Christian Democratic parties also argued, without any supporting evidence, that 'the presence of squatted buildings is often accompanied by a lot of disturbance and degradation … The quality and value of the surrounding housing decreases, with the result that the quality of life in the neighbourhoods is affected' (quoted by Dadusc & Dee 2015: 117). Although Manjikian (2013: 157–160, 168) highlights a particular strand of the xenophobic and racist narratives against squatting that demanded a 'defensive move' to anticipate an overwhelming flow of squatters once all the European countries have criminalised them, this dimension of the moral panic did not take the lead among the many stigmatising attributes in circulation.

240 Criminalisation and Counter-Hegemony

Based on parliamentary debates, government documents and politicians' statements to the press in the UK between 2010 and 2012, when the criminalisation of squatting in England and Wales came into force, Middleton (2015) confirms how effective the rhetoric of homogenisation is in successfully supporting a law change. She goes into more detail and distinguishes three tactics within that general rhetoric: (a) squatters are not fair because they 'are getting so much for free' when most people 'are struggling to get by' (Middleton 2015: 101); (b) 'squatters are criminal and lazy' because they are not 'virtuously hard-working and law-abiding' as most homeowners are (Middleton 2015: 101–102); and (c) squatters are a consolidated and even 'professional' subculture that must be eradicated:

> They display 'arrogant behaviour', believing themselves superior to the rest of society, and in particular believing themselves to be 'above the law'. They are 'web-savvy', they have a predilection for high-value properties, they deceive us with their 'guilt and tenacity' and they are carefree, continuing 'on their merry way' when they are evicted. The term squatter is also frequently prefaced by 'prolific' and 'professional', qualifiers which connote success, implying that squatters view their activities with pride.
>
> *(Middleton 2015: 103–104)*

Most observers noted that stigmatising discourses about squatters in the UK were intensified during the 2000s, but they were already circulating since the mid-1960s when organised public campaigns were initiated (Bailey 1973). For example, stereotypes of squatting as a 'social problem' and squatters as 'feckless, irresponsible and politically motivated' (Cobb 2015: 22) reached a peak in 1975. In fact, partial criminalisation of squatting was in effect since 1977 and amended in 1994 with the provision of a fast-track eviction process once squatters were requested to leave (Finchett-Maddock 2016: 61, Manjikian 2013: 86–87). Notwithstanding the risks of evictions and criminal charges, the practice of squatting was widely tolerated. The law changes regarding 'adverse possession' in 1980 and 2002 shook again the public debate on squatting. These regulations motivated the rise of the squatters perceived as 'thefts' and 'parasitic deviants' according to a Home Office Report (1991) but also as 'wily', 'clever' and deliberately organised in order to illegitimately achieve property titles. During the 2000s 'newspaper coverage had begun to "essentialize" the squatter, presenting him as a monolithic type' (Manjikian 2013: 88). In short, even if squatters enjoyed well-established rights and conventional aspirations to access property, they were still labelled as organised criminals by conservative outlets such as the Evening Standard and the Daily Mail (Manjikian 2013: 105). This homogenisation rhetoric was more advanced and abundant in the years before the squatting ban of 2012 by conflating all kinds of squatting (for example, short-term rough sleeping and long-term residential occupations) in the 'lifestyle' stereotype: '[O]ne who has alternate living arrangement available to him, but who makes an ideological decision to squat rather than to pay rent ... . Aggressive squatters or groups of people in housing need contentedly living in a communal nirvana' (Manjikian 2013: 107, Dadusc & Dee 2015: 115). A similar stereotype criticising squatters as a subculture of partygoers and organisers of raves preceded the legal reform in 1994 (Vasudevan 2017: 64).

Similar generalisations about squatters as a whole are found in Spain as well. Before the 'usurpation' of empty properties was made a criminal offence by a legal reform passed in 1995, media news about squatting were scarce and usually limited to the local sections (Alcalde 2004). Most journalists did not overtly attack squatters, although the 'okupa' stereotype associated to punk-style dress, youth, unemployment, and political radicalism was increasingly gaining public attention as an 'urban tribe' among others (Martínez 2002: 140–153). Moral panic about squatters before 1995 was not especially acute, but targeted youth radical movements in general such as the peace activists (*insumisos*) opposing military conscription, who regularly frequented squats (Seminario 2015: 193–196). Since the mid-1980s autonomist and anarchist squatted social centres took hold in the major cities and numbers rapidly soared by the early 1990s as the grassroots campaigns against the Olympics in Barcelona and the 'International Exposition' in Seville were firmly based on squatters' networks. Despite the initial ambivalence or ignorance of squatting by most mass media (Alcalde 2004), conservative newspapers such as ABC and La Vanguardia led the promotion of a negative framing: '[squatters are] violent youngsters, unemployed and active delinquents ... little hordes of rootless people who raze and invade alien properties' (quoted by Martínez 2002: 151). Given the upsurge of squatting immediately after the criminalisation came into effect, the moral panic and aggressive categorisation of squatters in the media also became more intense in the following years (Asens 2004, Debelle 2017, Dee & Debelle 2015) with a strong support of police agents who, in turn, sought to suppress left-libertarian and independentist activists and regularly infiltrated squats (Fernández 2009). The rise of squatting during the last economic recession, after 2008, infuriated the most conservative voices. In particular, the right-populist party Ciudadanos launched a parliamentary attempt to increase the prosecution and punishment of squatting. In the op-ed of an online newspaper (September, 2017), the leader of this party in Madrid, Begoña Villacís, combined all the above-mentioned stereotypes in a single column:

> No 'good morning', no introduction to their new neighbours—those simpletons who paid for live in a house like theirs in a neighbourhood like theirs and, up to now, with the same tranquillity than theirs ... For years we have produced laws that protect usurpers and opportunists, which allow some to 'live for free' and ... evict this man [a legitimate owner] from their own home. ... Squatters impose fear and intimidation to deteriorate neighbourhood life. Some streets are now in the hands of gangs and

242 Criminalisation and Counter-Hegemony

> bullies. There are now [occupied] drug-dealing flats ... brothels and nests of terrorists. The phenomenon becomes viral ... There is no such a dichotomy between the right to housing and the right to property. ... We should not wait a minute more in order to get rid of our condition of a paradise country for squatters.[1]

According to this politician, all squatters are unfair, unlawful, criminal and a plague that should be supressed immediately because the criminalisation in force does not suffice. She only compares squatters with homeowners and presents the latter as the principal representatives of society as a whole. Private property rights and homeowners' rights, then, are the priority to be protected. Squatters are bad neighbours (no hello to others), outsiders, they do not pay rent, do not pay mortgage instalments, and do not comply with the legislation, which is assumed to be outdated and inefficient. In an effort to raise alarm (a 'sense of urgency' and moral panic), she also exaggerates her hard line approach by suggesting that squatters can occupy principal homes when their regular residents are away — although this is not a proper case of squatting empty properties, but a completely different and more serious criminal infraction: housebreaking and intrusion into one's private home. The association of squatters with delinquents, drug trafficking, prostitution and terrorism are not chosen randomly. Without any evidence, these activities are attributed to all squatters and not distinguished from the practice of squatting itself. The newspaper contributes to the creation of panic by including four pictures without any actual squatters in them, as if they were unknown and dangerous ghosts that oblige owners to wall their front doors (photo 1) and keep a wary eye on their middle-class townhouses (photo 2), mansions with swimming pools (photo 3) and low-middle class developments (photo 3), where a group of eight new buyers in their thirties represent the 'idiots who pay a mortgage' (according to the author's headline) as the lawful rivals, and potential victims, of squatters. Both discourse and images pursue the same pragmatic aim — instilling a revanchist mood in public opinion which would justify harsher criminalisation.

Soft Gentrifiers

The above discourses stigmatise and homogenise squatters as a whole or 'other' against a 'society' which is always idealised and defined vaguely, as most legal documents name it. However, not so frequently, dominant narratives about squatters can also be expressed in apparently less negative terms. The reason of this apparent contradiction is that this positive framing is made up of squatters as functional to the capitalist regeneration of urban spaces. The stereotype of squatters as artists (cultural workers and professionals) and, eventually, gentrifiers of dilapidated urban areas is usually produced by wealthy groups as a homogenising label (all the squatters they know are 'soft gentrifiers') but is also widespread

IMAGE 6.2 After-squat New Yorck in Bethanien, Berlin, 2011
Source: Author

among political (left-libertarian) squatters as a very controversial and polarising category, as we will show later (Aguilera 2018). For example, an editor of an architecture magazine emailed me with the following message:

> [The area] in London where our office is based was once full of squatting artists and designers who gradually transformed the area from one that was quite dangerous to one that is now home to Google, Facebook and a myriad of trendy bars.
>
> *(Martínez 2015: 34)*

Cities such as Amsterdam, where squatting enjoyed many decades of tolerance, and Berlin, where a rapid gentrification process occurred in formerly squatted neighbourhoods, have often shaped the paradigmatic imaginary for the dissemination of this discourse (azozomox & Kuhn 2018, Holm & Kuhn 2017, Novy & Colomb 2012, Owens 2009, Pruijt 2013a, Uitermark 2004, Vasudevan 2017). Although exceptional, this can be designated as the 'improvement frame' according to Manjikian (2013: 57–58). Another indicator of how squatting is portrayed in mainstream media is the graffiti murals on the walls of long lasting squats. These are used by tourist guides, airlines and fashion magazines as identity signs of cities, an evident turn to the homogenisation of the squatting culture, social life and politics by incorporating these flagship images into city branding and urban marketisation strategies (Mayer 2016). Freetown Christiania, in Copenhagen, occupied since 1971, also became a very well-known tourist attraction internationally (Thörn et al. 2011).

244 Criminalisation and Counter-Hegemony

Recently, a report in the *Elle Décor Italia* magazine represented this general association of squatters with artistic venues and hip spots that eventually—against their will, though— paved the way for subsequent urban gentrification:

> SiViaggia.it, the Italian travel website, published a review of the most beautiful and socially influential European squats ... Between Louvre and Centre Pompidou, in one of the most important commercial streets of Paris's historical centre, they [Rivoli 59] created more than thirty artist studios, visited by thousands of people every week, and an art gallery that sells the works of artists from all over the world... . In 2014, a spectacular mobilisation pressured the city hall of Altona district [in Hamburg, Germany] to rule that the edifice [Rota Flora] will not be demolished and it will remain an active cultural centre. ... The Snakehouse, in Spuitstraat, in the heart of Amsterdam, it is a four storey squat occupied in 1983, where dozens of artists worked and lived together. ... The building was recently bought by the De Key construction company ... The edifice will be turned into a complex of luxury apartments. ... After countless eviction attempts and notices, the Tacheles [in Berlin] was closed in 2012, and it is now under restoration as part of the renovation plan of the surrounding area. ... Kukutza III [in Bilbao, Spain] filled an institutional void on cultural and entertainment issues, providing spaces for dance, climbing, martial arts, a library, a canteen, a theatre, and a workshop for craft beer production. After the definitive eviction—one of the most difficult in history, with more than 140,000 euros in damages, dozens of people wounded, and 64 arrests—even the area's shop-owners complained about the loss of the effervescent atmosphere that made the neighbourhood vibrant.[2]

Another journalistic account also echoing the controversy around Tacheles but with an eye in the coming criminalisation of squatting in England and Wales, was even more directly concerned about the outlook of squatters as gentrifiers. In the article gentrification is not seen as a negative process in which poor and vulnerable population are forcibly displaced, but as an opportunity to bring about economic vibrancy in a neighbourhood. Therefore, squatters are represented with an extraordinary capacity to boost business and tourism in the areas where they occupy:

> The Tacheles building in central Berlin (pictured above) has been occupied by artists for 20 years. Originally built to be a department store, it became a Nazi prison before being squatted in 1990. Now it's a celebrated institution, attracting hundreds of thousands of visitors each year. It is credited with playing a key part in Berlin's rebirth as a cultural capital and has regenerated the local area whose businesses reap rewards from the tourism it brings. For these reasons, the mayor of Berlin and the state

secretary for culture have been determined to prevent the insolvent owner's creditors, HSH Nordbank, from repossessing it—despite the building's obvious commercial potential, worth millions of euros ... There's a history to how squatting can sow the seeds of cultural success. Boy George, Mario Testino and Jamie Hince are all ex-squatters. The Sex Pistols' Jonny Rotten, in fact the entire punk movement, arguably, has its roots in squatting ... Catherine Garrity, a squatter with the Well Furnished group, claims that 'gentrification begins with squatting'. Garrity believes that squatting is an extension of the old maxim that 'artists move to an area because it's affordable, make it cool, and then the affluent arrive'. She cites the recent transformations of Shoreditch, London Fields, Dalston and Peckham Rye. All one-time no go areas, each district became home to artists and musicians who moved into the abandoned warehouses and large, empty properties that were abundant. The squatting communities contributed to local areas by opening up the spaces they squatted. Open-house art shows, theatre productions and music events in squats made the localities fashionably desirable, drawing in new crowds to help regenerate flat micro-economies. And, as if you didn't know, property prices in Shoreditch, London Fields, Dalston and Peckham Rye have all crept up rather nicely in the years since the more creative of the squat communities brought their artistic and fashionable influences to the areas.[3]

Although there are many types of squatted buildings and squatters, Pruijt (2013b: 1124) argues that 'entrepreneurial squatters' who promote studios, exhibition venues and gathering spaces for artists, and other cultural producers, hold the most positive image for local authorities. This often prompts legalisation agreements, state subsidies and the co-optation of former activists although squatters can also manipulate the discourse of creativity to convince authorities about how valuable they are for the sake of economic growth while, internally, keeping and promoting a middle-class discourse of leftist radicalism (Fraeser 2015, Novy & Colomb 2012, Valli 2015). Nonetheless, the media and political manipulation of this supposedly positive image does not consist of a mere partial and deeply biased representation of squatters, but it promotes a role model for more radical or destitute squatters. To date there is more evidence about the nuanced diversity of squatters and their radical questioning of gentrification processes, than their purposive, complicit and effective involvement in such a speculative urban change (Lees et al. 2016).

In sum (see Figure 6.1), the homogenising rhetoric unfolds in two directions: a) 'full stigmatisation' by accusing squatters of disturbing social order and behaving as 'evil others' (morally unfair, legally criminal and too socially tolerated); and b) 'partial stigmatisation' by selecting the portion of squatters which is more functional to the reproduction of the capitalist city—artists and middle-class creative squatters able to contribute to the vibrancy of urban life and the attraction of private capital investment by pioneering gentrification processes.

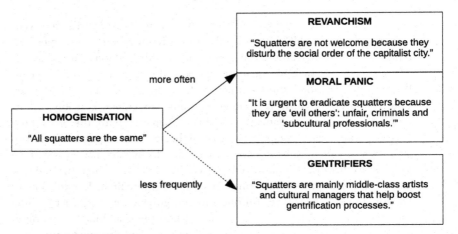

FIGURE 6.1 'Homogenisation' narratives that stigmatise squatters
Note: Quotations are only paradigmatic discourses from my own recreation (based on the gathered data) in order to illustrate the meaning of each category.
Source: Author

Are There Good and Bad Squatters?

Labelling and stigmatisation processes are not simple outcomes of interactions between different social groups. The concerned groups do not enjoy similar living conditions and resources that allow them to circulate their narratives against each other in a fair competition (Lamont 2018, Tyler & Slater 2018). Since social groups are hierarchically distributed and embedded into power relations, stigmas and spectacular narratives can be conceptualised as weapons of 'symbolic violence' (Bourdieu 1991) that those at the top of social structures spread in order to achieve the discipline, compliance, normalisation, and integration of those at the bottom (Foucault 1975 [1995], Scott 1990). In so doing, if successful, elites can avoid the regular use of physical violence and police repression against those who challenge the status quo. In our case, stigmas are used against the internal diversity of squatters as a social group or urban movement. The main purpose of these stratagems is to undermine the squatters' political leverage and to reproduce the elite's wealth and privileges. This applies to both homogenisation and polarisation rhetoric. The latter can be more accurately described as a 'divide and rule' tactic because the major attacks towards squatters take the paradigmatic form of a split between 'good' and 'bad' squatters (Bouillon 2013, Dee 2013, Dee & Debelle 2015).

Four predominant axes are drawn here, according to the evidence collected from various European countries. First, the more squatters resort to socially perceived violent means of protest, or are unilaterally accused of doing so, the more they are classified as 'bad' squatters.

Second, ideological and political radicalism is usually seen as a 'bad' thing. Conversely, the more squatters show restraint with their social, political, urban

Criminalisation and Counter-Hegemony **247**

and cultural criticisms (or these are only expressed through harmless artistic means), the more they are categorised as 'good' squatters. Their disposition to talk to journalists and be reported on and recorded by mass media may be used as an additional distinction between 'moderate' and 'radical' squatters. Involvement of squatters in formal organisations with non-squatters and their own political agenda helps condemn them compared to only-squatters self-help initiatives.

Third, squatters' attitudes towards negotiations with private owners and political and judicial authorities determine another bottom line for the divide. There are different kinds of negotiations, including interactions with the police, although the issue of reaching legal agreements regarding the status of the squat represents the highest stake (Martínez 2014). A plain refusal to accept the prevailing legal system as an extension of economic and political unbalance tends to label squatters as unreasonable outsiders who should not deserve recognition. In contrast, 'good' squatters are deemed and expected to, sooner or later, obtain legal status and durable arrangements for their illegal condition. This will to negotiate is proof that they are another acceptable social category among the diversity of 'city stakeholders'.

A fourth categorical cleavage directly frames squatters as either socially integrated (normalised) or attached to a marginal status (deviated). There are plenty of traits that fall under either side, so this frame stresses a supposedly resilient and original 'wild' nature versus the eventual process of 'taming' squatters in order to comply with socially accepted conventions. For example, their public outlook, the way they dress, how clean or dirty are the squats, their lifestyle in relation to drugs and partying, their gender and ethnic identity, their jobs and education, whether there are children and elderly involved, their relationship with welfare services, politeness with neighbours, etc. I will further elaborate these axes in more detail.

Mass media plays a key role in the diffusion of the 'divide and rule' repertoire. Dee (2013) compared media representations of squatting in the UK and the Netherlands and found striking differences. For instance, the negative stereotypes of squatters as drug-users who trash buildings prevailed more in the UK than in the Netherlands, where 'krakers' developed cordial relations with the police, had expert knowledge about the occupied buildings and the planning legislation, and usually behave non-violently unless provoked (Dee 2013: 251). Polarisations among squatters in the UK date back to the 1960s and 1970s around an axis of deserving or undeserving poor. On the one hand, positive stories were told about homeless families who occupied council properties and were led by non-homeless activists. On the other, negative stories encompassed squatting actions by 'single people, "outsiders", "hippies" ... particularly if they turned their attentions towards empty privately-owned properties or were seen to have some sort of wider political agenda' (Platt quoted by Dee 2013: 252).

Dee provides more illustrations of the divide. One of the squatters of an expensive mansion in London declared to the *Daily Telegraph*: 'I don't mind being called a squatter, but I am a good one. We are normal people, we go to work' (Dee 2013: 257). A neighbour of squatters in Brighton was quoted as

248 Criminalisation and Counter-Hegemony

saying: 'They look like scruffy students ... [b]ut they are very polite and well-spoken. They seem like your typical middle-class dropouts' (Dee 2013: 257). Another squatter plays the game of normalisation by insisting on the favourable label when talking to journalists: 'We are good squatters. We treat the places we live with respect. We keep the place clean and tidy' (Dee 2013: 258). On the other hand, marginal and deviant attributions are placed upon the bad squatters, according to the media highlights: '[A] gang ... and mostly in their early 20s and [Southern and Eastern] European ... They were intelligent students, not impoverished ... anarchist collectives living rent-free in Georgian townhouses' (Dee 2013: 258–260).

In France, Bouillon interviewed policemen who confirmed that squats occupied by 'people seen as marginals ... isolated adolescents without papers from Maghreb ... [and] Roma [people] ... have the shortest life expectancy' (Bouillon 2013: 236). Racism and preventive stereotypes placed upon social groups who generate 'a strong feeling of insecurity among neighbours' (ibid.) prompted police to swiftly evict the 'bad' squatters, even without granting them due rights to legal assistance and juridical procedure. This extends to squatters who are ignorant of the legislation, are intimidated by landlords and neighbours, and are subject to forced mobility due to asylum or job seeking. According to her research, in 75% of cases, court sentences determined immediate eviction (Bouillon 2013: 237), which is a sign of the predominance of such negative stereotypes.

She also found that court trials are a privileged stage to test how effective stereotypes are. Judges distinguished first between good and bad landlords based on three conditions: (a) Small private landlords may experience a higher loss than big corporations or state agencies when their properties are occupied; (b) The longer the period of vacancy, the more prone judges are to blame the owner and acquit the squatters; (c) The less active owners are in repairing, hiring or selling their property, the more favourable judges are towards squatters. But the burden may also fall on the side of squatters; if they are judged to be 'genuine poor' and 'good poor', they have more chance of avoiding eviction and further punishment (fines or imprisonment). Accordingly, defensive tactics in court trials play with these four arguments:

> [a)] They are not usurpers but 'truly poor' ... [b)] The judge will be all the more indulgent if the occupants have exhausted all legal solutions [to find accommodation]. ... [c)] They are not 'drug addicts', they 'don't steal' ... [d)] The question is to prove that they suffer from marginality and do not represent a danger for the collectivity.
>
> *(Bouillon 2013: 238–239)*

The appointment of an 'anti-squatters police chief' by the Spanish central government in 2016, which could operate across the Madrid region, was announced with the overt intention of speeding up lawsuits and increasing the penalties for what is already considered a criminal offence according to the Spanish penal code

Criminalisation and Counter-Hegemony 249

IMAGE 6.3 Squat Scup, Rome, 2014
Source: Author

(1995). In a meeting he held with residents' organisations, the police officer said they had identified 1,300 squatted houses in the region, and they classified them roughly as 'social squatters' (homeless people who occupy out of necessity or 'deserving poor'), 'ethnic squatters' (gypsies–Roma people), 'foreign squatters' (poor migrants) and 'anti-systemic and 15M squatters' (political squatters who help others to squat and organise social activities) [15M refers to the *Indignados* movement that rose up in 15 May 2011].[4] Only the 'deserving poor' did not represent a serious threat. Madrid's supposedly progressive mayor also condemned 'mafia-style squatters' while expressing concerns about the 'needy squatters' who face homelessness.[5] Many local activists commented informally and online that those views were completely biased, misrepresented the actual diversity of squatters and created artificial divides to spread fear and justify repression (Coordinadora de Vivienda 2017).

Other accounts of 'bad' and 'good' squatters in Barcelona confirmed the patterned boundary between 'artists, bohemians … peaceful, eager to negotiate … with a visible spokesperson' and 'rioters, violent … punks with dreadlocks … foreigners … far left, anarchists, independentist' squatters (Dee & Debelle 2015: 123–128). The most extreme attribution to 'bad squatters' is a link with terrorism, which is exceptional but not completely avoided by politicians and journalists (most recently via a diffused fear of migrants, refugees and clandestine jihadists: Manjikian 2013, Mudu & Chattopadhyay 2017). Media stories about terrorists hidden in Spanish

250 Criminalisation and Counter-Hegemony

squats or disguised as radical squatters were common in two periods, 1999–2001 (Asens 2004: 320–327) and 2015–16 (Debelle 2017: 181), although they were mainly based on specific police raids and followed by politicians and journalists' declarations instilling a sense of panic. These incidents added to the general negative discourse on squatting, but the terrorist connotation hardly contaminated the public identity of Spanish squatters in the other periods, from the mid-1980s to date (as verified in the three cities examined in Martínez 2018c).

More frequently, especially during the 1970s and 1980s, the characterisation of political squatters as 'terrorists', 'extremists' and 'violent activists' was very acute, for example, in Italy, Germany, The Netherlands and Denmark when militant actions and street clashes with the police were not unusual, and also due to the sympathy of some squats with armed groups such as the RAF (*Rote Armee Fraktion*, Red Army Faction) and the BR (*Brigate Rosse*, Red Brigades) (Katsiaficas 2006). For example:

> Roman Herzog, then minister of the interior in Baden-Würtemberg (and, from 1994 to 1999, president of Germany), publicly charged that the RAF was infiltrating and recruiting from the squatters' movement. Authorities claimed to be able to link 70 of 1,300 known squatters to armed groups.
>
> *(Katsiaficas 2014: xi)*

Similar labels were attached to Greek squatters because of the long-lasting involvement of militant anarchists in occupations of buildings (Kritidis 2014).

Middleton (2015) identified a similar hegemonic divide in the UK when both conservative and labour politicians sought to dissociate homelessness from squatting. She provides many samples to illustrate this point:

> Squatters do not fit the profile of the kind of vulnerable people we should be looking after ... [I]t is 'a FACT' that squatters are politically motivated and anti-establishment, 'not genuinely destitute'. ... In squats they [homeless people] have no protection.
>
> *(Middleton 2015: 103, 105)*

Although poor people may be excluded from the category of 'bad squatters', according to UK politicians, the homeless should not dare to take matters into their own hands and cross the line towards self-housing themselves. If they dare to squat, they risk losing face, subsidies and any help from the authorities. To some extent, this discourse praises homeless people for continuing to sleep in the streets and marginalises them should they aim to find a proper roof (Reeve 2011). However, 'in the absence of an alternative, it is highly probable that the persons concerned will sooner or later occupy a new building. Eviction thus contributes to producing the very situation it was supposed to end' (Bouillon 2013: 243).

Polarisation between deserving and underserving poor is by no means the only dichotomous frame at play. The analysis of four cases in Western

Europe (the UK, France, Denmark, and the Netherlands), including Roma settlements, distinguished nine frames that shifted over time towards an increasing 'exclusionary narrative' (Manjikian 2013: 32). This dominant discourse leads to waging a 'war on squatting' based on the assumption that squatters have become a security issue for nation states. Internal borders are erected and increasing police stop-and-frisk operations target migrants who squat (Manjikian 2013: 11). All squatters, then, are likely to be demonised. As a consequence, this frame justifies the 'politics of emergency' that ends up in the criminalisation and quick evictions of squatters, while replacing standard democratic procedures and rights to housing. For example, she gathers abundant media samples where squatters are pictured as 'free riders' (selfish, lazy, rent free), 'blight' (guilty of damaging the home value and investments made by homeowners), 'barbarian' (uncivilised, vandals, intruders, illegal tenants), 'deviated' (nomads, hobos, hippies, living in communes, unemployed and not seeking jobs, alternative lifestyles and dress-hair codes, anarchists, refugees, nuisance to neighbours), 'security threats' (gangsters, invaders, army, 'dangerous scourge', weapon-tool wielders). Although the exclusionary narrative takes the lead, Manjikian argues that there is also a subordinate 'inclusionist narrative' that entices public policies to support, subsidise, integrate and understand the squatters' motivations based on their legitimate response to housing needs. However, this approach is rooted in a view of the 'good' squatter as a passive victim of systemic conditions, in opposition to the 'empowered squatters' who actively challenge the system that excludes them (Manjikian 2013: 18–32) (see Figure 6.2).

Internal Cleavages

Whether in court facing lawsuits or while interacting with neighbouring residents and journalists, some squatters also play the game and strategically take sides—they may pretend to be considered 'good' (or even 'bad') squatters according to the potential benefits they expect from that categorisation. Furthermore, stigmas and stereotypes enjoy a performative power within the squatting scenes, especially in the most militant ones (Adilkno 1990 [1994], Dee 2013: 256, Kadir 2016). However, social, cultural, ideological and even economic diversity are the daily life experience of most squatters. That is to say, there are many possible categories to distinguish squatters, and the moral good–bad polarisation can hardly help to grasp them. Even the same individuals may go through different categories or combine their features (azozomox 2014, Mudu & Chattopadhyay 2017, Pattaroni 2014, Polanska & Piotrowski 2016). A paradigmatic case is the Metropoliz squat in a peripheral area of Rome where migrants, natives, militants and artists cooperate with each other and live together on the same premises, a former salami factory (Grazioli 2017, Mudu 2014: 152).

In Paris, the conflicts between the 'autonomous' (radical left-libertarian squatters who see squats as an end rather than a means to a legal place) and the 'institutional'

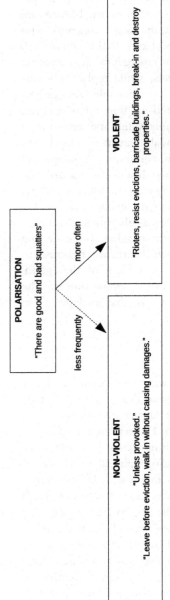

FIGURE 6.2 'Polarisation' narratives that stigmatise squatters

Note: Quotations are only paradigmatic discourses from my own recreation (based on the gathered data) in order to illustrate the meaning of each category.

Source: Author

wing (artists and housing activists in favour of legalisation of the squats, some even eager to fully participate in political parties) prompted Aguilera (2018: 135–140) to argue that this internal cleavage (and diversity) represents a strength of the movement. In interviews held with public officials from housing and cultural departments, he confirmed that the distinctions had practical consequences:

> They tolerate and legalise the 'animators' [who create services and house the needy,] who accept to negotiate, who are institution-friendly and officially organised through tangible structures like associations. They evict the 'troublemakers' [autonomous, survival and recognition squatters] who perpetuate a strong anti-institutional discourse and who self-organise in fluid and decentralised networks.
>
> *(Aguilera 2018: 137)*

After examining the reciprocal accusations, the two *opposed* types of squatters express about each other, Aguilera observes that 'every group of squatters attempts to represent itself as the "good ones" while simultaneously denouncing the process of categorisation … . [All] emphasise that they "truly" need to squat' (Aguilera 2018: 138). His argument is that the radical wing helps the moderate one to negotiate and achieve its goals because the former represents a more critical threat unable to be managed by the authorities who, forced to choose, prefer to give concessions to the moderate squatters. Radical squatters contribute to the rejuvenation of the movement with their libertarian insight in terms of self-management. On their side, moderate squatters help to soften the repression against squatting by attracting the attention of more favourable media and policymakers.

> Municipal officials consider them collaborators: 'They help me in my job to find vacant spaces in Paris. … They are experts, they have lists. We call them, they squat, we implement projects with them and then we build social housing.'
>
> *(Aguilera 2018: 140)*

Similar disputes at the heart of squatters' movements occurred in other countries. For example, Mudu (2012) examined the divides between two distinct branches of political squatting in Italy—'autonomists' rooted in a heterodox interpretation of Marxism, and 'anarchists' with fewer numbers of militants. It is worth noting that these two strands of radical politics among squatters are not so neatly separated in Northern Europe and the English-speaking countries. Fortunately, this internal divide in Italy offers more nuanced considerations regarding violence, leadership, use of humour, relations with the music industry, workers' struggles, self-management alternatives, employment inside squatted social centres, etc. than the conventional label of 'radicalism' represents. Sub-factions among these two radical groups were also significant and amplified with the

254 Criminalisation and Counter-Hegemony

splits created by the available opportunities to legalise some occupations and the involvement of squatters in municipal elections (Mudu 2012: 420).

Discursive Struggles and Counter-Hegemonic Discourse

Both the dominant homogenisation and polarisation rhetoric intend to undermine squatting, hide its social diversity and make squatters speechless. As shown above, this operates by more frequently pointing out 'bad squatters', revanchism and moral panic. On a subordinate hierarchical level (that is, less frequently), the hegemonic narrative sometimes frames squatting as a (potential) 'positive' contribution thanks to gentrifiers, artists, moderate housing activists and normalised 'good squatters' in general. This hierarchy and frequency is verified, for example, by the examination of media news in the UK showing the frequency of negative views as double when compared to positive categorisations (Dee & Debelle 2015: 120). Hence, it is worth asking: how do squatters face these dilemmas or escape them?

Dee and Debelle identify two major counter-tactics: (1) 'trying to produce a positive image' of squatting by spreading the features of the 'good squatters' and by emphasising the social benefits of squats; and (2) a 'refusal to engage with the media' and its categorisations by embracing otherness, difference and subjectivity while 'sidestepping subjectivities imposed from above', which may also entail an intense dedication to underground, face-to-face, independent and grassroots' communication (Dee & Debelle 2015: 135).

They also mention more ambivalent tactics in which squatters adopted different identities to detach themselves from the prevailing stereotypes. This, for instance, has proved somewhat successful in the squatting actions carried out by the PAH in Spain (Coordinadora de Vivienda 2017, García-Lamarca 2016, Martínez 2018b). Instead of using 'squatting' or 'occupation', they promoted their actions as 'recuperations' of public assets for those with a lifelong debt after forced evictions due to foreclosures. PAH squatters were also favourable to negotiations, legal arrangements and even the payment of affordable rents. In a similar vein, Dee argues that there is a certain social sympathy for those squatters 'mythologised [as] "Robin Hood" figures, taking back from the people what has been stolen from them by the ultrarich' (Dee 2013: 253). This figure, even without taking explicit anti-capitalist stances, may help to break down the dominant polarisations while justifying squatting as a necessary direct action.

Provos and situationists in the Netherlands, and the *Indiani Metropolitani* in Italy (Mudu 2012: 418) also played with political ambivalence, humour, and communicative guerrilla as tactics to mislead dominant interpretations. In many other cases, squatters unfold banners warning that they are not squatters. This happened, for instance, when the survivors of the Grenfell Tower fire in London, June 2017, occupied first a council-owned community centre, locally known as 'The Village', and empty apartments in a former college building afterwards, named 'the City'. Both places were located nearby the site of the

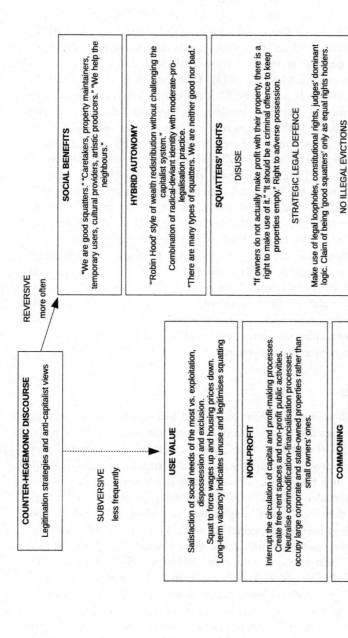

FIGURE 6.3 Counter-hegemonic narratives that legitimise squatting

Note: Quotations are only paradigmatic discourses from my own recreation (based on the gathered data) in order to illustrate the meaning of each category.

Source: Author

tragedy, in a wealthy borough (Kensington and Chelsea), although the residents from the Grenfell Tower were much poorer than the average of the area. While intending to prevent an immediate eviction by the authorities, to gain wide solidarity, and to make a statement about their claims to alternative homes, the squatters placed the sign 'Take note. This is not a squat' at the entrance of 'the City'.[6]

Figure 6.3 compiles these and other responses (see below) to confront the hegemonic discourse on squatting according to the available research and my own observations (e.g. Cattaneo & Martínez 2014). Drawing on Hodkinson (2012), we could group them in two large groups: (a) additional; and (b) oppositional. He employed these categories to distinguish squatting (as 'oppositional') from housing co-operatives (as 'additional') without, however, delving into the discursive struggles around squatting I am scrutinising here. In my view, both categories hold potentials to dispute the hegemonic logic of capitalism and its attached discourses of legitimation, although only the 'oppositional' alternatives would confront them at its core. In order to avoid the traditional distinction between reform and revolution, moderate and radical struggles, etc. that those terms may entail, I refer to them as 'reversive' and 'subversive' (Martínez 2008). In short, reversive strategies take advantage of system cracks, expand them, and drive the masters crazy. Guerrilla warfare, insurrections, and everyday life resistance to domination fall under this category. Subversive strategies critically point to the pillars of the system and aim at prefiguring full alternatives to it. New forms of language, social organisation, and practices, even placed within strongholds, are possible manifestations. As far as they both encompass a counter-hegemonic nature able to dispute the dominant stigmas and spectacular narrations, we could also name them as 'radical reforms' and 'radical experiments', respectively.

Reversive Responses

1. 'Social benefits'. Squatters can fight their usual bad reputation by claiming they contribute to society in very peculiar ways. Instead of parasites, many squatters argue that they take care of and rehabilitate the properties they occupy, which, otherwise, would continue to deteriorate (Dee 2013, Pruijt 2013a). Vacancy in a building or urban area is also considered negative in terms of the potential cooperation among residents, so some squatters are welcome when they help other neighbours with their daily issues. This logic applies to 'squatted social centres' as well. The more public activities are organised in the squats for visitors, the more squatters use them as proof of their altruism. This explains why even the most radical squatted social centres keep record of the concerts, talks, workshops and many other events they organised. The squatters' lawyers may use these portfolios as an evidence of their social contribution in case of litigation.

2. 'Hybrid autonomy'. The main battle here is waged around the distinction between the temporary occupation of disused properties and 'stealing'. Discursive tactics employed by squatters vary from appealing to those in society

critical of rich people who own many properties, to demands of more just housing policies and affordable real-estate prices for the many. This opens up a fruitful avenue to legitimise squatting through various combinations of positive and negative traits which are invigorated by 'spectacular narratives'. A regular illustration of 'hybrid autonomy' (Martínez 2016) consists of embracing radical and deviant identities proudly while, at the same time, expressing the will to pay rent and reach legal agreements (Coordinadora de Vivienda 2017, García-Lamarca 2016, Martínez 2018b). Equally, a refusal to identify squatters' spokespersons when engaging with the media and politicians, and the spread of confusing messages by all means possible (in a situationist-inspired fashion), may contribute to a certain political ambiguity that is able to erode the stigmatisation process.

3. 'Squatters' rights'. In this dimension, squatters use their legal expertise in order to remind both the authorities and the public of the owners' duties regarding the conservation and management of their properties. The lack of maintenance, ruin and vacancy are not tolerated in many legal codes, and 'adverse possession' was a historical means to grant squatters' rights to remain or even acquire or purchase the occupied property (Fox et al. 2015). Disuse is often considered a source of problems for the building, the neighbours and the urban area at large. Squatters also address their legal rights to be informed in due time, to legal assistance and relocation in case of eviction. They also reveal the large number of illegal evictions worldwide, executed by police and private owners, to which courts turn a blind eye. By knowing the details of the applicable law, their constitutional rights as citizens and the judge's prevailing arguments, squatters can strategically plan their legal defence (Bouillon 2013, Cattaneo & Martínez 2014). This 'rights discourse' also rules in some cases of 'conservational squatting' (Pruijt 2013a: 32–36) when heritage buildings and urban areas are threatened with demolition, and activists claim that illegal occupations are the only means to effectively comply with the legal duties to preserve them.

4. 'Alternative knowledge'. In general, a common resource that squatters, especially those more politicised, manage is a detailed knowledge of the targeted property, the state of the building and the economic conditions and behaviours of its owner. This research serves to assess the pros and cons of the occupation, but also to publicly justify the action. In addition, squatters can relate this key information to other alarming political and economic circumstances (corruption, housing shortage, gentrification processes, etc.). References to consolidated practices of squatting over decades in the same city or country have the advantage of cooling down the news inducing panic about single incidents (Martínez 2018c, Steen et al. 2014). Many fanzines, handbooks and the Dutch *White Book* of squatting take up this 'facts-based discourse' to show an amicable face of what might be seen dangerous or criminal.

IMAGE 6.4 Squat Rozbrat, Poznan, 2014
Source: Author

Subversive Alternatives

All the 'reversive' strategies (i.e. the narratives and the associated actions) can legitimate squatting, undermine stigmas and turn artificial splits upside down. However, there is no intrinsic content in them that is genuinely anti-capitalist, aiming to challenge the systemic conditions that foster squatting. Even the appeal to completely abolish private property, endorsed by left-libertarian squatters, is seldom realistic because squatters are focused on a specific contradiction of the capitalist system—the social management of empty properties, both privately and state-owned. In order to enhance the 'oppositional' or anti-capitalist nature of counter-hegemonic discourses, Hodkinson proposes various packages of prefigurative, defensive, and circulating forms of commoning (Hodkinson 2012: 438–440). Similarly, Madden and Marcuse define 'radical' or 'transformative demands' as 'system-challenging ... non-reformist reforms: not attempts to make the current system more resilient, but actions that improve present conditions while also progressively enabling the building of a different world' (Madden & Marcuse 2016: 200). Regarding squatting, its radicalism entails a discourse with potential performative capacities in line with the 'oppositional' and 'transformative' practices suggested by Hodkinson, Madden and Marcuse, not only in the field of housing, but also in other facilities such as countercultural, anarchist, and refugee squats. Without dismissing the radical potential of the squatters' reversive strategies, we can also envision three major dimensions of its subversive attempts, although both may be combined in practice. According to my own pool of pamphlets, fanzines, banners, and articles written by squatters, and other researchers' analyses, we can group the dispersed pieces of subversive discourses in the following three categories: use value, non-profit, and commoning (Martínez 2018b: 76–81).

1. 'Use value'. Capitalism works due to underlying processes of exploitation of the labour force within given social structures. Capitalists also manipulate the reproduction of the labour force (health, education, residential needs, non-working time, etc.). Some of their profits can be invested in the 'secondary circuit of capital', i.e. the production of the urban fabric. All these activities are driven by the pursuit of 'exchange value' at the expense of 'use values'. When squatters occupy empty properties, they claim a right to satisfy their needs for social reproduction, but also they resist exploitation as waged workers (Cattaneo & Martínez 2014). They also dispute the appropriation of resources by real-estate developers and speculators. The alternative to focusing on the specific portion of vacancy among properties subject to profit-making in the real-estate market means direct opposition to their extension. Given the primitive accumulation of capital that gave birth to private property, current forms of 'accumulation by dispossession' (Harvey 2006: 90–115) and privatisations of public assets such as social housing stocks, squatters argue that capitalists always illegitimately *squatted* larger spaces than the ones that are taken back into the hands of the exploited, dispossessed and excluded. As a consequence, squatting is truly anti-capitalist when it is practised by homeless people and others who cannot access social housing or affordable and decent shelters (Reeve 2011). Even for those who are not homeless, to buy or rent an expensive dwelling may imply the serious erosion of other aspects of a buyer or tenant's well-being. People with low or unstable income, such as unemployed people, students and the elderly, may resort to squatting as a solution to their urgent economic needs, especially in the absence of any state measures that suit them. Squatting can mitigate these undesirable effects and erode capital accumulation in both the real-estate and job market. In short, the better the living conditions enjoyed by the many, the less probable capitalists will force wages down and housing prices up. As Madden and Marcuse (2016: 207) advocate: 'Privilege inhabitants … rather than investors, owners and landlords.'

2. 'Non-profit'. When squatters are not so deprived economically, their refusal to pay high rents, selling prices and mortgage loans directly challenges the interests of capitalists, real-estate financialisation, and state policies that facilitate capital accumulation. Well-off political squatters (from the middle or well-paid working classes) may, remarkably, reject the argument of extreme necessity in their own case by stating that wealthier owners ought not to profit from their empty properties. Manipulated vacancy only boosts speculation and inflation, which results in higher living costs for all urban dwellers and inhabitants. This is especially justified when the targets of squatting are spaces left unused in convenient locations for collective gatherings and activities supplied by

squatters at no or low cost. They could not be performed by paying market prices, and the right to the city centre (Cattaneo & Martínez 2014, Madden & Marcuse 2016) would be just a privilege of the wealthy. Theoretically, regulations of land planning, welfare services, financial transfers and taxation are intended to limit the absolute powers of real-estate owners. However, these limitations have not been sufficient in impeding the commodification and financialisation of housing. Furthermore, state agencies may also set up for-profit housing corporations, urban plans and policies that reveal the failures of the capitalist system to properly accommodate everyone. By 'breaking the monopoly of for-profit developers' (Madden & Marcuse 2016: 207), squatters can grant access to houses and social facilities to those more in need as well as to those that defy capitalism on different flanks. This approach implies that squatters cannot make any profit either by renting, subletting, or selling the occupied property to others. Selling food, beverages, books, clothes, or handicrafts is deemed legitimate when it is not for profit and democratically managed among the squatters.

3. 'Commoning'. Squatting contributes to creating 'commons' in direct opposition to the continuing enclosures and appropriations of all spheres of life and nature operated by capital. Inequality is not only an outcome of capital accumulation, but also an intrinsic feature of capitalist production at the workplace and in all markets at large. Without equal conditions of work and consumption, common properties and an orientation of productive-reproductive activities to satisfy everybody's needs, there is no way out of capitalism. Historically, the commons encompassed portions of land and resources in a community-managed 'third space' between the state and the market. The notion of commons, however, entails much more: 'Daily acts of producing alternative forms of sociality that protect against enclosure and accumulation' (Hodkinson 2012: 437). Therefore, instead of authoritarian forms of production and the organisation of domestic and social life, commoning processes comprehend every collectively self-managed practice, institution, good, infrastructure, and struggle able to overcome the duality of state-owned and privately-owned modes of tenure and government. Squats are thus precious strongholds 'of non-hierarchical, small-scale, directly democratic, egalitarian and collective forms of housing in our everyday lives' (Hodkinson 2012: 438) whenever they avoid the reproduction of economic, social and cultural oppressions within their walls. Their example can also amplify the cry to democratise the planning, provision and management of state-owned assets such as housing (Madden & Marcuse 2016: 211–215). In addition, commoning practices extend the social benefits of squatting to the surrounding residential communities not just as mutual aid, but also as a contribution to the self-management of common goods, historical experiences, institutions and struggles within their boundaries. This includes vacant spaces subject to the conflict between economic speculation, government decisions and grassroots claims. Moreover, squatters may be

Criminalisation and Counter-Hegemony **261**

highly resourceful and valuable to the local community when they disclose the speculative processes underway.

An illustration of this counter-hegemonic framing is a poster published by Dutch activists with the title 'Squatting continues, with or without the ban':

> Squatting continues because vacancy and speculations are the crimes. Squatting continues as long as living spaces are regulated through the free market, and profit is placed above social needs. ... Squatting continues because youth and other people in need of housing cannot be exploited by landlords nor anti-squatting agencies. ... Squatting continues because property is not a vital necessity while a roof above your head is. Squatting continues because free and assertive people do not let their way be stopped by a strangle mortgage. Squatting continues break-opening spaces for initiatives based on solidarity, creativity and autonomy, in place of the market, control and capital.
>
> *(Dadusc 2017: 8)*

In a similar vein, a Spanish handbook to guide and help squatters justified squatting as follows:

IMAGE 6.5 Squat Barrilonia, Barcelona, 2012
Source: Author

262   Criminalisation and Counter-Hegemony

There are many evidences that labour and property are not related. An average household needs between 30 and 40 years to acquire homeownership
(and before paying off their mortgage, their home belongs to the bank). In
contrast, those living at the expenses of others' work can buy many houses.
Those who lend ten times the money others saved in their bank, charging
lucrative interest rates in every loan, can also buy many houses. You can also
purchase many houses if your family owns a company and can make investments. If you become a 'representative of the people' you will enjoy the
right to adjudicate public commissions, change land use and ask for bribes so
you can also buy many houses. Squatting is not only a means to get housing
but also to create a social centre, to gather, to share, to learn, and to fight.
By using an abandoned house you are questioning the capitalist system by
denying private property.

(Manual de Okupación 2014: 14)

The Criminalisation of Squatting Invigorates Class Domination

Stigmas contribute to the criminalisation of squatting but this does not imply that
this process starts there and simply ends with the implementation of a legal
change. Let's return to the British example to further elaborate this argument.
Above all, capitalist crises are the main drivers of mass squatting, although squatters' movements can remain or even flourish in less significant numbers as
a response to more specific conditions such as urban renewal plans, real-estate
speculation, housing bubbles, and the unmet social needs of affordable urban
space for dwelling, meeting, performing and organising grassroots politics. Stigmas
and stereotypes like the ones revisited before are especially prominent when the
capitalist class and the state elites from the executive, legislative and judiciary
powers, react to the 'squatting problem' in order to secure capitalist class control
(Cobb 2015: 21). The practice of squatting may constitute 'a direct barrier to
flows of capital accumulation' (ibid.) if the occupied assets are valuable for profit-
making, while the ideological discourse of squatting questions class inequalities,
the legitimacy of housing distribution and the rights of exclusive possession
(ibid.). The partial criminalisation of squatting in England and Wales by 1977
revealed how the government and the dominant mass media managed the economic recession by blaming the squatters of stealing the homes of ordinary
people or occupying social housing 'with the reality that squatters almost always
occupied long-term empty properties where they were less likely to be discovered' (Cobb 2015: 22).

According to Vasudevan (2017: 53, 59) there were 3,000 licensed squatters
and 7,000 unlicensed squatters in London by the end of 1974 ('licensed squatting' was a precarious concession granted by some city councils to active
organisations of homeless and poor families). Other estimations suggested the
figure of 50,000 squatters around 1975. According to him, the movement
shifted from mainly focusing on housing until the late 1970s to more 'localised

Criminalisation and Counter-Hegemony **263**

micro-communities and subcultures' (Vasudevan 2017: 61) in the 1980s and 1990s, although residential squatting was still a major component of this type of activism in London and countercultural social centres were never as pivotal as in Italy and Spain, for example. This explains that the last criminalisation of squatting that came into force by 2012 established a greater protection of residential properties and left the occupation of empty commercial premises out of the same regulation. However, as Cobb notes (2015: 23–29), three decades of neoliberal policies since the victory of the conservative party led by Margaret Thatcher in 1979, were as efficient as the 2008 global financial crisis to deploy a new round of moral panic about squatting that ended up in its criminal prosecution by 2012. In particular, the privatisation of social housing and the deregulation of financial markets gave rise to an enduring crisis of dispossession, displacement, and precarity in working conditions for those unable to access homeownership, especially the young people, immigrants, and the racialised population intersecting with the working class. The hegemony of the neoliberal ideology was not enough to prevent people from squatting so the legal change still targeted a practice capable of interference in an increasingly commodified housing market, in particular in urban regions or 'global cities' with high price inflation and demand such as London.

Accordingly, Cobb argues that the criminalisation of squatting is an 'ideological tool' used by the state to defend class hegemony from the squatters' threat since squatting 'is a potent symbol of housing market dysfunction' (2015: 30). However, when comparing the crises of the 1970s and the 2000s he appreciates that recent discursive struggles involve not only moral panic about squatting but also 'neoliberal anxieties' related to a different context of class struggles and also, I would add, of increasing fragmentation of urban movements (Mayer 2016). First, neoliberal policies promoted homeownership among middle and working classes as an investment to compensate welfare cuts so, after decades of relative success, the conservative government was able to manipulate the fear of squatters who could damage that asset-based welfare. Second, Cobb suggests that the criminalisation of squatting served the government to justify ongoing and deeper welfare reforms not only driven by austerity measures but also by an axiomatic rule of the market. If those who cannot afford to buy or rent privately in an expensive part of the city are forced to move away, how could welfare recipients and squatters still reside there? More accurately, moral panic shifts to a discourse of neoliberal 'moral unfairness', which represents a justification of class hegemony: only the wealthy should enjoy residential freedom because they have purchase power to do so; their locations and residential investments determine the leftovers for the rest; the state should not alter the market rules by subsidising households and allowing squatters to occupy highly demanded property. Third, the racist and xenophobic rhetoric behind the banning of squatting tries to exploit the social discontent about unemployment and labour precariousness by blaming poor foreigners who squat as unfair competitors of middle and working classes.

264 Criminalisation and Counter-Hegemony

In my view, more than a security or national identity threat (as argued by Manjikian 2013), foreign squatters here represent workers with a stronger bargain power when their residential needs are, at least temporarily, met. The criminalisation of squatting does not eliminate migrants or expel them from the country, but increases their vulnerability and labour exploitation.

Although I essentially agree with Cobb's analysis, we should add the increasing financialisation of housing (sub-prime mortgages as an extreme indicator) and university education (students' indebtedness as one striking indicator) (Fernández & Aalbers 2016, Lazzarato 2012) to the context in which the criminalisation of squatting occurs in 2012. These processes started before the economic crisis of 2008 and have been reinforced by conservative governments and neoliberal policies afterwards. As far as they contribute to intensify the precarious conditions of life, work, and housing of many more social groups, they also motivate squatting. Criminalisation, thus, tries to placate these social responses to financialisation. However, once the criminalisation is implemented squatters usually continue active, although subject to a more repressive environment (Cattaneo & Martínez 2014, Martínez 2018c). Squatters may lose one battle and would face new obstacles, but it is not unusual that they rise up again. Their contribution to class struggles has been eroded but not vanished. Their discursive responses, which are not scrutinised in Cobb's analysis as I have done above, serve to extend the ideological battle despite the legal defeats. On the one hand, investments and transactions in the housing markets are eased with the criminalisation of squatting. On the other, the reproductive needs of the labour force are aggravated when squatting is not an easy or feasible option, so wages can be lowered. Stigmas, stereotypes and criminalisation of squatting, thus, result in worsening class domination in a broader extent, although squatters' counter-hegemonic discourses can partially neutralise its worst effects (see a similar interpretive approach, albeit in a different context: Mitchell 2003).

Whether they like it or not, squatters are subject to a pervasive stigmatisation process in which the negative contents take priority over the occasional positive ones. Research across many European cities reveals three significant patterns: (a) the stigmatisation process is performed according to a twofold rhetoric consisting of 'homogenisation' and 'polarisation' narratives; (b) each dominant narrative always includes, as a subordinate dimension less often expressed in public, a relatively positive depiction (or 'partial stigmatisation', more precisely) of squatters; and (c) the hegemonic 'spectacular narrations' about squatting are, at least in the long-term, performative, i.e. effective in terms of their prosecution, criminalisation and social exclusion. In particular, the divides between 'good' and 'bad' squatters are drawn out according to the dichotomies of 'non-violence/violence', 'moderation/radicalism', 'pro-legalisation/anti-legalisation' and 'normalisation/deviation'. However, squatters' agency also plays a significant role in defying the circulation of negative stereotypes so they take part in discursive struggles where their own practices and the state repressive measures are at play too.

IMAGE 6.6 Squat Mare Street, London, 2010
Source: Author

Going back to the literature on the topic, my analysis shows the limited scope that squatters enjoy when they engage with the media, politicians, and juridical instances to overcome stigma and artificial splits, as some authors suggest (Bouillon 2013, Dee 2013, Dee & Debelle 2015). As these researchers also show, both the refusal to play the communication game in the media realm and political ambivalence may strengthen squatters' identity and discourse but, I would argue, without challenging the hegemonic system of categorisation and the capitalist structures that such a system of 'spectacular narrations' obscures. In my view, Manjikian's (2013) main virtue is to delve into multiple discursive frames that underpin the increasing 'exclusionary narratives' about squatting. She also recognises the subordinate place of 'inclusionary narratives'. However, compared to other studies and my own analysis above, all these frames indicate more a plurality of squatters and hegemonic categorisations rather than a priority of the security-related ones (especially when associated to terrorism and violence, although her argument can partially apply to poor international migrants and refugees from Asia and the Middle East: Mudu & Chattopadhyay 2017). In contrast, I suggest fewer dichotomies in order to map the divide between 'good' and 'bad' squatters, and the need to look at how squatters react to them, by following, for example, Aguilera (2018), Dee (2016) and Pruijt (2013b). More specifically, Dee (2016) proposes to conduct inquiries able to disclose facts and alternative voices which were dismissed by the dominant narratives. Pruijt (2013b) also encourages the introduction of public opinion polls, the scrutiny of the diversity among politicians and media, and the squatters' own accounts such as the

266 Criminalisation and Counter-Hegemony

Dutch *White Book*, in which they tell positive stories about their practice and social contributions. What I miss in their analyses is a tighter connection of these and other counter-hegemonic tactics with the structural conditions of power and economic relationships within the capitalist system as proposed by Cattaneo and Martínez (2014) and Cobb (2015).

As a consequence, I identified two main strands of discursive responses performed by squatters—'reversive' and 'subversive' (Hodkinson 2012, Madden & Marcuse 2016). 'Use value', 'non-profit' and 'commoning' principles would be, in my view, the main components of the most radical-experimental approach taken by the squatters' discourses, while also considering the more moderate responses (or 'radical reforms') a crucial source for a broader legitimation of squatting. This distinction is useful, although neither Hodkinson nor Madden and Marcuse delve into the specific variations among squatters' practices and discourses. These authors contribute a general framework that helps the understanding of how squatters root their anti-capitalist discourse among various housing struggles, despite its exceptional occurrence according to the evidence examined here and more general trends in European social movements (Mayer 2016). Finally, I mainly agree with Cobb's (2015) analysis that illuminates how the criminalisation process is articulated with economic crises and neoliberal policies so squatters are targeted not only as deviated or dangerous groups, but mainly as both symbols and practitioners of subversive threats to the capitalists' rule in the housing and labour markets.

Notes

1 https://blogs.elconfidencial.com/espana/mirada-ciudadana/2017-09-19/una-de-listos-y-tontos-hipotecados_1445886/
2 www.elledecor.it/en/architecture/the-most-beautiful-squats-in-the-world
3 https://londonlovesbusiness.com/the-untold-story-of-squats-gentrification-and-regeneration/
4 www.diagonalperiodico.net/global/30611-dancausa-general-contra-la-okupacion.html
5 www.eldiario.es/sociedad/Cerco-okupacion-Madrid-coordinador-policial_0_504650296.html
6 www.theguardian.com/uk-news/2017/dec/13/this-is-not-a-squat-how-the-grenfell-community-is-taking-control-of-its-destiny

References

Adilkno (1990 [1994]) *Cracking the Movement. Squatting beyond the Media*. New York: Autonomedia.
Aguilera, Thomas (2018) The Squatting Movement(S) in Paris: Internal Divides and Conditions for Survival. In Miguel A. Martínez (Ed.) *The Urban Politics of Squatters' Movements*. New York: Palgrave Macmillan, 121–144.
Alcalde, Javier (2004) La batalla de los medios: la definición de la problemática okupa en los medios de comunicación de masas. In Ramón Adell & Miguel Martínez (Eds) ¿*Dónde*

Criminalisation and Counter-Hegemony 267

están las llaves. *El movimiento okupa: prácticas y contextos sociales.* Madrid: Catarata, 227–266.

Asens, Jaume (2004) La represión al "movimiento de las okupaciones": del aparato policial a los *mass media*. In Ramón Adell & Miguel Martínez (Eds) *¿Dónde están las llaves? El movimiento okupa: prácticas y contextos sociales.* Madrid: Catarata, 293–337.

azozomox (2014) Squatting and Diversity: Gender and Patriarchy in Berlin, Madrid and Barcelona. In Claudio Cattaneo & Miguel Martínez (Eds) *The Squatters' Movement in Europe. Commons and Autonomy as Alternatives to Capitalism.* London: Pluto, 189–210.

azozomox & Armin Kuhn (2018) The Cycles of Squatting in Berlin (1969–2016). In Miguel A. Martínez (Ed.) *The Urban Politics of Squatters' Movements.* New York: Palgrave Macmillan, 145–164.

Bailey, Ron (1973) *The Squatters.* Harmondsworth: Penguin.

Bouillon, Florence (2013) What Is a "Good" Squatter? Categorization Processes of Squats by Government Officials in France. In SqEK (Squatting Europe Kollective) (Ed.) *Squatting in Europe. Radical Spaces, Urban Struggles.* Wivenhoe: Minor Compositions, 231–245.

Bourdieu, Pierre (1991) *Language and Symbolic Power.* Cambridge: Polity Press.

Cattaneo, Claudio & Miguel Martínez (Eds) (2014) *The Squatters' Movement in Europe: Commons and Autonomy as Alternatives to Capitalism.* London: Pluto.

Cobb, Neil (2015) The Political Economy of Trespass. Revisiting Marxist Analysis of the Law's Response to Squatting. In Lorna Fox O'Mahony, David O'Mahony & Robin Hickey (Eds) *Moral Rhetoric and the Criminalisation of Squatting. Vulnerable Demons?* Abingdon: Routledge, 13–37.

Coordinadora de Vivienda de la Comunidad de Madrid (2017) *La vivienda no es delito. Recuperando un derecho. Quién y por qué se okupa en Madrid.* Barcelona: El Viejo Topo.

Dadusc, Deanna (2017) *The Micropolitics of Criminalisation: Power, Resistance and the Amsterdam Squatting Movement.* Amsterdam: University of Kent [PhD Dissertation].

Dadusc, Deanna & ETC Dee (2015) The Criminalisation of Squatting. Discourses, Moral Panics and Resistances in the Netherlands and England and Wales. In Lorna Fox O'Mahony, David O'Mahony & Robin Hickey (Eds) *Moral Rhetoric and the Criminalisation of Squatting. Vulnerable Demons?* Abingdon: Routledge, 109–132.

Debelle, Galvão (2017) *Representación de conflictos de clase antes y después de la crisis: análisis crítico comparativo del discurso de procesos de securización acerca de rescates financieros y usurpación de propiedades privadas.* Barcelona: Universidad Autónoma de Barcelona [PhD Thesis].

Debord, Guy (1967) *The Society of the Spectacle.* New York: Zone Books.

Dee, E.T.C. (2013) Moving Towards Criminalisation and Then What? Examining Dominant Discourses on Squatting in England. In SqEK (Ed.) *Squatting in Europe. Radical Spaces, Urban Struggles.* Wivenhoe: Minor Compositions, 247–267.

Dee, E.T.C. (2016) The Production of Squatters as Folk Devils: Analysis of a Moral Panic that Facilitated the Criminalization of Squatting in the Netherlands. *Deviant Behavior* 37: 784–794.

Dee, E.T.C. & Galvão Debelle (2015) Examining Mainstream Media Discourses on the Squatters' Movements in Barcelona and London. *Interface* 7(1): 117–143.

Di Feliciantonio, Cesare (2017) Social Movements and Alternative Housing Models: Practicing the "Politics of Possibilities" in Spain. *Housing, Theory and Society* 34(1): 38–56.

Fernández, David (2009) *Crónicas del 6 y otros trapos sucios de la cloaca policial.* Barcelona: Virus.

Fernández, Rodrigo & Manuel Aalbers (2016) Financialization and Housing: Between Globalization and Varieties of Capitalism. *Competition & Change* 20(2): 71–88.

Finchett-Maddock, Lucy (2016) *Protest, Property and the Commons. Performances of Law and Resistance*. Abingdon: Routledge.

Foucault, Michel (1975 [1995]) *Discipline and Punish. The Birth of the Prison*. New York: Vintage.

Fox, Lorna; David O'Mahony & Robin Hickey (2015) Introduction: Criminalising Squatting. Setting an Agenda. In Lorna Fox O'Mahony, David O'Mahony & Robin Hickey (Eds) *Moral Rhetoric and the Criminalisation of Squatting. Vulnerable Demons?* Abingdon: Routledge, 3–10.

Fraeser, Nina (2015) Gängerviertel, Hamburg. In Alan Moore & Alan Smart (Eds) *Making Room. Cultural Production in Occupied Spaces*. Barcelona: Other Forms & Journal of Aesthetics and Protest, 172–177.

García-Lamarca, Melissa (2016) From Occupying Plazas to Recuperating Housing: Insurgent Practices in Spain. *International Journal of Urban and Regional Research* 41(1): 37–53.

Goffman, Erving (1963) *Stigma. Notes on the Management of Spoiled Identity*. Englewood Cliffs, N.J.: Prentice-Hall.

Grazioli, Margherita (2017) From Citizens to Citadins? Rethinking Right to the City inside Housing Squats in Rome, Italy. *Citizenship Studies* 21(4): 393–408.

Harvey, David (1990) *The Condition of Postmodernity. An Enquiry into the Origins of Cultural Change*. Oxford: Blackwell.

Harvey, David (2006) *Spaces of Global Capitalism. Towards a Theory of Uneven Geographical Development*. New York: Verso.

Hodkinson, Stuart (2012) The Return of the Housing Question. *Ephemera* 12(4): 423–444.

Holm, Andrej & Armin Kuhn (2017) Squatting and Gentrification in East Germany since 1989/90. In F. Anders & A. Sedlmaier (Eds) *Public Goods versus Economic Interests. Global Perspectives on the History of Squatting*. New York: Routledge, 278–304.

Jessop, Bob (1982) *The Capitalist State. Marxist Theories and Methods*. Oxford: Martin Robertson.

Kadir, Nazima (2016) *The Autonomous Life? Paradoxes and Authority in the Squatters Movement in Amsterdam*. Manchester: Manchester University Press.

Katsiaficas, Georgy (2006) *The Subversion of Politics. European Autonomous Social Movements and the Decolonization of Everyday Life*. Oakland: AK Press.

Katsiaficas, Georgy (2014) Preface. In Bart Van Der Steen, Ask Katzeef & L. Leendert Van Hoogenhuijze (Eds) *The City Is Ours. Squatting and Autonomous Movements in Europe from the 1970s to the Present*. Oakland: PM, ix–xii.

Kritidis, Gregor (2014) The Rise and Crisis of the Anarchist and Libertarian Movement in Greece, 1973–2012. In Bart Van Der Steen, Ask Katzeef & L. Leendert Van Hoogenhuijze (Eds) *The City Is Ours. Squatting and Autonomous Movements in Europe from the 1970s to the Present*. Oakland: PM, 63–93.

Lamont, Michèle (2018) Addressing Recognition Gaps: Destigmatization and the Reduction of Inequality. *American Sociological Review* 83(3): 419–444.

Lazzarato, Maurizio (2012) *The Making of the Indebted Man. An Essay on the Neoliberal Condition*. Amsterdam: Semiotext(e).

Lees, Loretta; Hyun Bang Shin & Ernesto López-Morales (2016) *Planetary Gentrification*. Cambridge: Polity Press.

Madden, David & Peter Marcuse (2016) *In Defense of Housing. The Politics of Crisis*. London: Verso.

Manjikian, Mary (2013) *Securitization of Property. Squatting in Europe*. New York: Routledge.

Manual de Okupación (2014) *Manual de Okupación*. Segunda edición. Madrid: self-published.

Martínez, Miguel A. (2002) *Okupaciones de viviendas y centros sociales. Autogestión, contracultura y conflictos urbanos*. Barcelona: Virus.

Martínez, Miguel A. (2008) Complexity and Participation: The Path of Strategic Invention. *Interdisciplinary Science Reviews* 33(2): 153–177.

Martínez, Miguel A. (2014) How Do Squatters Deal with the State? Legalization and Anomalous Institutionalization in Madrid. *International Journal of Urban and Regional Research* 38(2): 646–674.

Martínez, Miguel A. (2015) Squatting for Justice: Bringing Life to the City. In Alan Moore & Alan Smart (Eds) *Making Room. Cultural Production in Occupied Spaces*. Barcelona: Other Forms & Journal of Aesthetics and Protest, 34–39.

Martínez, Miguel A. (2016) Between Autonomy and Hybridity: Urban Struggles within the 15M Movement in Spain. In Margit Mayer, Catharina Thörn & Håkan Thörn (Eds) *Urban Uprisings. Challenging Neoliberal Urbanism in Europe*. London: Palgrave Macmillan, 253–281.

Martínez, Miguel A. (2018a) Introduction: The Politics of Squatting, Time Frames and Socio-Spatial Contexts. In Miguel A. Martínez (Ed.) *The Urban Politics of Squatters' Movements*. New York: Palgrave Macmillan, 1–21.

Martínez, Miguel A. (2018b) Urban Emptiness, Ghost Owners and Squatters' Challenges to Private Property. In Maja Hojer Bruun, Patrick Joseph Cockburn, Bjarke Skærlund Risager & Mikkel Thorup (Eds) *Contested Property Claims. What Disagreement Tells Us About Ownership*. Abingdon: Routledge, 74–91.

Martínez, Miguel A. (Ed.) (2018c) *The Urban Politics of Squatters' Movements*. New York: Palgrave Macmillan.

Mayer, Margit (2016) Neoliberal Urbanism and Uprisings across Europe. In Margit Mayer, Catharina Thörn & Håkan Thörn (Eds) *Urban Uprisings. Challenging Neoliberal Urbanism in Europe*. London: Palgrave Macmillan, 57–92.

Middleton, Theodora (2015) The Role of Rhetoric in the Criminalisation of Squatting. In Lorna Fox O'Mahony, David O'Mahony & Robin Hickey (Eds) *Moral Rhetoric and the Criminalisation of Squatting. Vulnerable Demons?* Abingdon: Routledge, 87–108.

Mitchell, Don (2003) *The Right to the City. Social Justice and the Fight for Public Space*. New York: The Guilford Press.

Mudu, Pierpaolo (2012) At the Intersection of Anarchists and Autonomists: Autogestioni and Centri Sociali. *ACME. An International E-Journal for Critical Geographies* 11(3): 413–438.

Mudu, Pierpaolo (2014) 'Ogni Sfratto Sarà Una Barricata': Squatting for Housing and Social Conflict in Rome. In Claudio Cattaneo & Miguel Martínez (Eds) *The Squatters' Movement in Europe: Commons and Autonomy as Alternatives to Capitalism*. London: Pluto, 136–154.

Mudu, Pierpaolo & Sutapa Chattopadhyay (Eds) (2017) *Migration, Squatting and Radical Autonomy*. Abingdon: Routledge.

Novy, Johannes & Claire Colomb (2012) Struggling for the Right to the (Creative) City in Berlin and Hamburg: New Urban Social Movements, New 'Spaces of Hope'? *International Journal of Urban and Regional Research* 37(5): 1816–1838.

Owens, Lynn (2009) *Cracking under Pressure. Narrating the Decline of the Amsterdam Squatters' Movement*. Amsterdam: Amsterdam University Press.

Pattaroni, Luca (2014) 'The Fallow Lands of the Possible': An Enquiry into the Enacted Criticism of Capitalism in Geneva's Squats. In Claudio Cattaneo & Miguel Martínez (Eds) *The Squatters' Movement in Europe: Commons and Autonomy as Alternatives to Capitalism*. London: Pluto, 60–84.

270 Criminalisation and Counter-Hegemony

Polanska, Dominika & Grzegorz Piotrowski (2016) Poland: Local Differences & the Importance of Cohesion. *Baltic Worlds* IX(1–2): 46–56.

Pruijt, Hans (2013a) The Logic of Urban Squatting. *International Journal of Urban and Regional Research* 37(1): 19–45.

Pruijt, Hans (2013b) Culture Wars, Revanchism, Moral Panics and the Creative City. A Reconstruction of A Decline of Tolerant Public Policy: The Case of Dutch Anti-Squatting Legislation. *Urban Studies* 50(6): 1114–1129.

Reeve, Kesia (2011) *Squatting: A Homelessness Issue. An Evidence Review.* London: Crisis & CRESR–Sheffield Hallam University.

Rossi, Ugo (2017) *Cities in Global Capitalism.* Cambridge: Polity Press.

Scott, James C. (1990) *Domination and the Arts of Resistance: Hidden Transcripts.* Yale: Yale University Press.

Seminario de Historia Política y Social de las Okupaciones en Madrid Metrópolis (2015) *Okupa Madrid (1985–2011). Memoria, reflexión, debate y autogestión colectiva del conocimiento.* Madrid: Diagonal.

Smith, Neil (1999) Which New Urbanism? the Revanchist '90s. *Perspecta* 30: 98–105.

Steen, Bart van der; Ask Katzeef & L. Leendert Van Hoogenhuijze (Eds) (2014) *The City Is Ours. Squatting and Autonomous Movements in Europe from the 1970s to the Present.* Oakland: PM.

Therborn, Göran (1980) *The Ideology of Power and the Power of Ideology.* London: Verso–NLB.

Thörn, Håkan; Cathrin Washede & Tomas Nilson (Eds) (2011) *Space for Urban Alternatives? Christiania 1971–2011.* Vilnius: Gidlunds Förlag.

Tyler, Imogen & Tom Slater (2018) Rethinking the Sociology of Stigma. *The Sociological Review Monographs* 66(4): 721–743.

Uitermark, Justus (2004) The Co-Optation of Squatters in Amsterdam and the Emergence of A Movement Meritocracy: A Critical Reply to Pruijt. *International Journal of Urban and Regional Research* 28(3): 687–698.

Valli, Chiara (2015) When Cultural Workers Become an Urban Social Movement: Political Subjectification and Alternative Cultural Production in the Macao Movement, Milan. *Environment & Planning A* 47: 643–659.

Vasudevan, Alexander (2017) *The Autonomous City. A History of Urban Squatting.* London: Verso.

METHODOLOGICAL NOTE

The journal articles that constitute the main pillars of this book are based on different methodological resources. In general, this 20-year dedication to the study of squatting mainly relies on qualitative methods, although I also embraced more quantitative analyses that informed other publications. While updating and rewriting my previous articles, I realised that the comparative impulse lying at the core of this book had to be reinforced with more empirical evidence. Thus I improved the arguments by using a selection of the available research works and also data I have collected over the last two decades. Additionally, I decided to include some of my own reflections and fieldwork notes from my in situ visits to squats in European cities so as to illustrate my analysis with the narration of case studies.

The academic character of this book implies that my arguments and observations are discussed according to the relevant scholarship on the topic of squatting. The main topics of each chapter determine the discussion. Apart from the case studies that provide in-depth accounts and a socio-spatial situated knowledge of the selected cities, the book does not intend to examine one by one all the mentioned urban areas and squats. Yet, my comparative approach aims at understanding patterns and singularities across many European cities and also, importantly, according to specific structural contexts. Hence, careful attention has been paid to the possibility of generalising the major statements of the book. Most of the reasoning lies on assumptions of probable dynamics in relationship to my own research and other scholars' accounts.

Above all, I have conducted an empirical analysis of squatting in Spain since the late 1980s. The two major sources during the initial stages were independent media and frequent visits to squats. The thousands of independent media items or so-called counter-informative sources provided the basic information for the first database of squats I created with a national scope. The same material offered

272 Methodological Note

an invaluable discursive pool to understand motives, protest repertoires, and the political interactions of squatters. This was supplemented with a specific survey that had only 20 responses before the 2002 book was published, and another 20 more in the following years; I therefore stopped using it as a research tool. In fact, my visits to the squats and my attendance at demonstrations gave me the opportunity to hold hundreds of informal talks with participants in the movement. I usually took notes of these conversations and also from the messages spread on the walls, banners, rooms, etc. Since 1999, I have participated in workshops, debates, assemblies, radio programmes, and public presentations in which I was able to test my initial hypotheses and discuss my arguments about squatting with both insiders and outsiders of the movement. Again, many of these discussions were recorded in my notebooks.

Until the mid-2000s most of the squats did not have their own websites. Instead, many of them produced short clips and documentaries that I also collected. Once, a colleague and I made a systematic discourse analysis of around 20 of these video recordings. When websites and blogs became more generalised, these were the main *emic* sources of empirical information. However, many of them were poorly maintained and updated or were very short-lived. As happened with other Spanish counter-information, not much was said about squatting in other European countries, so I started exploring and translating, when needed, websites from squats all over Europe even before travelling there. Without a doubt, squat.net was the main reference to follow.

Given the reluctance of most squatters to fill in surveys, I convinced many of them to allow in-depth interviews. Between 2002 and 2016 I conducted 49 formal interviews (17 with the help of assistants) in Spanish cities, sometimes with more than one respondent at the same time, and 13 in London, Amsterdam, Berlin, and Rome. Collective debates during the SqEK meetings in most of the cities we visited (Madrid, Milan, London, Berlin, New York, Paris, Amsterdam, Rome, Barcelona, Rotterdam, Prague, Stockholm, and Catania) were occasionally audio-recorded when permission was agreed upon. In most cases, I took written notes on the comments and cases under scrutiny. There were many historical references mentioned during those debates, so a further desktop enquiry was needed to follow up the cases and understand the contextual circumstances. Furthermore, I also found various online clips, audio podcasts, and debates about squatting that I listened to and, sometimes, transcribed partially. However, the most rewarding experience was to stay for a week or more in the cities I visited due to the SqEK meetings or because I had met people there, allowing me to return several times (especially in London, Amsterdam, Berlin, Rome, and Paris); it was usually a tight schedule, with visits and debates every day. Many locals helped us to identify buildings—current and former squats—to enter them and participate in some activities (or even to stay overnight when sleeping space was available), and to talk to hundreds of activists over the years.

Between mid-2007 and mid-2013 I was regularly involved in the Madrid squatting scene. I participated as a full member in several projects (above all,

Malaya, Mácula, and Casablanca) but was also an active visitor of many others, especially when there were parties, talks, meetings, workshops, campaigns, new occupations, and solidarity actions. When the Plataforma de Afectados por las Hipotecas (PAH, Platform for People Affected by Mortgages) started to call for blockades of foreclosures (*stop evictions*), I also joined enthusiastically between 2011 and 2013. This period represents the bulk of my ethnographic approach to the squatting movement, although there was no research plan made in advance—above all, I approached the squats as an activist, supporter, or participant. By 2008, I made a proposal for activist-research in one squat, Malaya, in order to write collectively the history of squatting in the metropolitan region of Madrid. The members of this social centre and ensuing projects run by almost the same group (Mácula and Casablanca), and a different social centre (Patio Maravillas), were informed about this project, allowed us room space to develop it, and sometimes attended our meetings. We transcribed all the public meetings and edited them to be published as a choral book with short analyses and comments to frame the conversations. However, my direct observations as an active partici-pant in the squats offered me much more information about the participants' points of view, incidents, legal strategies, social networks, themes discussed in assemblies and email lists, etc. Very often, I took notes and wrote my own reflective comments about what I observed. These notes were used to further reflect on the specific topics I wrote about later on (the global justice move-ment, migrant squatters, negotiations with authorities, etc.), but I always tried to avoid personal details and to reveal conflicts that might endanger activists' safety and confidentiality. Hence, my analyses aimed to address and disclose the more general dynamics of the movement's history and political struggles.

Although many members of the squats knew about my previous research on squatting, it was almost impossible to inform everyone that I intended to keep writing on the same subject. In addition to the *history project*, which was openly disseminated and presented to the squats involved, when I was personally asked or during informal conversations, I declared my current interest in continuing to research squatting, especially in times that I had institutional funding for doing so. Irrespective of that, my teaching duties, other research projects, and my dedication to activism as a priority over any specific study on squatting made my engagement as a participant observer a sort of part-time and unsteady work.

Since my involvement in occupations for housing was less intense than in squatted social centres, I also conducted formal in-depth interviews with PAH activists all over Spain—with a total of 63 interviews before 2018. I focused on their squatting campaigns, but not exclusively. In order to continue my investi-gations on squatting in Europe while living in Asia, beginning in 2013 I gathered media news on a regular basis, mostly from Spain, but also from all European countries. Around 400 media items were related to the PAH; more than 3,000 were related to squatting in Spain broadly; roughly 400 came from squatting in various European countries; 91 news items and other documents (especially from solidarity organisations) were connected to squatting by migrants

274 Methodological Note

in Spain and Europe before 2015. A critical discourse analysis of both mass media and independent media has been more systematically conducted in the case studies about migrants and squatting for housing, albeit a careful reading of all the material collected served to provide significant evidence and to underpin my theoretical arguments.

In sum, this methodological approach confers priority to the views provided by the movement insiders, including myself as a regular participant, but widens the picture by means of introducing the analyses of other researchers, mass media coverage, documents from institutional sources and civic organisations, historical accounts and databases, and especially a comparative insight ranging from temporary visits to squats in many European cities, to informal talks and semi-structured interviews, and collective debates. All this empirical information is relevant to meet the major goals of this research project (despite the ups and downs it has experienced over 20 years): to (1) understand the socio-spatial and political conditions favourable to the emergence and development of squatting; to (2) know the nature of the interactions between squatters and their opponents; and to (3) explain the main outcomes the movements have contributed to producing.

INDEX

15M movement 1, 171–177, 194, 215–231, 249, 269
59 Rivoli 157, 179, 208, 244

abolitionism 152–155
activist networks 11, 38, 97–99, 118–122, 124, 150
adverse possession 10, 99, 117, 190, 240, 257
Advisory Service for Squatters 55, 117, 210
anomalous institutions 212–216
anti-squatting 101–103, 123, 127, 235, 238, 248, 261
anti-vacancy measures 43, 101–103
artistic squat 9, 84, 110, 180–183
assembly 49, 69–84, 129, 150, 153, 207, 225, 226
Astra 211, 218
asylum 121, 160–164, 177, 210, 248
Ateneu 9 Barris 218
authoritarianism 4, 12, 20, 28, 34, 55, 65–85, 106, 107, 196, 260

Barocchio Occupato 199
Berlin Line 89, 111
black dwelling 98
Blocchi Precari Metropolitani 52
B-Rat 206
Brunnenstraße 114

Cambalache 171
Can Batlló 218

Can Masdeu 196
Can Tintorer 122
Candela 147
Casa Invisible 83, 147, 211, 218, 223
Casablanca 2, 170, 173, 224–228, 228, 273
Centri Sociali 45, 67
cession 131, 207
Christiania 113, 114, 147, 154, 206, 207, 243
Circoli del Proletariato Giovanile 69
City Plaza 163
class struggle 12, 17–19, 28–39, 48, 67, 70, 72, 84, 85, 234, 235, 263, 264
Colapesce 145
Collectif Artistique Tranquille 180
collective consumption 21, 24, 30–38, 86, 200
communalism 153–155
conservational squatting 15, 16, 146, 149, 150, 152, 257
co-optation 32, 36, 46, 75, 134, 164, 202, 203, 212–216, 245
Coordinadora de Inmigrantes 167
Coordinamento Citadino di Lotta per la Casa 52
counter-hegemony 19, 254–262

Datscha 53
dependent hierarchy 14, 18, 40
deprivation-based squatting 15, 16, 149, 157–160, 164, 176
direct action 5, 7, 44, 65, 72–79, 143, 150, 193, 200, 214, 254

276 Index

Disobbedienti 159
Droit Au Logement 15, 156, 164, 180–185

Eco-Box community garden 181
El Paso Occupato 199
Eskalera Karakola 79, 147, 158, 169,
    220, 221, 229
Ex Hotel Commercio 68

fascism 86, 166
feminism 18, 30, 34, 35, 50, 56, 63–88,
    119, 145, 158, 169, 209, 210, 220–222
flexible institutionalisation 201, 202, 212
foreclosure 1, 8, 51, 54, 153, 172,
    174, 254, 273
Forte Prenestino 52, 53
free spaces 84, 122, 148, 213
FUGA 122

Gängeviertel 50, 78, 84
Grenfell Tower 254, 256

homelessness 5, 53, 110, 164–173, 236,
    247–250, 259, 262
homogenisation 234–246, 254, 264
human rights 4, 55, 161, 171, 177, 236

Indiani Metropolitani 69, 254
intersectionality 13, 20, 52
institutionalisation 12, 23, 34–44, 56, 75,
    190–194, 201–233
International Monetary Fund 54, 120, 6
International Women's Space 160
Intersquat 182, 214
Italian *Autonomia* 68

Jardin d'Alice 181, 184
Jeudi Noir 156, 180, 183, 184, 185
Jour et Nuit Culture 180

Klinika 196
Kraakmoskee 162
Kraakspreekuur 55, 117, 127–133, 214
kraker 65, 247
Kukutza 106, 135, 244

La Barraka 171
La Cantine des Pyrénées 183
La Eskuela Taller 170
La Ingobernable 52, 105, 208

La Juli 171
La Mácula 171
La Miroiterie 183
La Prospe 219, 220, 228
Laboratorio 80, 168, 197, 222,
    223, 226, 227
Ladronka 195, 196
Las Corralas 153
Le Gare XP 180
Le Shakirail 181
Le Transfo 178, 182
legalisation 114, 115, 158–160, 191–227
LGBTIQ 22, 50, 67, 81, 84, 86,
    150, 209, 221, 223
licensed 43, 91, 208, 262
Liotru 145
Localia 122
London Action Resource Centre 120
Louise Michel 183
Lucha Autónoma 79, 221, 222
Lupo 145

Mbolo Moy Dole 173, 186
Metropoliz 66, 71, 155, 251
migrants 160–184
Movimenti Per Il Diritto All'Abitare 15
Mujeres Preokupando 80

negotiations 193–200
New Yorck 89, 115, 243
Nieuwmarkt 51, 111, 239

Obra Social 55, 172, 173
Od:zysk 196
ODS 169–176
Oficina de Okupación 55, 225
Olympics 241

PAH 54, 55, 83, 141, 153,
    172–176, 254, 273
Palacete Okupado 167
Palestra Popolare Polisportiva Etnea 9
Patio Maravillas 82, 172, 197, 211,
    219, 223, 273
political squatting 15, 16, 78, 141–144,
    167, 176, 177, 222, 253
pragmatism 153–155
protest waves 11, 34, 36,
    39, 45, 69
Provos 65, 66, 254
Przychodnia 53

Reclaim the Streets 51, 120
Refugee Strike House 160, 161
Rompamos el Silencio 147
reversive strategies 256–258
right to the city 48–55, 150–158, 209, 260
Rote Flora 50, 77, 78, 157

safe spaces 27, 28, 150, 158
Seco 147, 168, 169, 221, 229
social autonomy 65–84
social production of space 10, 16, 37, 39
socio-spatial structures 11, 40, 43, 45,
    97–133
SOS Racismo 168, 171
spatial claims 25, 27, 32
Spontis 74, 75
SQUASH 117, 123, 124, 212
Squatters Handbook 117, 135, 210
Squatting Europe/Everywhere Kollective
    4, 135, 226
strategic squatting 11–15, 143–154
structural power 17–19
Studentato 145
subcultural 46, 53, 110, 210–218

subversive strategies 256, 258, 266
Syrena 53
systemic power 18, 37

Tabacalera 147, 219, 223,
    226, 230
tactical squatting 15, 143–153
Teatro Coppola 108, 145, 211
terminal institutionalisation 191, 201,
    202, 214
The Refugees 163
The Village 254
Théâtre de Verre 180, 181
trespassing 117, 118, 235

Ungdomshuset 154
unitarianism 153–155

Villa Amalias 100

We Are Here 162
workerism 67, 68
winter truce 54, 115, 178, 183, 185

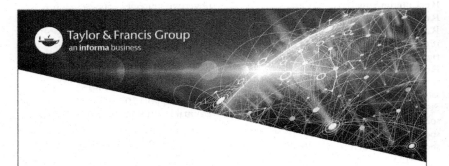